I0124698

Rachel Harriette Busk

Roman Legends

A Collection of the Fables and Folk-Lore of Rome

Rachel Harriette Busk

Roman Legends
A Collection of the Fables and Folk-Lore of Rome

ISBN/EAN: 9783744675390

Printed in Europe, USA, Canada, Australia, Japan

Cover: Foto ©Thomas Meinert / pixelio.de

More available books at **www.hansebooks.com**

ROMAN LEGENDS

A COLLECTION OF

THE FABLES AND FOLK-LORE

OF

ROME

BY

R. H. BUSK

AUTHOR OF 'SAGAS FROM THE FAR EAST' &c. 'HOUSEHOLD STORIES FROM
THE LAND OF HOFER' &c.

BOSTON

COPYRIGHT AND PUBLISHED BY

ESTES AND LAURIAT

1877

PREFACE.

I HAD HEARD it so often positively asserted that modern Italy had no popular mythology, and no contribution of special versions to offer to the world's store of Tradition- ary Tales, that, while possessing every opportunity, I was many years without venturing to set myself against the prevailing opinion so far as to attempt putting it to the proof.

A certain humble friend, however, used time after time so to impress me with the fancy that she had all the qualifications for being a valuable repository of such lore if it only existed, that I was finally led to examine her on the subject. She gave me a capital opportunity one day when, during a visit to a bedridden cripple whom she nursed, she was flapping the dust off the pictures and ornaments with a feather-brush according to the Roman idea of dusting. 'I never do any dusting,' she said the while, 'but I always think of *Monsignor Delegato* dusting the altar of the holy house of Loreto. And now I think of it, he was not called Monsignor Delegato, but Mon- signor Commissario. But every evening of my life while I was young and living at Loreto, I have seen him dust the altar of the *Santa Casa* at 23 o'clock,[1] before they shut

[1] An hour before the evening Ave.

up the church, saying a *Salve Regina* for the benefactors
of the spot.' If she was so familar with Loreto, I concluded, and had so noticed and remembered its customs,
probably she was not ignorant of its Legends either, and
I commenced my inquisition at once.

I have not given her Legends of Loreto in the text
because, being tolerably familiar, they were among those
which could best be sacrificed to the exigencies of space.
I gathered on that day, however, one version of S. Giovanni
Bocca d'oro, with two stories of Padre Filippo : and her
subsequent testimony concerning the crucifix of Scirollo
came in usefully (pp. 193, 195) in illustration of the Legend
of Pietro Bailliardo ; but, what was precious to me above
all, I gained the proof and earnest that there was certainly
a vein of legendary lore underlying the classic soil of Rome,
and that it only remained to find the means of working it.

I first lazily set myself to hunt through the bookshops,
new and old, to find any sort of collection of traditionary
tales ready made ; but only with the effect of establishing
the fact that no Italian Grimm had yet arisen to collect
and organise them, and put them into available shape.[1]

It is true the erudite and indefatigable Cesare Cantù
has found time in the midst of his more important labours

---

[1] Professor de Gubernatis (whose work was not published till my collection had long been in progress) fills a far more important place than
that of a mere collector of legends. His vast generalisations, indeed, touch
less upon the household tales of Italy than those of any other country, and
those which he does introduce are entirely from Tuscany and Piedmont. I
had not the advantage of seeing either his book on ' Zoological Mythology,'
or Mr. Cox's ' Mythology of the Aryan Nations,' till after my MS. was in
the printer's hands, and was not able, therefore, to give references in my
notes to the places where their interpretation may be found, though each
group to which my stories respectively belong has been treated by them.
It is a treatment, however, which requires to be studied as a whole, and
could hardly be understood under any piecemeal reference.

to illustrate some few remnants of mediæval customs and sayings yet lingering in the north of Italy, in his 'Novelle Lombarde;' and he tells me that the Balio Benvenuti, also of Milan, is bringing out another little volume about Lombard customs; but even these have not approached the fairy tales, and leave Central and Southern Italy altogether untouched.[1]

The nearest approach to the material of which I was in search was afforded in the roughly printed rimed legends which itinerant venders sell at the church doors on festa days. Among the collection I have made of these, are many whose quaintness gives them special interest, notwithstanding their baldness of style and diction; but the matter which came to me first hand seemed to have the first claim to publication; and I have, therefore, put these among my reserve for a second series.[2]

No repository of Roman Folklore was to be found ready-formed. 'Who among us,' writes Cesare Cantù in his preface to his 'Novelle Lombarde,' 'knows anything about these matters? If they were the things of Scotland or Touraine we should all have read them long ago in the

---

[1] There are, of course, the older collections of Straparola and Basile, referred to by Mr. Campbell and Professor De Gubernatis, not to speak of those of Boccaccio and Sacchetti; but these were made for quite different purposes than that of supplying Italy's quota to the study of Comparative Mythology. The comparatively recent 'Collection of Sicilian Tales,' by Laura Gonzenbach, mentioned by Professor De Gubernatis, I did not know of, and have not been able to see. Straparola's collection seems, in Rome at least, to have fallen into the oblivion which Mr. Campbell says is its merited lot. At least, not only was it not mentioned to me at any of the depôts where rare books are a *spécialité*, but my subsequent inquiry for it by name failed to produce a copy.

[2] I gave a translation of one of them, containing legendary details of the 'Flight into Egypt,' together with some verses of a Spanish version of the same, in a paper on 'Street Music in Rome,' in the 'Monthly Packet' of December, 1868.

pages of Scott or Balzac. But here among us there are neither writers who care to describe nor readers who take any interest in learning the ways of our own country. People like to seem above giving their attention to such homely matters, and only care for what they must look at through a telescope.'

I was thus thrown back on my own powers of collecting, and found the process, however fascinating where success-ful, much more uphill work than it had promised to be at the outset. Legends, it is true, there was less difficulty in obtaining. There might be some sense and some moral in them, and I found people were not ashamed of knowing them; but it long remained impossible to convince per-sons who had even betrayed to me indications that they possessed what I wanted, to own fully to a knowledge of *bonâ fide* Fairy Tales, or to believe that I could be serious in wishing to listen to such childish nonsense.

'But suppose you had a child to amuse,' I would say at last, ' I am sure you would sometimes tell it a marvellous story.'

' Ah, a *creatura*,[1] yes ! But I haven't the face to tell such nonsense to your *signoria*.'

'Never mind that, if I want to hear it. Imagine I am the *creatura*, and tell me one of your tales. I want something about transformations, fairy gifts, and marvels of all sorts.'

In some such way, after due precaution taken to con-vince me that such things were only allowed a place in the memory for the sake of amusing children, and not because anyone believed in them, one tale after another would be suffered reluctantly to ooze out.

---

[1] Roman vernacular for a child of either sex.

But you cannot make application for such wares to the first person you meet. The class in which such lore is stored away is not indeed so exclusive that introductions to it are a very difficult matter, but introduction of some sort you must have ; some claim for taking up a person's time, where time is money ; and some means of compensation you must devise, the more difficult to invent where direct payment would be an offence. Your modern Romans are very independent; I cannot say whether the quality is more an inheritance from their ancient forefathers, or adopted from the continental spread of French revolutionary ideas of '93. True, they are singularly urbane and deferential, but only so long as you are urbane and deferential towards them. If you omit any of their peculiar forms of politeness, they are suspicious of you, and scarcely know how to make allowance for the well-meaning inexperience of a foreigner. If you want to learn anything from them you must submit to become one of them. You must converse first on the subject uppermost in their minds, from the price of bread and meat to the latest change in the political atmosphere; only when all is exhausted may you venture to come round to the matter of which you are in search. Many, too, in whose memories such stories have lain dormant since childhood, for more than half a century, have not the power of recalling them in due form or order for narration on abrupt application, but will yet bring them out unconsciously if patiently led up to an appropriate starting point.

Nor is it every application, made with all precautions, that will be successful. Often you must submit to be put off with the tantalising experience that a person knew plenty of stories, but was quite incapable of putting them into shape. This happened once with an intelligent old lady from Siena, whom, after allowing her to indulge her irony at my expense concerning my childishness in seeking such things, I brought to confess that she had heard in her youth a strange story of a cat which wore *stivali di cacciatore* (hunter's boots), but she could not succeed in recalling a single incident of it; and I was obliged to content myself with the information (no small encouragement in the early days of my work, however!) that 'Puss in Boots' had actually travelled to Tuscany.

At another time one would have to spend hours in listening to detached incidents altogether lacking a thread to connect them, or stories of which the point had been so completely lost that they could only have been made available by means of a reconstruction too integral to be honestly attempted. As, e.g., 'Oh yes! I know a story of an enchantress who had a gown which made her invisible, and a pair of boots which would carry her a thousand miles without walking, but I quite forget what she did with them.' Or else it might be, 'I knew a story of a king whose wife had been *fatata* (subjected to magic influence), and maligned by her mother-in-law while the king was gone to the wars; but that's all I remember, except that in the end the queen was rehabilitated, and the mother-in-law punished'—incidents of stories recurring in every collection, but tantalisingly lacking all means of further particular identification with any. Sometimes, too, it would be only a title that could be recalled, and nothing more, as in the case of a certain 'Uccello Biverde,'[1] which I

---

[1] Whatever *Biverde* may mean. Possibly *bel-verde*, such, at least, is the title of Pellicciaio's Madonna with the 'beautiful green' dress, at the

have been several times assured is 'a most beautiful story,' but I have never yet succeeded in meeting with any one who could supply the narrative. I have further felt called sometimes to exercise a difficult forbearance in withholding some specimens which at first promised to afford singular instances of interchanged episodes, but which there afterwards appeared reason to conclude were merely jumbled in the bad memory of the narrator, and had, therefore, no individual interest, but were rather calculated to mislead.[1]

One of my worst disappointments was the case of a very old woman, who, I am assured, knows more of such things than anyone in the world, but whom nothing can induce to repeat them now. She has grown so toothless and tremulous and inconsecutive, that it is not easy to understand her ; but I think her arguments are not difficult to appreciate in the following way,—that having had a long run of weary bad fortune, she had rather not dwell on stories where things turned out as one could wish to have them. She wants to go to heaven, she says, and so she believes in God, and whatever else she *must* believe ; but for anything more, for special interpositions of Providence, and anything one is not obliged to believe, she had rather say nothing about all that. 'But don't tell them then as if you believed them ; tell them only as a pastime ; just to oblige me.' I thought I had moved her, but the utmost she would yield was to promise to think about it before I came again : and when I came

Servite Church, Siena. The title may also be compared with 'The Maid of the Bright-Green Kirtle,' in Campbell's 'West Highland Tales.'

[1] This, I am inclined to think, is the case with some published stories, as e.g. the singular medley contained in the third of the 'Tales of the West Highlands,' vol. i.

again she was as rigid as ever. It is vexatious to think
that a vast store is going to the grave with her under
one's very eyes and that one cannot touch it.

It is further to be remarked, that while there are thus
a vast number of persons holding the store of traditional
myths, it by no means includes the generality of the population; there is a still larger class among whom every
trace of such lore is lost. So destitute are they of all
knowledge of the kind, that it would be interesting to
trace back the antecedents of each, and so discover, if it
might be, the origin of this discrepancy; for not only
have I found it impossible myself to stir up any memory
of such stories in half the people I have applied to,
(though, to all appearance, similarly circumstanced with
those who have proved the most communicative), but old
'gossips,' sitting by while the stories in the text were
being poured out, have, time after time, displayed a won-
derment which proved that their very style was something
quite new to them.

Nevertheless, in spite of all difficulties, a few years'
patience has put me in possession of a goodly bulk of
popular stories not yielding in interest, I think, to those
of any other country. The tales included in the present
collection are but a portion of those which I have gathered
within the limits of the Roman State. I hope to be able
to complete at some future day the remainder that I have
gathered both there and from other divisions of the
former Heptarchy of Italy. The localities from which
these have been chiefly drawn are Palombara, Capranica,
Loreto, Sinigaglia, Viterbo, Cori, Palestrina, and, above
all, Rome itself. One of my chief contributors had passed
her whole existence—infancy, married life, and widow-

hood—within the limits of one parish in the heart of Rome.

The collection has arranged itself, according to the spontaneous titling of the narrators, into four categories, and it may not be unimportant to note that Romans, always precise in their choice of language, keep rigidly to these designations. I have, for instance, been on the very verge of passing over a whole mine of 'Esempj,' or 'Ciarpe' by only asking for 'Favole' (and *vice versâ*). Remembering afterwards to say, 'I daresay you can, at all events, recall some " Esempj," or " Ciarpe,"' I have received for answer, 'To be sure; why didn't you say sooner that such would suit you?'

The said four categories are,—

1. ESEMPJ, or those stories under which some religious or moral lessons might be conveyed, answering to what we call Legends. Though the word *Leggenda* exists in the dictionary, and is not altogether unused, I have never once met it among the people.

2. Ghost stories and local and family traditions. The latter are much more carefully preserved than among our own people,[1] and the Roman poor will tell the tale (more or less accurately) of the virtues and vices of their great families, with a gusto which shows that they look upon them as something specially belonging to themselves ; but the former do not appear to have any recognised title, and the contempt in which they are held makes it very difficult to get hold of them, so that it is not very easy to avoid giving offence in approaching the subject. Only by a prolonged and round-about conversation one may

[1] Except perhaps among the Scotch Highlanders. See Campbell's 'Tales,' Preface to vol. i.

sometimes elicit excellent specimens brought in as matters
of curious personal experience by the very persons who,
on direct questioning, had repudiated all knowledge of
anything of the sort.

3. FAVOLE. The word universally appropriated in
Roman dialect for 'Fairy Tales,' a not unclassical application of the term, I think, and continued in the 'Fabliaux'
of the mediæval period. But when asking for them I have
never had any given me belonging to the class which we
call 'fables' in English.

4. CIARPE, expounded by Bazzarelli as *parole vane,
ciance; ciance* being said, on the authority of Petrarch,
to stand for *parole vane, lontane dal vero, chiacchiera;
chiacchiera* being the equivalent for gossip. Versions of
some stories in this category, notably No. 6, ' L'Uccelletto '
(The Little Bird), and 21, ' The Value of Salt,' we all
heard in our English nurseries, while those under the
heading of ' La Sposa Cece' (The Simple Wife) belong to
the same class as ours of the man who being told to give
his wife her medicine in a convenient vehicle, wheeled her
about in a hand-barrow, while she swallowed it; or that of
the idiotic couple who wasted their three precious chances
in wishing three yards of black pudding on each other's
noses, and then wishing it off again; but I do not know
that we have any special technical designation for such.
All the headings of which I have given the Italian are
those used by the narrators themselves.

It is impossible, in making acquaintance with these
stories in their own language, not to regret having to put
them into another tongue. Much of what is peculiar in
them, and distinguishes them from their counterparts in
other lands, is, of course, wrapped up in the form of ex-

pression in which they are clothed. Divested of this, they run the risk of losing the national character they have acquired during their residence on Italian soil. I had purposed, therefore, originally, to print an Italian version, side by side with the English rendering, but was obliged to renounce the arrangement, as it would have proved too voluminous. I have only been able to preserve some few of the vernacular idiosyncrasies in the notes, for the benefit of those who take an interest in the people's characteristic utterances.

I think I may safely say that the whole of the stories are traditional. There were only two of my contributors who could have read them had they even existed in print. The best-instructed of them was the one who gave me ' Prete Olivo' and ' Perchè litigano i cani ed i gatti;' both of which I am clear, from ' asides' which accompanied them concerning her father's manner of telling, she had heard from his lips, even as she said.

With the exception of some of the Legends, Local Traditions, and Ciarpe, there are few, either printed in this collection or among those I still hold in MS., the leading episodes of which (if not the entire story) are not to be found in the collections of other countries; but certain categories common in other countries are wanting in the Roman. One could not in making the collection but be struck with the almost complete absence of stories of heroism and chivalry. There are some, indeed, in which courageous deeds occur; but there is none of the high-souled mettle which comes out so strong in Hungarian, Gaelic, and Spanish tradition, in many of the Teutonic and Breton, and some Norse and Russian tales. Several, we shall find, are identical stories, with the grand and fierce element left out. I have never come across a single story of knightly prowess in any shape. I have in MS. one or two dragon stories, but no knights figure even in these. At the same time, tales of horror seem equally to have failed to fascinate the popular imagination, and we can trace again the toning down process in many instances. I have in MS. several versions of the rather ghastly story of the boy who went out to discover Fear, but the Roman mind does not often indulge in such scenes as it presents. Similarly, horrid monsters are rare. ' Orco ' himself is not painted so terrible as in other countries. Giants and dwarfs, again, being somewhat monstrous creations, are not frequent. The stories about the *Satiri* were only told me spontaneously by one narrator ; one other owned to having heard of such beings on being questioned, but there is no general popular conception corresponding to the German ideas of wild men. I have never met anyone who believed in the present existence of any supernatural being of this class,[1] and rarely with any who imagined such had ever existed. ' The stories always say, " there was a fairy who did so and so : " but *were* there ever fairies ? Perhaps there were, perhaps there weren't,' soliloquised an old woman one day at the end of a tale ; that was the strongest expression of opinion in their favour that came in my way. Another said once, ' If there ever were such beings there would be now ; but there certainly are not any now, so I don't believe there ever were any.'[2]

Again, religious legends, with admixture of pagan super-

---

[1] See remarks in Preface to Campbell's ' Tales of the West Highlands,' vol. i. p. c. Dr. Dasent's ' Popular Tales from the Norse,' pp. xliv, xlv, &c.

[2] It has been observed to me that these words furnish a remarkable, because unconscious, parallel to the well-known dictum of Minucius Felix, on the mythical exploits of the old heathen gods and heroes, ' Quæ si facta essent fierent ; quia fieri non possunt ideò nec facta sunt.'

stitions, seem rare. English readers may say that there is superstition in some of the legends in the text; but they only exaggerate the literalness with which they deal with Gospel promises; there is little at variance with it. The false-tale of the pilgrim husband, pp. 355–6, is the most devious from Christian doctrine that I have come across in Rome. I cannot fancy a Roman, however illiterate, gravely telling such stories as some of those which Mr. Ralstone gives us from Russia. The story of ' Pret' Olivo ' is doubtless derivatively the same as Dr. Dasent's ' Master Smith'; but the Roman version presents vastly less of the pagan element.

In winding up his general remarks on the migrations of myths, Prof. de Gubernatis gives as his opinion that ' the elementary myth was the spontaneous production of imagination and not of reflection;' . . . that 'morals have often been made an appendix to fables, but never entered into the primitive fable;' that ' art and religion have made use of the already existing myths (themselves devoid of moral conscience) as allegories for their own æsthetic and moral ends.' And it appears to me that the Romans, in adapting such elementary myths to legendary use, have christianised them more than some other peoples.

Pacts with the Devil, in which the Germans revel, are rare; the story of ' Pietro Bailliardo ' is one of the very few. It would seem that witchcraft never at any time obtained any great hold upon the people of Rome, nor were witches ever treated with the same severity which befell them in other parts of Europe. It is true that some stories about witch-stepmothers wind up with ' e la brucciorno in mezzo alla Piazza,' [1] but I am inclined to think it is rather a ' tag ' received from other coun-

[1] (' And they burnt her to death in the public square.')

tries, than an actual local tradition; and certainly by cross-questioning I failed to awaken in the memory of the 'oldest inhabitants' with whom I have had the opportunity of conversing any tradition of anything of the sort having actually taken place.

'What do *you* know about burning witches *in mezzo alla Piazza?* I thought such things were never done in Rome?' I observed one day to one who ended a story thus. 'Who said the story took place in Rome?' was the ready reply. I received the same reply to the same observation from another, with the addition of 'There was something about a king and a queen in the story and in other stories I have told you, and we never had a king or a queen of Rome—the one may belong to the same country as the other. Who knows what sort of a country such stories come from!' A third answered, 'No; I don't believe witches were ever burnt by law in Rome; I have always heard say that our laws were less fierce than those of some other countries; but I can quite fancy that if the people found a witch doing such things as I have told you, they would burn her all by themselves, law or no law.'

Of course I have no pretension that my researches have been exhaustive, nor have I been, properly speaking, searching for superstitions, but in a good deal of intercourse with the uneducated, I have certainly *come across* less of superstitious beliefs in Rome than collectors of Folklore seem to have met in other countries. The saying exists,

> Giorno di Venere,
> Giorno di Marte,
> Non si sposa,
> E non si parte.[1]

[1] 'Don't marry or set out on a journey on a Friday or Tuesday;' and under the two heads brought under the rime, any other undertaking is equally proscribed: some servants, for instance, dislike going to a new situation on those days.

But I have seldom heard the lines quoted without the addition of, ' But *I* don't believe in such things;' and a reference to the column of marriage announcements in the ' Times ' will show that the prejudice against marrying in the month of May is, to say the least, quite as strong among our own most highly-educated classes.

It is not altogether uncommon at the Parochial Mass, to hear along with banns of marriage and other announcements, a warning pronounced against such and such a person whom private counsel has failed to deter from ' dabbling in black arts ; ' but from the observations which I have had the opportunity of making such persons find their dupes chiefly among the dissolute and non-believing. I know a very consistently religious woman, and also singularly intelligent, who appeared to have a salutary contempt for certain practices in which her husband, a worthless fellow, who had long ago abandoned her and his religion together, indulged. ' He actually believes,' she told me one day, ' that if you go out and stand on a cross road—not merely where two roads happen to cross each other, but where they actually make a perfect cross—and if at the stroke of *mezzogiorno in punto*, you call the Devil he is bound to come to you.'

' He always kept a bag of particular herbs,' I heard from her another time, ' hung up over the door, all shred into the finest bits. As he was very angry if I touched them, I one day said, " Why *do* you want that bundle of herbs kept just there ? " and then he told me that it was because no witch could pass under them without first having to count all the minute bits, and that though it was true she might do so by her arts without taking them down and handling them, it was yet so difficult when they were shred into such an infinite number that it was the best preservative possible against evil influences.'

Another class of infrequent occurrence in the Roman stories is that in which animals are prominent actors, other than those in which they are transformed men. The tátos, the enchanted horse which excites so great enthusiasm in the Hungarian, and whose counterpart does great wonders also in the Gaelic tales, seems to be absolutely unknown,[1] as I think is also the class not uncommon in the Gaelic (*e.g.* 'Tales of the West Highlands,' i. 275 *et seq.*), also in the Russian Folklore, p. 338, of birds made to pronounce articulate words analogous in sound to their own cries.[2] Such traditions would naturally find a hold rather among countrypeople than townspeople.

Fairies and witches are frequent enough, but the limits between the respective domains assigned to them are not so marked as with us. Roman fairies, it will be seen, are by no means necessarily 'fairy-like.' At the same time fairies, such as those described by Mr. Campbell, 'West Highland Tales,' p. ci., are altogether unknown.

[1] In the story of 'Filagranata,' *infra*, pp. 6 *et seq.*, he is divested in a marked manner of the individuality and importance attaching to his part in the corresponding versions of other countries.

[2] The Rev. Alfred White told me, however, an English story of the sort, picked up from a countryman in Berkshire. The Magpie was one day building her nest so neatly, and whispering to herself after her wont as she laid each straw in its place, 'This upon that, this upon that,' when the Woodpigeon came by. Now the Woodpigeon was young and flighty, and had never learnt how to build a nest; but when she saw how beautifully neat that of the Magpie looked, she thought she would like to learn the art. The busy Magpie willingly accepted the office of teaching her, and began a new one on purpose. Long before she was half through, however, the flighty Woodpigeon sang out, 'That'll doooo!' The Magpie was offended at the interruption, and flew away in dudgeon, and that's why the Woodpigeon always builds such ramshackle nests. Told well; the 'This upon that!' and the 'That'll do!' takes just the sound of the cry of each of the birds named.

CONTENTS.

LEGENDARY TALES AND ESEMPJ.

GHOST AND TREASURE STORIES AND FAMILY AND LOCAL TRADITIONS.

Contents. xxiii

APPENDICES.

FAVOLE.

B

LA FOLLE

ONCE upon a time [1] there was a poor woman who had a great fancy for eating parsley. To her it was the greatest luxury, and as she had no garden of her own, and no money to spend on anything not an absolute necessity of life, she had to go about poaching in other people's gardens to satisfy her fancy.

Near her cottage was the garden of a great palace, and in this garden grew plenty of fine parsley; but the garden was surrounded by a wall, and to get at it she had to carry a ladder with her to get up by, and, as soon as she had reached the top of the wall, to let it down on the other side to get down to the parsley-bed. There was such a quantity of parsley growing here that she thought it would never be missed, and this made her bold, so that she went over every day and took as much as ever she liked.

But the garden belonged to a witch,[2] who lived in the palace, and, though she did not often walk in this part of the garden, she knew by her supernatural powers that some one was eating her parsley; so she came near the place one day, and lay in wait till the poor woman came. As soon, therefore, as she came, and began eating the parsley, the witch at once pounced down, and asked her, in her gruff voice, what she was doing there. Though dreadfully frightened, the poor woman thought it best to own the whole truth; so she confessed that she came down by the ladder, adding that she had not taken anything except the parsley, and begged forgiveness.

'I know nothing about forgiveness,' replied the witch.

and the thought quickly ran through Filagranata's head—
' I have been taught to loose my hair whenever those words
are said; why should not I loose it to draw up such a
pleasant-looking cavalier, as well as for the ugly old hag ?'
and, without waiting for a second thought, she untied the
ribbon that bound her tresses and let them fall upon the
prince. The prince was equally quick in taking advantage
of the occasion, and, pressing his knees firmly into his
horse's flanks, so that it might not remain below to betray him, drew himself up, together with his steed, just
as he had seen the witch do.

Filagranata, half frightened at what she had done the
moment the deed was accomplished, had not a word to
say, but blushed and hung her head. The prince, on the
other hand, had so many words to pour out, expressive of
his admiration for her, his indignation at her captivity,
and his desire to be allowed to be her deliverer, that the
moments flew quickly by, and it was only when Filagranata found herself drawn to the window by the power of
the witch's magic words that they remembered the dangerous situation in which they stood.

Another might have increased the peril by cries of
despair, or lost precious time in useless lamentations ; but
Filagranata showed a presence of mind worthy of a prince's
wife by catching up a wand of the witch, with which she
had seen her do wonderful things. With this she gave
the prince a little tap, which immediately changed him
into a pomegranate, and then another to the horse, which
transformed him into an orange.[4] These she set by on
the shelf, and then proceeded to draw up the witch after
the usual manner.

The old hag was not slow in perceiving there was something unusual in Filagranata's room.

' What a stink[5] of Christians ! What a stink of Christians !' she kept exclaiming, as she poked her nose into
every hole and corner. Yet she failed to find anything to

reprehend; for as for the beautiful ripe pomegranate and the golden orange on the shelf, the Devil himself could not have thought there was anything wrong with them. Thus baffled, she was obliged to finish her inspection of the state of the pigeons, and end her visit in the usual way.

As soon as she was gone Filagranata knew she was free till the next day, and so once more, with a tap of the wand, restored the horse and his rider to their natural shapes.

'And this is how your life passes every day! Is it possible?' exclaimed the prince; 'no, I cannot leave you here. You may be sure my good horse will be proud to bear your little weight; you have only to mount behind me, and I will take you home to my kingdom, and you shall live in the palace with my mother, and be my queen.'

It is not to be supposed but that Filagranata very much preferred the idea of going with the handsome young prince who had shown so devoted an appreciation of her, and being his queen, to remaining shut up in the doorless tower and being the witch's menial; so she offered no opposition, and the prince put her on to his good horse behind him, and away they rode.

On, on, on,[6] they rode for a long, long way, until they came at last to a wood; but for all the good horse's speed, the witch, who was not long in perceiving their escape and setting out in pursuit, was well nigh overtaking them. Just then they saw a little old woman[7] standing by the way, making signs and calling to them to arrest their course. How great soever was their anxiety to get on, so urgent was her appeal to them to stop and listen to her that they yielded to her entreaties. Nor were they losers by their kindness, for the little old woman was a fairy,[8] and she had stopped them, not on her own account, but to give them the means of escaping from the witch.

To the prince she said: 'Take these three gifts, and

when the witch comes very near throw down first the mason's trowel ; and when she nearly overtakes you again throw down the comb; and when she nearly comes upon you again after that, throw down this jar[9] of oil. After that she won't trouble you any more.' And to Filagranata she whispered some words, and then let them go. But the witch was now close behind, and the prince made haste to throw down the mason's trowel. Instantly there rose up a high stone wall between them, which it took the witch some time to climb over. Nevertheless, by her supernatural powers she was not long in making up for the lost time, and had soon overtaken the best speed of the good horse. Then the prince threw down the comb, and immediately there rose up between them a strong hedge of thorns, which it took the witch some time to make her way through, and that only with her body bleeding all over from the thorns. Nevertheless, by her supernatural powers she was not long in making up for the lost time, and had soon overtaken the best speed of the good horse. Then the prince threw down the jar of oil, and the oil spread and spread till it had overflowed[10] the whole country side ; and as wherever you step in a pool of oil the foot only slides back, the witch could never get out of that, so the prince and Filagranata rode on in all safety towards the prince's palace.

'And now tell me what it was the old woman in the wood whispered to you,' said the prince, as soon as they saw their safety sufficiently secured to breathe freely.

'It was this,' answered Filagranata ; 'that I was to tell you that when you arrive at your own home you must kiss no one—no one at all, not your father, or mother, or sisters, or anyone—till after our marriage. Because if you do you will forget all about your love for me, and all you have told me you think of me, and all the faithfulness you have promised me, and we shall become as strangers again to each other.'

'How dreadful!' said the prince. 'Oh, you may be sure I will kiss no one if *that* is to be the consequence; so be quite easy. It will be rather odd, to be sure, to return from such a long journey and kiss none of them at home, not even my own mother; but I suppose if I tell them how it is they won't mind. So be quite easy about that.'

Thus they rode on in love and confidence, and the good horse soon brought them home.

On the steps of the palace the chancellor of the kingdom came out to meet them, and saluted Filagranata as the chosen bride the prince was to bring home; he informed him that the king his father had died during his absence, and that he was now sovereign of the realm. Then he led him in to the queen-mother, to whom he told all his adventures, and explained why he must not kiss her till after his marriage. The queen-mother was so pleased with the beauty, and modesty, and gentleness of Filagranata, that she gave up her son's kiss without repining, and before they retired to rest that night it was announced to the people that the prince had returned home to be their king, and the day was proclaimed when the feast for his marriage was to take place.

Then all in the palace went to their sleepingchambers. But the prince, as it had been his wont from his childhood upwards, went into his mother's room to kiss her after she was asleep, and when he saw her placid brow on the pillow, with the soft white hair parted on either side of it, and the eyes which were wont to gaze on him with so much love, resting in sleep, he could not forbear from pressing his lips on her forehead and giving the wonted kiss.

Instantly there passed from his mind all that had taken place since he last stood there to take leave of the queen-mother before he started on his journey.

His visit to the witch's palace, his flight from it, the life-perils by the way, and, what is more, the image of Filagranata herself,—all passed from his mind like a vision of the night, and when he woke up and they told him he was king, it was as if he heard it for the first time, and when they brought Filagranata to him it was as though he knew her not nor saw her.

'But,' he said, 'if I am king there must be 'a queen to share my throne;' and as a reigning sovereign could not go over the world to seek a wife, he sent and fetched him a princess meet to be the king's wife, and appointed the betrothal. The queen-mother, who loved Filagranata, was sad, and yet nothing that she could say could bring back to his mind the least remembrance of all he had promised her and felt towards her.

But Filagranata knew that the prince had kissed his mother, and this was why the spell was on him; so she said to her mother-in-law: 'You get me much fine-sifted flour [11] and a large bag of sweetmeats, and I will try if I cannot yet set this matter straight.' So the queen-mother ordered that there should be placed in her room much sifted flour and a large bag of sweetmeats. And Filagranata, when she had shut close the door, set to work and made paste of the flour, and of the paste she moulded two pigeons, and filled them inside with the comfits. Then at the banquet of the betrothal she asked the queen-mother to have her two pigeons placed on the table; and she did so, one at each end. But as soon as all the company were seated, before any one was helped, the two pigeons which Filagranata had made began to talk to each other across the whole length of the table: and everybody stood still with wonder to listen to what the pigeons of paste said to each other.

'Do you remember,' said the first pigeon, 'or is it possible that you have really forgotten, when I was in that

doorless tower of the witch's palace, and you came under
the window and imitated her voice, saying,—

> Filagranata, thou maiden fair,
> Loose thy tresses of golden hair:
> I, thy old grandmother, am here,

till I drew you up?'
And the other pigeon answered,—
' Si, signora, I remember it now.'

And as the young king heard the second pigeon say
' Si, signora, I remember it now,' he, too, remembered
having been in a doorless tower, and having sung such
a verse.

' Do you remember,' continued the first pigeon, ' how
happy we were together after I drew you up into that
little room where I was confined, and you swore if I would
come with you we should always be together and never be
separated from each other any more at all?'

And the second pigeon replied,—
' Ah yes! I remember it now.'

And as the second pigeon said ' Ah yes! I remember it now,' there rose up in the young king's mind the
memory of a fair sweet face on which he had once gazed
with loving eyes, and of a maiden to whom he had sworn
lifelong devotion.

But the first pigeon continued :—
' Do you remember, or have you quite forgotten, how
we fled away together, and how frightened we were when
the witch pursued us, and how we clung to each other,
and vowed, if she overtook us to kill us, we would die in
each other's arms, till a fairy met us and gave us the
means to escape, and forbad you to kiss anyone, even your
own mother, till after our marriage?'

And the second pigeon answered,—
' Yes, ah yes! I remember it now.'

And when the second pigeon said, ' Yes, ah yes! I remember it now,' the whole of the past came back to his

mind, and with it all his love for Filagranata. So he rose up [12] and would have stroked the pigeons which had brought it all to his mind, but when he touched them they melted away, and the sweetmeats were scattered all over the table, and the guests picked them up. But the prince ran in haste to fetch Filagranata, and he brought her and placed her by his side in the banquet-hall. But the second bride was sent back, with presents, to her own people.

'And so it all came right at last,' pursued the narrator. 'Lackaday! that there are no fairies now to make things all happen right. There are plenty of people who seem to have the devil in them for doing you a mischief, but there are no fairies to set things straight again, alas!'

---

[1] This story comes from Palombara.

[2] The expression employed in this place was 'Orca;' as this is a word of most frequent, but somewhat capricious use, I interrupted the narrator to inquire her conception of it. 'Well, it means a species of beast,' she said: 'but you see it must have been a bewitched ('fatata') beast, because the story says it was so rich, and had a palace, and spoke and did all the things you shall hear.' She did not, however, seem to identify it with the evil principle according to its undoubted derivation, nor did she allow either that it had any connexion with 'orso,' a bear, as the narrator of the 'il Vaso di Persa' had expounded it, and indeed as the details of that story required; it will be seen, therefore, that popular fancy invests the monster with various shapes. The story of 'The Pot of Marjoram,' it will be seen, contains one or two incidents in common with this one. The apparently insignificant detail of the little plant—on which, however, both stories rest for a foundation—is noteworthy, the narrator in each instance being most positive that it was the one she had named and no other, and in both cases insisting on showing me the plant, that there might be no mistake about it. (See note to the word 'Persa,' infra, p. 54.)

[3] Filagranata bella bella,
  Tira giù le bionde trecce,
  Ch' io son nonna vecchiarella.

'Tira giù,' or 'butta giù,' as in the next repetition, mean equally 'throw down.' 'Biondo' expresses particularly the yellow tint in hair. Bazzarini, 'Ortografia Enciclopedica Universale,' defines it, 'colore tra il giallo e bianco ed è proprio di capelli,' on the authority of Petrarch's use of the word. He has also 'biondeggiante, che biondeggia, che ingiallisce,'

turning or tending to yellow; and it is thus the yellow Tiber gets called
' il biondo Tevere.'

⁴ ' Portogallo ' is now the ordinary word for an orange, and points to the
introduction of the fruit from the Portuguese colonies in the sixteenth century. The ' arancia,' ' melarancia,' or ' merangola,' the ungrafted orange-
tree, was, however, indigenous in Italy; and the fruit, which has even a
finer appearance than the edible orange, is still grown for ornament in
Roman gardens.

⁵ ' Puzzo,' stink. There is no neutral word in Italian for a smell; you
must define a good or a bad smell either as a perfume or a stink.

⁶ ' Camninando, camminando, camminando.' This threefold repetition of this verb, according to the tense and person required by the
story, I have found used as a sort of sing-song refrain by all the tellers of
tales I have had to do with.

⁷ ' Vecchiarella,' little old woman.

⁸ ' Fata ;' ethnologically Fata is the same as ' Fairy,' ' Fée,' &c., &c.,
and ' fairy ' is the only translation; but it will be observed the Italian
' fata ' has always different characteristics from the English ' fairy.'

⁹ ' Buzzica ' is a homely word for a lamp-filler; it probably comes from
' buzzicare,' to move gently or slowly. The narrator used the word because
she would, according to local custom, keep her oil in a ' buzzica,' without
perceiving that it was most inappropriate for the purpose of the story, which
required that the oil should be poured out quickly.

¹⁰ ' Allagato,' inundated. I preserve the word on account of its
expressiveness—literally making a lake of the country.

¹¹ ' Fior di farina.'

¹² As the story was told me the dialogue was broken, and every incident of the journey was made the subject of a separate question and
answer; all the furniture in the room also here entered into conversation
with the pigeons, brooms being particularly loquacious; but as it became
tedious, and by no means added to the poetry of the situation, I condensed
it to the dimensions in the text.

[I have placed this story first in order, as its incidents ramify
into half the traditionary tales with which we are acquainted.

(1.) ' Rapunzel,' No. 12 in ' Grimm,' is the most like it among
the German in the beginning, and has the most dissimilar ending.
The counterpart form, in which it is some misdeed or ill-luck of
the father instead of the mother, which involves the surrender of
the first-born, is the more frequent opening, as in ' The Water
King,' Ralston's ' Russian Folk Tales,' p. 120. ' The Lassie and
her Godmother,' in Dr. Dasent's ' Norse Tales,' has an opening like
' Filagranata,' which, as it proceeds, connects it with ' Marienkind,'
No. 4 in ' Grimm ;' and the prohibition to open the room, in that

one, carries on the connexion to another group, the Bluebeard group, represented in this series by 'Monsoo Mostro,' 'Rè Moro,' &c.; while, further on, 'Lassie and her Godmother' evolves the incident of the reflection in the well, which connects it with the following story in this collection, and in this round-about way, though not in direct form, with the termination of 'Filagranata.'

(2.) The introduction of an orange as a help to defy the 'orca,' connects the story again with the two next (though the fruit is used differently), and with a vast number of myths, as pointed out in Campbell's 'Tales of the West Highlands,' Introduc-tion, pp. lxxx–lxxxv. I was rather put off the scent by the narrator using the word portogallo: melagranata, though pro-perly a pomegranate, is, I think, used in old Italian for an orange, being simply a red, or golden, apple.

(3.) The three gifts of the trowel, the comb, and the oil-filler, again bring this story in connexion with another vast group. Compare 'Campbell,' iv. 290; also his remarks, i. 58–62, on the 'Battle of the Birds,' which story this resembles in the main, but, as will be found throughout this collection, the Roman form is milder. The prince wins his bride without performing tasks, and the couple, in escaping, have only to kill a strange 'orca,' and not the girl's own father. In the third version of the tale in Mr. Campbell's series, the girl becomes a poultry-maid, and has three fine dresses, constituting a link with another group—that of Cinderella (I have given the Tirolean one as 'Klein-Else' in 'Household Stories from the Land of Hofer'); and the three dresses there (though not in the Gaelic story) representing the sun, moon, and stars, give it another connexion with 'Marien-kind.' 'The Master Maid,' in Dr. Dasent's collection, again, has the golden apple (though it assists in a different way) and the ending of the Roman version (a golden cock there taking the part of the two paste pigeons), but begins with the tasks in the 'Giant's House' of the Gaelic version, which the Roman ignores.

In the Russian story of 'Baba Yaga' (Ralston's 'Russian Folk Tales,' pp. 139) we have the three magic gifts. Though Mr. Campbell has a very ingenious solution for the idea of the supernatural attaching to swords (i. lxxii), the same does not seem at all to explain the introduction of supernatural combs;

when I once found a comb transformed into a mountain in a Tirolean story, I thought, as Mr. Ralston has also suggested (p. 144), that it fitted very well with the German expression for a mountain-ridge; but he does not tell us whether the metaphor holds good in Russ, where he finds it used; and in the present instance it is a hedge of thorns into which the comb resolves itself. I have another Roman story, in which the comb ' swelled and swelled till every one of its teeth became a pier, and the spaces between them were arches, and it was a bridge by which one could pass over.'

(4.) The kiss which brings forgetfulness, again, is found in the myths of every country. It occurs in the Tirolean story I have given as the ' Dove-Maiden ' in ' Household Stories from the Land of Hofer,' though I had to omit it there for want of space; but the remaining episodes of that story are nearly identical with those of the Russian story of ' The Water-King;' and in the Tirolean story the maiden is fetched from a heathen magician's house by the aid of saints, while in the others it is from giants' or witches' abodes, by aid of other giants and witches. Mr. Ralston supplies, at pp. 132–7, a long list of variants of this story, and in a Russian one, at p. 133, comes a ride on a Bear, which is one of the incidents in the ' Dove-Maiden,' though, if I remember right, it does not occur in any of the others. In Mr. Campbell's notes to ' The Battle of the Birds ' are also collected notices of variants of this episode.

The affinity of this story with others again will be found in Mr. Cox's ' Mythology of the Aryan Nations,' ii. p. 301.]

THE THREE LOVE-ORANGES.[1]

They say there was a king's son who went out to hunt.[2] It was a winter's day, and the ground was covered with snow, so that when he brought down the birds with his arquebuse the red blood made beautiful bright marks on the dazzling white snow.

' How beautiful!' exclaimed the prince. ' Never will

I marry till I find one with a complexion fair as this snow, and tinted like this rosy blood.'

When his day's sport was at an end, he went home and told his parents that he was going to wander over the world till he found one fair as snow, tinted like rosy blood. The parents approved his design and sent him forth.

On, on, on he went, till one day he met a little old woman, who stopped him, saying: 'Whither so fast, fair prince?'

He replied, 'I walk the earth till I find one who is fair as snow, tinted like rosy blood, to make her my wife.'

'That can I help you to, and I alone,' said the little old woman, who was a fairy; and then she gave him the three love-oranges, telling him that when he opened one such a maiden as he was in search of would appear, but he must immediately look for water and sprinkle her, or she would disappear again.

The prince took the oranges, and wandered on. On, on, on he went, till at last the fancy took him to break open one of the oranges. Immediately a beautiful maiden appeared, whose complexion was indeed fair as snow, and tinted like rosy blood, but it was only when she had already disappeared that he recollected about the water. It was too late, so on he wandered again till the fancy took him to open another orange. Instantly another maiden appeared, fairer than the other, and he lost no time in looking for water to sprinkle her, but there was none, and before he came back from the search she was gone.

On he wandered again till he was nearly home, when one day he noticed a handsome fountain standing by the road, and over against it a fine palace. The sight of the fountain made him think of his third orange, and he took it out and broke it open.

Instantly a third maiden appeared, far fairer than either of the others; with the water of the fountain he sprinkled her the moment she appeared, and she vanished not, but staid with him and loved him.

Then he said, ' You must stay here in this bower while I go on home and fetch a retinue worthy to escort you.'

In a palace opposite the fountain lived a black Saracen woman,[3] and just then she went down to the fountain to draw water, and as she looked into the water she said, ' My mistress says that I am so ugly, but I am so fair, therefore I break the pitcher and the little pitcher.'[4]

Then she looked up in the bower, and seeing the beautiful maiden, she called her down, and caressed her, and stroked her hair, and praised her beauty; but as she stroked her hair she took out a magic pin, and stuck it into her head, and instantly the maiden became a dove and perched on the side of the fountain.

Then she broke the pitcher and the little pitcher, and the prince came back.

When the prince saw the ugly black woman standing in the bower where he had left his beautiful maiden, he was quite bewildered, and looked all about for her.

' I am she whom you seek, prince,' said the woman. ' It is the sun has changed me thus while standing here waiting for you; but all will come right when I get away from the sun.'

The prince did not know what to make of it, but there was no help for it but to take her and trust to her coming right when she got away from the sun. He took her home, therefore, and right grand preparations were made for the royal marriage. Tapestries were hung on the walls, and flowers strewed the floor, while in the kitchen was the cook as busy as a bee, preparing I know not how many dishes for the royal banquet.

Then, lo, there came and perched on the kitchen window a little dove, and sang, ' Cook, cook, for whom are you cooking; for the son of the king, or the Saracen Moor? May the cook fall asleep, and may all the viands be burnt!'[5]

After this nothing would go right in the kitchen; every day all the dishes got burnt, and it was impossible to give the wedding banquet, because there was nothing fit to send up to the table. Then the king's son came into the kitchen to learn what had happened, and they showed him the dove which had done all. 'Sweet little dove!' said the prince, and, catching it in his hand, began to caress it; thus he felt the pin in its head, and pulled it out. Instantly his own fair maiden stood before him, white as snow, rosy as blood. Then the mystery was cleared up, and there was great rejoicing, and the old witch was burnt.

[1] 'I tre Melangoli di amore;' melangolo or merangolo, or merangola, an ungrafted orange. See note to 'Filagranata.'

[2] 'Caccia,' though usually translated by 'hunt,' is used for all kinds of sport. Bazzarini says it even includes 'pallone' and other games; but it is in common use for shooting small birds as for hunting quadrupeds.

[3] 'Mora Saracena,' a black Saracen woman; 'mora' is in constant use for a dark-coloured person. Senhor de Saraiva tells me that a so-called 'Mora encantada' figures as one of the favourite personages in Portuguese traditionary tales; but she is less often an actual Moor than a princess held in thrall by Moorish art, to be set free by Christian chivalry. She is often represented as bound at the bottom of a well.

[4]
Mia padrona dice che son tanta brutta,
E son tanta bella,
Io rompo la brocca e la brocchetta.

This verse would be hardly comprehensible but that the incident is better explained in the more detailed versions of other countries mentioned in note to the last tale. The ugly 'Mora' sees the reflection of the face of the beautiful maiden who sits in the tree overlooking the fountain, and takes it for her own. See Campbell's *Tales of the W. Highlands*, pp. 56-7, &c.

[5]
Cuoco, cuoco, per chi cucinate,
Pel figlio del rè o per la mora Saracena?
Il cuoco si possa dormentar',
E le vivande si possano bruciar'.

[This story, besides its similarities with those mentioned in note of the foregoing, is substantially the same as 'Die weisse u. die schwarze Braut' in Grimm (with his 'Schneeweisschen u. Rosenroth' it seems to have nothing in common, though the words 'Snow-white and rose-red' suggest it); but its commencement is different The German Tale of Sneewittchen (Grimm,

p. 206) has also much similarity with it : a queen sat working in a window framed with ebony ; she pricks her finger, and three drops of blood that fall on the snow suggest the wish that her child may be fair as snow, red as blood, and her hair as dark as ebony. Her wishes are fulfilled, and she dies. She is succeeded by a witch-stepmother, from whom the child of wishes suffers many things, but the witch is ultimately danced to death in red-hot iron shoes. A link between them is supplied by the next following, in which the opening agrees with the German story. In Schneller's ' Legends of the Italian Tirol' are two, with a title similar to the Roman one. In the first (' I tre aranci ') the girl becomes the property of a fairy, as in Filagranata. She is sent to fetch three oranges, which she does by the help of five gifts given her by an old man ; but the whole ends in the good child wishing as her only reward to be restored to her mother. The other is called ' L'amor dei tre aranci.' In this the prince breaks a witch's milkjug while playing at ball, and in revenge she tells him he shall not marry till he finds ' the Love of the three oranges,' which he similarly obtains by the help of five gifts received of an old woman ; when he opens them, the story goes on just like the Roman one, the verse of the dove being a little different :—

> Cogo, bel cogo,
> Endormeazate al fogo,
> Che l'arrosto se possa brusar,
> E la fiola (figlia) della stria non ne possa magnar.

and there is nothing about ' fair as snow, rosy as blood,' in it. He has another, ' Quel dalla coda di oro,' in which three golden apples or balls play a prominent part, but it belongs to another group. A second version of this, entitled ' I pomi d'oro,' however, is a strange mixture of the various Tirolean and Roman versions.

The Hungarian story of ' Vas Laczi ' (Iron Ladislas) begins, like ' L'amor dei tre aranci,' by a young prince getting into a scrape with a witch, this time by breaking her basket of eggs. His punishment is the fulfilment of his first wish, and his first wish happens to be a pettish one, that the earth might swallow up his three sisters ; as one of them is said to be always dressed like the sun, the second like the moon, and the third like the stars, we have a link with the German Marienkind and the Tirolean Klein-Else. Afterwards Iron Ladislas goes in search of his sisters, and encounters many heroic adventures and many transformations, in one of which a tree in a dragon's garden with golden apples is a prominent detail.

A tree with golden fruit is also an important incident in the principal and most popular of Hungarian myths, that of 'Tünder Illona' (Fairy Helen). As it is seen depicted on the thirteen compartments of the grand staircase walls of the National Club at Pest, Tünder Illona appears in the first as the Goddess or Queen of Summer held in thrall by the stern witch the Goddess or Queen of Winter. She is seen planting in the territory of the Earth-King a tree which represents her earnest longings after freedom, and committing it to the benign influence of the Sun-King.

The second shows this mystical tree bearing its golden fruit, which the beautiful Fairy, as if ashamed of her boldness, is hasting to pluck off, borne on a chariot formed of obedient swans. The Wind-genius wafts poppy seeds over the eyes of the armed guard the Winter-Queen had set round the tree, and lulls them to sleep.

In the third Argilus, the Earth-Prince, is seen surprising in his (up till then vain) nightly attempt to gather the golden fruit, Tünder Illona's departing convoy. He aims an arrow at the coy plunderer; then suddenly a glance from her pierces his heart instead, and he lets the arrow harmlessly strike the ground.

The fourth portrays the happy union of Illona and Argilus, Summer and Earth; but the Winter-Queen comes by enraged at their successful defiance of her, and cuts off Illona's beautiful golden locks. (The people have it that these locks borne along by the winds planted the Puszta with the beautiful long feathery grass which they call ' Orphan-girl's hair '). In the distance are seen the parents of the Earth-Prince hurrying forward in search of their son.

The fifth shows Tünder Illona waking from her delicious slumber, and on discovering the loss of the mantle of her hair, hasting back in agony to her swan-chariot. Argilus in vain stretches out his arms after her, and prays her to remain always with him.

In the sixth the scene is changed to the dwelling of the Earth-King. Prince Argilus is taking leave of his parents as he starts on his perilous journey, determined to deliver the captive Fairy.

In the seventh the Earth-Prince has advanced on his journey as far as the dwelling of a giant, of whom he asks counsel, and who appoints him three witches to show the way to regain the Tünder.

In the eighth he is seen victorious in a late conflict with three giants, from each of whom he has succeeded in gaining an instrument necessary for his purpose; from one a switch, from another a pipe, from the third a conjuring mantle. The giants throw down masses of rock upon him, but he spreads out the conjuring mantle, and committing himself to it, floats securely through the air.

In the ninth Argilus has reached the Winter-Witch's border, and prepares to engage in combat with the dragon who guards it.

The tenth is highly sensational. The Winter-Witch has thrown a deep sleep over him, and the poor Summer-Fairy strives to awaken him in vain.

In ·the eleventh the ardent desires of Tünder Illona have prevailed over all the enchantments of the Winter-Witch, and at her prayer there rises up from the innermost region of the earth the fairy Iron-Queen, who brings the Tátos, the winged magic horse who is to bear the Prince through all dangers to certain victory.

The twelfth shows Argilus and Illona once more united, enthroned side by side, and subjects bearing them offerings.

The thirteenth is a large composition symbolising the mystic union of Earth and Summer, whence sprang, says the myth, Autumn with her abundant fruits, and the great god Pan, the author of all productiveness, who called the land of his birth after his own name and blessed it with fecundity above all nations of the earth. The tree of golden fruit, the first occasion of the auspicious meeting which led to this union, is again introduced, and Tünder Illona is again clothed in her luxuriant mantle of golden hair.]

PALOMBELLETTA.¹

THEY say there was a peasant whose wife had died and
left him one little girl, who was the most beautiful creature that ever was seen; no one on earth could compare
with her for beauty. After a while the peasant married
again : this time he married a peasant-woman who had a
daughter who was the most deformed object that ever was
seen; no cripple on earth could compare with her for
deformity; and, moreover, her skin was quite black and
shrivelled, and altogether no one could bear to look at
her, she was so hideous.

One day when everyone was out, and only the fair
daughter at home, the king came by from hunting thirsty,
and he stopped at the cottage and asked the fair maid for
a glass of water. When he saw how fair she was and with
what grace she waited on him, he said, 'Fair maiden, if
you will, I will come back in eight days and make you
my wife.' The maiden answered, 'Indeed I will it, your
Majesty!' and the king rode away.

When the stepmother came home the simple maiden
told her all that had happened, and she answered her
deceitfully, congratulating her on her good fortune.
Before the day came round, however, she shut the fair
maiden in the cellar. When the king came she went out
to meet him with a smiling face, saying, 'Good day, Sire !
What is your royal pleasure?' And the king answered,
'To marry your daughter am I come.' Then the stepmother brought out her own daughter to him, all wrapped
up in a wide mantle, and her face covered with a thick
veil, and a hood over that.

'Rest assured, good woman, that your daughter will
be my tenderest care,' said the king; 'but you must take
those wrappers off.'

'By no means, Sire !' exclaimed the stepmother.

' And beware you do it not. You have seen how fair she is above all the children of earth. But this exceeding beauty she has on one condition. If one breath of air strike her she loses it all. Therefore, Oh, king! let not the veil be removed.'

When the king heard that he called for another veil, and another hood, and wrapping her still more carefully round, handed her into the carriage he had brought for her, shut the door close, and rode away on horseback by her side.

When they arrived at the palace the hideous daughter of the stepmother was married to the king all wrapt up in her veils.

The stepmother, however, went into her room, full of triumph at what she had done. ' But what am I to do with the other girl! ' she said to herself ; ' somehow or other some day she will get out of the cellar, and the king will see her, and it will be worse for my daughter than before.' And as she knew not what to do she went to a witch to help her. ' This is what you must do,' said the witch ; ' take this pin ' (and she gave her a long pin with a gold head), ' and put it into the head of the maiden, and she will become a dove. Then have ready a cage, and keep her in it, and no one will ever see her for a maiden more.'

The stepmother went therefore, and bought a cage, and taking the large pin [2] down into the cellar, she drove the pin into the fair maiden's head, holding open the cage as she did so.

As soon as the pin entered the maiden's head she became a dove, but instead of flying into the cage she flew over the stepmother's head far away out of sight.

On she flew till she came to the king's palace, right against the window of the kitchen where the cook was ready preparing a great dinner for the king. The cook looked round as he heard the poor little dove beating its frightened breast against the window, and, fearful lest it should hurt itself, he opened the window.

In flew the dove as soon as he opened the window, and
flew three times round his head, singing each time as she
did so :—'O cook! O cook! of the royal kitchen, what
shall we do with the Queen ?   All of you put yourselves to
sleep, and may the dinner be burnt up!'[3]

As soon as she had sung this the third time the cook
sank into a deep sleep ; the dinner from want of attention
was all burnt up; and when the king sat down to table,
there was nothing to set before him.

'Where is the dinner?' exclaimed the king, as he
looked over the empty table to which he had brought his
bride, still wrapt up in her thick veils.

'Please your Majesty, the dinner is all burnt up as
black as charcoal,' said the chamberlain; 'and the cook
sits in the kitchen so fast asleep that no one can wake
him.'

'Go and fetch me a dinner from the inn,' said the
king ; 'and the cook, when he comes to himself, let him
be brought before me.'

After a time the cook came to himself, and the chamberlain brought him before the king.

'Tell me how this happened,' said the king to the
cook.   'All these years you have served me well and
faithfully ; how is it that to-day, when the dinner should
have been of the best in honour of my bride, everything
is burnt up, and the king's table is left empty?'

'Indeed, the dinner had been of the best, Sire,' answered
the cook. 'So had I prepared it.   Only, when all was
nearly ready, there came a dove flying in at the window,
and flew three times round my head, singing each time,

> Cook of the royal kitchen,
> What shall we do with the Queen ?
> Sleep ye all soundly, and burnt be the meal
> Which on the King's board should have been.

After that a deep sleep fell on me and I know nothing
more of what happened.'

'That must have been a singular dove,' said the king; 'bring her to me and you shall be forgiven.'

The cook went down to look for the dove, and found her midway, flying to meet him.

'There is the dove, Sire,' said the cook, handing the dove to the king.

'So you spoilt my dinner, did you palombelletta,' said the king. 'But never mind; you are a dear little dove, and I forgive you,' and he put her in his breast and stroked her. Thus, as he went on stroking and fondling her, calling her 'palombelletta bella!' he felt the gold head of the stepmother's big pin through the feathers. 'What have you got in your head, palombelletta dear?' he said, and pulled the pin out.

Instantly the fair maiden stood before him in all her surpassing beauty as he had seen her at the first. 'Are you not my fair maiden who promised to marry me?' exclaimed the king.

'The very same, and no other,' replied the maiden.

'Then who is this one?' said the king, and he turned to the stepmother's daughter beside him, and tore off her veil. Then he understood the deceit that had been played on him, and he sent for the stepmother, and ordered that she and her daughter should be punished with death.

---

[1] 'Palombelletta,' dear little dove.

[2] 'Spillone,' big pin. This magic use of long pins driven into the head is one of the frequent charges against witches. See numerous instances at various epochs given by Del Rio, 'Disquisitionum Magicarum,' lib. iii. p. 1, 2 iv. s. II., where he mentions among others the cases of two midwives who were convicted in Germany of having destroyed, the one forty, the other innumerable, new-born infants in this manner.

[3]
        Cuoco! cuoco! di reale cucina
        Che faremo della regina?
        Tutti posse a dormentar',
        E la pranza posse bruciar'.

The words have been clipt in repetition. 'Posse,' in the third line, must be a corruption of 'si pongono,' from the verb 'ponere;' and in the third line, of 'si può,' from the verb 'potere.'

[The next group most prolific in variety of incidents is that in which the stepmother represents the evil genius of the story; sometimes there is a daughter only, sometimes a daughter and a son, and sometimes, but less frequent, a son only. Allied to it is that in which the character devolves on two elder sisters, not specified to be stepsisters, and the incidents in these two branches are closely interwoven. I give the first place to Cinderella, because it has acquired a homely importance.]

LA CENORIENTOLA.[1]

THEY say there was a merchant who had three daughters. When he went out into foreign countries to buy wares he told them he would bring them rare presents whatever they might ask for. The eldest asked for precious jewels, the second for rich shawls, but the youngest who was always kept out of sight in the kitchen by the others, and made to do the dirty work of the house, asked only for a little bird.

'So you want a little bird, do you! What is the use of a little bird to you!' said the sisters mocking her, and 'Papa will have something else to think of than minding little birds on a long journey.'

'But you *will* bring me a little bird, won't you, papa?' pleaded the little girl; 'and I can tell you that if you don't the boat you are on will stand still, and will neither move backwards nor forwards.'

The merchant went away into a far country and bought precious wares, but he forgot all about the little bird. It was only when he had got on board a boat to go down a mighty river on his homeward way, and the captain found the boat would not move by any means, that he remembered what his daughter had said to him. Then while the captain was wondering how it was the boat would not move, he went to him and told him what he had done. But the captain said, 'That is easily set right. Here close by is a garden full of thousands of birds; you can easily creep in and carry off one. *One* will never be missed among so many thousands.'

The merchant followed his directions and went into the garden where there were so many thousand birds that he easily caught one. The captain gave him a cage, and he brought it safely home and gave it to his daughter.

That night the elder sisters said as usual, ' We are going to the ball; you will stay at home and sweep up the place and mind the fire.'

Now all the birds in the garden which the captain had pointed out to the merchant were fairies; so when the others were gone to the ball and the youngest daughter went into her room to her bird, she said to it:

> Give me splendid raiment,
> And I will give you my rags.[2]

Immediately, the bird gave her the most beautiful suit of clothes, with jewels and golden slippers, and a splendid carriage and prancing horses. With these the maiden went to the ball which was at the king's palace. The moment the king saw her he fell in love with her, and would dance with no one else. The sisters were furious with the stranger because the king danced all night with her and not with them, but they had no idea it was their sister.

The second night she did the same, only the bird gave her a yet more beautiful dress, and the king did all he could to find out who she was, but she would not tell him. Then he asked her name and she said,—

' They call me *Cenorientola.*'

' *Cenorientola,*' said the king; ' what a pretty name! I never heard it before.'

He had also told the servants that they must run after her carriage and see where it went; but though they ran as fast as the wind they could not come near the pace of her horses.

The third night the sisters went to the ball and left

her at home, and she staid at home with her little bird
and said to it,—

> Give me splendid raiment,
> And I will give you my rags.'

Then the bird gave her a more splendid suit still, and the
king paid her as much attention as ever. But to the
servants he had said, ' If you don't follow fast enough to-
night to see where she lives I will have all your heads cut
off.' So they used such extra diligence that she in her
hurry to get away dropped one of her golden slippers ;
this the servants picked up and brought to the king.

The next day the king sent a servant into every house
in the city till he should find her whom the golden slipper
fitted, but there was not one ; last of all he came to the
merchant's house, and he tried it on the two elder daughters
and it would fit neither. Then he said,—

' There must be some other maiden in this house ; ' but
they only shrugged their shoulders. ' It is impossible ;
another maiden there must be, for every maiden in the city
we have seen and the slipper fits none, therefore one there
must be here.'

Then they said,—

' In truth we have a little sister who sits in the kitchen
and does the work. She is called *Cenorientola*, because
she is always smutty. We are sure she never went to a
ball, and it would only soil the beautiful gold slipper to
let her put her smutty feet into it.'

' It may be so,' replied the king's servant, ' but we
must try, nevertheless.'

So they fetched her, and the king's servant found that
the shoe fitted her ; and they went and told the king all.

The moment the king heard them say *Cenorientola*
he said,—' That is she ! It is the name she gave me.'

So he sent a carriage to fetch her in all haste. The
bird meantime had given her a more beautiful dress than
any she had had before, and priceless jewels, so that when
they came to fetch her she looked quite fit to be a queen.

Then the king married her; and though her sisters had behaved so ill to her she gave them two fine estates, so that all were content.

¹ 'Cinderella' is a favourite in all countries, with its promise of compensation to the desolate and oppressed. I only came across it once, however, while making this collection, in its own simple form, and with a name as near its own as *Cenorientola*. Of course the construction of such words is quite arbitrary, and any Italian can make a dozen such out of any name or word: even in the dictionary the following variations are to be found—'Cenericcio,' 'Cenerognolo,' 'Cenerino,' 'Ceneroso,' 'Cenerugiolo.'

²   Da mi tu panni belli,
       Ed io te do i cencirelli.

³   Da mi tu abiti belli
       Ed io te do i stracciarelli.

The same as above: 'abiti' and 'panni' are convertible, so are 'cenci and 'straccj.'

[The counterparts to the story are endless. In Grimm's 'Aschenputtel' (p. 93), the nominal German counterpart, there is a stepmother as well as two sisters, and the story turns upon the gifts each daughter craves of the father, an episode which occurs in Roman versions with different titles. His 'Die drei Männlein im Walde' ('Three Little Men in the Wood') is like it, and the other versions too, and the episode in it of the good daughter receiving the faculty of dropping a gold coin from her mouth at every word she utters, is like a Hungarian story, in which no stepmother figures, but the evil genius of the story (the Lady-in-Waiting) is plainly called a witch. In this story it is a princess, from whose footsteps rise gold pieces, her tears are pearls, and her smiles rosebuds. In one of the Siddhi Kür Stories which I have translated as 'Sagas from the far East' (p. 49) is a similar incident, and a Spanish equivalent in Note 3. A friend of mine met with a very similar legend in a convent at Quito, concerning a nun called 'the Rose of Quito,' out of whose grave a rose-tree is said to have sprung and blossomed on the morrow of her burial. It seems, however, to have an independent origin, as 'the Rose of Quito' died within the last 150 years. In the Tirolean 'Klein-Else,' or 'Aschenpfödl,' to which allusion has already been made, and which answers to it in name, we have a connexion with the last group (as in some of the succeeding Roman versions) in the sun, moon, and star dresses.

Among the Tales of Italian Tirol we find it as *Zendrarola*, and with a good deal of variation from any other form I have met. The story opens with a dying father as in the North Tirolean ' Klein-Else,' but it is only a rich man, not a warrior-baron, and he has three daughters instead of one. He bids them choose what gifts he shall bestow on them before he dies, and the eldest asks for a pair of earrings; the second for a dress; and the youngest for his magic sword, which gives whatever the possessor wishes for. The story is singular in this, that the elder sisters seem to have no spite. The father does not die; but, notwithstanding his recovery, he has nothing more to do with the story further than to give an unwilling consent that the youngest daughter, though his favourite, shall go forth with her sword and roam the world till she finds a husband. She only takes service in a large house in a big town, however; but there falls in love with a melancholy youth, son of a count, who lives opposite. For the sake of being nearer him, she obtains the place of kitchen-maid in his palace, and thus acquires her title of Zendrarola in a very different way from her counterparts in other lands. One day she hears he is going to a ball, and she makes her wishing-sword give her a dress like the sky; and the young Count, who has never admired anyone before, of course falls in love with her. When he comes back, he confides to his lady mother what has occurred, and Zendrarola, now again dressed as a dirty drudge, interposes that the fair one he was extolling was not prettier than herself. He silences her indignantly by giving her a poke with the shovel, and when she meets him next night in some beautiful attire, and he asks her where she comes from, she answers ' *dalla palettada* ' (from shovel-blow). The next day the same thing happens, and he gives her a blow with the tongs, and when he asks her in the evening what her country is, she answers ' *majettada* ' (tongs-blow); answering to *Frustinaia* and *Stivalaia* in the second Roman version of ' Maria di Legno.' He gives her a ring, which she sends up in his broth, as Klein-Else does in the pancake, and so he recognises and marries her. In one or two of the Roman versions also, the means of recognition is a ring in place of a slipper.

I do not remember any Cinderella among the Russian Tales, though there are stepmother stories, which pair off with others of the Roman. For Scotch versions I must refer the reader to Campbell's ' Highland Tales,' i. 226, and ii. 292.]

VACCARELLA.[1]

THEY say there was once a husband and a wife; but I don't mean that they were husband and wife of each other. The husband had lost his wife, and the wife had lost her husband, and each had one little daughter. The husband sent his daughter to the wife to be brought up along with her own daughter, and as the girl came every morning to be trained and instructed, the wife used to send a message back by her every evening, saying, 'Why doesn't your father marry me? then we should all live together, and you would no longer have this weary walk to take.'

The father, however, did not see it in the same light; but the teacher[2] continued sending the same message. In short,[3] at last she carried her point, having previously given a solemn promise to him that Maria, his little girl, should be always as tenderly treated as her own.

Not many months elapsed, however, before she began to show herself a true stepmother. After treating Maria with every kind of harshness, she at last sent her out into the Campagna to tend the cow, so as to keep her out of sight of her father, and estrange him from her. Maria had to keep the cow's stall clean with fresh litter every day; sometimes she had to take the cow out to grass, and watch that it only grazed over the right piece of land; at other times she had to go out and cut grass for the cow to eat. All this was work enough for one so young; but Maria was a kind-hearted girl, and grew fond of her cow, so that it became a pleasure to her to attend to it.

When the cruel stepmother saw this she was annoyed to find her so light-hearted over her work, and to vex her more gave her a great heap of hemp to spin. It was in vain that Maria reminded her she had never been taught to spin; the only answer she got was, 'If you don't bring it home with you to-night all properly spun you will be finely punished;' and Maria knew to her cost what that meant.

When Maria went out into the Campagna that day she was no longer light-hearted; and as she littered down the stall she stroked the cow fondly, and said to her, as she had no one else to complain to, 'Vaccarella! Vaccarella! what shall I do? I have got all this hemp to spin, and I never learnt spinning. Yet if I don't get through it somehow I shall get sadly beaten to-night. Dear little cow, tell me what to do!'

But the cow was an enchanted cow,[4] and when she heard Maria cry she turned round and said quickly and positively:—

> Throw it on to the horns of me,
> And go along, cut grass for me![5]

Maria did as she was told, went out and cut a good basketful of grass, and imagine her delight on coming back with it to find all the whole lot of hemp beautifully spun.

The surprise of the stepmother was still greater than hers, at finding that she had got through her task so easily, for she had given her enough to have occupied an ordinary person a week. Next day, therefore, she determined to vex her with a more difficult task, and gave her a quantity of spun hemp[6] to weave into a piece of fine cloth. Maria's pleadings were as fruitless as before, and once more she went to tell her tale of woe to her 'dear little cow.'

Vaccarella readily gave the same answer as before:—

> Throw it on to the horns of me,
> And go along, cut grass for me!

Once more, when Maria came back with her basket of grass, she found all her work done, to her great surprise and delight. But her stepmother's surprise was quite of another order. That Maria should have woven the cloth, not only without instruction, but even without a loom, proved clearly enough she must have had some one to help her—a matter which roused the stepmother's jealousy in the highest degree, and wherein this help consisted she determined to find out. Accordingly, next day she gave her a shirt to make up, and then posted herself out of sight in a corner of the cow-house to see what happened. Thus she overheard Maria's complaint to her dear little cow, and Vaccarella's reply :—

> Throw it on to the horns of me,
> And go along, cut grass for me!

She thus also saw, what Maria did not see, that as soon as she had gone out the cow assumed the form of a woman, and sat down and stitched and stitched away till the shirt was made, and that in a surprisingly short space of time. As soon as it was finished, and before Maria came in, the woman became a cow again.

The cruel stepmother determined that Maria should be deprived of a friend who enabled her to set all her hard treatment at defiance, and next morning told her that she was going to kill the cow. Maria was broken-hearted at the announcement, but she knew it was useless to remonstrate ; so she only used her greatest speed to reach her ' dear little cow,' and warn her of what was going to happen in time to make her escape.

' There is no need for me to escape,' replied Vaccarella ; ' killing will not hurt me. So dry your tears, and don't be distressed. Only, after they have killed me, put your hand under my heart, and there you will find a golden ball. This ball is yours, so take it out, and whenever you are tired of your present kind of life, you have only to say to it on some fitting occasion—"Golden ball, golden ball, dress me in gold and give me a lover," [7] and you shall see what shall happen.'

Vaccarella had no time to say more, for the stepmother arrived just then with a man who slaughtered the cow at her order.

D

Under Vaccarella's heart Maria found the promised golden ball, which she hid away carefully against some fitting occasion for using it arose.

Not long after there was a *novena*⁸ of a great festival, during which Maria's stepmother, with all her disposition to overwork her, durst not keep her from church, lest the neighbours should cry ' Shame !' on her.

Maria accordingly went to church with all the rest of the people, and when she had made her way through the crowd to a little distance from her stepmother, she took her golden ball out of her pocket and whispered to it— ' Golden ball, golden ball, dress me in gold and give me a lover.'

Instantly the golden ball burst gently open and enveloped her, and she came out of it all radiant with beautiful clothing, like a princess. Everybody made way for her in her astonishing brightness.

The eyes of the king's son were turned upon her, no less than the eyes of all the people ; and the prayers were no sooner over than he sent some of his attendants to call her and bring her to him. Before they could reach her, however, Maria had restored her beautiful raiment to the golden ball, and, in the sordid attire in which her stepmother dressed her, she could easily pass through the crowd unperceived.

At home, her stepmother could not forbear talking, like everyone else in the town, about the maiden in glittering raiment who had appeared in the midst of the church ; but, of course, without the remotest suspicion that it was Maria herself. But Maria sat still and said nothing.

So it happened each day of the Novena; for, though Maria was not at all displeased with the appearance and fame of the husband whom her ' dear little cow ' seemed to have appointed for her, she did not wish to be too easy a prize, and thought it but right to make him take a little trouble to win her. Thus she every day restored all her bright clothing to the golden ball before the prince's men could overtake her. Only on the last day of the Novena, when the prince, fearful lest it might also be the last on which he would have an opportunity of seeing her, had told them to use extra diligence, they were so near overtaking her that, in the hurry of the moment, she dropped a slipper.[9] This the prince's men eagerly seized, feeling no compunction in wresting it from the mean-looking wench (so Maria now looked) who disputed possession of it with them, not in the least imagining that she could be the radiant being of whom they were in search.

The Novena over, Maria once more returned to her ceaseless toil; but the stepmother's hatred had grown so great that she determined to rid herself of her altogether and in the most cruel way.

Down in the cellar there stood a large barrel,[10] which had grown dirty and mouldy from neglect, and wanted scalding out. ' Get into the barrel, Maria girl,' she bid her next morning for her task, ' and scrape it and rub it well before we scald it.'

Maria did as she was bid, and the stepmother went away to boil the water.

Meantime, the prince's men had taken Maria's slipper to him, and he, delighted to have any token of his fair one, appointed an officer to go into every house, and proclaim that the maiden whom the slipper might fit should be his bride. The officer went round from house to house, trying the slipper on everybody's foot. But it fitted no one, for it was under a spell.

But the stepmother's own daughter[11] had gone down to the cellar to help Maria, unbeknown to her mother; and it so happened that, just as she was inside the barrel and Maria outside, the king's officer happened to come by that way. He opened the door,[12] and, seeing a damsel standing within, tried on the sandal without waiting to ask leave. As the sandal fitted Maria to perfection, the

officer was all impatience to carry her off to the prince,
and placed her in the carriage which was waiting outside,
and drove off with her before anyone had even observed
his entrance.

Scarcely had all this passed than the stepmother came
back, with her servants, each carrying a can of boiling
water. They placed themselves in a ring round the barrel,
and each emptied her charge into it. As it was the stepmother's daughter who was inside at the time, instead of
Maria, it was she who got scalded to death in her place.

By-and-by, when the house was quiet, the bad stepmother went to the barrel, intending to take out the body
of Maria and hide it. What was her dismay when she
found, instead of Maria's body, that of her own daughter !
As soon as her distress and grief subsided sufficiently to
enable her to consider what she had to do, the idea suggested itself to conceal the murder by putting the blame
of it on some one else. For this purpose she took the
body of her daughter, and, dressing it in dry clothes, seated
it on the top of the stairs against her husband's return.[13]

Presently, home he came with his ass-load of wood,
and called to her daughter to come and help him unload
it, as usual. But the daughter continued sitting on the
top of the stairs, and moved not. Again and again he
called, louder and louder, but still she moved not ; till at
last, irritated beyond all endurance, he hurled one of his
logs of wood at her, which brought the badly-balanced
corpse rolling and tumbling all the way down the stairs,
just as the stepmother had designed.

The husband, however, was far from being deceived by
the device. He could see the body presented no appearance of dying from a recent fall.

' Where's Maria ? ' he asked, as soon as he got up into
the room.

' Nobody knows ; she has disappeared ! ' replied the
stepmother ; nor was he slow to convince himself she was
nowhere in the house.

'This is no place for me to stay in,' said the husband to himself. 'One child driven away, and one murdered; who can say what may happen next?'

Next morning, therefore, he called to him the little daughter born to him since his marriage with Maria's stepmother, and went away with her for good and all. So that bad woman was deprived, as she deserved, of her husband and all her children in one day.

Just as the father and his daughter were starting to go away, Maria drove by in a gilded coach with the prince her husband; so he had the satisfaction, and her stepmother the vexation, of seeing her triumph.

----

[1] 'Vaccarella,' 'dear little cow,' 'good little cow.' The endearment is expressed in the form of the diminutive.

[2] 'Maestra.'

[3] 'Basta,' 'enough,' 'to cut a long story short.'

[4] 'Fatata.'

[5]
> Butta sopr' alle corna a me,
> E vatene far l'erba per me.

'Corno' is one of the words which (as 'muro,' 'novo,' 'braccio,' 'dito,' &c.), masculine in the singular, have a feminine plural.

[6] 'Carrèvale,' or 'corrèvale'—I could not very well distinguish which, and do not know the word. The narrator explained it as like 'cànapa'—hemp, only finer. 'Refe' is used in the same sense in Tuscany.

[7]
> Pallo dorato! Pallo dorato!
> Vestimi d'oro e dammi l'innamorato.

'Dorato' is used for 'golden' as well as for 'gilt.' The change from 'palla,' a ball, to 'pallo' is a very considerable license, for the sake of making it rime with 'innamorato;' though some words admit of being spelt either way, as 'mattino' or 'mattina,' 'botto' or 'botta' (a blow), and others can be used with either gender without alteration, as 'polvere.' I have never met with 'pallo' elsewhere, though it is one of the words which take a masculine augmentative ('pallone').

[8] 'Novena,' a short service, with or without a sermon, said for nine days before some great festival, in preparation for it.

[9] 'Pianella,' a sandal, or slipper without a heel. '*In those days* they used to wear such things instead of shoes,' commented the old lady as she told the tale.

[10] 'Botte,' a very large wine-barrel of a certain measure.

[11] Here called 'buona figlia,' 'good daughter.' There did not seem any reason for this designation. Possibly the narrator had forgotten some incident of the story, introducing it.

83825

[12] That the cellar should be, as thus appears, on the ground-floor, is very characteristic of Rome, though there are, of course, plenty of underground cellars too; but the one is properly ' cantino' and ' canova,' and the other ' grottino.' The distinction is, however, not very rigidly observed in common parlance. To have an underground cellar is so far a *specialité*, that it has been taken to be a sufficiently distinctive attribute to supply the sign or title to those inns which possess it. Rufini gives examples of above a dozen thus called ' Del Grottino.'

[13] The ground-floor being used as a cellar, the family lives upstairs. This is a very common arrangement.

[The introduction of the wonder-working cow in this second version of the story of Cinderella cannot fail to suggest the idea that it may find its prototype in Sabala, the heavenly cow of the Ramayana.[1]

I have another Stepmother story, the place of which is here, but it is too long to give in its entirety. It begins like the last, and the next, and many others, with a widower, the teacher of whose children, a boy and girl, insists on marrying him. Soon after, of course, she turns the children out of doors; the boy is made the slave of a witch, and comes well at last out of many adventures; it is one of the nearest approaches to a heroic story that I have met with in Rome. There are details in it, however, like Filagranata and others, not actually of the Stepmother group. The girl gets taken into a Brigand's cave, and goes through adventures which befall the youngest of *three* sisters (without a stepmother) in the Italian-Tirolese tale of ' Le tre Sorelle,' and that, again, is precisely like another Roman story I have, in many respects different from the present one, called ' The Three Windows.' One of the adventures in the present story is, that the witch, instead of killing the girl, gives her the appearance of death, and she is shut up in a box instead of being regularly buried, and a prince, as he goes by hunting, finds her, and the means of restoring

[1] The reader who has not access to a better rendering of this beautiful legend will find one I have given from Bopp, in 'Sagas from the Far East,' pp. 402–3; but Mr. Ralston gives us a Russian version, in which a doll or puppet is the agent instead of the cow (pp. 150–9). It is true, on the other hand, that he has (p. 115) another rather different story, in which a cow also gives good gifts; and mentions others at p. 260. In a story of the Italian Tirol, ' Le due Sorelle,' which I shall have occasion to notice later, a cow has also a supernatural part to play, somewhat like that of Vaccarella; only there she acts at the bidding of a fairy, not of her own motion.

her, and marries her. This is a very common incident in another group, and occurs in the ' Siddhi Kür ' story which I have given as ' The Prayer making suddenly Rich,' in ' Sagas from the Far East ; ' and in the third version of ' Maria de Legno, *infra*, where also the girl is not even seemingly dead. I cannot forbear subjoining a quaint version of the story of Joseph, which was told me, embodying the same incident, though the story of Joseph has usually been identified with the group in which a younger brother is the hero ; by Dr. Dasent, among others, who gives several examples, under the name of ' Boots.' In the Roman series this group is represented by ' Scioccolone.']

GIUSEPPE L'EBREO.

' Do you know the story of Giuseppe l'Ebreo ?'

' Not by that name. Tell it me, and I'll tell you if I've heard it before.'

' There was once a *moglie e marito* who had seven sons.'

' Oh, do you mean the Machabees ?'

' No. I don't think they were called Machabees—I don't know. But the youngest of the seven was called Joseph, and he was his father's Benjamin, and that made the others jealous of him. They used to go out in the Campagna together to feed the flocks, for in those days all were shepherds ; and when the others had Joseph out there all alone they said, " Let us kill him ;" and they were going to kill him ; but one said, " No, we must not kill him : we will put him down a well ;" and so they did.

' The next day it happened that a great king went by hunting, and as his dogs passed the well where Joseph was they scented human blood and made a great barking, and the king said, " See what the dogs have found." So they took the stone from the mouth of the well and let a cord·down, and behold a beautiful boy came up—for Joseph was a beautiful boy— and he pleased the king, and he took him home and kept him as a precious jewel, he was so fair. So handsome was he, that the Queen fell in love with him ; and when he wouldn't listen to her she accused him of having insulted her, and had him put into prison.

' After that the King had a strange dream : he saw three lean cows and three fat cows ; and he saw the three lean cows eat up the three fat cows ; and he sent for all the *theologians* in the country, and none of them could tell what the dream meant ; but Joseph said, " I can tell what the dream means." . . . The rest as in the Bible.'

[Dr. Dasent gives one Norse story of a stepmother, with a stepson and daughter, which begins like the one of which I have given an abstract, but runs off into quite different incidents.]

THE KING WHO GOES OUT TO DINNER.[1]

THEY say there was a well-to-do peasant whose wife died leaving him two children—a boy and a girl. Both were beautiful children, but the girl was of the most inconceivable beauty.

As both were still young, and the father did not know how to supply a mother's place to them, he sent them to a woman, who was to teach them and train them, and do all that a mother would have done for them. So to her they went every day. The woman, however, was bent on marrying their father, and used to send a message every day to ask why he did not marry her. The father sent in answer that he did not want to marry; but the woman continued to repeat the same message so frequently that, wearied by her importunity, he sent an answer to the effect that when a pair of strong woollen stockings, which he also gave the children to take to her, were rotted away he would marry her, and not before. The woman took the pair of stockings and hung them up in a loft and damped them with water twice a day till they were soon quite rotted ; then she showed them to the children, and told them to tell their father what they had seen. When the children went home they said, ' Papa ! we saw your pair of stockings to-day; they are all rotted away.' But the father said, ' Nonsense ! Those thick stockings could not have rotted in this time ; there must be some unfair play.'

The next morning he gave them a large pitcher of water, and told them to take it to their teacher, saying that when all the water had dried up he would marry her, and not before. The teacher took the children up every day to see how rapidly the water diminished in the jug; but the fact was she used to go first and pour out a little every day.[2] At last she showed them the pitcher empty, and bid them tell their father that they had seen it so. 'Impossible!' said their father; but when they assured him they had seen the water in it gradually diminish day by day, he saw there was no way of disputing the fact, and that he was bound by the condition he himself had fixed.

Accordingly he married the teacher. No sooner, however, was she in possession of the house than she told the father she would not have the children about the place; they were not her children, and she could not bear the sight of them. The father expostulated, saying he had no place to send them to, but the stepmother continued so persistently in her representations that, for the sake of peace, he ceased to oppose her, and she took upon herself the task of disposing of them.

One day, therefore, she made them a large cake,[3] and putting it in a basket with a bottle of wine, she took them for a walk outside the gates. When they had gone a long, long way, she proposed that they should sit down and lunch off their cake and wine. The children were nothing loth; but, while they were eating, the stepmother slipped away unperceived, and left them alone, thinking that they would be lost. But the fact was the boy had overheard their father and mother talking about getting rid of them, and he had provided himself with a paper parcel[4] of ashes, and had strewn them all along the road they had come, unperceived by his stepmother, and so now by this track they found their way home again.

The stepmother was furious at seeing them come back, but she said nothing in order not to rouse their suspicions. A few days after, however, she made another cake and proposed to take them another walk. The children accompanied her willingly; but the little boy provided himself with a parcel of millet, and strewed the grain on the ground as they walked along. They were in no haste, therefore, to finish their refection. But, alas! when they came to trace the track by which they were to return,

there was no means of finding it, for the birds had come
meanwhile and eaten up all the grain. The little girl
was appalled when she saw they were lost, and sat down
to cry; but the little boy said, 'Never mind; our stepmother was very cross and unkind to us; perhaps we shall
meet with some one who will behave better to us. Come,
let us look for shelter before night comes on.' The little
girl took courage at her brother's words, and, joining
hands, they walked on together.

Before night they came to a little cottage, the only
one in sight; so they knocked at the door. 'Who's there?'
said a voice within, and when they answered 'Friends,' an
old man opened the door. 'Will you please take us in
and give us shelter for the night, for our stepmother has
turned us out of our home?' said the little boy. 'Come
in, and welcome,' answered the old man, 'and you shall
be my children.' So they went in and lived with him as
his children.

When they had been living there some time, it
happened that one day when the old man and her brother
were both out, the king came by hunting, and he came
to the hut and asked for some water to drink. The extraordinary beauty of the maiden astonished the king, and
he asked her whence she was, and so learnt all her story.
When he went home he told his mother, saying, 'When I
was out to-day I saw the most beautiful maiden that ever
was created. You must come and see her.' The queen-
mother did not like going to the poor hut, but the prince
urged her so much that at last she consented to accompany
him. The king drove out beforehand to the cottage and
gave notice that he would like to dine there, and, giving
the maiden plenty of money, told her to prepare the best
dinner that ever she could for him and the queen-mother.
The maiden tidied up the cottage so neatly, and prepared
the dinner so well, and did the honours of it so gracefully,
that the queen-mother was won to admire her as much as

her son had been, and when the king told her of his intention to make the girl his wife she was well pleased. So
Albina (such was her name) was married to the king, and
her brother was made viceroy.

In the meantime, the stepmother had begun to wonder
what had become of the children. But she was a
witch, and had a divining rod;[5] this rod she struck, and
asked it where the children were. The answer came,
' The girl is married to the king, and the lad is made
viceroy.'

When she heard this she went to her husband and said,
' Do you know a sort of remorse has taken me that we let
those poor children go we know not whither. I am
resolved to put on a pilgrim's dress and go and seek them
that I may bring them home to us again.' The father
was very glad to hear her speak thus, and gave his consent
to her taking the journey. The next day, therefore, she
put on a pilgrim's dress and went forth.

On, on, on she went till she came to the city where
Albina was married to the king. Here she took up her
stand opposite the palace windows, and with her divining
rod she called up a golden hen with golden chickens,[6] and
made them strut about under the palace window. When
Queen Albina looked out and saw the wonderful brood, she
sent down at once to call the pilgrim-woman to her and
offered to buy them of her. ' My hen and chickens I
neither sell nor pledge,' answered the pretended pilgrim;
' I only part with them at one price.'

' And what is the price, good pilgrim, say ? ' answered
the queen.

' My price is that the queen herself take me down to
the palace garden and show me the whale which I know
there is in the fish-pond.'[7]

' That is a condition easily accepted,' answered Albina.
' I will take you there at once, good woman.'

The queen and the pretended pilgrim then went down

together to the pond. The pretended pilgrim no sooner came in sight of the whale than she touched the water with her rod and bade the whale swallow the queen. The whale obeyed the stroke of the wand imparted through the water, and the stepmother went up and threw herself on the queen's bed. When she had well wrapped herself in the coverlets so as to be hidden, she called the maids to her and bid them tell the king that the queen was sick. The king immediately came in all haste to assure himself of the state of the queen. 'I am ill indeed, very ill!' cried the pretended queen, groaning between whiles; 'and there is no hope for me, for there is only one remedy for my malady, and that I cannot take.'

'Tell me the one remedy at least,' said the king.

'The one only remedy for me is the blood of the viceroy, and that I could not take.'

'It is a dreadful remedy indeed,' said the king; 'but if it is the only thing to save your life, I must make you take it.'

'Oh, no! I could not take it!' exclaimed the pretended queen, for the sake of appearing genuine.

But the king, bent on saving her life at any price, sent and had the viceroy taken possession of and secured, ready to be slain,[8] in one of the lower chambers of the palace. The windows of this chamber looked out upon the fish-pond.

The viceroy looked out of the window on to the fish-pond, and immediately there came a voice up to him, speaking out of the whale, and saying, 'Save me, my brother, for here am I imprisoned in the whale, and behold two children are born to me.'

But her brother could only answer, 'I can give help to none, for I also am in peril of death, being bound and shut up ready to be slain!'

Then a voice of lamentation came up from within the

whale saying, ' Woe is me that my brother is to be slain, and I and my children are shut up in this horrible place! Woe is me!'

Presently, the gardener hearing these lamentations, went to the king, saying, ' O, king! come down thyself and hear the voice of one that waileth, and the voice cometh as from within the whale.'

The king went down, and at once recognised the voice of the queen; then he commanded that the whale should be ripped open; no sooner was this done than the queen and her two children were brought to light. The king embraced them all, and said, ' Who then is she that is in the queen's bed?' and he commanded that she should be brought before him. When the queen had seen her she said, ' This is my stepmother;' and when the pilgrim's weeds, which she had taken off, were also found, and it was shown that it was she who had worked all this mischief, the king pronounced that she was a witch, and she was put to death, and the viceroy was set at liberty.

[1] ' Il Rè che va a Pranzo.'

[2] I am inclined to think there was some forgetfulness here on the part of the narrator; such artifices always fulfil the conditions they evade in some underhand way—they never set them utterly at defiance, as in the instance in the text. Such conditions also always go in threes; the third was probably forgotten in this instance.

[3] ' Pizza,' a cake made of Indian corn.

[4] ' Cartoccio,' a conical paper parcel.

[5] ' Bacchettino da comando.'

[6] ' Biocca cogli polsini d'oro,' a hen and chickens all of gold; ' biocca' is a word used by peasants for ' gallina,' and ' polsini' for ' pollastri.'

[7] ' Pescheria,' ordinarily ' fish-market,' but sometimes, as in this place, a tank or piece of water for preserving fish for table. That so large a fish as a whale should be kept in one, is only one of the exaggerations proper to the realm of fable.

[8] The very incident which occurs in the stepmother story of ' How the Serpent-gods were Propitiated,' in ' Sagas from the Far East.'

[I now come to three stories more strictly of the Cinderella type than the two last, but no stepmother appears in them.]

THE POT OF MARJORAM.[1]

THEY say there was once a father who was a rich, very rich, merchant, and the daughters had been used all their lives to have every thing that money could buy them, so that one day when the father was going to a distant mart where he expected to find the choicest wares, and asked them what he should bring home, they scarcely knew what to ask. But when he told them he expected to find shawls of such brilliant hues as they had never seen, with gold threads interwoven, the eldest instantly begged him to bring her one of these; and when he said he expected to find coverlets of bird plumage vieing with the rainbow in brilliancy, the second entreated him to bring her one of these.

The third daughter, however, who was distinguished by stay-at-home habits, and by her distaste for vanity of every kind, would not have any of these gay ornaments, though he not only offered her shawls and coverlets such as her sisters revelled in the idea of possessing, but precious jewelry, sparkling rubies, and rarest pearls. She would have none of these, but asked him only to bring her a pot of marjoram, which she wanted for household uses as none was to be got in the country where they were living.

The father soon after set out on his travels, and having reached his destination did not fail, while laying in his rare and precious stock, to select the choicest specimens to bestow on his two eldest daughters.

But the homely pot of marjoram quite went out of his head, and he returned homewards without having so much as thought of it.

He was nearly home when he was accosted on the way by a strange-looking man one evening, who asked him if he would not buy of him a pot of marjoram.

'A pot of marjoram!' The words brought back his youngest daughter's request whom he would not have disappointed for all the world.

'A pot of marjoram, say you? Yes, it's just what I want. Give it here, and there's something extra because it is just what I want;' and throwing him money to three or four times the ordinary value of the article, he called to an attendant to stow the pot on to the pack-saddle of one of the mules.

But the stranger held back the pot and laughed in his face.

'I had thought you were a trader,' he said, 'and knew enough of the rules of trade to let a man fix his own price on his own wares.'

The merchant laughed in his turn at what seemed to him an insolent comparison.

'When a trader goes thousands of miles, through a thousand perils to bring home precious wares from afar which those at home scarcely know the use of, true, then, he alone can fix the price. But a pot of marjoram, every one knows the price of that.'

'Perhaps not,' replied the stranger, binding his cloak about him with the pot tightly held under his arm. 'At all events it is clear *you* don't;' and he took a step forward as if he considered the negotiation at an end.

The merchant was vexed; he would not on any account miss taking back a pot of marjoram, and he knew he was now so near home that no other chance would there be of procuring one. Swallowing down his annoyance as well as he could, therefore, he led his horse nearer to the strange man and said,—

'You make me quite curious to hear your price named, friend, as till this moment I had not thought there could be two ideas on the subject.'

'My price is three hundred thousand scudi,' replied the strange man, who was really a magician; 'and if you knew its powers you would know, too, it is cheap at that.'

And again he made as if he would have gone on his way, indifferent whether the bargain were concluded or not.

The merchant was quite puzzled how to act. The pot of marjoram he must have, and his knowledge of the art of bargaining convinced him that the man's manner meant he would not rebate an iota of his price. Whatever awkwardness he felt in suddenly giving three hundred thousand scudi for an article he had just appraised at a paul it was even more apparent to him that any attempt at haggling would only have added to the absurdity of the situation by its futility. Therefore, assuming a magnificent air, as if the vast price were after all no matter to him, he called to his steward to count out the sum demanded and rode on.

Arrived at home, his showy presents were received with raptures by his two eldest daughters, while the youngest received her modest-seeming share of his generosity with an expression of surprise and admiration, which gave the good merchant a secret satisfaction in imagining that she was not altogether ignorant of its immense value.

As days went by, however, everything fell back into the usual routine. The elder sisters continued the same round of gaiety in which they had ever been immersed, the younger remained as of old, quietly absorbed in her household duties; but if she had any pastime it was that of diligently cultivating her pot of marjoram. By degrees, however, through the steward's gossip with the servants, it came round to the knowledge of the sisters that, though their younger sister had seemed to frame so humble a request, its satisfaction had cost their father's treasury a fabulous sum. The discovery excited their utmost indignation, and their jealousy being roused, they determined to inflict a condign and appropriate punishment for what they deemed her presumption, by destroying the illstarred pot of marjoram.

To get at it, however, was no easy matter, as its guardian seldom left the house, and was always watching over it with jealous care. At last they resolved, by way of pretext for securing her absence, to represent to their father that it was not good for a young girl to remain so shut up ; that whether she had a taste for it or not, she ought to see the world ; and urged their arguments so efficaciously that he quite admitted their cogency, and one evening, calling his youngest daughter to him, imperatively required that she should accompany him to an evening engagement.

The poor child dared not disobey her father, but parted from her pot of marjoram with a heavy heart, as if some foreboding of evil possessed her. No sooner had she left the house than the sisters went up into her room, and taking the pot of marjoram, flung it out of the window, so that it all lay broken and shattered on the highroad, where it was soon trampled under foot and every vestige of it dispersed.

When she came in and saw what was done her grief was unbounded, and no sooner was the house sunk in slumber than, determining to live no longer under the same roof with those who had treated her so unfeelingly, she set out to wander forth absorbed in sorrow, and not caring whither she went.

On, on, on she went, taking no heed of the way, all through the night, and when the morning dawned she found herself in the midst of a vast plain, at a place where many roads met. As she hesitated for a moment which she should take, there suddenly appeared before her a fairy,[2] though the last time she looked up she had not seen a speck anywhere between herself and the horizon.

‘ Where are you going so early, my pretty maiden, and

E

why weep you ?' said the fairy, in a soothing voice that seemed made to charm an answer out of the most reluctant.

Nevertheless, it was no easy question to answer, for the maiden had no sort of idea whither she was going; therefore she took the second question first and poured out the whole tale of her sisters' harshness and her late terrible disappointment.

'That is not so very bad after all,' replied the fairy, when she had finished her tale. 'I see you have been trying to be a sensible girl, but you must be brave as well as sensible. Men say of us women, "Women always look at the dark side of things;"[3] there is always a bright side which you must try to look out for, even when, as in this instance, you couldn't possibly see it; for all the evil that befalls us does not work evil in the end.[4] Now it happens that there is a particularly bright side to this case of yours, and the evil that was done you will bring you no ultimate harm. But you must exercise fortitude and stedfastness in what you will have to do. For this I will give you a man's clothing, as it would not be seemly for a young girl like you to be going about the world alone, and it will save you from many dangers.'

So saying, though she had no bundle of any sort about her, she produced a complete suit of male attire, travelling cloak and all, and in the girdle were bound weapons, and many articles of which the maiden did not even know the use or the name, but the fairy assured her she would want them all by and by. Then, having pointed out which was the road she should take, she again bid her be of good heart, and disappeared almost before the maiden had time to utter her heartfelt thanks.

The fairy had no sooner vanished than the whole face of the country wore a different aspect; instead of being surrounded by a vast plain, mighty mountains rose on the right hand and on the left, while before her, straight along her path, was a dense forest. The maiden's heart misgave her at the sight, but she remembered the fairy's advice and walked steadily along. Notwithstanding her conversation had not seemed to last many minutes too, the sun was already high in the heavens, and its rays beat so fiercely upon her that she was glad even of the gloomy forest's shade. Arrived at the first trees she was pleased to hear the trickling of a little brook over the stones, and to find that the good fairy had not failed to give her a supply of provisions of which she now gladly availed herself.

As the afternoon grew cooler she rose and walked on till nightfall without further adventure, and then disposed herself to rest for the night, climbing first into the spreading boughs of a large tree, that she might be out of the way of any wild beasts which the forest might harbour.

In the middle of the night her sleep was disturbed by a horrible growling; and what was her surprise when she fully woke to find that though it proceeded from a common he-, and she-bear⁵ stretched out under the very tree she had chosen for her resting-place, she could understand all the meaning it contained just as if they had spoken in words; and she recognised the new power as another gift of the good fairy.

'Where have you been all this long time?' growled the she-bear; 'it is quite abominable what a long time you stay away now continually; I have been hunting through the whole forest for you.'

'That was quite waste of trouble,' replied the he-bear testily, 'for I have been a long way from the forest.'

'Where were you, then?' growled the she-bear again, with a tone that showed she was determined to know all about it.

'If you must know, I went twenty miles along the side of the river, then over the back of the rocky mountains, and then skirting round the forest till I came to the kingdom of Persia. And out of the kingdom of Persia there went up a great wail, for last night, from his high tower, the king of Persia fell out of window and broke all his bones, moreover his flesh is all cut with the glass, which has entered into his wounds. Therefore the land of Persia bewails her king.'

'Then let them get another king,' growled the she-bear.

'That is not so easy,' rejoined the he-bear. 'For over all the face of the earth was no king so comely in person as the king of Persia. But that is not the worst, for the matter concerns us more nearly than you have any idea of.'

'How can it concern us?' retorted the she-bear.

'It concerns us so much that if anyone only knew of us we should both be killed. For the only remedy for his wounds is that we should both be killed, the fat of our bodies be melted together, an ointment made of it with honey and wax, and be smeared over the king's body, and then bathe him in warm baths, doing this alternately for the space of three days he will be made well again. And now he has sent a proclamation into all lands inviting any physician to come to heal him by his art, and if any of them by their books and their divination should discover this we both shall certainly be put to death.'

'Nonsense! do come and go to sleep,' replied the she-bear testily; 'how should anyone find us out in the midst of this forest?'

'It's not very likely certainly,' growled the he-bear.

And in consequence of this happy feeling of security both brutes were soon fast asleep.

How gladly the maiden listened to their snoring, when she found she could understand it just as well as their growling.

'I'm sound asleep,' snored the she-bear.

'I'm so tired I don't want ever to wake again,' snored her mate.

'Neither shall you,' said the maiden as she noiselessly let herself down from the tree.

'Only think of that old king of Persia wanting our fat; long may he wish for it!' snored the she-bear.

'Now it would be a fine thing to give back all his strength and his beauty to the king of Persia, but the price of one's life is too much for the honour,' snored the he-bear.

'Nevertheless, you shall have that honour,' whispered the maiden, as she drew two sharp two-edged knives with which her girdle was furnished, and, taking her stand firmly, plunged one with each hand deep into the throat of each beast. A mingled stream of blood gushed forth, and the two huge carcases rolled over without so much as a grunt, so neatly had the execution been performed.

By the first morning's light she once more called all her courage to her assistance, and cut up the carcases, extracting the fat. Then she lit a fire and melted it down together, nor was she without the requisite wax and honey, for the good fairy had provided her with enough of each. The ointment made, she set out to follow the line of travel the bear had indicated, and not without much toil and weariness at last found herself in the kingdom of Persia. Strong in belief in the efficacy of her remedy, she presented herself at once at the palace gate and demanded admission on the score of her ability to effect the desired cure of the ailing king.

'Though I may not have the high-sounding fame of which I daresay many can boast who have come at the summons of your king, yet so certain am I of the powers of my treatment that I put my life in your hands, and give you leave to torture me to death if I succeed not.'

'Fear not, fair sir,' replied the chamberlain; 'no difficulty will be made in admitting you, for you alone have

applied to heal the king. Every other mediciner throughout the whole world, on reading the description of the
king's ailments given in the proclamation, has pronounced his health past recovery, and not one will even
make the attempt.'

Pale, emaciated, and agonised as he was, the maiden
at once recognised on her admission to the presence of
the king the justice of the bear's account of his personal
attractions, and now more earnestly than ever desired her
success.

The king very willingly submitted to her medicaments,
and at the end of three days was, as the bear had predicted,
quite sound in limb and restored to all his beauty of
person. If his personal attractions had been an object
of admiration to the maiden, those of his supposed physician had not been lost on the king, and when she came
on the fourth day to take her leave of him, he told her at
once he could not think of parting with her; she must
remain attached to his court, and be always his physician
in attendance. The flush of joy which she could not
conceal at the proposal sufficed to convince the king of
the justice of certain suspicions he had already entertained, that his supposed physician was no physician, but
a maiden worthy to be his queen.

For the moment he said nothing further, but only
assigned to the stranger apartments in the palace, and a
suite of his own, and a yearly stipend on the most liberal
scale. As days went by, being continually in each other's
presence, with that familiarity which their new relations
allowed, each had the opportunity of growing more and
more fond of the other. At last the king called his chamberlain to him one day and told him it was his desire that
the state physician should appear before him dressed in
queenly robes, and attended by a train of ladies of the
court, and damsels and pages of honour.

The chamberlain fancied that the life-peril through

which the prince had so lately passed had injured his brain, and only undertook the commission with a visible reluctance. Nevertheless, as he durst not disobey any command of his sovereign, how strange soever, all was done as he had directed; though what puzzled the chamberlain the more was that the physician seemed as nearly demented as the king, for, instead of testifying any reluctance in submitting to such a travesty, his countenance had betrayed the most unmistakable joy at hearing the king's pleasure.

The king had further given orders for the attendance of all the great officers of state and all the nobles of the land, as well as his guards of various degrees, all in brilliant gala dress. Before going into the state hall to receive their homage, however, he entered alone into his private cabinet, whither he commanded the attendance of his physician. Both meeting thus, each habited to the greatest advantage in their own appropriate dress, each was more than ever smitten with the attractions of the other. The king was not very long in winning from the maiden the confession that the robes she now wore were those of her sex, or that she shared his own desire that they should be united by that tie which would bind them together inseparably for ever. No sooner had he thus obtained her consent than he led her into the midst of the assembled court and required the homage of all his people to her as their queen.

As for the wicked sisters, his first act was to send for them and have them burnt to death.

---

[1] 'Il vaso di persa.' Marjoram goes by the name of 'persa' in the vernacular of Rome. Parsley, which sounds the more literal translation, is 'erbetta.' I think the narrator believed it to be connected with Persia.

[2] 'Fata' is a powerful enchantress. I know no English equivalent but 'fairy,' though there is this difference that a 'fata' is by no means invariably an airy and beautiful being; she more often wears a very ordinary appearance, and not unfrequently that of a very old wrinkled woman, but is always goodnatured and benevolent, as distinguished from the malevolent 'strega,' a nearer counterpart of our 'witch.'

³ 'Le femmine sempre pigliano il peggio.'
⁴ 'Non tutto il male vien' per nuocere.'
⁵ 'Orgo,' the vernacular form of the classic 'Orco,' is the Italian equivalent for 'Old Bogey;' but it is also used in place of 'orso,' a bear (as in the precise instance of this tale being told to me), when it is desired to give terror to his character in a tale.

['How well I remember,' added the narrator, 'the way my mother used always to end that story when she told it to me.'

'And how was that?' asked I eagerly, not at all sorry to come across some local addition at last.

'But it has nothing to do with the tale, really,' she replied, as deeming it too unimportant to trouble me with.

'Never mind, I should like to hear it,' said I.

'Well then, it used to run thus: "Never was such a banquet made in all the world as for the nuptials of this king of Persia. The *confetti* were as big as eggs; and, do you know, I had five of them given to me." '

'O mamma,' I used to say then, 'why didn't you keep them for me? what splendid *confetti* they must have been!'

'Stop, and you shall hear what I did with them,' she would reply.

Uno lo dava al gallo	One I gave to the cock
Che mi portava a cavallo,	Who carried me on his back,¹
Una a la gallina	And one to the hen
Che m' insegnò la via.	Who showed me the way,
Uno al porco	And one to the pig
Che m' insegnò la porta.	Who pointed out the door;
Uno ne mangiai,	One I ate myself,
E uno ne misse là,	And one I put by there,
Che ancora ci sarà.	Where no doubt it still remains.

And she used to point as she spoke at an old glass cabinet, where I would go and rummage, always expecting to find the sweetmeat, till one day, getting convinced it had no existence, I got very angry, and threw a big key at one of the panes and broke it, and she never would tell me that story any more.]

¹ Has this anything to do with 'riding the *cock-horse*'?

THE POT OF RUE.[1]

THEY say there was once a rich merchant who had three daughters. Two of them were very gay and fond of dancing and theatres, but the youngest was very stay-at-home and scarcely ever went beyond the garden.

One day when the father was going abroad to buy merchandise, he asked his three daughters what he should bring them home. The two eldest asked for all manner of dresses and ornaments, but the youngest asked only for a pot of rue.

'That's a funny fancy,' said the father, 'but an easy one to satisfy at all events; so be sure you shall have it.'

'Not so easy, perhaps, as you think,' replied the maiden; 'only now you have promised it, mind you bring it, as you will find you will not be able to get home unless you bring it with you.'

The father did not pay much heed to her words, but went to a far country, bought his merchandise, taking care to include the fine clothes and jewels for his two eldest daughters, and, forgetting about the pot of rue, set out to come home.

They were scarcely a day's journey out at sea when the ship stood quite still, nor was the captain able by any means to govern it, for neither sail nor oar would move it an inch.

'Some one on board has an unfulfilled promise on him,' declared the captain; and he called upon whoever it was to come forward and own it, that he might be thrown overboard, and that the lives of all the passengers and crew should not be put in jeopardy by his fault.

Then the merchant came forward and said it was true he had forgotten to bring with him something he had promised to his little daughter, but that it was so slight a matter he did not think it could be that which was stopping the ship.

As no one else had anything of the sort to accuse themselves of, the captain judged that it was indeed the merchant's fault that had stopped the ship; only, as he was such a great merchant and a frequent trader by his vessel, he agreed to put back with him instead of throwing him overboard. He first, however, asked,—

'And what may the thing be that you have to take to your daughter?'

'Nothing but a pot of rue,' replied the merchant.

'A pot of rue!' answered the captain; 'that is no easy matter. In the whole country there is no one has a plant of it but the king, and he is so choice over it that he has decreed that if anyone venture to ask him only for a single leaf he shall instantly be put to death.'

'That is bad hearing,' said the merchant. 'Nevertheless, as I have promised to get it I must make the trial, and if I perish in the attempt I might have had a worse death.'

So they landed the merchant, and he went straight up to the king's palace.

'Majesty!' he said, throwing himself on his knees before the throne. 'It is in no spirit of wantonness I break the decree which forbids the asking a single leaf of the precious plant of rue. A promise was on me before I knew the king's decree, and I am bound thereby to ask not merely a single leaf but the whole plant, of the king, even though it be at peril of my life.'

Then said the king,—

'To whom hadst thou made this promise?'

And the merchant made answer,—

'Though it was only to my youngest daughter I made the promise, yet having made it, I will not leave off from asking for it.'

Then the king answered,—

'Because thou hast been faithful to thy promise, and courageous in risking thy life rather than to break thy

word, behold I give the whole plant at thy desire; and
this without breaking my royal decree. For my decree
said that whoso desired a single leaf should be put to
death, but in that thou hast asked the whole plant thou
hast shown a courage worthy of reward.'

So he took the plant of rue and gave it to the merchant
to give to his daughter; moreover, he bade him tell her
that she should every night burn a leaf of the plant.
With that he dismissed him.

The merchant returned home and distributed the
presents he had brought to his daughters, and not more
pleased were the elder ones with their fine gifts than was
the younger with her simple pot of rue. In the evening
they went with their father to the ball as usual, but the
youngest staid at home as she was wont to do, and this
night she burnt a leaf of the rue as the king had bidden her.
But the king had three beautiful sons, and no sooner had
she burnt the rue leaf than the eldest son of the king
appeared before her, and sitting beside her, said so many
kind things that no evening had ever passed so pleasantly.
This she did every evening as the king had bidden.

But the other merchants said to the merchant her
father,—

'How is it that only two daughters come to the
balls?'

And the merchant, not knowing how to account for
the youngest daughter's preference for staying at home,
answered,—

'I have only two daughters old enough to come to the
balls?'

But the other merchants said,—

'Nay, but bring now thy youngest daughter.'

So the next evening the merchant made the youngest
daughter go with him to the ball, and the two elder
daughters were left at home.

As the youngest was wont never to leave her room, the

others, how jealous soever they were of her, were never
able to do her any harm.   But now that they felt secure
she was absent for a considerable space, they went into
her apartment and set fire to it, and the whole place was
burnt, and also the garden, and the plant of rue.

If the king's son had come in haste for the burning of
a single leaf, I leave it to be imagined with what speed he
came for the burning of the whole plant.   With such im-
petus, indeed, he came, that he was bruised and burnt all
over with the flaming beams of which the apartment was
built, and cut all over with the broken glass ; so that
when he reached home again he was in a sorry plight
indeed.

But the youngest daughter, coming home with her
father from the ball, and finding all her apartment burnt
to the ground, as well as all the plants in the garden, and
with them the pot of rue, she said, ' I will stay no more in
this place.'   So she dressed herself in man's clothes and
wandered forth.

On, on, on, she went, till night came, and she could
go no further, but she laid herself to sleep under a tree.
In the middle of the night came an ogre and an ogress,[2]
and laid themselves down also under the tree.   Then she
heard the ogre speaking to the ogress, and saying, ' Our
king's eldest son, the flower of the land, is sore ill and like
to die, having fallen through the window of the highest
story of the palace, and is cut with the glass, and bruised
all over.   What shall be done to heal the king's eldest
son, the flower of the land ? '

And the ogress made answer : ' This is what should be
done—but it is well no one knows it.   They should kill
us, and take the fat that is round our hearts and make an
ointment, and anoint therewith the wounds of the king's
son.'

When the merchant's daughter heard this, she waited
till the ogre and ogress were gone to sleep ; then she took

out a brace of pistols—for with the man's dress she had also a brace of pistols—and with one in each hand she killed the ogre and ogress together, and with her knife she ripped them open, and took out the fat that was round their hearts. Then she journeyed on till she came to the king's palace. At the door of the palace stood a guard, who told her there was no entrance for such as her; but she said, ' To heal the wounds of the king's eldest son am I come.'

Then the sentinel laughed, and said, ' So many great and learned surgeons have come, and have benefited him nothing; there is no entrance for a mountebank like thee. Begone! begone!'

But she, knowing certainly that she had the only means of healing, would not be sent away; and when the sentinel would have driven her off she struggled so bravely that he had to call out all the guard to resist her; and when they all used their strength against her, she protested so loudly that the noise of the struggle made the king himself begin to inquire what was the matter. Then they told him, ' Behold, there stands without a low and base fellow, who would fain pretend to heal the wounds of the king's son.'

But the king answered : ' As all the great and learned surgeons have failed, let even the travelling doctor try his skill; maybe he knows some means of healing.'

Then she was brought into the apartment of the king's son, and she asked for all she needed to make the ointment, and linen for bandages, and to be left alone with him for the space of a week. At the end of a week the king's son was perfectly cured and well. Then she dressed herself with care, but still in the garb of a travelling doctor—for she had no other—and stood before him, and said, ' Know you me not ?' And when he looked at her he said, ' Ah ! yes ; the maiden of the rue plant !' For till then she had been so soiled with the dust of travel that he could not

recognise her. Then when he had recognised her he protested he would marry her, and, sending to the king his
father, he told him the same.

When the king heard of his resolve, he said, ' It is well
that the prince is healed of his wounds; but with the
return of bodily health it is evident he has lost his reason,
in that he is determined to marry his surgeon. Nevertheless, as nothing is gained in this kind of malady by
contradiction, it is best to humour him. We must get
this surgeon to submit to be dressed up like a princess,
and we must amuse him by letting him go through the
form of marrying her.'

It was done, therefore, as the king had said. But
when the ladies of the court came to attend the supposed
surgeon, and saw her dressed in her bridal robes, they saw
by the way they became her that she was indeed a woman
and no surgeon, and that the prince was by no means dis-
tempered in his mind.

But the prince silenced their exclamations, saying:
' Nay, but say nothing; for perchance if my father knew
that this should be a real marriage, and no mere make-
believe to humour a disordered whim, he might withhold
his consent, seeing the maiden is no princess. But I
know she is the wife destined for me, because my mother,
before she died, told me I should know her by the pot of
rue; and because, by devoting herself to healing me, she
has deserved well of me. So let the marriage go through,
even as the king my father had devised.'

So the marriage was celebrated, and when the king learnt
afterwards that the pretended surgeon was a real maiden,
he knew the thing could not be altered, and said nothing.
So the merchant's daughter became the prince's wife.

[1] ' Il Vaso di Ruta.'
[2] ' Orco ed orchessa.'

[The following is a third variant of this story, but so like the
last, that I only give an abbreviated version of it.]

KING OTHO.[1]

In this case the merchant, when he goes out to buy his wares, asks his three daughters what he shall bring them. The eldest asks for fine dresses, the second for beautiful shawls, the third for nothing but some sand out of the garden of King Otho. The king had registered sentence of death against anyone who should ask for the sand. But in consideration of a bribe of three hundred scudi the gardener gives him a little.

When she gets it, the daughter burns a little in the evening, when the sisters are gone to a ball. Instantly King Otho comes, and falls in love with her. She gives him a most exquisite pair of knee-bands she has embroidered, before he goes away. The second night she gives him a handkerchief of her work, and the third a beautiful necktie.

After this, her father insists one evening that she should go to the ball. Her sisters say that if she goes they shall stay away. When she is gone they burn down her room, and in it all the sand of King Otho's garden. If the king came quickly for the burning of a little pinch, he naturally comes in exceeding greater haste at the burning of the whole quantity: in such haste that he is wounded all over with the blazing beams and broken glass. There is a great explosion.[2] As he knew nothing about the spite of the sisters, he could only think that the mischief arose from the misconduct of her to whom the sand had been given, and determines accordingly to have nothing more to do with her.

When she comes home, and finds what has happened, she is in despair. She dresses like a man and goes away. In the night, in a cave where she takes shelter, she hears an ogre and ogress talking over what has happened, and they say that the only cure is an ointment made of their blood.[3] She shoots them both, and takes their blood and

heals the king with it. The king offers any kind of reward the supposed doctor will name; but she will have
nothing but some of the sand of the garden. She contrives, however, to discover the knee-bands, the handkerchief, and the necktie she had given him, and asks him
what they are. 'Oh, only the presents of a faithless lover,'
he replies. She then insists he should give them up to
her, which he does, and she goes away.

When she gets home she burns a pinch of the sand,
and the king is forced by its virtue to appear; but he
comes in great indignation, and accuses her of wounding
him. She replies it was not she who wounded him, but
who healed him. He is incredulous; and she shows him
the knee-bands, handkerchief, and necktie, which convince
him he owes his healing to her. They make peace, and
are married.

¹ This was pronounced 'Uttone,' but was doubtless intended for 'King
Otho.' Words which in Latin were spelt with a *u*, as 'Bollo,' 'pollo,'
retain the sound of *u* in the mouth of the people; but I know of no
reason for it in the present instance.

² 'Precipizio,' equivalent to 'an explosion,' 'a terrible kick-up,' &c.

⁸ The blood instead of the fat is one of the variations of this version.
It is not easy to see how blood can enter into the composition of an ointment, yet one of the most frequent charges to be met in processes against
witches was taking the blood of infants to make various ointments.

[Mr. Ralston gives a very pretty counterpart of so much of
this story as relates to the transformation of a human being into a
flower, at p. 15 of the story commencing at page 10, and
'Aschenputtel,' Grimm, p. 93, has something like it; but I do
not recall any European story in which a person is actually
wounded and half-killed by damage done to a tree mysteriously
connected with him. There is something like it in the 'trees of
life' which people plant, and their withering is to be a token
that harm has befallen them.

Overhearing the advice of supernatural beasts under a tree
occurs in the Norse 'True and Untrue,' and is very common in
all sorts of ways, everywhere. It enters, too, into the analogous
Italian Tirolean tale of 'I due cavallari,' where witches figure
instead of the orco and orchessa.

Next, are four stories in which many incidents of the Cinderella type are set in a different framework; they are represented in the Gaelic by ' The King who wanted to marry his Daughter; ' at the end of which reference will be found to other versions, where are details occurring in one or other of the following : that from Straparola is naturally the most like the Roman, but it is not like any one of them all throughout, and forms a remarkable link between the first Roman and the two Gaelic versions. The girl's answer, that she ' came from the country of candlesticks,' in the second version, is noteworthy, because it connects it with the Roman story of the ' Candeliera,' at the same time that it conveys no sense in its own. The box in the Gaelic versions recalls, just as Mr. Campbell says, the fine old chests which served for conveying home the *corredo* (including much more than *trousseau* in its modern use) of the bride, which are not only preserved as heirlooms and curiosities in many an Italian palace, but in many a museum also; there are some very handsome ones at Perugia. And yet it is just in the Italian versions that the box loses this character. In Straparola's, it is a wardrobe; in the two versions of ' Maria di Legno,' a wooden statue : in ' La Candeliera,' it has the shape of a candlestick. In the third version of ' Maria di Legno,' the box used is only an old press that happens to be in the deserted tower.

Mr. Ralston, pp. 77–8, supplies a Russian counterpart, in which it is a prince, and not a maiden, who is conveyed in a provisioned box, and this is linked hereby with the Hungarian story of Iron Ladislas, who descends by such means to the underground world in search of his sisters; and this again connects this story both with those in which I have already had occasion to mention him and with one to follow called ' Il Rè Moro,' one I have in MS. called ' Il Cavolo d'oro, &c. The first and more elaborate of the four Roman stories, ' Maria di Legno,' does the same.]

MARIA WOOD.[1]

ONCE again my story is of a widower father; this time, however, a king, and having one only daughter, Maria, the apple of his eye and the pride of his heart. The one concern of his life was to marry her well and happily before he died.

The queen, whom he believed to be wise above mortal women, had left him when she died a ring, with the advice to listen to the addresses of no one on Maria's behalf but his whose finger a gold ring which she gave him should fit, for that he whom it alone should fit would be a noble and a worthy husband indeed.

Maria's teacher was very different from those we have had to do with hitherto; she was a beneficent fairy, whose services her good and clever mother had obtained for her under this disguise, and all her lessons and actions were directed entirely for her benefit, and she was able to advise and look out for her better than her father himself.

Time went by, and no one who came to court Maria had a finger which the ring would fit. It was not that Maria was not quite young enough to wait, but her father was growing old and feeble, and full of ailments, and he hasted to see her settled in life before death called him away.

At last there came to sue for Maria's hand a most accomplished cavalier, who declared himself to be a prince of a distant region, and he certainly brought costly presents, and was attended by a brilliant retinue well calculated to sustain the alleged character.

The father, who had had so much trouble about fitting the ring, was much disposed not to attend any more to this circumstance when the prince objected to be subjected to so trivial a trial. After some days, however, as he hesitated finally to make up his mind to bestow her on him without his having fulfilled this condition, he suddenly consented to submit to it, when, lo and behold, the ring could not be found!

' If you have not got the ring,' said the prince, ' it really is not my fault if it is not tried on. You see I am perfectly willing to accept the test, but if you cannot apply it you must not visit it on me.'

' What you say is most reasonable,' said the father. ' But what can I do? I promised her mother I would not let the girl marry anyone but him the ring fitted.'

' Do you mean then that the girl is never to marry at all, since you have lost the ring! That would be monstrous indeed. You may be sure, however, in my case, the ring *would* have fitted if you had had it here, because I am so exactly the kind of husband your wife promised the ring *should* fit. So what more reasonable than to give her to me? However, to meet your wishes and prejudices to the utmost, I am willing to submit to any other test, however difficult, the young lady herself likes to name. Nay, I will say—three tests. Will that satisfy you?'

All this was so perfectly reasonable that the father felt he could not but agree to it, and Maria was told to be ready the next day to name the first of the tests which she would substitute for that of the ring.

Though the prince was so handsome, so accomplished, so rich, and so persevering with his suit, Maria felt an instinctive dislike to him, which embarrassed her the more that she had no fault of any sort to find with him which she could make patent to her father.

To the compassionate and appreciative bosom of her teacher she poured out all her grief, and found there a ready response.

The teacher, who by her fairy powers knew what mortals could not know, knew that the prince was no other than the devil,[2] and that the marriage must be prevented at any price, but that it would be vain for her to give this information to the father, as he would have laughed in her face, and told her to go and rule copybooks and knit stockings. She must, therefore, set to work in a different way to protect her charge from the impending evil.

In the first instance, however, and without mentioning the alarming disclosure of who her suitor really was, she merely bid Maria to be of good courage and all would come right; and for the test she had to propose, she bid her ask him to produce a dress woven of the stars of heaven.

The next morning, accordingly, when the prince came to inquire what her good pleasure was, she asked him to bring her a dress woven of the stars of heaven.

The prince bit his lip, and a look of fierceness it had never worn before stole over his face at hearing this request. And though he instantly put on a smile, there was much suppressed anger perceptible in the tone with which he answered,

'This is not your own idea. Some one who has no good will towards me has told you this.'

'It was no part of the condition, I think, that I should act without advice, and certainly no part of it that I should say whether I took advice or not,' replied Maria discreetly; and then her desire to break from the engagement making her bold, she added, 'But, you know, if you do not like the test, or consider it in any way unfair, I do not press you to accept it. You will meet with no reproach from me if you renounce it.'

'Oh dear no! I have no such wish,' the prince hastened to reply. 'The dress woven of the stars of heaven will be here by to-morrow morning, and you have only to be ready by the same time to name what is the second test you propose.'

Maria hastened back to her teacher to recount the

story of the morning's work; to tell of the moment of hope she had had that the prince would renounce the attempt, and then his final acceptance of the undertaking. ' Dear teacher mine! Cannot you think of something else so very, very difficult I can give him to do to-morrow that he may be obliged to refuse it ? '

' To-morrow I would have you ask him for a dress woven of moonbeams,' replied the teacher; 'which will be very difficult to supply ; but I fear he will yet find the means of accomplishing it.'

The next morning the dress woven of the stars of heaven was brought in by six pages, and it was all they could do to carry it, for the dazzling of the rays of the stars in their eyes. When the dress of moonbeams was asked for, the prince showed little less impatience than at the first request, but yet undertook to supply it, and reminded Maria that the next day she must be ready with her third test.

Once more Maria had recourse to her sage teacher's counsels, and this time was advised to ask for a dress woven of sunbeams.

The next day the dress woven of moonbeams was produced, but it required twelve pages to bring it in, for it was so dazzling they could only hold it for ten minutes at a stretch, and they had to carry it in relays, six at a time. When Maria now asked for the dress woven of sunbeams, the prince grew so angry that she was quite frightened, and at the same time entertained for a moment a confident hope that now, at last, he would own himself baffled. Nevertheless, at the end of a few moments' hesitation, he pronounced his intention of complying, but added in almost a threatening tone, ' And remember that when it comes to-morrow morning you will not then have any more ridiculous tests to prefer, but will belong to me for ever, and must be prepared to go away with me in the carriage that will be at the door.' He turned on his heel as he spoke and stalked away, without saying good-bye, or so much as turning to look at her, or he would have seen she had sunk down on the ground in an agony of despair.

Her father came in and found her thus, and asked her what could possibly put her into such a state on the eve of such a brilliant marriage. Maria threw herself in his arms and told him all her distress, but when it was told it sounded childish and unreasonable.

'Can anything be more absurd?' replied the old man. 'To-morrow I may be dead, and what will become of you? What can you desire more than a husband suited to you in age and person, with every advantage the world can offer? And you would throw all this away for the sake of a foolish fancy you cannot even explain! Dry your tears and do not listen to such fancies any more, and keep your pretty little face in good order for looking as smiling and as pleasing as such a devoted husband deserves you should look on your wedding morning. It is I who have to lament; I who shall be left alone in my old age; but I do not repine, I shall be quite happy for my few remaining days in knowing that you have all the happiness life can afford you;' and as he spoke he clasped her fondly in his arms.

Maria, reassured by his words, began to think he was in the right, and she was thus as cheerful as he could wish that last night they were to spend together.

But when night came and she found the teacher who understood her so well, waiting to put her to bed for the last time, all her own true feelings came back, and, bursting into tears, she entreated her to find some way of delivering her.

'The time has come,' replied the teacher, 'that I should tell you all. The innocence and truthfulness of your heart guided you right in believing that the prince was no husband for you. You did not, and could not, know who he was; but now I must tell you he is the devil himself. Nay; do not shudder and tremble so; it remains entirely with yourself to decide whether you shall be his or not; he can have no sort of power over any against their will.'

' But, of course, I will have nothing to do with him,' replied the child, simply. ' Why don't you tell papa, and make him send him away ? '

' Because, for one thing, he would not believe me. As I have said, the prince being what he is can have no power over you against your own will. Your breaking from him must be your own act. Further, you must understand the terms of the struggle. Power is given him to deceive, and thus he has deceived your father. I have been set by your mother to watch over you, and I can tell you what he is, but I have no power to undeceive your father. If I were to attempt it it would do no good, he would not believe me, and it would break his heart to see you renounce so promising an union. On the other hand, you must understand that when the devil wooes a maiden in this form he does not suddenly after appear with horns and hoofs and carry her off to brimstone and fire. For the term of your life he will behave with average kindness and affection, and he will abundantly supply you with the good things of this world. After that I need not say what the effect of his power over you will be. On the other hand, if you give him up you must be prepared to undergo many trials and privations. It is not merely going on with your present life such as it has been up till now. Those peaceful days are allowed for youthful strength to mature, but now the time has come that you have to make a life-choice. What do you say ? Have you courage to renounce the ease and enjoyment the prince has to offer you and face poverty, with the want and the insults which come in its train ? '

Poor little Maria looked very serious. She had never

felt any great attraction for the prince, it is true, but now the question was placed upon a new issue. She had learnt enough about duty and sacrifice, and she had always intended to do right at all costs, but now that the day of trial had come it seemed so different from what she had expected, she knew not what to say.

'You are tired to-night, my child; and it is late,' said the teacher. 'We will say no more till the morning. I will wake you betimes and you shall tell me your mind then.'

In the morning Maria's mind was made up. She had chosen the good part; but how was she to be delivered from the prince?

'This is what you will have to do,' replied the teacher, after commending her good resolution. 'I have had made ready for you a wooden figure of an old woman, inside which I will stow away all that you have valuable, for it may be of use some day, but especially I will bestow there the dresses woven of the stars of heaven, of moonbeams, and that of sunbeams, which, I doubt not, the prince will bring you, according to promise, in the morning. When you have driven with him in his carriage all day, towards evening you will find yourself in a thick wood. Say to him you are tired with sitting in the carriage all day, and ask to be allowed to walk a little way in the wood before sundown. I, meantime, will place ready my wooden figure of an old woman, which you will find there, and, watching for a moment when he has his head turned, place yourself inside the figure and walk away. There is another thing which you must do, which is very important. When the ring was lost, you must know it was he who took it, and, though he kept it studiously concealed all the while he was in your father's palace, he will now carry it boldly slung on the feather in his cap; this you must find means of possessing yourself of during the journey, because it is essential to you that you should have it in your own hands. And fear nothing either, in making your escape, for the ring is your own property, which he has falsely taken ; and, in leaving him, remember he can have no power over you against your will. I may not inform you what may befall you in your new character as poor Maria Wood, but be good and courageous ; always, as now, choose the right bravely in all questions and doubts, and you shall not go unrewarded.'

There was little time for leave-taking between the good teacher and her affectionate pupil, for the prince almost immediately after came to claim his bride, and all the neighbours and friends came, too, to the festivities. The dress woven of sunbeams was brought by four-and-twenty pages, for it was so dazzling they could not hold it for more than five minutes at a time, and they had to carry it by relays.

At last leave-takings and festivities were over, and, amid the good-wishes and blessings of all, Maria drove away in the prince's carriage. On they drove all day, and towards the end of it, as it was getting dark, Maria contrived to twitch the ring from the prince's cap without his being aware of it ; presently after she exclaimed, ' Oh dear ! how cramped I feel from sitting all day in this carriage ; cannot I walk a little way in this wood before it gets dark ? '

' Most certainly you can, if you wish,' replied the prince, who, having everything his own way, was in a very accommodating humour.

When they had walked a little way down the forest-path, Maria espied the wooden form she was to assume, placed ready under a tree.

' That old woman will have a longish way to go to get a night's shelter, I fancy,' exclaimed the prince, with a laugh which made Maria shudder, both from its heartlessness and also because it reminded her that she would soon find herself alone, far from shelter, in that dark wood.

But was it not better to be alone in the dark than in such company as that she was about to leave, she said to herself. Then she turned once more to look at it. The figure looked so natural she could not forbear saying mechanically, ' Poor old woman ! give me a little coin to bestow on her that she may wish us Godspeed on our night-journey.'

' Nonsense!' replied the prince. ' Never let me hear you talk such idle stuff. And, come, it is time to go back into the carriage; it is getting quite dark.'

' Oh ! what a beautiful firefly !' exclaimed Maria, reminded by the speech to hasten her separation from her uncongenial companion, ' Oh, do catch it for me!'

The prince lifted his cap, and ran a few steps after the insect. ' Oh, I see another, and I shall catch it before you catch yours—you'll see!' So saying, she darted towards the tree where the wooden figure stood ready, and placing herself inside, walked slowly and freely along, counterfeiting the gait of an aged and weary woman.

The prince had soon caught the firefly and was bringing it back in triumph, when, to his dismay, Maria was nowhere to be seen. He ran this way and that, called and shouted in vain. The servants with the carriage were too far off to have seen anything; there was no witness to appeal to but the old woman.

' Which way did the young lady run who was walking with me just now ?' he eagerly inquired.

' Down that path there to the right, as fast as the firefly itself could fly, and if she comes back as quickly as she went she will be back presently,' replied Maria Wood, feigning the voice of an old woman.

The prince ran in the direction indicated, and was soon himself lost in the mazes of the forest, where he wandered hopelessly all night ; and only when the morning light came was he able to make his way back to his carriage, and drive home ashamed and crestfallen, giving up his conquest in despair, and vowing useless vengeance against the fairy godmother, whose intervention he now recognised it was had baffled him.

Maria meantime walked steadily and fearlessly along, guided by the stars which peeped here and there through the tall trees. Nor was shelter so far off as the prince had said. Before very long a party of charcoal-burners hailed her, and offered a share of such poor hospitality as they could command. It was very different from the comforts of her father's house ; but Maria took it as the first instalment of the hardships she had accepted.

Maria's wooden form was very skilfully made; the limbs had supple joints, which could be moved by the person inside just like those of a living being; and the clothes the teacher had provided being just like those of the country people about, no one entertained the least suspicion that Maria Wood, as she had now become, was anything different from themselves.

The charcoal-burners were kind, simple people, and, finding Maria willing to assist them in their labours to the extent of her powers, proposed to her to stay and cast in her lot with them as long as the season for their work lasted ; and she did their hard work and shared their poor fare with never a word of complaint.

At last, one day, when she was on I know not what errand, at some distance from the encampment, the young king of the country, who had lately been called to the throne, came through the forest hunting, with a large retinue of followers. Crash, crash, like thunder, went the brushwood as the wild boar trampled it down, and the eager dogs bounded after him with lightning speed. They passed close to Maria, who was as much alarmed as if she had really been the old woman she seemed to be : but when she saw the riders bearing down upon her, their horses' hoofs tearing up the soil, and the branches everywhere giving way before their impetuosity, her heart failed her entirely, and she swooned away upon the grass. The king, however, was the only one whose course passed over the spot where she was, and he only perceived her in time to rein up his mount just before it might have trampled on her.

'See here to this old body, whom we have nearly frightened to death,' he cried; and the huntsmen came and lifted her up.

'Some of you carry her home to the palace, that she may be attended to,' said the king further; and they carried her home to the palace, and laid her on a bed, and restored her senses.

When the king came home from the hunt, he would go himself to see how it had fared with her; and when he found her almost restored he asked her whither she would wish to be sent.

'Little it matters to me where I go,' replied Maria Wood, in the saddened voice of grief-stricken age; 'for home and kindred have I none. Little it matters where I lay my weary bones to rest.'

When the king heard her speak thus he compassionated her, and inquired if there was any service in the household that could be offered her.

'Please your Majesty, there is not much strength in her for work,' replied the steward; 'but, if such is your royal will, she can be set to help the scullions in the kitchen.'

'Will that suit you, old dame?' inquired the king. 'They shall not ask too much of you, and a good table and warm shelter shall never be wanting.'

'All thanks to your Majesty's bounty. My heart could desire nothing more than to live thus under the shadow of your Majesty,' replied Maria, making a humble obeisance.

And thus Maria, from a princess, became a servant of servants.

' What's the use of giving us such a cranky old piece as that for a help ?' said the scullion to the turnspit, as Maria was introduced to her new quarters.

' Why, as to that, as she has taken the service she must do it, cranky or not cranky,' answered the turnspit.

' Aye, I dare say we shall be able to get it out of her one way or another,' replied the scullion.

And they *did* get it out of her; and Maria had more put upon her, and less of kind words and scarcely better food than with the charcoal-burners. But she took it all in silence and patience, and no complaint passed her lips. She had no fixed duties, but one called her here and another there; she was at everyone's bidding, but she did her best to content them all.

Then came the Carneval; and on the last three days every servant had license to don a domino and dance at the king's ball. What an opportunity for Maria Wood! After serving in her unbecoming disguise with so much endurance and perseverance for now a full year, here was one day on which she might wear a becoming dress, and enjoy herself according to the measure of her age and sex, and due position in the world.

All the household, all royal as it was, was in a hubbub of confusion. No one was at work—no one at his post; and there was no one to notice that Maria Wood was absent, like the rest.

Locking herself into the loft which served her for a sleeping-place, Maria not only came out of her wooden disguise, but took out of it the garment woven of the stars of heaven—a most convenient dress for the occasion. At a masqued ball no one can recognise anybody else, except by a guess suggested by familiar characteristics which the domino fails to disguise. But no one at the king's court was familiar with the characteristics of Maria Wood; and wherever she passed the whole company was in an excitement to know whose was the elegant figure shrouded in such a marvellous costume. But there was so much majesty in her air, that no one durst ask her to dance or so much as approach her.

Only the king himself felt conscious of the right to offer to lead her to the dance; and she, who had not forgotten how handsome he was, and how kind he had been on the night that his huntsmen had nearly frightened her to death in the forest, right willingly accepted the favour. But even he was so awed by her grace and dignity, that, charmed as he was with her conversation, and burning to know her style and title, he yet could not frame the question that would ascertain whence she had come.

Very early in the evening, while the other masquers reckoned the amusement was only beginning, Maria, with characteristic moderation, chose an opportunity for withdrawing unperceived from the ballroom.

It will readily be imagined that the next night every one was full of curiosity, and the king most of all, to know whether the lady in the starry dress would appear again; and the more that, though everybody had been talking of her to the exclusion of everyone else the whole intervening day through, no one could offer a satisfactory conjecture as to who she could possibly be.

While all eyes were full of expectation, accordingly, the second evening, suddenly and unannounced there appeared in their midst a form, graceful and mobile like hers they had so much admired, but draped in a still more dazzling dress (for Maria this night wore her garment woven of moonbeams); and it was only the king who had the certainty that it was really the same person.

'Why did you take away all the light of our ball so early last night?' inquired the king, as they were dancing together.

'I have to be up early, and so I must go to bed early,' replied Maria.

'And what can a sylph-like creature like you have to

get up early in the morning for? You are only fit to lie on a bed of roses, with nightingales to sing to you,' pursued the king.

' My occupations are very different, I can assure your Majesty,' said Maria, with a hearty laugh.

' What can those occupations possibly be?' inquired the king eagerly; ' I am dying to know.'

' Oh, fie! You must not ask a domino such a direct question as that; it is as bad as asking her name, and that is against all rules. But see, the dancers await your Majesty; we are putting them all out.'

Thus she put him off, and she fenced so well that he succeeded no better in searching out the mystery in all his subsequent attempts. Though he had determined, too, never to leave her side all the evening, that he might certainly observe which way she went, she was so alert that she defeated his plans. Kings have a certain etiquette to observe, even at a Carneval ball; and while social exigencies demanded that he should bestow a salute on one and another of the distinguished personages present, Maria contrived to gather her shining raiment round her so as to invert its dazzling folds, and glide away unperceived.

The king was beside himself with vexation when he found she was gone; nor could he sleep all the succeeding night, or rather those hours which must be stolen out of the day to make a night of when the real night has been spent in revels. One thought occupied him, which was that the succeeding night was the last in which he could expect to have the chance of obtaining an explanation from his fair partner of the dance. The next day began the gloom of Lent, and she would disappear from his sight for ever. He arranged in his head a dozen forms of conversation by which to entrap her into some admission by which he could find out who she could possibly be; he determined to be more vigilant than ever in observing her movements; and, to provide against every possible chance of failure, he stationed guards at every exit of the ballroom, with strict orders to follow her when she passed.

In the midst of the ball on the third night Maria entered more radiant than ever, having on her dress woven of sunbeams. The masquers put their hands up to shade their eyes as she passed, and the chandeliers and torches were paled by its brilliance. The king was at her side immediately, but though he put in requisition all the devices he had prepared, Maria succeeded in evading them all, and the evening passed away without his being a bit wiser about how to see more of her than he had been at the beginning. The only thing that gave him a little hope that she did not mean absolutely to abandon him, was that in the course of the evening she took out a ring, which she told him had never fitted anyone yet, and begged him, as a matter of curiosity, to try it on his hand; and then when it strangely happened that it fitted him perfectly, she could not altogether conceal the pleasure it seemed to give her. Nevertheless, she put up the ring again, and wo..ld give no further explanation about it any more than about herself.

By-and-by, choosing her moment as dexterously as before, she made her escape without exciting the king's attention. The guards, however, were all expectation, and notwithstanding that she had taken the precaution of turning the sunbeams inwards, they recognised her, and followed softly after her as they had been bidden. Maria, however, did not fail to perceive they were following her, and, to divert their attention, took off a string of precious pearls she wore round her throat, and, unthreading them on the ground, escaped swiftly to her loft while the guards were occupied in gathering up the treasure.

The king was disconsolate beyond measure when he found that all his schemes were foiled, and that his radiant maiden had passed away like the rays in which she was clothed, leaving only darkness and weariness for him.

So disconsolate he grew that nothing could distract him. He would no more occupy himself with the affairs of the state, still less with any minor occupations. He could not bear the light of the sun because its beams reminded him of his loss, and he dreaded similarly the sight of the moon or the stars, but, shut up in a dark room almost hopeless, he wept the weary days away.

So remarkable a change in the habits of the young king became the subject of general comment, and could not fail to reach the ears of even so insignificant a menial as Maria. She, indeed, had every reason to hear of it, for scarcely could the afflicted king be induced to take the simplest food, and the attendants of the kitchen were reduced to complete inactivity. Maria was no longer called hither and thither at everyone's pleasure, and as long as this inactivity lasted she knew the king was still of the same mind about herself. But at last the talk of the kitchen took a more alarming character; it was reported that physicians had been called in, and had pronounced that unless means were found to distract him his state of despondency would prove fatal, but that nothing which had been tried had the least effect in rousing him from his melancholy.

Meantime Lent was passing away and Easter was close at hand. Maria thought she might now be satisfied with his constancy, and determined to take the step which she had good reason to believe would restore all his vigour.

Accordingly, while the cooks and scullions were all dispersed about one thing and another, she went into the kitchen and made a cake, into which she put the ring, and took it up herself to the queen-mother. It was not very easy for such a haggard old woman to obtain admission to the private apartments, but when she declared she had come about a remedy for the king, she was made welcome. Having thus obtained the ear of the queen-mother, she assured her, with many protestations, that if the king could be made to eat the whole of the cake, without giving the least piece of it to anyone, he would be immediately cured. But that if he gave away the least piece the virtue might be lost. This was lest he should thus give away the ring to anyone. The ladies waiting on the queen laughed at the old woman's pretensions, and would have driven her away with contumely, but the queen said: 'Nay, who knows but there may be healing in it. Experience often teaches the old remedies which science has failed to discover.'

Then she dismissed Maria with a present, and took the cake in to the king, trying to amuse him with the old woman's story; but the king refused to be amused, and let the cake be. Only as he took no notice of what food he ate, and they gave him this cake for all his meals, he took it as he would have taken anything else that had been set before him. When he cut it, his knife struck against something hard, and when he had pulled this out, he found it was the very ring his sylphlike partner had given him the night she wore the dress woven of sunbeams.

At the sight he started like one waking from a trance.

'How came this ring here?' he exclaimed; and the queen-mother, who had stood by to see the effect of the remedy, replied,

'A certain old woman, whom you befriended in the forest and told the servants to shelter in the palace, brought me the cake, saying it would prove a remedy for your melancholy, which she had prepared out of gratitude.'

'Let her be called instantly hither,' then said the king; and they went to fetch Maria Wood; but Maria could nowhere be found.

The king was at this announcement very nearly relapsing into his former condition ; but the idea came to his mind to find something out by means of the ring itself. Therefore he summoned together all the gold-smiths, and refiners, and alchemists of his kingdom, and bid them tell him the history of the ring.

At the end of seven days' trial the oldest of the alchemists brought it back to the king and said :

'We find, O King, that this ring is made of gold which comes from afar. Moreover, that the workman-ship is such as is only produced in the kingdoms of the West, and the characters on it pronounce that its owner is a princess of high degree, whose dominions exceed greatly those of the King's Majesty in magnitude.'

The king now ordered a more urgent search to be made for Maria Wood, as the only clue by which to reach the fair owner of the ring ; and Maria, having heard by report of the alchemists' announcement, thought it was time to let herself be known. Habiting herself, therefore, in becoming attire, with jewels befitting her rank, with all of which the fairy had amply provided her, she entered for the last time her wooden covering, and went up to the king in answer to his summons.

'Come·hither, good woman,' said the king encourag-ingly ; ' you have indeed done me good service in sending me this ring, and have repaid a hundredfold the little favour I bestowed on you in taking you into the palace. If, now, you will further bring me hither her to whom this ring belongs, or take me where I may find her, you shall not only live in the palace, but shall live there in royal state and luxury, and whatsoever more you may desire.'

At these words Maria stepped out of her wooden case, and stood before the king in all her youthful beauty, telling him all her story.

The proofs that supported it were sufficient to silence every doubt ; and when the people were called together to celebrate her marriage with the king, the whole nation hailed her accession as their queen with the greatest delight.

Soon after, the royal pair went to visit Maria's father, who had the joy of knowing that his child was really well established in life. They stayed with him till he died; and then his dominions were added to those of the king, Maria's husband. Maria did not forget to inquire for her good mistress, but she had long ago gone back to Fairy-land.

SECOND VERSION.

Another version of this, differing in many details, was given me in the following form. The former was from Loreto; this, from Rome itself.

THEY say, there was a king, whose wife, when she came to die, said to him,

'When I am dead, you will want to marry again; but take my advice: marry no woman but her whose foot my shoe fits.'

But this she said because the shoe was under a spell, and would fit no one whom he could marry.

The king, however, caused the shoe to be tried on all manner of women; and when the answer always was that it would fit none of them, he grew quite bewildered and strange in his mind.

After some years had passed, his young daughter, having grown up to girl's estate, came to him one day, saying,

'Oh, papa; only think! Mamma's shoe just fits me!'

'Does it!' replied the simple king; 'then I must marry you.'

'Oh, that cannot be, papa,' said the girl, and ran away.

But the simple king was so possessed with the idea that he must marry the woman whom his wife's shoe fitted, that he sent for her every day and said the same thing.

But the queen had not said that he should marry the woman whom her shoe fitted, but that he should not marry any whom it did not fit.

When the princess found that he persevered in his silly caprice, she said at last,

'Papa, if I am to do what you say, you must do something for me first.'

'Agreed, my child,' replied the king; 'you have only to speak.'

'Then, before I marry,' said the girl, 'I want a lot of things, but I will begin with one at a time. First, I want a dress of the colour of a beautiful noontide sky, but all covered with stars, like the sky at midnight, and furnished with a parure to suit it.' ³

Such a dress the king had made and brought to her.

'Next,' said the princess, 'I want a dress of the colour of the sea, all covered with golden fishes, with a fitting parure.'

Such a dress the king had made, and brought to her.

'Next,' said the princess, 'I want a dress of a dark blue, all covered with gold embroidery and spangled with silver bells, and with a parure to match.'

Such a dress the king had made and brought to her.

'These are all very good,' said the princess; 'but now you must send for the most cunning artificer in your whole kingdom, and let him make me a figure of an old woman ⁴ just like life, fitted with all sorts of springs to make it move and walk when one gets inside it, just like a real woman.'

Such a figure the king had made, and brought it to the princess.

'That is just the sort of figure I wanted,' said she; 'and now I don't want anything more.'

And the simple king went away quite happy.

As soon as she was alone, however, the princess packed all the three dresses and many of her other dresses, and all her jewellery and a large sum of money, inside the figure of the old woman, and then she got into it and walked away. No one seeing an old woman walking out of the palace thought she had anything to do with the princess, and thus she got far away without anyone thinking of stopping her.

On, on, on, she wandered till she came to the palace of a great king, and just at the time that the king's son was coming in from hunting.

'Have you a place in all this fine palace to take in a poor old body?' whined the princess inside the figure of the old woman.

'No, no! get out of the way! How dare you come in the way of the prince!' said the servants, and drove her away.

But the prince took compassion on her, and called her to him.

'What's your name, good woman?' said the prince.

'Maria Wood is my name, your Highness,' replied the princess.

'And what can you do, since you ask for a place?'

'Oh, I can do many things. First, I understand all about poultry, and then——'

'That'll do,' replied the prince; 'take her, and let her be the henwife,⁵ and let her have food and lodging, and all she wants.'

So they gave her a little hut on the borders of the forest, and set her to tend the poultry.

But the prince as he went out hunting often passed by her hut, and when she saw him pass she never failed to come out and salute him, and now and then he would stop his horse and spend a few moments in gossip with her.

Before long it was Carneval time; and as the prince came by Maria Wood came out and wished him a 'good Carneval.'⁶ The prince stopped his horse and said, his young head full of the pleasure he expected,

'To-morrow, you know, we have the first day of the feast.'

'To be sure I know it; and how I should like to be there: won't you take me?' answered Maria Wood.

'You shameless old woman,' replied the prince, 'to think of your wanting to go to a *festino* [7] at your time of life!' and he gave her a cut with his whip.

The next day Maria put on her dress of the colour of the noontide sky, covered with stars like the sky at midnight, with the parure made to wear with it, and came to the feast. Every lady made place before her dazzling appearance, and the prince alone dared to ask her to dance. With her he danced all the evening, and fairly fell in love with her,[8] nor could he leave her side; and as they sat together, he took the ring off his own finger and put it on to her hand. She appeared equally satisfied with his attentions, and seemed to desire no other partner. Only when he tried to gather from her whence she was, she would only say she came from the country of Whipblow,[9] which set the prince wondering very much, as he had never heard of such a country. At the end of the ball, the prince sent his attendants to watch her that he might learn where she lived, but she disappeared so swiftly it was impossible for them to tell what had become of her.

When the prince came by Maria Wood's hut next day, she did not fail to wish him again a 'good Carneval.'

'To-morrow we have the second *festino*, you know,' said the prince.

'Well I know it,' replied Maria Wood; 'shouldn't I like to go! Won't you take me?'

'You contemptible old woman to talk in that way!' exclaimed the prince. 'You ought to know better!' and he struck her with his boot.

Next night Maria put on her dress of the colour of the sea, covered all over with gold fishes, and the parure made to wear with it, and went to the feast. The prince recognised her at once, and claimed her for his partner all the evening, nor did she seem to wish for any other, only when he tried to learn from her whence she was, she would only say she came from the country of Bootkick.[10] The prince could not remember ever to have heard of the Bootkick country, and thought she meant to laugh at him; however, he ordered his attendants to make more haste this night in following her; but what diligence soever they used she was too swift for them.

The next time the prince came by Maria Wood's hut, she did not fail to wish him again a ' good Carneval.'

'To-morrow we have the last festino!' exclaimed he, with a touch of sadness, for he remembered it was the last of the happy evenings that he could feel sure of seeing his fair unknown.

'Ah! you must take me. But, what'll you say if I come to it in spite of you?' answered Maria Wood.

'You incorrigible old woman!' exclaimed the prince; 'you provoke me so with your nonsense, I really cannot keep my hand off you;' and he gave her a slap.

The next night Maria Wood put on her dress of a dark blue, all covered with gold embroidery and spangled with silver bells, and the parure made to wear with it. The prince constituted her his partner for the evening as before, nor did she seem to wish for any other, only when he wanted to learn from her whence she was, all she would say was that she came from Slapland.[11] This night the prince told his servants to make more haste in following her, or he would discharge them all. But they answered, 'It is useless to attempt the thing, as no mortal can equal her in swiftness.'

After this, the prince fell ill of his disappointment, because he saw no hope of hearing any more of the fair domino with whom he had spent three happy evenings, nor could any doctor find any remedy for his sickness.

Then Maria Wood sent him word, saying, 'Though the prince's physicians cannot help him, yet let him but take a cup of broth of my making, and he will immediately be healed.'

'Nonsense! how can a cup of broth, or how can any medicament, help me!' exclaimed the prince. 'There is no cure for my ailment.'

Again Maria Wood sent the same message; but the prince said angrily,

'Tell the silly old thing to hold her tongue; she doesn't know what she's talking about.'

But again, the third time, Maria Wood sent to him, saying, 'Let the prince but take a cup of broth of my making, and he will immediately be healed.'

By this time the prince was so weary that he did not take the trouble to refuse. The servants finding him so depressed began to fear that he was sinking, and they called to Maria Wood to make her broth, because, though they had little faith in her promise, they knew not what else to try. So Maria Wood made ready the cup of broth she had promised, and they put it down beside the prince.

Presently the whole palace was roused; the prince had started up in bed, and was shouting,

'Bring hither Maria Wood! Quick! Bring hither Maria Wood!'

So they ran and fetched Maria Wood, wondering what could have happened to bring about so great a change in the prince. But the truth was, that Maria had put into the cup of broth the ring the prince had put on her finger the first night of the feast, and when he began to take the broth he found the ring with the spoon. When he saw the ring, he knew at once that Maria Wood could tell where to find his fair partner.

'Wait a bit! there's plenty of time!' said Maria, when the servant came to fetch her in all haste; and she waited to put on her dress of the colour of the noontide sky.

The prince was beside himself for joy when he saw her, and would have the betrothal celebrated that very day.

THIRD VERSION.

IN another version, on the princess refusing to do what the king wishes, he sends his servants to take her to a high tower he has out in the Campagna, and bids them carry her to the top and drop her down.

They take her there; but have not the heart to throw her down. In a corner of the upper story of the tower they see a large case or press.

'Suppose we shut her up in this great press, and leave her in the middle of the open Campagna, a long way off, to the providence of God? It will be better than killing her,' says one of them.

'We have nothing against the plan,' answered the others; 'provided we take her so far that she cannot possibly come back to our king's country.'

So they locked her up in the great box, and carried the box a long, long way out in the open Campagna, and left it there to the providence of God.

The poor princess was very glad to have escaped death; but she felt very desolate in the box. As she was wondering what would happen to her, she was suddenly frightened by a great barking of dogs round the box. A king's son had come by hunting, and his dogs had smelt human blood in the box.

'Call the dogs off, and let's see what's in the box,' said the prince.

So they opened the box; and when they saw the princess inside, they saw she was no common maiden, for she had a stomacher and earrings of brilliants. So they brought her to the prince, and she pleased him, and he married her.

[This way of introducing the box incident is more like Straparola's, and again connects this group with the former one in which I have had occasion to mention it.]

¹ Maria di Legno.

² This is one of the very rare instances in which the Devil appears in Roman stories in this kind of character, so common in Northern popular tales.

³ 'Colle gioie compagne.'

⁴ 'Vecchiarella.'

⁵ 'Gallinara.'

⁶ A 'buon carnevale' chiefly implies the wish that the person to whom it is addressed should have good success with partners at the balls, &c.

⁷ A 'festino' is the common name for a public masqued ball commencing at midnight. There are three principal ones in the Roman Carneval; in other parts of Italy, where the Carneval is longer, there are probably more. It is also called 'Veglione,' because it keeps people awake at a time when they ought to be in bed.

⁸ 'How quick princes always were in falling in love in those days!' was the running comment of the narrator.

⁹ To understand the implied satire of this word it is necessary to observe that 'Frusta' is a whip; the princess therefore says she came from 'Frustinaia,' Whip-blow.

¹⁰ 'Stivale,' a boot. As the prince had struck her with his boot, she says she comes from 'Stivalaia,' Boot-kick.

¹¹ 'Schiaffaia' from schiaffa, a slap. The prince had given her a slap, so she says she comes from Slap-land.

LA CANDELIERA.¹

THEY say there was once a king who wanted to make his beautiful young daughter marry an old, ugly king. Every time the king talked to his daughter about this marriage, she cried and begged him to spare her; but he only went on urging her the more, till at last she feared he would command her to consent, so that she might not disobey; therefore at last she said: 'Before I marry this ugly old king to please you, you must do something to please me.'

'Oh, anything you like I will do,' replied he.

'Then you must order for me,' she replied, 'a splendid

candelabrum, ten feet high, having a thick stem bigger than a man, and covered all over with all kinds of ornaments and devices in gold.'

'That shall be done,' said the king; and he sent for the chief goldsmith of the court, and told him to make such a candelabrum; and, as he was very desirous that the marriage should be celebrated without delay, he urged him to make the candelabrum with all despatch.

In a very short space of time the goldsmith brought home the candelabrum, made according to the princess's description, and the king ordered it to be taken into his daughter's apartment. The princess expressed herself quite pleased with it, and the king was satisfied that the marriage would now shortly take place.

Late in the evening, however, the princess called her chamberlain to her, and said to him: 'This great awkward candlestick is not the sort of thing I wanted; it does not please me at all. To-morrow morning you may take it and sell it, for I cannot bear the sight of it. You may keep the price it sells for, whatever it is; but you had better take it away early, before my father gets up.'

The chamberlain was very pleased to get so great a perquisite, and got up very early to carry it away. The princess, however, had got up earlier, and had placed herself inside the candlestick; so that she was carried out of the palace by the chamberlain, and thus she escaped the marriage she dreaded so much with the ugly old king.

The chamberlain, judging that the king would be very angry if he heard of his selling the splendid candelabrum he had just had made, did not venture to expose it for sale within the borders of his dominions, but carried it to the capital of the neighbouring sovereign. Here he set it up in the market-place, and cried, 'Who'll buy my candelabrum? Who'll buy my fine candelabrum?' When all the people saw what a costly candelabrum it was, no one would offer for it. At last it got bruited about till it reached the ears of the son of the king of that country, that there was a man standing in the market-place, offering to sell the most splendid candelabrum that ever was seen; so he went out to look at it himself.

No sooner had the prince seen it than he determined that he must have it; so he bought it for the price of three hundred scudi, and sent his servants to take it up into his ˙apartment. After that, he went about his affairs as usual. In the evening, however, he said to his body-servant, 'As I am going to the play to-night, and shall be home late, take my supper up into my own room.' And the servant did as he told him.

When the prince came home from the play, he was very much surprised to find his supper eaten and all the dishes and glasses disarranged.

'What is the meaning of this?' he exclaimed, calling his servant to him in a great fury. 'Is this the way you prepare supper for me?'

'I don't know what to say, your Royal Highness,' stammered the man; 'I saw the supper properly laid myself. How it got into this condition is more than I can say. With the leave of your Highness, I will order the table to be relaid.'

But the prince was too angry to allow anything of the sort, and he went supperless to bed.

The next night the same thing happened, and the prince in his displeasure threatened to discharge his servant. The night after, however, his curiosity being greatly excited as he thought over the circumstance, he called his servant, and said: 'Lay the supper before I go out, and I will lock the room and take the key in my pocket, and we will see if anyone gets in then.'

But, though this is what he said outloud, he determined to stay hidden within the room; and this is what he did. He had not remained there hidden very long when, lo and behold, the candelabrum, on which he had never bestowed a thought since the moment he bought it, opened, and there walked out the most beautiful princess he had ever seen, who sat down at the table, and began to sup with hearty appetite.

'Welcome, welcome, fair princess!' exclaimed the astonished prince. 'You have heard me from within your hiding-place speaking with indignation because my meal had been disturbed. How little did I imagine such an honour had been done me as that it should have served you!' And he sat down beside her, and they finished the meal together. When it was over, the princess went away into her candelabrum again; and the next night the prince said to his servant: 'In case anyone eats my supper while I am out, you had better bring up a double portion.' The next day he had not his supper only, but all his meals, brought into his apartment; nor did he ever leave it at all now, so happy was he in the society of the princess.

Then the king and queen began to question about him, saying: 'What has bereft our son of his senses, seeing that now he no more follows the due occupations of his years, but sits all day apart in his room?'

Then they called him to them and said: 'It is not well that you should sit thus all day long in your private apartments alone. It is time that you should bethink yourself of taking a wife.'

But the prince answered, 'No other wife will I have but the candelabrum.'

When his parents heard him say this they said: 'Now there is no doubt that he is mad;' and they spoke no more about his marrying.

But one day, the queen-mother coming into his apartment suddenly, found the door of the candelabrum open, and the princess sitting talking with the prince. Then she, too, was struck with her beauty, and said: 'If this is what you were thinking of when you said you would marry the candelabrum, it was well judged.' And she took the princess by the hand and led her to the presence of the king. The king, too, praised her beauty, and she was given to the prince to be his wife.

And the king her father, when he heard of the alliance, he too was right glad, and said he esteemed it far above that of the ugly old king he wanted her to have married at the first.

[1] Among the licenses which Italians take with the terminations of their words, not the least is altering the gender. ' Candeliere ' (masc.), otherwise ' candelliere,' is the proper form ; and I do not think ' candeliera ' will be found in any dictionary ; but as the story requires the female gender, the word is readily coined.

[The mode of telling adopted by Roman narrators makes a way out of the difficulty which this group of stories presents at first sight in the king seeming to be fated by supernatural appointment to marry his daughter. One says, 'the queen did not say he was to marry her the ring fitted, but he was not to marry any it did not fit.' The other says, the slipper was a supernatural slipper, and would not fit anyone whom he could marry. Whether this was a part of the traditional story or the gloss of the repeater, I do not pretend to decide. In the ' Candeliera,' though similar in the main, this difficulty does not arise.

My Roman narrators seem to have been fonder of stories of maidens than of youths. I have only one of the latter, and by no means an uncommon one, to set off against all the Stepmother stories of the former. It, however, is the male counterpart of a prolific family in which the girls figure under similar circumstances. Grimm gives several, particularly ' Frau Holle,' p. 104. Dr. Dasent gives ' The two Stepsisters.' In the Tales of Italian Tirol are two, ' Cölla döllö doi sores ' and ' Le due sorelle.' And among the Russian Tales, 'Frost,' p. 214. It has also been connected with the large group in which a rich brother (sometimes the elder, sometimes the younger) leaves his poor brother to starve, and ultimately gets terribly punished for enviously grasping at the poor one's subsequent good fortune : but the structure of these is very different.]

THE TWO HUNCHBACKED BROTHERS.[1]

THERE was once a man who had one son, who married a widow who also had one son, and both were hunchbacks. The wife took very good care of her own son, but the son of her husband she used to put to hard work and gave him scarcely anything to eat. Her son, too, used to imitate his mother, and sadly ill-treat his stepbrother.

After treating him ill for a long time, she at last sent him away from the house altogether.

The poor little hunchback wandered away without knowing where to go.

On, on, on he went, till at last he came to a lonely hut on a wide moor. At his approach a whole host of little hunchbacks came out and danced round him, chanting plaintively—

Sabbato!
Domenica!

a great number of times. At last our little hunchback felt his courage stirred, and, taking up the note of their chant, chimed in with—

Lunedì!

Instantly the dancing ceased, all the little hunchback dwarfs became full-grown, well-formed men, and, what was better still, his own hump was gone too, and he felt that he, too, was a well-grown lad.

‘ Good people,’ said our hunchback—now hunchbacked no more—‘ I thank you much for ridding me of my hump and making me a well-grown lad. Give me now some work to do among you, and let me live with you.’

But the chief of the strange people answered him and said : ‘ This favour we owe to you, not you to us ; for it was your chiming in with the right word on the right note which destroyed the spell that held us all. And in testimony of our gratitude we give you further this little wand, and you will not need to work with us. Go back and live at home, and if ever anyone beats you as heretofore, you have only to say to it, "At 'em, good stick!"² and you will see what it will do for you.'

Then all disappeared, and the boy went home.

' So you've come back, have you ? ' said the stepmother. ' What, and without your hump, too ! Where have you left that ? '

Then the good boy told her all that had happened, without hiding anything.

' Do you hear that ? ' said the stepmother to her own son. ' Now go you and get rid of your hump in the same way.'

So the second hunchback went forth, and journeyed on till he came to the lonely hut on the moor.

A tribe of hunchbacks came out and danced round him, and sung—·

> Sabbato !
> Domenica !
> Lunedi !

to which the bad son of the stepmother added in his rough voice, all out of tune—

> Martedi !

Immediately all the hunchbacks came round him and gave him a drubbing, and the chief of them stuck on him a hump in front as well as behind.

Thus they sent him home to his mother.

When his mother saw him come home in this plight, she turned upon the stepson and abused him for having misled her son to injure him ; and both mother and son set upon him and belaboured him after their wont. But he had only told the truth, without intention to deceive; and the stepmother's son had incurred the anger of the dwarfs by his discordant addition to their chant. So the first hero took out his wand and said, ' At' em, good stick ! ' and

the wand flew out of his hand and administered on mother
and son a sounder drubbing than that they had themselves
been administering. Ever after that he was able to live
at home in peace, for everyone was afraid to injure him
because of the power of his stick.

¹ 'I due Fratelli Gobbi.'

² 'Bachettone mena!' Perhaps the greatest stumbling-block in the way
of acquiring familiarity with the art of conversing in Italian is the capricious use of the augmentative and diminutive terminations of words.
Scarcely any substantive or adjective comes out of the mouth of an Italian
without qualifications of this sort, making the spoken quite different from
the written language. A foreigner can never arrive at the right use of
these, because they have to be made up at the moment of use, upon no
established laws, but entirely by a sort of instinctive perception of fitness.
At Note 1 and 3 to 'Il Poveretto,' and other places, I have given some
specimens of some of the most ordinary of these transformations. In
the instance before us, 'bacchettone,' from 'bacchetta,' a rod, presents
two distinct irregularities. The augmentative of a feminine noun never
ought strictly to be '*ona*;' but there are numerous instances, scarcely to be
remembered under the largest practice, in which a feminine noun takes a
masculine augmentative. 'Bacchetta' happens to be one of these. Next,
the addition '*one*' would ordinarily express that the thing to whose
designation it was added was particularly big; yet in this instance it is
applied to a *little wand*; it is clear, therefore, that it no longer means 'big,'
but 'singular,' 'remarkable' in some way or other; best rendered in
English by 'good stick.' 'Menare,' whence 'mena,' is a word of
many meanings, which, though they may be all traced to the same original
idea, must not be confounded. In common parlance, as in the present
case, it means to beat; and 'menar moglie' is a common expression too;
but it does not mean 'to beat your wife,' but 'to lead home a wife,' or, as
we say, to 'take a wife.' The primary meaning is 'to lead;' hence, to
govern; hence, to govern harshly; hence, to govern with violence; hence,
to spite, to beat. One sentence in which it is used recalls a capricious use
of our own word 'to beat.' 'Menar' il cane per l'aja' (literally, to lead the
dog all about the threshing-floor), answers exactly to our expression, 'to
beat about the bush' in talking. 'Menare' and 'dimenare, la coda,' is
said also of a dog wagging his tail. On the other hand, 'menare per il
naso' (literally, 'to lead one by the nose'), has by no means the signi-
fication those words bear in English, but implies a roundabout way of
giving an account of anything.

[Next we have a group where a younger sister of three
comes to supernatural good fortune, without any previous envy
or ill-treatment on the part of her elders.]

THE DARK KING.[1]

THEY say there was once a poor chicory-gatherer who went out every day with his wife and his three daughters to gather chicory to sell for salad. Once, at Carneval time, he said, ' We must gather a fine good lot to-day,' and they all dispersed themselves about trying to do their best. The youngest daughter thus came to a place apart where the chicory was of a much finer growth than any she had ever seen before. ' This will be grand ! ' she said to herself, as she prepared to pull up the finest plant of it. But what was her surprise when with the plant, up came all the earth round it and a great hole only remained !

When she peeped down into it timidly she was further surprised to find it was no dark cave below as she had apprehended, but a bright apartment handsomely furnished, and a most appetising meal spread out on the table, there was, moreover, a commodious staircase reaching to the soil on which she stood, to descend by.

All fear was quickly overcome by the pleasant sight, and the girl at once prepared to descend, and, as no one appeared, to raise any objection, she sat down quite boldly and partook of the good food. As soon as she had finished eating, the tables were cleared away by invisible hands, and, as she had nothing else to do she wandered about the place looking at everything. After she had passed through several brilliant rooms she came to a passage, out of which led several store-chambers, where was laid up a good supply of everything that could serve in a house. In some there were provisions of all sorts, in some stuffs both for clothes and furniture.

' There seems to be no one to own all these fine things,' said the girl. ' What a boon they would be at home ! ' and she put together all that would be most useful to her mother. But what was her dismay when she went back to the dining-hall to find that the staircase by which she had descended was no longer there !

At this sight she sat down and had a good cry, but by-and-by, supper-time came, and with it an excellent supper, served in as mysterious a way as the dinner ; and as a good supper was a rare enjoyment for her, she almost forgot her grief while discussing it. After that, invisible hands led her into a bedroom, where she was gently undressed and put to bed without seeing anyone. In the morning she was put in a bath and dressed by invisible hands, but dressed like a princess all in beautiful clothes.

So it all went on for at least three months; every luxury she could wish was provided without stint, but as she never saw anyone she began to get weary, and at last *so* weary that she could do nothing but cry. At the sound of her crying there came into the room a great black King.[2] Though he was so dark and so big that she was frightened at the sight of him, he spoke very kindly, and asked her why she cried so bitterly, and whether she was not provided with everything she could desire. As she hardly knew herself why she cried, she did not know what to answer him, but only went on whimpering. Then he said, ' You have not seen half the extent of this palace yet or you would not be so weary ; here are the keys of all the locked rooms which you have not been into yet. Amuse yourself as much as you like in going through them ; they are all just like your own. Only into the room of which the key is not among these do not try to enter. In all the rest do what you like.'

The next morning she took the keys and went into one of the locked rooms, and there she found so many things to surprise and amuse her that she spent the whole day there, and the next day she examined another, and so on for quite three months together, and the locked room of which she had not the key she never thought of trying to enter. But all amusements tire at last, and at the end of this time she was so melancholy that she could do nothing but cry. Then the Dark King came again and asked her tenderly what she wanted.

'I want nothing you can give me,' she replied this time. 'I am tired of being so long away from home. I want to go back home.'

'But remember how badly you were clothed, and how poorly you fared,' replied the Dark King.

'Ah, I know it is much pleasanter here,' said the girl, 'for all those matters, but one cannot do without seeing one's relations, now and then at least.'

'If you make such a point of it,' answered the Dark King, 'you shall go home and see papa and mamma, but you will come back here. I only let you go on that condition.'

The arrangement was accepted, and next day she was driven home in a fine coach with prancing horses and bright harness. Her appearance at home caused so much astonishment that there was hardly room for pleasure, and even her own mother would hardly acknowledge her; as for her sisters, they were so changed by her altered circumstances and so filled with jealousy they would scarcely speak to her. But when she gave her mother a large pot of gold which the Dark King had given her for the purpose, their hearts were somewhat won back to her, and they began to ask all manner of questions concerning what had befallen her during her absence. So much time had been lost at first, however, that none was left for answering them, and, promising to try and come back to them soon, she drove away in her splendid coach.

Another three months passed away after this, and at the end of it she was once more so weary, her tears and cries again called the Dark King to her side.

Again she confided to him that her great grief was the wish to see her friends at home. She could not bear being so long without them. To content her once more he promised to let her drive home the next day; and the next day accordingly she went home.

This time she met with a better reception, and having brought out her pot of gold at her first arrival, everyone was full of anxiety to know how it came she had such riches at her disposal.

'What that pot of money!' replied the girl, in a tone of disparagement. 'That's nothing. You should see the beautiful things that are scattered about in my new home, just like nothing at all;' and then she went on to describe the magnificence of the place, till nothing would satisfy them but that they should go there too.

'That's impossible,' she replied. 'I promised him not even to mention it.'

'But if he were got rid of, *then* we might come,' replied the elder sisters.

'What do you mean by "got rid of"?' asked the youngest.

'Why, it is evident he is some bad sort of enchanter, whom it would be well to rid the earth of. If you were to take this stiletto and put it into his breast when he is asleep, we might all come down there and be happy together.'

'Oh, I could never do that!'

'Ah, you are so selfish you want to keep all for yourself. If you had any spirit in you, you would burst open that locked door where, you may depend the best of the treasure is concealed, and then put this stiletto into the old enchanter, and call us all down to live with you.'

It was in vain she protested she could not be so ungrateful and cruel; they over-persuaded her with their arguments, and frightened her so with their reproaches that she went back resolved to do their bidding.

The next morning she called up all her courage and pushed open the closed door. Inside were a number of beautiful maidens weaving glittering raiment.

'What are you doing?' asked the chicory-gatherer.

'Making raiment for the bride of the Dark King against her espousals,' replied the maidens.

A little further on was a goldsmith and all his men working at all sorts of splendid ornaments filled with pearls and diamonds and rubies.

'What are you doing?' asked the girl.

'Making ornaments for the bride of the Dark King against her espousals,' replied the goldsmiths.

A little further on was a little old hunchback sitting crosslegged, and patching an old torn coat with a heap of other worn-out clothes lying about him.

'What are you doing?' asked the maiden.

'Mending the rags for the girl to go away in who was to have been the bride of the Dark King,' replied the little old hunchback.

Beyond the room where this was going on was a passage, and at the end of this a door, which she also pushed open. It gave entrance to a room where, on a bed, the Dark King lay asleep.

'This is the time to apply the stiletto my sisters gave me,' thought the maiden. 'I shall never have so good a chance again. They said he was a horrid old enchanter; let me see if he looks like one.'

So saying she took one of the tapers from a golden bracket and held it near his face. It was true enough; his skin was black, his hair was grizly and rough, his features crabbed and forbidding.

'They're right, there's no doubt. It were better the earth were rid of him, as they say,' she said within herself; and, steeling herself with this reflection, she plunged the knife into his breast.

But as she wielded the weapon with the right hand, the left, in which she held the lighted taper, wavered, and some of the scalding wax fell on the forehead of the Dark King. The dropping of the wax [3] woke him; and

when he saw the blood flowing from his breast, and perceived what she had done, he said sadly,

'Why have you done this? I meant well by you and
really loved you, and thought if I fulfilled all you desire,
you would in time have loved me. But it is over now.
You must leave this place, and go back to be again what
you were before.'

Then he called servants, and bade them dress her
again in her poor chicory-gatherer's dress, and send her up
to earth again; and it was done. But as they were about
to lead her away, he said again,

'Yet one thing I will do. Take these three hairs;
and if ever you are in dire distress and peril of life with
none to help, burn them, and I will come to deliver
you.'

Then they took her back to the dining-hall, where the
staircase was seen as at the first, and when they touched
the ceiling, it opened, and they pushed her through the
opening, and she found herself in the place where she had
been picking chicory on the day that she first found the
Dark King's palace.

Only as they were leading her along, she had considered that it might be dangerous for her, a young girl,
to be wandering about the face of the country alone, and
she had, therefore, begged the servants to give her a
man's clothes instead of her own; and they gave her the
worn-out clothes that she had seen the little old hunchback sitting crosslegged to mend.

When she found herself on the chicory-bed it was in
the cold of the early morning, and she set off walking towards her parents' cottage. It was about midday when
she arrived, and all the family were taking their meal.
Poor as it was, it looked very tempting to her who had
tasted nothing all the morning.

'Who are you?' cried the mother, as she came up to
the door.

'I'm your own child, your youngest daughter. Don't you know me?' cried the forlorn girl in alarm.

'A likely joke!' laughed out the mother; 'my daughter comes to see me in a gilded coach with prancing horses!'

'Had you asked for a bit of bread in the honest character of a beggar,' pursued the father, 'poor as I am, I would never have refused your weary, woebegone looks; but to attempt to deceive with such a falsehood is not to be tolerated;' and he rose up, and drove the poor child away.

Protests were vain, for no one recognised her under her disguise.

Mournful and hopeless, she wandered away. On, on, on, she went, till at last she came to a palace in a great city, and in the stables were a number of grooms and their helpers rubbing down horses.

'Wouldn't there be a place for me among all these boys?' asked the little chicory-gatherer, plaintively. 'I, too, could learn to rub down a horse if you taught me.'

'Well, you don't look hardly strong enough to rub down a horse, my lad,' answered the head-groom; 'but you seem a civil-spoken sort of chap, so you may come in; I dare say we can find some sort of work for you.'

So she went into the stable-yard, and helped the grooms of the palace.

But every day the queen stood at a window of the palace where she could watch the fair stable-boy, and at last she sent and called the head-groom, and said to him, 'What are you doing with that new boy in the stable-yard?'

The head-groom said, 'Please your Majesty he came and begged for work, and we took him to help.

Then the queen said, 'He is not fit for that sort of work, send him to me.'

So the chicory-gatherer was sent up to the queen, and

the queen gave her the post of master of the palace, and appointed a fine suite of apartments and a dress becoming the rank, and was never happy unless she had this new master of the palace with her.

Now the king was gone to the wars, and had been a long time absent. One day the queen said to the master of the palace that very likely the king would not come back, so that it would be better they should marry.

Then the poor chicory-gatherer was sadly afraid that if the queen discovered that she was a woman she would lose her fine place at the palace, and become a poor beggar again without a home; so she said nothing of this, but only reasoned with the queen that it was better to wait and see if the king did not come home. But as she continued saying this, and at the same time never showed any wish that the king might not come back, or that the marriage might take place, the queen grew sorely offended, and swore she would be avenged.

Not long after, the king really did come back, covered with glory, from the wars. Now was the time for the queen to take her revenge.

Choosing her opportunity, therefore, at the moment when the king was rejoicing that he had been permitted to come back to her again, with hypocritical tears she said,

'It is no small mercy, indeed, that your Majesty has found me again here as I am, for it had well-nigh been a very different case.'

The king was instantly filled with burning indignation, and asked her further what her words meant.

'They mean,' replied the queen, 'that the master of the palace, on whom I had bestowed the office only because he seemed so simple, as you too must say he looks, presumed on my favour, and would have me marry him, urging that peradventure the king, who had been so long absent at the wars, might never return.'

The king started to his feet at the words, placing his hand upon his sword in token of his wrath; but the queen went on:

'And when he found that I would not listen to his suit, he dared to assume a tone of command, and would have compelled me to consent; so that I had to call forth all my courage, and determination, and dignity, to keep him back; and had the King's Majesty not been directed back to the palace as soon as he was, who knows where it might have ended!'

It needed no more. The king ordered the master of the palace to be instantly thrown into prison, and appointed the next day for him to be beheaded.

The chicory-gatherer was ready enough now to protest that she was a woman. But it helped nothing; they only laughed. And who could stand against the word of the queen?

Next day, accordingly, the scaffold was raised, and the master of the palace was brought forth to be beheaded, the king and the queen, and all the court, being present.

When the chicory-gatherer, therefore, found herself in dire need and peril of life, she took out one of the hairs the Dark King had given her, and burnt it in the flame of a torch. Instantly there was a distant roaring sound as of a tramp of troops and the roll of drums. Everyone started at the sound, and the executioner stayed his hand.

Then the maiden burnt the second hair, and instantly a vast army surrounded the whole place; round the palace they marched and up to the scaffold, and so to the very throne of the king. The king had now something to think of besides giving the signal for the execution, and the headsman stayed his hand.

Then the maiden burnt the third hair, and instantly the Dark King himself appeared upon the scene, clothed in shining armour, and fearful in majesty and might. And he said to the king,

'Who are you that you have given over my wife to the executioner?'

And the king said,

'Who is thy wife that I should give her to the executioner?'

The Dark King, taking the master of the palace by the hand, said,

'This is my wife. Touch her who dares!'

Then the king knew that it had been true when the master of the palace had alleged that she was not guilty of the charge the queen had brought against her, being a woman; and seeing clearly what had been the malice of the queen, he ordered the executioner to behead her instead, but the chicory-gatherer he gave up to the Dark King.

Then the Dark King said to the chicory-gatherer,

'I came at your bidding to defend you, and I said you were my wife to save your life; but whether you will be my wife or not depends on you. It is for you to say whether you will or not.'

Then the maiden answered,

'You have been all goodness to me; ungrateful indeed should I be did I not, as I now do, say "yes."'

As soon as she said 'yes,' the earth shook, and she was no longer standing on a scaffold, but before an altar in a splendid cathedral, surrounded by a populous and flourishing city. By her side stood the Black King, but black no longer. He was now a most beautiful prince; for with all his kingdom he had been under enchantment, and the condition of his release had been that a fair maiden should give her free consent to marry him.[4]

---

[1] 'Il Rè Moro.'

[2] 'Moro' does not necessarily mean a Moor, it is continually used for any dark-complexioned person; also commonly for dark or black, as a pet name for a black dog, &c.

³ The 'moccolaio.'
⁴ The narrator ended this story with the following stanza :—

> Si faceva le nozze
> Con pane e tozze,
> E polla vermiciosa,
> E viva la sposa!

This is one of those rough verses with which such stories abound, and they have been rendered rougher than they originally were by substituting words which serve to retain the jingle after those conveying the sense are forgotten, like many of our own nursery-rhymes. The literal rendering of this one would be, 'So the marriage was celebrated with bread and hunches of bread, and a chicken stuffed with vermicelli. Long live the bride!' 'Vermiciosa' is not a dictionary word; 'vermicoloso' is the nearest, and probably a corruption of the same. Of course, primarily it means 'full of worms;' but as all the forms of words compounded out of the diminutive of 'verme,' a worm, may be applied to the fine kind of maccaroni which bears the same name, I am more inclined to think a fowl stuffed or served up with maccaroni is meant here—if it have any meaning at all beyond the purpose of a rhyme—rather than 'a wormy fowl,' the literal interpretation.

I have met this same 'tag' again and again in the mouths of various narrators at the end of stories which end in a marriage. Another such, familiarly used by every Roman narrator, is :—

> 'Stretta la foglia,
> Larga la via (often, 'Stretta la via'),
> Dite la vostra, Larga la foglia,
> Ch' ho detto la mia.'

('Narrow the leaf, broad the way. Tell me your tale, for I've told you mine.') Perhaps originally it was 'Larga la voglia' (my willingness is ample, but my means of amusing you are restricted).

MONSU MOSTRO.[1]

THERE was a father who had three daughters, and when all trades failed, he said he would go and gather chicory, and called his daughters to go with him. But it was a wet day, and they begged to be left at home ; so he went alone.

He went out into the fields till he came to a place where was the biggest plant of chicory that ever was seen. 'That will do for me,' he said, and began to pull it up.

Up it came by the root and left a hole in the ground, and a voice came up through the hole, and said, 'Who's there?'

'Friends!'² answered the chicory-gatherer; and then One sprang up through the hole on to the ground. This was Monsu Mostro. The poor man was rather frightened at his aspect, but he dared say nothing.

'Come along with me,' said Monsu Mostro and the poor man followed till they came to a palace in the Campagna, where he gave him a horse to ride home upon and a heap of money. 'I give you all this,' said Monsu Mostro; 'but you must give me one of your daughters in return.' The poor man was too frightened to refuse, so he said he would.

When he came home all his three daughters came jumping round him with delight at seeing him come home riding on horseback. 'Papa! papa!³ where have you been?' And when they saw what a lot of money he had brought home, their questions increased tenfold. But, in spite of his riches, the chicory-gatherer did not seem in good spirits. He did not know how to announce that he had to take one of his daughters to Monsu Mostro, and so he was very slow at answering their inquiries. It was not till next morning that he made up his mind to break this dreadful matter; and then, when the time had come for him to go forth, and there was no putting it off any longer, he made a great effort and said at last, 'I have found a husband for one of you; which shall it be?'

'Not I!' said the eldest; 'I'm not going to marry a husband whom I havn't seen. Oibo!'

'Not I!' said the second. 'I'm not going to marry a husband whom I havn't seen. Oibo!'

'Take me, papa! take me! I'll go!' said the youngest. So the father remounted the horse, and put her behind him. Thus they arrived at the palace of Monsu Mostro, and knocked.

'Who's there?' said a voice within.

'Friends!' answered the father; and they were shown in.

'Here's my daughter, as I promised,' said the father.

'All right!' said Monsu Mostro; and, giving him another large sum of money, sent him away.

When the father was gone, he said to the girl, 'I'm not going to marry you as your father thought. I want you to do the service of the house. But mind when there is anyone here you always call me " papa." '

The girl promised to do as she was bid, and soon after there was a knock at the door, and some hunters who had got belated in the Campagna came to seek hospitality.

'Let them in, set supper before them; and give them a change of clothes,' said Monsu Mostro; and the girl did as she was bid. While they were at supper one of the huntsmen kept looking at her, for she was a beautiful girl, and afterwards he asked her if she would marry him, for he was the king's son. 'Oh, shouldn't I like it!' said the girl, 'but you must ask papa.' The prince asked Monsu Mostro, and as he made no objection, he went and fetched a great cortége, and took her to the palace to marry her. As she was going away Monsu Mostro gave her a comb, wrapped up in paper, and said, ' Take care of this, and don't forget you have got it.' The girl was too full of her happiness to pay much heed, but she put it in her bosom and went away.

As she drove along, a pair of horns like a cow's began to grow on her head, and they had already attained a considerable size before she arrived at the royal palace. The queen was horrified at her appearance, and refused to let her come in. 'How can it possibly be that such a beautiful girl should have all of a sudden got a pair of horns?' said the prince. But it was no use saying anything, for there were the horns, and the queen was determined that she should not be admitted into the royal palace.

The prince was very much distressed, and would on no account let her be turned adrift as the queen wished, but sent her to a house in the Campagna, where he sent a servant every day to ask how she was, and to take her some present, but also to observe if the horns had not perchance gone away as suddenly as they had come. But, instead of going away, they went on growing every day bigger.

In the meantime the queen sent a servant out with three little puppy-dogs in a basket, saying that whoever trained them best should marry the prince. One of these the servant brought to her, and the two others to two other girls, who were princesses, either of whom the queen would have preferred her son should marry.

'Train puppy-dogs!' said each of the other two girls. 'I know nothing about training puppy-dogs! What can I do with them!' and they let them get into all manner of bad habits.

But *she* put hers in a basket and went back to the palace of Monsu Mostro, and knocked.

'Who's there?' said Monsu Mostro.

'It's I!'⁴ answered she; and then she told him all that had befallen her, and showed him the puppy-dog in the basket. He looked at it for a moment, but would not let her in, and only cried out, 'Go along! you ugly horned thing!'⁵

She went away crying; but having lifted up the cloth and peeped at the puppy-dog, she felt reassured, and sent it back by a servant to the queen.

When the queen uncovered the basket a beautiful little dog sprang out all of solid gold, yet it leaped about and performed all manner of tricks just as if it had been a real dog.

The prince was triumphant when he saw that *her* dog was so much better than the other two; but the queen was indignant, and said, 'It is no dog at all, that gold thing!' and she would not allow that the girl had won the trial.

After that the queen sent a servant out with three pounds of flax, and said that whoever could spin it best should marry the prince.

'What do I know about spinning!' said each of the other two; and they let the flax lie without touching it.

But *she* took hers in a basket and went to the palace of Monsu Mostro, and knocked.

'Who's there?' asked he.

'It's I!' she replied in her doleful voice, and told him her new difficulty. Monsu Mostro looked at the flax, but refused to admit her, and saying, 'Away with you, you horned wretch!' shut the door against her.

This basket, too, she sent by a servant to the queen, and when the queen opened it she found it full of gold thread.

'You must allow she has done better than the others this time!' said the prince.

'No! it is as bad as before,' answered the queen; 'it is not natural! It won't do for me!'

'After that the queen sent out a notice that whichever of them had her hair growing down to her heels should marry the prince.

'My hair does not reach down to my waist,' said each of the other two. 'How can I make it grow down to my heels?'

But *she* went to the palace of Monsu Mostro, and knocked.

'Who's there?' asked he

'It is I!' she replied, as dolefully as before, and told him what was required of her now.

'You see now what it is to have paid no attention to what I told you,' answered Monsu Mostro. 'I told you not to forget the comb I gave you. If you had not forgotten

I

that none of this would have happened. That comb is
your remedy now ;' and with that he shut the door.

But she went home and combed her hair with the
comb he had given her; and not only the horns went away,
but her hair grew down quite to her heels and swept the
ground. But the other two were jealous when they saw
that she had beaten them in all three trials, and they came
to her to ask how she made her hair grow, and she sent
them to the palace of Monsu Mostro to ask.

But as they only came out of jealousy, he told them to
make themselves two pitch nightcaps and sleep in them ;
and when they got up in the morning, instead of having
longer hair, all the hair they had came off.

But she was at length given to the prince, and they
were married amid great rejoicing.

¹ At what period the title of honour of 'Monsu' got appended to the
monster's name is more than I can fix.

² 'Chi è?' 'amicè.' See note 3, p. 187.

³ The reader will bear in mind, in this and other places, that 'papa'
and 'mama' are vernacular for 'father' and 'mother' among children of
the lowest classes in Italy.

⁴ 'Son' io.' I have generally found these stories told with a great deal
of effect, especially to suit the tone to the dialogues. It was particularly
the case with this one, *e.g.* the 'son' io' was said in the lamentable tone of
a person wearied with fatigue and disappointment.'

⁵ 'Vatene, brutta cornuda!'

[The two preceding stories represent the Roman contribution
to the stories of visits to the underground world and the Bluebeard group. I have others (particularly one called 'Il Cavolo
d Oro', the 'Golden Cabbage') more like the general run of
them. The two I have selected have this difference, that in
neither instance does the subterranean ruler represent the Devil.
'Monsu Mostro,' is most disinterested in his generosity. As
usual with the Roman versions, all that is terrible is eliminated.
For other versions, see Ralston, pp. 98–100 ; and for a somewhat
similar story, the 'Water Snake,' p. 116. Much in the Norse,
'East of the Sun and West of the Moon,' is like the 'Rè Moro;'
so is 'The Old Dame and her Hen,' though the later details of

that story are more like the Tirolean version, which I have given in ' Laxehale's Wives,' in ' Household Stories from the Land of Hofer.' The German version given as ' Fitchers Vogel,' Grimm, p. 177, has more of the horrid element than any of the others. In the version of ' Tünder Illona ' given in Graf Mailath's Magyarische Sagen ' (a rather different version from that told me at Pesth, which I have given at p. 20–1), Prince Argilus loses his bride and her kingdom, and has to begin all his labours over again, through looking into a closed chamber which Tünder Illrua had bid him not to open in her absence. But heroic action abounds in the Hungarian tales, just as it is wanting in the Roman ones, and in this, and in many details, particularly in the enthusiasm for magic horses, they are singularly like the Gaelic.

The ' Rè Moro ' is perhaps nearer ' Beauty and the Beast ' than ' Bluebeard.' I had a version of this given me in the following form, under the title of

THE ENCHANTED ROSE-TREE.[1]

THEY say there was once a merchant who, when he was going out to buy rare merchandise, asked his daughter what rich present he should bring home to her. She, however, would hear of nothing but only a simple rose-tree.

' ' That,' said her father, ' is too easy. However, as you are bent on having a rose-tree, you shall have the most beautiful rose-tree I can find in all my travels.'

In all his travels, however, he met with no rose-tree that he deemed choice enough. But one day, when he was walking outside the walls of his own city, he came to a garden which he had never observed before, filled with all manner of beautiful flowers.

' This is a wonderful garden indeed,' said the merchant to himself; ' I never saw it before, and yet these luxuriant plants seem to have many years' growth in them. There must be something wonderful about them, so this is just the place to look for my daughter's rose-tree.' In he went therefore to look for the rose-tree.

In the midst of the garden was a casino, the door of which stood open; when he went in he found a banquet spread with the choicest dishes; and though he saw no one, a kind voice invited him to sit down and enjoy himself. So he sat down to the banquet, and very much he did enjoy himself, for there was everything he could desire.[2]

When he had well eaten and drunk, he bethought him to go out again into the garden and seek a choice rose-tree.

' As the banquet was free,' he thought to himself, ' I suppose the flowers are free too.'

So he selected what seemed to him the choicest rose of all; while it had petals of the richest red in the world, within it was all shining gold, and the leaves too were overlaid with shining gold. This rose-tree, therefore, he proceeded to root up.

A peal of thunder attended the attempt, and with a noise of rushing winds and waters a hideous monster[3] suddenly appeared before him.

' How dare you root up my rose-trees?' said the monster; ' was it not enough that I gave you my best hospitality freely? Must you also rob me of my flowers, which are as my life to me? Now you must die!'

The merchant excused himself as best he could, saying it was the very freedom of the hospitality which had emboldened him to take the rose, and that he had only ventured to take it because he had promised the prettiest rose-tree he could find to his daughter.

' Your daughter, say you?' replied the monster. ' If there is a daughter in the case perhaps I may forgive you; but only on condition that you bring her hither to me within three days' time.'

The father went home sad at heart, but within three days he kept his promise of taking his daughter to the garden. The monster received them very kindly, and gave them the casino to live in, where they were well fed and lodged. At the end of eight days, however, a voice came to the father and told him he must depart; and when he hesitated to leave his daughter alone he was taken by invisible agency and turned out of the garden.

The monster now often came and talked to the daughter, and he was so gentle and so kind that she began quite to like him. One day she asked him to let her go home and see her friends, and he, who refused her nothing, let her go; but begged her to promise solemnly she would come back at the end of eight days, 'for if you are away longer than that,' he added, 'I know I shall die of despair.' Then he gave her a mirror into which she could look and see how he was.

Thus she went home, and the time passed quickly away, and eight days were gone and she had not thought of returning. Then by accident the mirror came under her hand, and, looking into it, she saw the monster stretched on the ground as if at the point of death. The sight filled her with compunction, and she hurried back with her best speed.

Arrived at the garden, she found the monster just as she had seen him in the mirror. At sight of her he revived, and soon became so much better that she was much touched when she saw how deeply he cared for her.

'And were you really so bad *only* because I went away?' she asked.

'No, not only because you went away, for it was right you should go and see your parents; but because I began to fear you would never come back, and if you had never come back I should quite have died.'

'And now you are all right again?'

'Yes, now you are here I am quite happy; that is, I should be quite happy if you would promise always to remain and never go away any more.'

Then when she saw how earnest and sincere he was in wishiug her to stay, she gave her consent never to leave him more.

No sooner had she spoken the promise than in the twinkling of an eye all was changed. The monster became a handsome prince, the casino a palace, the garden a flourishing country, and each several rose-tree a city. For the prince had been enchanted by an enemy, and had to remain transformed as a monster till he should be redeemed by the love of a maiden.

[1] ' La Rosa fatata.'

[2] According to the narrator, there was a dish of ' pasta ' heaped up like a mountain ; and ' souplis di riso con rigaglie' and ' capone con contorni,' and several kinds of wine. I give this description verbally, as it was given to me, as characteristic of the local colouring such legends receive. The dishes named are the favourites of the Roman middle class. ' Pasta ' is the Roman equivalent for the ' maccaroni ' of the Neapolitan. ' Rigaglie' is the liver, &c., of poultry minced, to put into the fried balls of rice. ' Contorni' means something more than 'garnish,' being something put round the dish, not merely for ornament, but more or less substantial, to be eaten with it, as sausages round a turkey.

[3] The word used in this place was ' mostro,' not ' orco,' marking a distinct idea in the tradition, where it is the Principle of Evil himself who is intended, and where, an unfortunate mortal subjected by malice to his influence.

[The three brothers who occupy so large a space in the household tales of other countries, do not seem to be popular favourites in Rome. I have come across them but seldom. There are plenty of them in the ' Norse Tales,' under the name of ' Boots ' for the unexpectedly doughty brother. The Spanish romance I have given as ' Simple Johnny and the Spell-bound Princesses,' in ' Patrañas,' makes him a knight. In the Siddhi Kür story of ' How the Schimnu Khan was Slain,' it is three hired companions (as in some other versions), who betray the hero ; and in all but this (which is its link with the usual Three-brother stories), it is a remarkably close repetition of the details of another Spanish romance, which I have given as ' The Ill-tempered Princess,' and this, in its turn, is like the Tirolean ' Laxhale's Wives ' and the Roman ' Diavolo che prese moglie.' Compare, further, a number of instances collected by Mr. Ralston, pp. 72–80, and 260–7. In many parts of Tirol you meet a Three-brother story different from any of these. Three brothers go out to hunt chamois on a Sunday morning, and get so excited with the sport that they make themselves too late to hear Mass, and get turned into stone, or some other dreadful punishment. The younger brother, who has all along urged them to go down, but has been overruled by the others, is involved in the same punishment. There are three peaks on the Knie Pass, leading from Tirol to Salzburg, called 'The Three Brothers,' from such a legend.]

SCIOCCOLONE.[1]

ONCE upon a time there were three brothers, who were woodmen; their employment was not one which required great skill, and they were none of them very clever, but the youngest was the least brilliant of all. So simple was he that all the neighbours, and his very brothers—albeit they were not so very superior in intelligence themselves— gave him the nickname of 'Scioccolone,' the great simpleton, and accordingly Scioccolone he was called wherever he went.

Every day these three brothers went out into the woods to their work, and every evening they all came home, each staggering under his load of wood, which he carried to the dealer who paid them for their toil: thus one day of labour passed away just like another in all respects. So it went on for years.

Nevertheless, one day came at last which was not at all like the others, and if all days were like it the world would be quite upside down, or be at least a very different world from what it is. *Oimè!* that such days never occur now at all! *Basta*, this is what happened. It was in the noontide heat of a very hot day, the three simple brothers

committed the imprudence of going out of the shelter of
the woods into the wold beyond, and there, lying on the
grass in the severest blaze of the burning sun, they saw
three beautiful peasant girls lying fast asleep.

' Only look at those silly girls sleeping in the full blaze
of the sun ! ' cried the eldest brother.

' They'll get bad in their heads in this heat,' said the
second.

But Scioccolone said : ' Shall we not get some sticks
and boughs, and make a little shed to shelter them ? '

' Just like one of Scioccolone's fine ideas ! ' laughed the
eldest brother scornfully.

' Well done, Scioccolone ! That's the best thing you've
thought of this long while. And who will build a shed
over us while we're building a shed for the girls, I should
like to know ? ' said the second.

But Scioccolone said : ' We can't leave them there like
that ; they will be burnt to death. If you won't help me
I must build the shed alone.'

' A wise resolve, and worthy of Scioccolone ! ' scoffed
the eldest brother.

' Good-bye, Scioccolone ! ' cried the second, as the two
elder brothers walked away together. ' Good-bye for ever !
I don't expect ever to see you alive again, of course.'

And they never did see him again, but what it was
that happened to him you shall hear.

Without waiting to find a retort to his brothers' gibes,
Scioccolone set to work to fell four stout young saplings,
and to set them up as supports of his shed in four holes
he had previously scooped with the aid of his bill-hook ;
then he rammed them in with wedges, which he also had
to cut and shape. After this he cut four large bushy
branches, which he tied to the uprights with the cord he
used for tying up his faggots of logs ; and as the shade of
these was scarcely close enough to keep out all the fierce
rays of the sun, he went back to the wood and collected all

the large broad leaves he could find, and came back and spread them out over his leafy roof. All this was very hard labour indeed when performed under the dreaded sun, and just in the hours when men do no work; yet so beautiful were the three maidens that, when at last he had completed his task, he could not tear himself away from them to go and seek repose in the shade of the wood, but he must needs continue standing in the full sun gazing at them open-mouthed.

At last the three beautiful maidens awoke, and when they saw what a fragrant shade had refreshed their slumbers they began pouring out their gratitude to their devoted benefactor.

Do not run at hasty conclusions, however, and imagine that of course the three beautiful maidens fell in love on the spot with Scioccolone, and he had only to pick and choose which of them he would have to make him happy as his wife. A very proper ending, you say, for a fairy tale. It was not so, however. Scioccolone looked anything but attractive just then. His meaningless features and uncouth, clownish gait were never at any time likely to inspire the fair maidens with sudden affection; but just then, after his running hither and thither, his felling, digging, and hammering in the heat of the day, his face had acquired a tint which made it look rougher and redder and more repulsive than anyone ever wore before.

Besides this, the three maidens were fairies, who had taken the form² of beautiful peasant girls for some reason of their own.

But neither did they leave his good deed unrewarded. By no means. Each of the three declared she would give him such a precious gift that he should own to his last hour that they were not ungrateful. So they sat and thought what great gift they could think of which should be calculated to make him very happy indeed.

At last the first of the three got up and exclaimed that

she had thought of her gift, and she did not think anyone could give him a greater one; for she would promise him he should one day be a king.

Wasn't that a fine gift!

Scioccolone, however, did not think so. The idea of *his* being a king! Simple as he was, he could see the incongruity of the idea, and the embarrassment of the situation. How should he the poor clown, everybody's laughingstock, become a king? and if he did, kingship had no attractions for him.

He was too kind-hearted, however, to say anything in disparagement of the well-meant promise, and too straightforward to assume a show of gratitude he did not feel; so after the first little burst of hilarity which he was not sufficiently master of himself to suppress, he remained standing open-mouthed after his awkward manner.

Then the second fairy addressed him and said :—

'I see you don't quite like my sister's gift; but you may be sure she would not have promised it if it had not been a good gift, after you have been so kind to us; and when it comes true, it will somehow all turn out very nice and right. But now, meantime, that I may not similarly disappoint you with my gift by choosing it for you, I shall let you choose it for yourself; so say, what shall it be?'

Scioccolone was almost as much embarrassed with the second fairy's permission of choosing for himself as he had been with the first fairy's choice for him. First he grinned, and then he twisted his great awkward mouth about, and then he grinned again, till, at last, ashamed of keeping the fairies waiting so long for his answer, he said, with another grin :—

'Well, to tell you what I should *really* like, it would be that when I have finished making up my faggot of logs this evening, instead of having to stagger home carrying it, it should roll along by itself, and then I get astride of it, and that *it* should carry *me.*'

'That *would* be fine!' he added, and he grinned again as he thought of the fun it would be to be carried home by the load of logs instead of carrying the load as he had been wont.

'Certainly! That wish is granted,' replied the second fairy readily. 'You will find it all happen just as you have described.'

Then the third fairy came forward and said :—

'And now choose; what shall *my* gift be? You have only to ask for whatever you like and you shall have it.'

Such a heap of wishes rose up in Scioccolone's imagination at this announcement, that he could not make up his mind which to select; as fast as he fixed on one thing, he remembered it would be incomplete without some other gift, and as he went on trying to find some one wish that should be as comprehensive as possible, he suddenly blurted out—

'Promise me that *whatever* I wish may come true; that'll be the best gift; and so if I forget a thing one moment I can wish for it the next. That'll be the best gift to be sure!'

'Granted!' said the third fairy. 'You have only to wish for anything and you will find you get it immediately, whatever it is.'

The fairies then took leave and went their way, and Scioccolone was reminded by the lengthening shades that it was time he betook himself to complete his day's work. Scarcely succeeding in collecting his thoughts, so dazzled and bewildered was he by the late supernatural conversation, he yet found his way back to the spot where he had been felling wood.

'Oh, dear! how tired I am!' he said within himself as he walked along. 'How I wish the wood was all felled and the faggots tied up!' and though he said this mechanically as he might have said it any other day of his life, without thinking of the fairy's promise, which was, indeed, too vast for him to put it consciously to such a practical test then, full of astonishment as he was, yet when he got back to his working-place the wood *was* felled and laid in order, and tied into a faggot in the best manner.

'Well to be sure!' soliloquised Scioccolone. 'The girls have kept their promise indeed! This is just exactly what I wished. And now, let's see what else did I wish? Oh, yes; that if I got astride on the faggot it should roll along by itself and carry me with it; let's see if that'll come true too!'

With that he got astride on the faggot, and sure enough the faggot moved on all by itself, and carried Scioccolone along with it pleasantly enough.

Only there was one thing Scioccolone had forgotten to ask for, and that was power to guide the faggot; and now, though it took a direction quite contrary to that of his homeward way, he had no means of inducing it to change its tack. After some time spent in fruitless efforts in schooling his unruly mount, Scioccolone began to reason with himself.

'After all, it does not much matter about going home. I only get laughed at and called "Scioccolone." Maybe in some other place they may be better, and as the faggot is acting under the orders of my benefactress, it will doubtless all be for the best.'

So he committed himself to the faggot to take him wherever it would. On went the faggot surely and steadily, as if quite conscious where it had to go; and thus, before nightfall, it came to a great city where were many people, who all came out to see the wonder of the faggot of logs moving along by itself, and a man riding on it.

In this city was a king, who lived in a palace with an only daughter. Now this daughter had never been known to laugh. What pains soever the king her father took to divert her were all unavailing; nothing brought a smile to her lips.

Now, however, when all the people ran to the windows to see a man riding on a faggot, the king's daughter ran to look out too; and when she saw the faggot moving by itself, and the uncouth figure of Scioccolone sitting on it, and heard all the people laughing at the sight, then the king's daughter laughed too; laughed for the first time in her life.

But Scioccolone passing under the palace, heard her clear and merry laugh resounding above the laughter of all the people, he looked up and saw her, and when he saw her looking so bright and fair he said within himself:—

'Now, if ever the fairy's power of wishing is to be of use to me, I wish that I might have a little son, and that the beautiful princess should be the mother.' But he did not think of wishing to stop there that he might look at her, so the faggot carried him past the palace and past all the houses into the outskirts of the city, till he got tired and weary, and just then passing a wood merchant's yard, the thought rose to his lips,—

'I wish that wood merchant would buy this faggot of me!'

Immediately the wood merchant came out and offered to buy the faggot, and as it was such a wonderful faggot, that he thought Scioccolone would never consent to sell it, he offered him such a high price that Scioccolone had enough to live on like a prince for a year.

After a time there was again a great stir in the city, everyone was abroad in the streets whispering and consulting. To the king's daughter was born a little son, and no one knew who the father was, not even the princess herself. Then the king sent for all the men in the city, and brought them to the infant, and said, 'Is this your father?' but the babe said 'No!' to them all.

Last of all, Scioccolone was brought, and when the king took him up to the babe and said, 'Is this your father?' the babe rose joyfully from its cradle and said, 'Yes; that is my father!' When the king heard this and saw what a rough ugly clown Scioccolone was, he was very angry with his daughter, and said she must marry him and go away for ever from the palace. It was all in vain that the princess protested she had never seen him but for one moment from the top of the palace. The babe protested quite positively that he was his father; so the king had them married, and sent them away from the palace for ever; and the babe was right, for though Scioccolone and the princess had never met, Scioccolone had wished that he might have a son, of whom she should be the mother, and by the power of the spell [3] the child was born.

Scioccolone was only too delighted with the king's angry decree. He felt quite out of place in the palace, and was glad enough to be sent away from it. All he wanted was to have such a beautiful wife, and he willingly obeyed the king's command to take her away, a long, long way off.

The princess, however, was quite of a different mind. She could not cease from crying, because she was given to such an uncouth, clownish husband that no tidy peasant wench would have married.

When, therefore, Scioccolone saw his beautiful bride so unhappy and distressed, he grew distressed himself; and in his distress he remembered once more the promise of the fairy, that whatever he wished he might have, and he began wishing away at once. First he wished for a pleasant villa,[4] prettily laid-out, and planted, and walled; then, a casino [5] in the midst of it, prettily furnished, and having plenty of pastimes and diversions; then, for a farm, well-stocked with beasts for all kinds of uses; for carriages and servants, for fruits and flowers, and all that can make life pleasant. And when he found that with all these things the princess did not seem much happier than before, he bethought himself of wishing that he might be furnished with a handsome person, polished manners, and an educated mind, altogether such as the princess wished. All his wishes were fulfilled, and the princess now loved him very much, and they lived very happily together.

After they had been living thus some time, it happened one day that the king, going out hunting, observed this pleasant villa on the wold, where heretofore all had been bare, unplanted, and unbuilt.

' How is this ! ' cried the king ; and he drew rein, and went into the villa intending to inquire how the change had come about.

Scioccolone came out to meet him, not only so transformed that the king never recognised him, but so distinguished by courtesy and urbanity, that the king himself felt ashamed to question him as to how the villa had grown up so suddenly. He accepted his invitation to come and rest in the casino, however ; and there they fell to conversing on a variety of subjects, till the king was so struck with the sagacity and prudence of Scioccolone's talk, that when he rose to take leave, he said :

' Such a man as you I have long sought to succeed me in the government of the kingdom. I am growing old and have no children, and you are worthy in all ways to wear the crown. Come up, therefore, if you will, to the palace and live with me, and when I die you shall be king.'

Scioccolone, now no longer feeling himself so ill-adapted to live in a palace, willingly consented, and a few days after, with his wife and his little son, he went up to the palace to live with the king.

But the king's delight can scarcely be imagined when he found that the wife of the polished stranger was indeed his very own daughter.

After a few years the old king died, and Scioccolone reigned in his stead. And thus the promises of all the three fairies were fulfilled.

[1] 'Sciocco,' a simpleton; 'scioccolone,' a great awkward simpleton.

[2] Even in this story, where the fairies really are described as fair to see, it will be observed it is only said they had assumed the forms of beautiful girls for one occasion, not that they were necessarily beautiful, like our fairies

[3] 'Fatatura,' the virtue of enchantment.

[4] 'Villa' is more often used to express a little estate—or, as we should say, the 'grounds' on which a country-house stands—than for the house itself, though we have borrowed the word exclusively in the latter sense.

[5] 'Casino' a tasteful little house.

[Among the Italian-Tirolese tales is one called 'I tre pezzi rari' (The Three Rare Things), which begins just like 'Scioccolone,' and then the fairies give the three gifts of a dinner-providing table-cloth, an exhaustless purse, and a resistless cudgel, which we so often meet with, as in Grimm's 'Tischchen deck dich,' p. 142; Campbell's 'Three Soldiers,' i. p. 176-93, who refers to numerous other versions, in which other incidents of the two next succeeding tales occur. The Spanish version I have given by the name of 'Matanzas' in 'Patrañas.'

In the Roman version of the 'Dodici palmi di naso,' it is singular that it is the second and not the youngest son who is the hero. There is another Italian-Tirolese story, entitled 'Il Zufolotta,' in which only one boy and two fairies are concerned, and they only give him the one gift of the Zufoletto, which, instead of supplying every wish as in 'Dodici palmi di naso,' has the power of the Zauberflöte, the pipe of the 'Pied Piper,' and kindred instruments in all times and countries, so that, when it has got its possessor into such trouble that he is condemned to be executed, it answers the same end as the cudgel, liberating its master by setting the judge and executioner dancing, instead of by thumping them.]

TWELVE FEET OF NOSE.[1]

THERE was a poor old father, who was very poor indeed, and very old. When he came to die, he called his three sons round his bed, and said they must summon a notary to make his will. The sons looked at each other, and thought he was doating. He repeated his desire, and then one of them ventured to say :

'But father, dear, why should we go to the expense of calling in a notary; there is not a single thing on earth you have to leave us ! '

But the old man told them again to call a notary, and still they hesitated, because they thought the notary would say they were making game of him.

At last the old man began to get angry when he found they would not do as he said, and, just not to vex him in his last moments, they called the notary, and the notary brought his witnesses.

Then the father was content, and called them all to his bedside.

'Now, pull out the old case under the bed, and take out what you find there.'

They found an old broken hat, without a brim, a ragged purse that was so worn you could not have trusted any money in its keeping, and a horn.[2]

These three things he bequeathed in due form of law, one to each of his sons ; and it was only because they saw that the man was in his death agony that those who were called to act as witnesses could keep from laughing. To the notary, of course, it was all one whether it was an old hat or a new one, his part was the same, and when he had done what was needful, he went his way, and the witnesses went with him ; but as they went out, they said one to another :

K

'Poor old man! perhaps it is a comfort to him in his last moments to fancy he has got something to leave.'

When they were all gone, as the three sons were standing by, very sad, and looking at each other, not knowing what to make of the strange scene, he called the eldest, to whose portion the hat had fallen, and said:

'See what I've given you.'

'Why, father!' answered he, 'it isn't even good enough to bind round one's knee when one goes out hoeing!'

But the father answered:

'I wouldn't let you know its value till those people were gone, lest any should take it from you; this is its value, that if you put it on, you can go in to dine at whatever inn you please, or sit down to drink at what wineshop you please, and take what you like and drink what you like, for no one will see you while you have it on.'

Then he called his second son, to whose lot the purse had fallen, and he said:

'See what I have given you.'

'Why, father!' answered the son, 'it isn't even good enough to keep a little tobacco in, if I could afford to buy any!'

But the father answered:

'I wouldn't tell you its value till those people were gone, lest any should take it from you; but this is its value; if you put your fingers in, you'll find a scudo there, and after that another, and another, as many as ever you will; there will always be one.'

Then he called his youngest son, and said:

'See what I have given you.'

And he answered:

'Yes, father, it's a very nice horn; and when I am starving hungry I can cheat myself into being content by playing on it.'

'Silly boy!' answered the father; 'that is not its use. I wouldn't tell you its value while those people were here, lest they should take it from you. Its value is this, that whenever you want anything you have only to sound it, and one will come who will bring whatever you want, be it a dinner, a suit of clothes, a palace, or an army.'

After this the father died, and each found himself well provided with the legacy he had given him.

It happened that one day as the second son[3] was passing under the window of the palace a waiting-maid looked out and said: ' Can you play at cards?'

' As well as most,' answered the youth.

' Very well, then; come up,' answered the waiting-maid; ' for the queen wants some one to play with her.'

Very readily he went up, therefore, and played at cards with the queen, and when he had played all the evening he had lost fifty scudi.

'Never mind about paying the fifty scudi,' said the queen, as he rose to leave. ' We only played to pass away the time, and you don't look by your dress as if you could afford fifty scudi.'

' Not at all!' replied the youth. 'I will certainly bring the fifty scudi in the morning.'

And in the morning, by putting his fingers fifty times into the ragged purse, he had the required sum, and went back with it to the palace and paid the queen.

The queen was very much astonished that such a shabby-looking fellow should have such command of money, and determined to find out how it was; so she made him stay and dine. After dinner she took him into her private room and said to him:

' Tell me, how comes it that you, who are but a shabby-looking fellow, have such command of money?'

' Oh!' answered he quite unsuspectingly, ' because my father left me a wonderful purse, in which is always a scudo.'

'Nonsense!' answered the queen. 'That is a very pretty fable, but such purses don't exist.'

'Oh, but it is so indeed,' answered the youth.

'Quite impossible,' persisted the queen.

'But here it is; you can see for yourself!' pursued the incautious youth, taking it out.

The queen took it from him as if to try its powers, but no sooner was she in possession of it than she called in the guard to turn out a fellow who was trying to rob her, and give him a good beating.

Indignant at such treatment, the youth went to his eldest brother and begged his hat of him that he might, by its means, go and punish the queen.

Putting on the hat he went back to the palace at the hour of dinner and sat down to table. As soon as the queen was served he took her plate and ate up all that was in it one course after another, so that the queen got nothing, and finding it useless to call for more dishes, she gave it up as a bad job, and went into her room. The youth followed her in and demanded the return of his wonderful purse.

'How can I know it is you if I don't see you?' said the queen.

'Never mind about seeing me. Put the purse out on the table for me and I will take it.'

'No, I can't if I don't see you,' replied the queen. 'I can't believe it is you unless I see you.'

The youth fell into the snare and took off his hat.

'How did you manage to make yourself invisible?' asked the queen.

'Just by putting on this old hat.'

'I don't believe that could make you invisible,' exclaimed the queen. 'Let me try.'

And she snatched the hat out of his hand and put it on. Of course she was now in turn invisible, and he sought her in vain; but worse than that, she rang the bell for the guard and bid them turn the shabby youth out and give him a bastonata.

Full of fresh indignation he ran to his youngest brother and told him all his story, begging the loan of his horn, that he might punish the queen by its means; and the brother lent it him.

He sounds the horn and One comes.[4]

'I want an army with cannons to throw down the palace,' said the youth; and instantly there was a tramp of armed men, and a rumble of artillery waggons.

The queen was sitting at dinner, but when she heard all the noise she came to the window; meantime the soldiers had surrounded the palace and pointed their guns.

'What's all this about! What's the matter!' cried the queen out of the window.

'The matter is, that I want my purse and my hat back,' answered the youth.

'To be sure! you are right; here they are. I don't want my palace battered down, so I will give them to you.'

The youth went up to receive them; but when he got upstairs he found the queen sunk half fainting in a chair.

'Oh! I'm so frightened; I can't think where I put the things. Only send away that army and I'll look for them immediately.'

The youth sent away the army, and the queen got up and began looking about for the things.

'Tell me,' she said, as she wandered from one cupboard to another, 'how did you, who are such a shabby-looking fellow, manage to call together such an army?'

'Because I've got this horn,' answered the youth. 'And with it I can call up whatever I want, and if you don't make haste and find the purse and the hat, I'll call up the army again and batter down the palace in right earnest.'

'You won't make me believe that!' replied the queen.
'That sorry horn can't work such wonders as that: let
me try.' And she took the horn out of his hands and
sounded it and One appeared. 'Two stout men!' she
commanded quickly; and when they came she bid them
drive the shabby-looking youth out of the palace and give
him a bastonata.

He was now quite undone, and was ashamed to go
back to his brothers. So he wandered away outside the
town. After much walking he came to a vineyard, where
he strolled in; and what struck him was, that though it
was January, there was a fine fig-tree covered with ripe
luscious figs.

'This is a godsend indeed,' he said, 'to a hungry
man,' and he began plucking and eating the figs. Before
he had eaten many, however, he found his nose had begun
to grow to a terrible size; a foot for every fig.

'That'll never do!' he cried, and left off eating the
figs and wandered on. Presently he came to another
vineyard, where he also strolled in: there, though it was
January, he saw a tree all covered with ripe red cherries. 'I
wonder what calamity will pursue me for eating them,'
he said, as he gathered them. But when he had eaten a
good many he perceived that at last his luck had turned,
for in proportion as he ate his nose grew less and less, till
at last it was just the right size again.

'Now I know how to punish the queen,' he said, and
he filled a bottle with the juice of the cherries, and went
back and gathered a basketful of figs.

These figs he cried under the palace window, and as he
had got more dusty and threadbare with his late wanderings
no one recognised him. 'Figs in January! that is a
treat!' and they bought up the whole basketful. Then
as they ate, their noses all began to grow, but the
queen, as she was very greedy, ate twelve for her share,
so that she had twelve feet of nose added to the length of

hers. It was so long that it trailed behind her on the ground as she walked along.

Then there was a hue and cry! All the surgeons and physicians in the kingdom were sent for, but could do no good. They were all in despair, when our youth came up disguised as a foreign doctor.

'Noses! I can heal noses! whoever has got too much nose let him come to me!'

All the inhabitants gathered round him, and the queen called to him loudest of all.

'The medicine I have to give is necessarily a very strong one to effect so extraordinary a cure; therefore I won't give it to the queen's majesty till she has seen it used on all her servants, beginning with the lowest.'

Taking them all in order, beginning with the lowest, he gave a few drops of cherry-juice to each, and all their noses came right.

Last of all the queen remained.

'The queen can't be treated like common people,' he said; 'she must be treated by herself. I must go into her room with her, and I can cure her with one drop of my cordial.'

'You think yourself very clever that you talk of curing with one drop of your cordial, but you're not the only person who can work wonders. I've got greater wonders than yours. I've got a hat which makes you invisible, a purse that never is empty, and a horn that gives you everything you call for.'

'Very pretty things to talk about,' answered the pretended doctor, 'but such things don't exist.'

'Don't they!' said the queen. 'There they are!'

And she laid them all out on the table.

This was enough for him. Taking advantage of the lesson she had given him by her example, he quickly put on the hat, making himself invisible; after that it was easy to snatch up the other things and escape; nor could anyone follow him. He lived very comfortably for the rest of his life, taking a scudo out of his purse for whatever he had to pay, and his brothers likewise got on very well with their legacies, for he restored them as soon as he had rescued them from the queen. But the queen remained for the rest of her life with TWELVE FEET OF NOSE.

[1] 'Dodici palmi di naso,' a nose twelve palms long. Twelve palms make a canna and a half, equal to three mètres.

[2] 'Ciuffoletto.' 'What is a '*ciuffoletto*?' I asked. 'Much the same as a *fravodo*,' the narrator answered; and I remembered that from another, in another tale, I had made out 'fravodo' to be a horn.

[3] That the second of the three sons should be the hero of the story is, I think, an unusual variation.

[4] See Note 4, p. 146.

A YARD OF NOSE.[1]

THERE was once a poor orphan youth left all alone, with no home, and no means of gaining a living, and no place of shelter.

Not knowing what to do he wandered away over the Campagna, straight on; when he had wandered all day and was ready to die of hunger and weariness, he at last saw a fig-tree covered with ripe figs.

'There's a godsend!' said the poor orphan; and he set to upon the figs without ceremony. But, lo! he had scarcely eaten half-a-dozen when his nose began to feel very odd; he put his hand up to it and it felt much bigger than usual; however, he was too hungry to trouble himself about it, and he ate on. As he ate on his nose felt queerer and queerer; he put his hand up and found it was quite a foot[2] long! But he was so hungry he went on eating still, and before he had done he had fully a yard of nose.

'A pretty thing I have done for myself now! As well might I have died of starvation as make myself such an object as this! Never can I appear among civilised beings again.' And he laid himself down to sleep, hiding himself in the foliage of the fig-tree lest anybody passing by should see his nose.

In the morning the first thing he thought of when he awoke was his nose ; he had no need to put up his hand to feel it for it reached down to his hand, a full yard of it waggling about.

' There's no help for it,' he said. ' I must keep away from all habitable places, and live as best I may.'

So he wandered on and on over the Campagna away from all habitations, straight on ; and when he had wandered all day and was ready to die of hunger and weariness he saw another fig-tree covered with ripe figs.

Right glad he was to see anything in the shape of food. ' If it had only been anything else in the world but figs!' he said. ' If I go on at this rate I shan't be able to carry my nose along at all! Yet starving is hard, too, and I'm such a figure now, nothing can make me much worse, so here goes!' and he began eating at the figs without more ado.

As he ate this time, however, his nose, instead of feeling queerer and queerer as it had before, began to feel lighter and lighter.

Less, less, and still less it grew,[3] till at last he had to put his hand up to feel where it was, and by the time he had done eating, it was just its natural size again.

' *Now* I know how to make my fortune!'[4] he cried, and he danced for delight.

With a basketful of the figs of the first tree he trudged to the nearest town, still clad in his peasant's dress, and cried, ' Fine figs! fine figs! who'll buy my beautiful ripe figs!'

All the people ran out to see the new fruit-seller, and his figs looked so tempting that plenty of people bought of him. Among the foremost was the host of the inn, with his wife and his buxom daughter, and every one of them, as they ate the figs their noses began to grow and grow till everyone of them had a nose fully a yard long.

Then there was a hue and cry through the whole town, everyone with his yard of nose dangling and waggling, came running out, calling, ' Ho! Here! Wretch of a fruit-seller!' [5]

But our fruit-seller had had the good sense to foresee the coming storm, and had taken care to get far out of the way of pursuit.

But the next day he dressed himself like a doctor, all in black, with a long false beard, and came to the same town, where he entered the druggist's [6] shop, and gave himself out for a great doctor.

'You come in good season!' said the druggist. 'A doctor is wanted here just now, if ever one was, for to everyone almost in the town is grown a nose [7] so big! so big! in fact, a full yard of nose! Anyone who could reduce these noses might make a fortune indeed!'

'Why, that's just what I excel at of all things. Let me see some of these people,' answered our pretended doctor.

The druggist looked incredulous at a real remedy turning up so very opportunely: but at the same moment a pretty peasant girl came into the shop to buy some medicine for her mother; that is, she would have been pretty if it had not been for the terrible nose, which made a fright of her. The false doctor was seized with compunction when he saw what a fright his figs had made of this pretty girl, and he took out some figs of the other tree and gave her to eat, and immediately her tremendous nose grew less, and less, and less, and she was a pretty girl again. Of course it need not be said that he did not give her the figs in their natural state and form; he had peeled and pounded, and made them up with other things to disguise them.

The druggist no sooner saw this wonderful cure than he was prompt to publish it, and there was quite a strife who should have the new doctor the first.

It was the innkeeper who succeeded in being the first to possess himself of him. 'What will you give me for the cure?' said the strange doctor.

'Whatever you have the conscience to ask,' replied the host, panting to be rid of the monstrosity.

'Four thousand scudi apiece,' replied the false doctor; and the host, his wife, and his buxom daughter stood in a row waiting to be cured. With the same remedy that had cured the peasant girl he cured the host first, and next his daughter. After he had cured her he said, 'Instead of the second premium of four thousand scudi, I will take the hand of your daughter, if you like?'

'Yes, if you wish; it's a very good idea,' replied the host.

'Never, while I live!' said the wife.

'Why not? He's a very good husband!' said the host.

'An ugly old travelling doctor, who comes no one knows whence, to marry my daughter indeed!' said the wife.

'I'm sure we're under great obligations to his cleverness,' said the husband.

'Then let him be paid his price, and go about his business, and not talk impudence!' said the wife.

'But I choose that he *shall* marry her!' said the husband.

'And *I* choose that he shan't,' said the wife; 'and you'll find that much stronger.'

Just then a customer came in, and the host had to go and attend upon him, and while he was gone the wife called the servants, and bade them turn the doctor out, and give him a good drubbing into the bargain, saying, 'I'll have some other doctor to cure me!'

So he left them, and went on curing people's noses all day, till he had made a lot of money. Then he went away, but limping all the time from the beating he had received. The next day he came back dressed like a Turk, so that no one would have known him for the same man, and he came back to the same inn, saying he, too, could cure noses.

The mistress of the inn gave him a hearty welcome, as she was very anxious to find another doctor who could cure her nose.

'My treatment is effectual, but it is rude,' said the pretended Turk. 'I don't know if you'll like to submit to it.'

'Oh yes! Anything, whatever it may be, only to be rid of this monstrous nose,' said the hostess.

'Then you must come into a room by yourself with me,' said the pretended Turk; 'and I have a stick here made out of the root of a particular tree. I must thump you on the back with it, and in proportion as I thump you the nose will draw in. Of course it will hurt very much, and make you cry out, so you must tell your servants and people outside that however much you may call they are not to come in. For if they should come in and interrupt the cure, it would all have to be begun over again, and all you had suffered would go for nothing.'

So the hostess gave strict orders, saying, 'I am going into this room with the Turk to be cured by him, and however much I may call out, or whatever I may say, mind none of you, on pain of losing your places, open the door, or come near the room.'

Then she took the Turk into a room apart, and shut the door. The Turk no sooner got her alone than he made her lie with her face downwards on a sofa, and then —whack, whack, whack![8] he gave her such a beating that she felt the effects of it to the end of her days.

Of course it was in vain she screamed and roared for help; the servants had had their orders, and none of them durst approach the room. It was only when she had fainted that the Turk left her alone and went his way.

But she never got her nose cured, and he married the pretty peasant girl who was the subject of his first cure.

¹ 'Mezza canna di Naso,' half a cane of nose. A cane is the former Roman standard measure, and was exactly equal to two mètres.

² 'Palmo,' was the expression used; the *Canna* was divided into eight palms.

³ 'Calava, calava, calava.'

⁴ 'Adesso eo' a cavallo.' 'Now I am on the way to fortune.'

⁵ 'Quell' fruttivendolo'; 'quell' uomo'! 'quella donna!' a vulgar way of calling after people.

⁶ 'Spezziale,' a druggist ('droghiere' is a grocer). It is the custom in Rome for the doctors of the poor to sit in the druggists' shops, ready to be called for.

⁷ 'Nasone,' a big nose.

⁸ 'Pimperte; Pămperte! Pūmperte!'

[The two following stories contain a jumbling mixture of the incidents of the three preceding, set in a different framework; more or less mixed up with those in the stories of other countries mentioned at p. 128. Some of those in 'The Transformation Donkey' occur in the Siddhi Kür story of 'The Gold-spitting Prince,' in 'Sagas from the Far East,' but they are constructed into a quite different tale.]

ThE CHICORY-SELLER AND THE ENCHANTED PRINCESS.¹

THERE was a chicory-seller, with a wife and a son, all of them dying of hunger, and sleeping on the floor because they couldn't afford a bed. Once when they went out in the morning to gather chicory, the son found such a large plant of it, never was such a plant seen, it took them an hour, working at it together, to pull it up, and it filled two great bags. What is more, when they had got it all up, there was a great hole in the ground.

'What can there be down in that hole?' said the son. 'I must go and see!' In he jumped,² and down he went.

Suddenly he found himself in the midst of a splendid palace, and a number of obsequious servants gathered round him. They all bowed to the ground, and said,

'Your lordship! your lordship!' and asked him what he 'pleased to want.'

So there he was, dressed like a clodhopper, and all these servants dressed like princes, bowing and scraping to him.

'What do I want?' said the lad; 'most of all, I want a dinner.'

Immediately they brought him a banquet of a dinner, and waited on him all the time. Dinner over, they dressed him like a prince.

By-and-by there came in an ugly old hag, as ugly as a witch, who said,

'Good morning, Prince; are you come to marry me?'

'I'm no prince; and I'm not come to marry you most certainly!' replied the youth.

But all the servants standing round made all sorts of gesticulations that he should say 'yes.'

'It's no use mouthing at me,' said the lad; 'I shall never say "yes" to *that!*'

But they went on making signs all round that he should say 'yes,' till at last they bewildered him so, that, almost without knowing what he did, he said 'yes.'

Directly he had said 'yes,' there were thunder and lightning, and thunderbolts, and meteors, and howling of wind, and storm of hail. The youth felt in great fear; but the servants said:

'It is all right. She you thought an old hag is indeed a beautiful princess of eighteen, but she was under a spell; by consenting to marry her you have ended that spell, if you can only stand through the fear of this storm for three days and three nights, no harm can come to you, and we also shall all be set free.'

The whole apartment now seemed on fire, and when that ceased for a time, it seemed to rain fire all around.

For two days he managed to endure, but on the third day he got so frightened that he ran away. He had not much bettered his condition, however; for, if he had got away from the magic storms of the under world, he had come into real storms in the actual world, and there he was alone in the Campagna, starving and destitute again.

At last an old man appeared, who said to him:

'Why were you so foolish as to run away? You were told no harm could happen to you. Now you have nearly lost all. There is, however, one remedy left. Go on to the top of that high mountain, and gather the grass that grows there, and bring back a large bundle of it, and give it to these people to eat, and that will finish what you have begun. You will marry the princess, and share her kingdom; and all her people will be set free. For all those who waited on you as servants are noblemen of her court, who are under a spell.'

'How am I to get up to the top of that high mountain?' said the youth; 'it would take me a life of weariness to arrive there!'

'Take this divining-rod,' said the old man, 'and whatever difficulty comes in your way, touch it with this wand, and it will disappear.'

The youth took the wand, and bent his steps towards the mountain. There were rivers to be crossed, and steep places to be climbed, and many perils to be encountered, but the wand overcame them all. Arrived at the top, he saw a plat of fine, long grass growing, which he made no doubt was the grass he had to take. But he thought within himself, 'If this wand can do so much, it can surely give me also a house and a dinner; and, then, why should I toil down this mountain again at all!'

'Rod! rod! give me a nice little house!' he commanded;[3] and there was a nice little house on the top of the mountain.

'Rod! rod! give me a good dinner!' and a good dinner was spread on the table.

And thus it was with everything he wanted; so he went on living on the top of the mountain, without thinking of those he had to deliver in the hole under the earth.

Suddenly, there stood the old man. 'You were not sent here to amuse yourself,' said he, severely. 'You were sent to fetch the means of delivering others;' and he took the wand away from him, and touched the casino, and it disappeared, and he was once more left destitute.

'If you would repair the past,' said the old man, as he went away, 'gather even now a bundle of grass and take it, and perhaps you will be in time yet; but you will have to toil alone, for you have forfeited the rod. And now, remember this counsel: whoever meets you by the way and asks to buy that grass, sell it to no man, or you are undone.'

As there was nothing else to be done, the youth set to work and cut some grass, and then terrible was the way he had to walk to get down again. Storms of fire broke continually over him, and every moment it seemed as though he would be precipitated to the bottom.

As he reached the plain a traveller met him.

'Oh, you have some of that grass,' said he. 'I was just going up the mountain to get some. If you will give it me, and save my journey, I will give you a prancing horse, all covered with gold trappings studded with precious stones.'

But this time the youth began to pay more attention to the injunctions laid upon him, and he shook his head, and walked on.

'Give it me,' continued the stranger, 'and I will give

you in return for it a casino of your own in the Campagna, where you may live all your life.'

But the youth shook his head, and continued his way, without so much as answering him.

'Give it me,' said the stranger the third time, 'and I will give you gold enough to make you rich all your days.'

But the youth stood out the third temptation as well as the other two, and then the stranger disappeared.

Without further hindrance he arrived at the chicory-hole, let himself down, and gave the grass to all the people to eat, who were half dead with waiting so long for him ; and as they ate, the spell ceased. Only as he had cut the grass in an indolent sort of way, he had not brought so large a quantity as he ought, and there was one poor maiden left for whose deliverance the provision sufficed not.

Meantime the whole face of the country was changed. The plain was covered with flourishing cities ; over the chicory-hole was a splendid palace, where the maiden, who had under the spell looked like an old hag, took up her abode, and where the old man had promised that he should live with her for his reward.

This reward he now came to claim.

'But you have not completed your task,' said the princess.

'I think I have done a pretty good deal,' answered the youth.

'But there is that one who is yet undelivered.'

'Oh, I can't help about *one*. She must manage the best way she can.'

'That won't do,' said the princess. 'If you want to have me, you must complete your work.'

So he had to toil all the way up to the top of the mountain, and all the way down again, and at last the work was complete.

Then the princess married him, and all went won-
drously well.[3]

[1] ' Il Cicoriaro e la Principessa fatata.'

[2] 'Fa una zompa ;' 'zompa' for 'zomba,' properly a blow, a thump ;
here, 'jumped down with a noise like a thump.'

[3] *Bacchettone di comando*, suits this use of it better than does the
English equivalent.

[4] ' Ecco il vecchio !' such abrupt interruptions, with change of tense, are
often introduced with dramatic effect by the narrators. A similar one
occurs at p. 133. 'He sounds the horn and One comes.'

[5] ' E tutto andava benone ;' 'bene,' well ; 'benone,' superlatively well.

THE TRANSFORMATION-DONKEY.[1]

THERE was once a poor chicory-seller : all chicory-sellers
are poor, but this was a very poor one, and he had a large
family of daughters and two sons. The daughters he left
at home with their mother, but the two sons he took with
him to gather chicory. While they were out gathering
chicory one day, a great bird flew down before them and
dropped an egg and then flew away again. The boys
picked up the egg and brought it to their father, because
there were some figures like strange writing on it which
they could not read ; but neither could the father read the
strange writing, so he took the egg to a farmer.[2] The
farmer read the writing, and it said :—

' Whoso eats my head, he shall be an emperor.

' Whoso eats my heart, he shall never want for money.'

' Ho, ho !' said the farmer to himself, ' it won't do
to tell the fellow this ; I must manage to eat both the
head and the heart myself.' So he said, ' The meaning of
it is that whoever eats the bird will make a very good
dinner ; so to-morrow when the bird comes back, as she
doubtless will to lay another egg, have a good stick ready
and knock her down ; then you can make a fire, and bake
it between the stones, and I will come and eat it with you
if you like.'

The poor chicory-seller thought his fortune was made when a farmer offered to dine with him, and the hours seemed long enough till next morning came.

With next morning, however, came the bird again. The chicory-seller was ready with his stick and knocked her down, and the boys made a fire and cooked the bird. But as they were not very apt at the trussing and cooking, the head dropped into the fire, and the youngest boy said: 'This will never do to serve up, all burnt as it is;' so he ate it. The heart also fell into the fire and got burnt, and the eldest boy said: 'This will never do to serve up, all burnt as it is;' so he ate that.

By-and-by the farmer came, and they all sat down on a bank—the farmer quite jovial at the idea of the immense advantage he was going to gain, and the chicory-seller quite elated at the idea of entertaining a farmer.

'Bring forward the roast, boys,' said the father; and the boys brought the bird.

'What have you done with the head?' exclaimed the farmer, the moment he saw the bird.

'Oh, it got burnt, and I ate it,' said the younger boy.

The merchant ground his teeth and stamped his foot, but he dared not say why he was so angry; so he sat silent while the chicory-seller took out his knife³ and cut the bird up in portions.

'Give me the piece with the heart, if I may choose,' said the merchant; 'I'm very fond of birds' hearts.'

'Certainly, any part you like,' replied the chicory-seller, nervously turning all the pieces over and over again; 'but I can't find any heart. Boys, had the bird no heart?'

'Yes, papa,' answered the elder brother, 'it had a heart, sure enough; but it tumbled into the fire and got burnt, and so I ate it.'

There was no object in disguising his fury any longer, so the farmer exclaimed testily, 'Thank you, I'll not

have any then ; the head and the heart are just the only
parts of a bird I care to eat.' And so saying he turned on
his heel and went away.

'Look, boys, what you've done! You've thrown away
the best chance we ever had in our lives!' cried the father
in despair.⁴ 'After the farmer had taken dinner with
us he must have asked us to dine with him, and, as one
civility always brings another, there is no saying what it
might not have led to. However, as you have chosen to
throw the chance away, you may go and look out for yourselves. I've done with you.' And with a sound cudgelling⁵
he drove them away.

The two boys, left to themselves, wandered on till they
came to a stable, when they entered the yard and asked to
be allowed to do some work or other as a means of sub-
sistence.

'I've nothing for you to do,' said the landlord ; 'but,
as it's late, you may sleep on the straw there, on the condition that you go about your business to-morrow first
thing.'

The boys, glad to get a night's lodging on any condition, went to sleep in the straw. When the elder brother
woke in the morning he found a box of sequins⁶ under his
head.

'How could this have come here,' soliloquised the boy,
'unless the host had put it there to see if we were honest?
Well, thank God, if we're poor there's no danger of either
of us taking what doesn't belong to us.' So he took the
box to the host, and said : 'There's your box of sequins
quite safe. You needn't have taken the trouble to test
our honesty in that way.'

The host was very much surprised, but he thought the
best way was to take the money and say nothing but 'I'm
glad to see you're such good boys.' So he gave them
breakfast and some provisions for the way.

Next night they found themselves still in the open

country and no inn near, and they were obliged to be content to sleep on the bare ground. Next morning when they woke the younger boy again found a box of sequins under his head.

'Only think of that host not being satisfied with trying us once, but to come all this way after us to test our honesty again. However, I suppose we must take it back to him.'

So they walked all the way back to the host and said: 'Here's your box of sequins back; as we didn't steal it the first time it was not likely we should take it the second time.'

The host was more and more astonished; but he took the money without saying anything, only he praised the boys for being so good and gave them a hearty meal. And they went their way, taking a new direction.

The next night the younger brother said: 'Do you know I've my doubts about the host having put that box of sequins under your head. How could he have done it out in the open country without our seeing him? To-night I will watch, and if he doesn't come, and in the morning there is another box of sequins, it will be a sign that it is your own.'

He did so, and next morning there was another box of sequins. So they decided it was honestly their own, and they carried it by turns and journeyed on. About noon they came to a great city where the emperor was lately dead, and all the people were in great excitement about choosing another emperor. The population was all divided in factions, each of which had a candidate, and none would let the candidate of the others reign. There was so much fighting and quarrelling in the streets that the brothers got separated, and saw each other no more.

At this time it happened that it was the turn of the younger brother to be carrying the box of sequins. When the sentinels at the gate saw a stranger coming in carrying a box they said, 'We must see what this is,' and they took him to the minister. When the minister saw his box was full of sequins he said, 'This must be our emperor.' And all the people said, 'Yes, this is our emperor. Long live our emperor!' And thus the boy became an emperor.

But the elder brother had entered unperceived into the town, and went to ask hospitality in a house where was a woman with a beautiful daughter; so they let him stay. That night also there came a box of sequins under his head; so he went out and bought meat and fuel and all manner of provisions, and gave them to the mother, and said, 'Because you took me in when I was poor last night, I have brought you all these provisions out of gratitude,' and for the beautiful daughter he bought silks and damasks, and ornaments of gold. But the daughter said, 'How comes it, tell me, that you, who were a poor footsore wayfarer last night, have now such boundless riches at command?' And because she was beautiful and spoke kindly to him, he suspected no evil, but told her, saying, 'Every morning when I wake now, I find a box of sequins under my head.'

'And how comes it,' said she, 'that you find a box of sequins under your head now, and not formerly?' 'I do not know,' he answered, unless it be because one day when I was out with father gathering chicory, a great bird came and dropt an egg with some strange writing on it, which we could not read. But a farmer read it for us; only he would not tell us what it said, but that we should cook the bird and eat it. While we were cooking it the heart fell into the fire and got burnt, and I ate it : and when the farmer heard this he grew very angry. I think, therefore, the writing on the egg said that he who ate the heart of the bird should have many sequins.'

After this they spent the day pleasantly together; but the daughter put an emetic in his wine at supper, and so made him bring up the bird's heart, which she kept for herself, and the next morning when he woke there was no box of sequins under his head. When he rose in the morning also the beautiful girl and her mother turned him out of the house, and he wandered forth again.

At last, being weary and full of sorrow, he sat down on the ground by the side of a stream crying. Immediately three fairies appeared to him and asked him why he wept. And when he told them, they said to him : 'Weep no more, for instead of the bird's heart we give you this sheepskin jacket, the pockets of which will always be full of sequins. How many soever you may take out they will always remain full.' Then they disappeared ; but he immediately went back to the house of the beautiful girl, taking her rich and fine presents; but she said to him, 'How comes it that you, who had no money left when you went away, have now the means to buy all these fine presents ? ' Then he told her of the gift of the three fairies, and they let him sleep in the house again, but the daughter called her maid to her and said : 'Make a sheepskin jacket exactly like that in the stranger's room.' So she made one, and they put it in his room, and took away the one the fairies had given him, and in the morning they drove him from the house again. Then he went and sat down by the stream and wept again ; but the fairies came and asked him why he wept ; and he told them, saying, ' Because they have driven me away from the house where I stayed, and I have no home to go to, and this jacket has no more sequins in the pockets.' Then the fairies looked at the jacket, and they said, ' This is not the jacket we gave you ; it has been changed by fraud :' so they gave him in place of it a wand, and they said, ' With this wand strike the table, and whatever you may desire, be it meat or drink or clothes, or whatsoever you may want, it shall come upon the table.' The next day he went back to the house of the woman and her daughter, and sat down without saying anything, but he struck the table with his wand, wishing for a great banquet, and immediately it was covered with the choicest dishes. There was no need to ask him questions this time, for they saw in what his gift consisted, and in the night, when he was asleep, they took his wand away. In the morning they drove him forth out of the house, and he went back to the stream and sat down to cry. Again the fairies appeared to him and comforted him; but they said, 'This is the last time we may appear to you. Here is a ring; keep it on your hand; for if you lose this gift there is nothing more we may do for you;' and they went away. But he immediately returned to the house of the woman and her beautiful daughter. They let him in, 'Because,' they said, 'doubtless the fairies have given him some other gift of which we may take profit.' And as he sat there he said, 'All the other gifts of the fairies have I lost, but this one they have given me now I cannot lose, because it is a ring which fits my finger, and no one can take it from my hand.'

'And of what use is your ring?' asked the beautiful daughter.

'Its use is that whatever I wish for while I have it on I obtain directly, whatever it may be.'

'Then wish,' said she, 'that we may be both together on the top of that high mountain, and a sumptuous *merenda*[7] spread out for us.'

'To be sure!' he replied, and he repeated her wish. Instantly they found themselves on the top of the high mountain with a plentiful *merenda* before them; but she had a vial of opium with her, and while his head was turned away she poured the opium into his wine. Presently after this he fell into a sound sleep, so sound that there was no fear of waking him. Immediately she took the ring from his finger and put it on her own; then she wished that she might be replaced at home and that he might be left on the top of the mountain. And so it was done.

In the morning when he woke and found himself all alone on the top of the high mountain and his ring gone, he wept bitter tears, and felt too weary to attempt the descent of the steep mountain side. For three days he remained here weary and weeping, and then, becoming faint from hunger, he took some of the herbs that grew on the mountain top for food. As soon as he had eaten these he was turned into a donkey,[8] but as he retained his human intelligence, he said to himself, this herb has its uses, and he filled one of the panniers on his back with it. Then he came down from the mountain, and when he was at the foot of it, being hungry with the long journey, he ate of the grass that grew there, and, behold! he was transformed back into his natural shape; so he filled the other basket with this kind of grass and went his way.

Having dressed himself like a street seller, he took the basket of the herb which had the property of changing the eater into a donkey, and stood under the window of the house where he had been so evil entreated, and cried, 'Fine salad! fine salad! who will buy my fine salad?'[9]

'What is there so specially good about your salad?' asked the maid, looking out. 'My young mistress is particularly fond of salad, so if yours is so very superfine, you had better come up.'

He did not wait to be twice told. As soon as he saw the beautiful daughter, he said, 'This is fine salad, indeed, the finest of the fine, all fresh gathered, and the first of its kind that ever was sold.'

'Very likely it's the first of its kind that ever was sold,' said she; 'but I don't like to buy things I haven't tried; it may turn out not to be nice.'

'Oh, try it, try it freely; don't buy without trying;' and he picked one of the freshest and crispest bunches.

She took one in her hand and bit a few blades, and no sooner had she done so than she too became a donkey. Then he put the panniers on her back and drove her all over the town, constantly cudgelling her till she sank under the blows. Then one who saw him belabour her thus, said, ' This must not be ; you must come and answer before the emperor for thus belabouring the poor brute ; ' but he refused to go unless he took the donkey with him ; so they went to the emperor and said, ' Here is one who is belabouring his donkey till she has sunk under his blows, and he refuses to come before the emperor to answer his cruelty unless he bring his donkey with him.' And the emperor made answer, ' Let him bring the beast with him.'

So they brought him and his donkey before the emperor. When he found himself before the emperor he said, ' All these must go away ; to the emperor alone can I tell why I belabour my donkey.' So the emperor commanded all the people to go to a distance while he took him and his donkey apart. As soon as he found himself alone with the emperor he said, ' See, it is I, thy brother ! ' and he embraced him. Then he told him all that had befallen him since they parted. Then said the emperor to the donkey, ' Go now with him home, and show him where thou hast laid all the things—the bird's heart, the sheepskin jacket, the wand, and the ring, that he may bring them hither ; and if thou deliver them up faithfully I will command that he give thee of that grass to eat which shall give thee back thy natural form.'

So they went back to the house and fetched all the things, and the emperor said, ' Come thou now and live with me, and give me of thy sequins, and I will share the empire with thee.' Thus they reigned together.

But to the donkey they gave of the grass to eat, which restored her natural form, only that her beauty was marred by the cudgelling she had received. And she said, ' Had I not been so wilful and malicious I had now been empress.'

[1] ' La Somara.'

[2] The 'mercante di Campagna' occupies the place of farmer in the

social system cf Rome; that is, he produces and deals in grain and cattle; there is ' buttaro' (cattle breeder) besides; but the characteristics of each are so different that the one does not well translate the other.

³ 'Cortello' for 'coltello' (a knife). The substitution of *r* for *l* in a good many words is a common Romanism.

⁴ 'Dishperato' for 'disperato' ('out of himself with vexation'), is another Romanism; as also

⁵ 'Bashtonata' for 'bastonata' (a cudgelling); at least many Romans, particularly old-fashioned people, when using some words in which *sp* and *st* occur, put in an *h* on occasions requiring great vehemence of expression.

⁶ Zecchini. The *zecchino* was the gold standard coin in Rome before that of the *scudo* was adopted. Its value was fixed in the reign of Clement XIII., 1758, at two scudi and twenty bajocchi—something between 10*s.* and 11*s.*; it was current till a few years back; and 'zecchini' is a common way of saying 'money' when a large sum is spoken of, just as we still talk of guineas.

⁷ 'Merenda' is a supplementary meal taken at any time of day. It is not exactly lunch, because the habit of taking lunch at one and dining late has not yet obtained to any great extent in Rome; and where it has, lunch is called 'déjeûner'; breakfast (i.e. a cup of coffee and a roll early in the morning) is always called 'colazione.' The established custom of Rome is dinner ('pranzo,' or 'desinare,') at twelve, and supper ('cena') an hour or two after the Ave, varying, therefore, according to the time of year, from six or seven till nine or ten, and even later. 'Merenda' is a light meal between 'pranzo' and 'cena' of not altogether general use, and chiefly on occasions of driving outside the gates to spend the afternoon at a country villa or casino.

⁸ 'Soma' is a burden; 'somaro' or 'somura' an ass used for carrying burdens. Thus in the next line it is spoken of as having panniers on as a matter of course.

⁹ 'Che bell' insalatina; chi vuol insalatina; che bell' insalatina!' a common form of crying. 'Che belle mela!' 'What fine apples!' 'Che belle persiche!' or 'What fine peaches!' may be heard all the year round.

[In these stories we have had the actions of three *Fate,* somewhat resembling English fairies; in the following, we meet with three who, as often happens in Roman stories, are nothing better than witches.]

SIGNOR LATTANZIO.

THEY say there was a duke who wandered over the world seeking a beautiful maiden to make his wife.

After many years he came to an inn where was a lady, who asked him what he sought.

'I have journeyed half the earth over,' answered the duke, 'to find a wife to my fancy, and have not found one ; and now I go back to my native city as I came.'

'How sad!' answered the lady. 'I have a daughter who is the most beautiful maiden that ever was made ; but three fairies have taken possession of her, and locked her up in a casino in the Campagna, and no one can get to see her.'

'Only tell me where she is,' replied the duke, 'and I promise you I'll get to see her, in spite of all the fairies in the world.'

'It is useless!' replied the lady. 'So many have tried and failed. So will you.'

'Not I!' answered the duke. 'Tell me how they failed, and I will do otherwise.'

'I have told so many, and all say the same as you, and all go to seek her, but none ever come back.'

'Never mind! Tell it once again, and I promise you it shall be the last time, for I will surely come back.'

'If you are bent on sacrificing yourself uselessly,' proceeded the lady, 'this is the story. You must go to the mountain of Russia, and at the foot of it there will meet you three most beautiful maidens, who will come round you, and praise you, and flatter you, and pour out all manner of blandishments, and will ask you to go into their palace with them, and will entreat you so much that you will not be able to resist; then you will go into their palace with them, and they will turn you into a cat, for they are three fairies. But, on the other hand, if you can resist only for the space of one hour to all they will say to you, then you will have conquered, and they will be turned into cats, and you will have free access to my daughter to release her.'

'I will go,' said the duke firmly; and he rose up and went his way to the mountain of Russia.

'Now, if all these other men have failed in this same

attempt,' he mused within himself as he went along, 'it behoves me to be prudent. I know what I will do; I will put a bandage over my eyes, and then I shan't see the fairies, and their blandishments will have no power over me.' And so he did.

Then the fairies came out to him and said, 'Signor Lattanzio! welcome, welcome! how fair you are; do take the bandage off and let us see you; how noble you look. Do let us see your face? We are dying to have you with us!'

But the duke remained firm, and seemed to take no heed, though their voices were so soft and persuasive that he longed to look at them, or even to lift up one corner of the bandage and take a peep. But he remained firm.

'Signor Lattanzio! Signor Lattanzio! Don't be so ungallant,' pursued the fairies. 'Here are we at your feet, as it were, begging you to give us your company, and you will not so much as speak to us, or even look at us!'

But the duke remained firm, and seemed to take no heed, though his head was turned by their accents, and he felt that if he could only go with them as they wished he should want no more. But he remained firm.

'Signor Lattanzio! Signor Lattanzio! Signor Lattanzio!' cried the three fairies disdainfully, for now they began to suspect in right good earnest that at last one had come who was too strong for them. 'The fact is you are afraid of us. If you are a man, show you have no fear, and come and talk with us.'

But the duke remained firm, though a vanity, which had nearly lost him, whispered that it would be a grander triumph to look them in the face and yet resist them, than to conquer without having ventured to look at them, yet prudence prevailed, and he remained firm.

So they went on, and the duke felt that the hour was drawing to a close. He took out his repeater and struck it, and the hour of trial was over.

'Traitor !' cried the three fairies, and in the same instant they were turned into cats.   Then the duke went into their palace, and took their wand, and with it he could open the gates of the casino where the lady's daughter was imprisoned.

When he saw her, he found her indeed fairer than the fairest; fairer even than his conception.

When, therefore, with the wand he had restored all the cats that were upon the mountain to their natural shapes as those that had failed in their enterprise, he took her home with him to be his wife.

[As this was told me, the sign by which the duke was to recognise the three fairies was, that they were to be sweeping the ground with their breasts. The incident seemed so extravagant, that I omitted it in writing out the story ; I mention it, however, now because I find the same in Note 1, on an Albanian story, to p. 177, in Ralston's ' Russian Folk Tales '; I met the incident subsequently in another Roman story.

The idea which has prompted this tale is apparently the same as that which has given rise to the story of ' Odysseus and the Seirens.'   See Cox's ' Aryan Mythology,' II. 242.]

HOW CAJUSSE WAS MARRIED.[1]

THERE was a poor tailor starving for poverty because he could get no work.   One day there knocked at his door a good-natured-looking old man; the tailor's son opened the door, and he won the boy's confidence immediately, saying he was his uncle.   He also gave him a piastre[2] to buy a good dinner.   When the father came home and found him installed, and heard that he called himself his son's uncle, and would, therefore, be his own brother, he was much surprised; but as he found he was so rich and so generous, he thought it better not to dispute his word.

The visitor stayed a whole month, providing all expenses so freely all the time that everyone was delighted with him, and when at last he came to take leave, and proposed that the tailor's boy should go with him and learn some business at his expense, the son himself was all eagerness to go, and the father, too, willingly gave his consent.

As soon as they had gone a good way outside the gates the stranger said to the boy, ' It is all a dodge about my calling myself your uncle. I am not your uncle a bit ; only I want a strong daring sort of boy to do something for me which I am too old to do myself. I am a wizard,[3] and if you do what I tell you I will reward you well ; but if you attempt to resist or escape you may be sure you will suffer for it.'

'Tell me what I have to do, before we talk about resisting and escaping,' replied the boy ; ' maybe I shan't mind doing it.'

They were walking on as they talked, and the boy observed that they got over much more ground than by ordinary walking, and they were now in a wild desolate country. The wizard said nothing till they reached a spot where there was a flat stone in the ground. Here he stopped, and as he lifted up the stone, he said, ' This is what you have to do. I will let you down with this rope, and you must go all along through the dark till you come to a place where is a beautiful garden. At the gate of the garden sits a fierce dog, which will fly out at you, and bark fearfully. I will give you some bread and cheese to throw to him, and, while he is devouring the bread and cheese, you must pass on. Then all manner of terrible noises will cry after you, calling you back ; but take no heed of them, and, above all, do not look back ; if you look back you are lost. As soon as you are out of sound of the voices you will see on a stone an old lantern, take that and bring it back to me.'

The boy showed no unwillingness to try his fortune,

and the magician gave him the bread and cheese he had promised, and let him down by a rope. He gave him also a ring, saying, 'If anything else should happen, after you have got the lantern, to prevent your bringing it away, rub this ring and wish at the same time for deliverance, and you will be delivered.'

The boy did all the wizard had told him, and something more besides; for when he got into the garden he found the trees all covered with beautiful fruits, which were all so many precious stones; with these he filled his pockets till he could hardly move for the weight of them; then he came back to the opening of the cave, and called to the wizard to pull him up.

'Send up the lantern first,' said the magician, 'and I'll see about pulling you up afterwards.'

But the boy was afraid lest he should be left behind; so he refused to send up the lantern unless the wizard hauled him up with it. This the wizard would by no means do.

'Ah! the youngster will be frightened if I shut him up in the dark cave a bit,' said he, and closed the stone, meaning to call to him by-and-by to see if he had come round to a more submissive mind. The boy, however, finding himself shut up alone in the cave, bethought him of the ring, and rubbed it, wishing the while to be at home. Instantly he found himself there, lantern in hand. His parents were very much astonished at all he told them of his adventures, and, poor as they were, were very glad to have him safe back.

'I wonder what the magician wanted this ugly old lantern for,' said the boy to himself one day. 'It must be good for something or he would not have been so anxious to have it; let me try rubbing it, and see if that answers as well as rubbing the ring.' He no sooner did so than One⁴ appeared, and asked his pleasure. 'A table well laid for dinner!' said the boy; and immediately a table appeared covered with all sorts of good things, with

real silver spoons and forks.⁵ Then he called on his mother
and father, and they made a good meal ; after that they
lived for a month on the price of the silver which the
mother took out and pawned.⁶ One day she found the
town all illuminated. ' What is going on ? ' she asked of
the neighbours. ' The daughter of the Sultan is going
to marry the son of the Grand Vizier, and there is a distri-
bution of alms to the people on the occasion ; that is why
they rejoice.' Such was the answer.

When she came home she told her son what she had
heard. He said, ' That will not be, because the daughter
of the Sultan will have to marry me ! ' but she only
laughed at him. The next day he brought her three neat
little baskets filled with the precious stones which he had
gathered in the under-ground garden, and he said, ' These
you must take to the Sultan, and say I want to marry
his daughter.' But she was afraid and would not go ;
and when at last he made her go, she stood in a
corner apart behind all the people, for there was a public
audience, and came back and said she could not get at
the Sultan ; but he made her go again the next two days
following, and she always did the same. The last day,
however, the Sultan sent for her, saying, ' Who is that
old woman standing in the corner quite apart ? bring her
to me.' So they brought her to him all trembling.

' Don't be afraid, old woman,' said the Sultan. ' What
have you to say ? '

' My son, who must have lost his senses, sent me to
say he wanted to marry the daughter of the Sultan,' said
the old woman, crying for very fear ; ' and he sends these
baskets as a present.'

When the Sultan took the baskets and saw of what
great value were the contents, he said, ' Don't be afraid,
old woman ; go back and tell your son I will give him an
answer in a month.'

She went back and told her son ; but at the end

M

of a week the princess was married, nevertheless, to the
son of the Grand Vizier.

'There!' said the mother, when she heard it; 'I
thought the Grand Sultan was only making game of you.
Was it likely that the daughter of the Sultan should
marry a beggar,[7] like you?'

'Don't be in too great a hurry, mother,' replied the
lad; 'leave it to me, leave it to me.'[8]

With that he went and took out the old lantern, and
rubbed it till One appeared asking his pleasure.

'Go to-night, at three hours of night,'[9] was his reply,
'and take the daughter of the Sultan and lay her in a
poor wallet in the out-house here.'

At three hours of night he went into the out-house
and found the princess on the poor wallet as he had commanded. Then he laid his sabre on the bed between
them, and sat down and talked to her; but she was too
frightened to answer him. This he did three nights
running. The princess, however, went crying to her
mother, and told her all that had happened. The Sultana
could not imagine how it was. 'But,' she said, 'something
wrong there must be;' and she went and told the
Sultan, and he, too, said it was all wrong, and that the
marriage must be annulled. Also the son of the Grand
Vizier went to his father and complained, saying, 'Every
night my wife disappears just at bed-time, and, though
the door is locked, I see nothing of her till the next
morning.'

His father too said, 'There must be something wrong,'
and when the Sultan said the marriage must be annulled,
the Grand Vizier was quite willing. So the marriage was
annulled.

At the end of the month, the lad made his mother go
back to the Sultan for his answer, and he gave her three
other baskets of precious stones to take with her. The
Sultan, when he saw the man had so many precious stones

to give away, thought he must be in truth a prince in disguise, and he answered, ' He may come and see us.' He also said, ' What is his name that I may know him ? '

And his mother said, ' His name is Cajusse.'

So she went home and told her son what the sultan had said. Then he rubbed the lantern and asked for a suit to wear, all dazzling with gold and silver, and a richly caparisoned horse, and six pages in velvet dresses, four to ride behind, and one to go before with a purse scattering alms to the people, and one to cry, ' Make place for the Signor Cajusse!' Thus he came to the sultan, and the sultan received him well, and gave him his daughter to be his wife; but Cajusse had brought the lantern with him, and he rubbed it, and ordered that there should stand by the side of the sultan's palace a palace a great deal handsomer, furnished with every luxury, and that all the windows should be encrusted round with precious stones, all but one. This was all done as he had said, and he took the princess home with him to live there. Then he showed her all over the beautiful palace, and showed her the windows all encrusted with gems, ' and in this vacant one,' said he, ' we will put those in the six baskets I sent you before the sultan consented to our marriage ; ' and they did so ; but they did not suffice.

But the magician meantime had learnt by his incantations what had happened, and in order to get possession of the lantern he watched till Cajusse was gone out hunting; then he came by dressed as a pedlar of metal work,[11] and offered to exchange old lanterns for new ones. The princess thought to make a capital bargain by exchanging Cajusse's shabby old lantern for a brand new one, and thus fell into his snare. The magician no sooner had possession of it than he rubbed it, and ordered that the palace and all that was in it should be transported on to the high seas.

The sultan happened to look out of window just as the

palace of Cajusse had disappeared. 'What is this?' he cried. And when he found the palace was really gone, he uttered so many furious threats that the people, who loved Cajusse well, ran out to meet him as he came home from hunting, and told him of all that had happened, and warned him of the sultan's wrath. Instead of going back to be put in prison by the sultan therefore, he rubbed his ring and desired to be taken to the place wherever the princess was. Instantly he found himself on a floating rock in mid ocean, at the foot of the palace. Then he went to the gate and sounded the horn.[12] The princess knew her husband's note of sounding and ran to the window. Great was her delight when she saw that it was really he, and she told him that there was a horrid old man who had possession of the palace, and persecuted her every day to marry him, saying her husband was dead. And she, to keep him at a distance, yet without offending him lest he should kill her, had said : 'No, I have always resolved never to marry an old man, because then if he dies I should be left alone, and that would be too sad.' 'But when I say that,' she continued, 'he always says, "You need not be afraid of that, for I shall never die !" so I don't know what to say next.'

Then the prince said, 'Make a great feast to-night, and say you will marry him if he tells you one thing: say it is impossible that he should never die, for all people die some day or other; it is impossible but that there should be some one thing or other that is fatal to him ; ask him what that one fatal thing is, and he, thinking you want to know it that you may guard him against it, will tell; then come and tell me what he says.'

The princess did all her husband had told her, and then came back and repeated what the magician had said : 'One must go into the wood,' she repeated, 'where is the beast called hydra, and cut off all his seven heads. In the head which is in the middle of the other six, if it is split open, will be found a leveret; if this leveret is caught and his head split open there is a bird; if this bird is caught and his head split open, there is in it a precious stone. If that stone is put under my pillow I must die.'

The prince did not wait for anything more : he rubbed the ring, and desired to be carried to the wood where the hydra lived. Instantly he found himself face to face with the hydra, who came forward spueing fire. But Cajusse had also asked for a coat of mail and a mighty sword, and with one blow he cut off the seven heads. Then he called to his servant to take notice which was the head which was in the middle of the other six, and the servant pointed it out. Then he said, 'Watch when I split it open, for a leveret will jump out. Beware lest it escapes.' The servant stood to catch it, but it was so swift it ran past the servant. The prince, however, was swifter than it, and overtook it and killed it. Then he said, 'Beware when I split open the head of the leveret. A little bird will fly out; mind that it escapes not, for we are undone if it escapes.' So the servant stood ready to catch the bird, but the bird was so swift it flew past the servant. The prince, however, was swifter than the bird, and he overtook it and killed it, and split open its head and took out the precious stone. Then he rubbed the ring and bid it take him back to the princess. The princess was waiting for him at the window.

'Here is the stone,' said the prince; and he gave it to her, and with it a bottle of opium. 'To-night,' he said, 'you must say you are ready to marry the wizard; make a great feast again, and have ready some of this opium in his wine. He will sleep heavily, and not see what you are doing; then you can put the stone uuder his pillow, and when he is dead call me.'

All this the princess did. She told the wizard that she was now ready to do as he wished. The magician was so delighted that he ordered a great banquet.

'Here,' said the princess at the banquet, 'is a little of my father's choicest wine, which I had with me in the palace when it was brought hither,' and she poured out to him to drink of the wine mixed with opium.

After this, when the wizard went to bed, he was heavy and took no notice what she did, and thus she put the stone under his pillow. No sooner did he, therefore, lay his head on the pillow than he gave three terrible yells, turned himself round and round three times, and was dead.

There was no need to call the prince, for he had heard the death yells, and immediately came up. They found the lantern, after they had hunted everywhere in vain, tied on to the magician's body under all his clothes, for he had hid it there that he might never part with it. By its power Cajusse ordered the palace to be removed back to its place, and there they lived happily for ever afterwards.

[1] 'Il Matrimonio di Cajusse,' I should imagine Caius was the right reading. Italians, though they are so fond of clipping off the final vowel of their own words, whenever they get hold of a foreign word ending in a consonant must needs always add a syllable on to it. The narrator in this instance could not spell, and I write the word as she pronounced it. Meeting with so close a counterpart of 'Aladdin's Lamp,' I cross-questioned the narrator very closely as to whether she had not read it, but she assured me most solemnly that her mother had told it her when she was not more than five years old; that it was impossible she could have read it, as she could only read very imperfectly, only a few easy sentences; she had never in her life read anything long. I further elicited that it was possible her mother might have read it; but I am inclined to think she said this rather to improve my idea of her family, than because she thought it was really the case.

[2] 'Piastra.' In Melchiorri's 'Guida Metodica di Roma,' ed. 1856, in the list of moneys current the half-scudo is put down as 'commonly called *mezza piastra.*' I do not remember to have heard it so used myself, though I have heard old people talk of piastres, the value of which would thus be the same as a scudo, or about five francs: an old inhabitant told me it was 7½ bajocchi, more than a scudo.

[3] 'Mago.' I asked the narrator what her idea of a 'mago' was, and she said, 'Something like a *stregone* (masculine of *strega*, witch), only not quite so bad.'

⁴ Genii having no place in modern Italian mythology, the 'Genius of the Lamp' loses his identity here.

⁵ 'Posate,' spoons and forks. I spare the reader the enumeration of the Roman dishes which were detailed to me as figuring on the table, as I have had to quote many of them in other stories.

⁶ 'I always used to wonder,' observed the narrator very pertinently, 'as my mother told me this, why they didn't rub the lamp again and ask for what they wanted, instead of going about pawning the *posate*. I suppose they had forgotten about it.'

⁷ 'Pezzente,' a sorry fellow; literally beggar.

⁸ 'Che ci penso io' is a saying ever in the mouth of a Roman. Whatever you may be giving directions about, they always stop you with 'Lasci far a me, che ci penso io' ('Leave it to me ; I'll manage it.')

⁹ 'Tre ore di notte' means three hours after the evening Ave. If it was summer-time this would be about 11 P.M. A subject of the 'Gran Sultan' being supposed to measure time by the Ave Maria is not one of the least bizarre of traditionary accretions.

¹⁰ 'Chincaglieria,' all kinds of small articles of metal-work.

¹¹ 'Frâvodo.' As I had never heard the word before, I was very particular in making the narrator repeat it, to take it down. She described it as a horn or trumpet, but I cannot meet with the word in any dictionary.

[The introduction into this story of the dog to be appeased with a sop, and the hydra to be slain, no trace of either occurring in ' Aladdin's Lamp,' is noticeable; the incident of the unjewelled window loses its point, probably through want of memory. The transporting the palace into the middle of the sea is a novel introduction ; but the most remarkable change is in the mode of compassing the death of the magician. This episode as here described enters into a vast number of tales. It occurs in a Hungarian one I have in MS. :—A king directs in dying that his three sons shall go out to learn experience by adventure before they succeed to the throne. The first two nights of the journey the two elder brothers keep watch in turn, while the others sleep, and each kills a dragon. The third night, István (Stephen), the youngest, keeps watch, and is enticed away by the cries for help of a frog, which he delivers, but when he comes back the watch-fire is out. He has now to wander in search of fresh fire ; he sees a spark in the distance and makes for it ; by the way he meets ' Dame Midnight,' who tells him the fire is a week's journey off, so he binds her to a tree, and the same with ' The Lady Dawn,' so that it might not be day before his return. In a week he reaches the fire, but three giants guard it, who are laying siege to a *vár* (fortress) to obtain possession of three beautiful maidens, whom they destined to be the brides of the King of the Dwarfs and of the very two dragons his brothers had killed. But before they give him of their fire they say he must help them in the siege. He, however, kills them by stratagem, and makes his way into the princesses' sleeping apartment, takes three pledges of his having been there, and returns to his brothers. They continue their wanderings till they come to an inn where the three princesses and the king their father have established themselves in disguise, and make all who pass that way tell the tale of their adventures as a means of discovering who it was delivered them from the giants. The princes make themselves known, and the king bestows his daughters on them. As they drive home with their brides, they pass the Dwarf-King in a ditch by the roadside, who implores them to deliver him. The two elder brothers take no notice. István stops and helps him out. The dwarf with his supernatural strength thrusts István back into the ditch, and drives off with his bride. István sets out to search after and recover her; he meets the frog he delivered, who gives him supernatural aid, and leads him through heroic adventures in which he does service to other persons and animals, who in turn assist him by directing him to the palace of the Dwarf-King Here exactly the same scene occurs between István and his bride as between Cajusse and the sultan's daughter, and they lay the same plan. But the Dwarf-King is more astute than the magician, and he at first tells her that his life's safety lies in his sceptre, on which she makes him give her the sceptre, 'that she may take care of it,' in reality intending to give it up to István. When he sees her so anxious for his safety, he tells her it is not in the sceptre, but he does not yet tell the truth; he next says it is in the royal mantle, and then in the crown (incidents proper to the version of Hungary, which sets so great store by the royal crown and mantle). Ultimately he confides that it resides in a golden cockchafer, inside a golden cock, inside a golden sheep, inside a golden stag, in the ninety-ninth *sziget* (island). She communicates all this to István. He overcomes the above-named series of golden animals by the aid of the animals he lately assisted, and thus recovers his bride.

All these incidents (somewhat differently worked in), occur in the Norse tale of 'The Giant who had no Heart in His Body,' and in the Russian 'Koschei the Deathless,' and in many others.

I have other of the 'Arabian Night' stories, told with the local colouring of characters and incidents proper to the neighbourhood of Rome ; particularly various versions of 'The Forty Thieves,' leading to a number of Brigand stories, for which I have not space left in this volume.]

LEGENDARY TALES AND ESEMPJ.

1

Oɴᴇ day the Madonna was carrying the Bambino through a lupin-field, and the stalks of the lupins rustled so, that she thought it was a robber coming to kill the Santo Bambino.[1] She turned, and sent a malediction over the lupin-field, and immediately the lupins all withered away and fell flat and dry on the ground, so that she could see there was no one hidden there. When she saw there was no one hidden there, she sent a benediction over the lupin-field, and the lupins all stood up straight again, fair and flourishing, and with tenfold greater produce than they had at the first.

2

Oɴᴇ day when Jesus Christ was grown up, and went about preaching, He came to a certain village and knocked at the first door, and said, 'Give me a lodging.'[2] But the master of the house shut the door in his face, saying, ' Here is nothing for you.' He came to the next house, and received the same answer; and the next, and the next, no one in all the village would take Him in. Weary and footsore, He came to the cottage of a poor little old woman, who lived all alone on the outskirts, and knocked there. ' Who is there?'[3] asked the old woman. ' The Master with the Apostles,' answered Jesus Christ. The old woman opened the door, and let them all in. ' Have you no fire?' asked Jesus Christ. ' No fire have I,' answered the old woman. Then Jesus Christ blessed the hearth, and there came a pile of wood on it,

and a fire was soon made. 'Have you nothing to give us
to eat?' asked Jesus Christ. 'Nothing worth offering
you,' answered the old woman; 'here is a little fish' (it
was a little fish, that, not so long as my hand) 'and
some crusts of bread, which they gave me at the eating-
shop in charity just now, and that's all I have;' and she
set both on the table. 'Have you no wine?' again asked
Jesus Christ. 'Only this flask of wine and water they
gave me there, too;' and she set it before Him.

Then Jesus Christ blessed all the things, and handed
them round the table, and they all dined off them, and at
the end there remained just the same as at the beginning.
When they had finished, He said to the old woman, 'This
fire, with the bread, and the fish, and the wine, will always
remain to you, and never diminish as long as you live.
And now follow Me a little way.'

The Master went on before with His Apostles, and the
old woman followed after, a little way behind. And behold, as they walked along, all the houses of that inhospi-
table village fell down one after the other, and all the
inhabitants were buried under them. Only the cottage
of the old woman was left standing. When the judgment
was complete, Jesus Christ said to her, 'Now, return
home.' [4]

As she turned to go, St. Peter said to her, 'Ask for the
salvation of your soul.' And she went and asked it of
Jesus Christ, and He replied, 'Let it be granted you!'

3

ONE day as He was going into the Temple, He saw
two men quarrelling before the door: a young man and
an old man. The young man wanted to go in first, and
the old man was vindicating the honour of his grey
hairs.

'What is the matter?' asked Jesus Christ; and they
showed Him wherefore they strove.

Jesus Christ said to the young man, ' If you are desirous to go in first, you must accept the state to which honour belongs,' and He touched him, and he became an old man, bowed in gait, feeble, and grey-haired, while to the old man He gave the compensation for the insult he had received, by investing him with the youth of the other.

4

In the days when Jesus Christ roamed the earth, He found Himself one day with His disciples in the Campagna, far from anything like home. The only shelter in sight was a cottage of wretched aspect. Jesus Christ knocked at the door.

' Who is there ? ' said a tremulous voice from within.

' The Master with the disciples,' answered Jesus Christ. The man didn't know what He meant ; nevertheless, the tone was too gentle to inspire fear, so he opened, and let them all in.

' Have you no fire to give us ? ' asked Jesus Christ.

' I'm only a poor beggar. I never have any fire,' said the man.

' But these poor things,' said Jesus Christ, ' are stiff with cold and weariness ; they must have a fire.'

Then Jesus Christ stood on the hearth, and blessed it, and there came a great blazing fire of heaped-up wood. When the beggar saw it, he fell on his knees in astonishment.

' Have you no food to set before us ? ' asked Jesus Christ.

' I have one loaf of Indian corn,⁶ which is at your service,' answered the beggar.

' One loaf is not enough,' answered Jesus Christ ; ' have you nothing else at all ? '

' Nothing at all about the place that can be eaten,' answered the beggar. ' Leastwise, I have one ewe, which is at your service.'

' That will do,' answered Jesus Christ; and he sent St. Peter to help the man to prepare it for dressing.

' Here is the mutton,' said the beggar; ' but I cannot cook it, because I have no lard.' [6]

' Look!' said Jesus Christ.

The beggar looked on the hearth, and saw everything that was necessary ready for use.

' Now, then, bring the wine and the bread,' said Jesus Christ, when the meat was nearly ready.

' There is the only loaf I have,' said the beggar, setting the polenta loaf on the table; ' but, as for wine, I never see such a thing.'

' Is there none in the cellar?' asked Jesus Christ.

' In the cellar are only a dozen empty old broken wine-jars that have been there these hundred years; they are well covered with mould.' Jesus Christ told St. Peter to go down and see, and when he went down with the beggar, there was a whole ovenful of fresh-baked bread boiling hot,[7] and beyond, in the cellar, the jars, instead of being broken and musty, were all standing whole and upright, and filled with excellent wine.

' See how you told us falsely,' said St. Peter, to tease him.

' Upon my word, it was even as I said, before you came.'

' Then it is the Master who has done these wonderful things,' answered St. Peter. ' Praise Him!'

Now the meat was cooked and ready, and they all sat down to table; but Jesus Christ took a bowl and placed it in the midst of the table and said, 'Let all the bones be put into this bowl;' and when they had finished he took the bones and threw them out of the window, and said, ' Behold, I give you an hundred for one.' After that they all laid them down and slept.

In the morning when they opened the door to go, behold there were an hundred sheep grazing before the door.

'These sheep are yours,' said Jesus Christ; 'moreover, as long as you live, neither the bread in the oven nor the wine in the cellar shall fail;' and He passed out and the disciples after Him.

But St. Peter remained behind, and said to the man who had entertained them, 'The Master has rewarded you generously, but He has one greater gift yet which He will give you if you ask Him.'

'What is it? tell me what is it?' said the beggar.

'The salvation of your soul,' answered S. Peter.

'Signore! Signore! add to all Thou hast given this further, the salvation of my soul,' cried the man.

'Let it be granted thee,'[8] answered the Lord, and passed on His way.

5

ANOTHER day Jesus Christ and His disciples dined at a tavern.[9]

'What's to pay?' said Jesus Christ, when they had finished their meal.

'Nothing at all,' answered the host.

But the host had a little hunchback son, who said to him, 'I know some have found it answer to give these people food instead of making them pay for it; but suppose they forget to give us anything, we shall be worse off than if we had been paid in the regular way. I will tell you what I'll do now, so as to have a hold over them. I'll take one of our silver spoons and put it in the bag that one of them carries, and accuse them of stealing it.'

Now St. Peter was a great eater, and when anything was left over from a good meal he was wont to put it by in a bag against a day when they had nothing. Into this bag therefore the hunchback put the silver spoon.

When they had gone on a little way the young hunchback ran after them and said to Jesus Christ,—

'Signore! one of these with you has stolen a spoon from us.'

N

' You are mistaken, friend; there is not one of them who would do such a thing.'

' Yes,' persevered the hunchback; 'it is *that* one who took it,' and he pointed to St. Peter.

' I ! ! ' said St. Peter, getting very angry.   ' How dare you to say such a thing of me ! '

But Jesus Christ made him a sign that he should keep silence.

' We will go back to your house and help you to look for what you have lost, for that none of us have taken the spoon is most certain,' He said; and He went back with the hunchback.

' There is nowhere to search,' answered the hunchback, ' but in that man's bag; I know it is there, because I saw him take it.'

' Then there's my bag inside out,' said St. Peter, as he cast the contents upon the floor.   Of course the silver spoon fell clattering upon the bricks.

' There ! ' said the hunchback, insolently.   ' Didn't I tell you it was there? You said it wasn't ! '

St. Peter was so angry he could not trust himself to speak ; but Jesus Christ answered for him :

' Nay, I said not it was not there, but that none of these had taken it. And now we will see who it was put it there.' With that He motioned to them all to stand back, while He, standing in the midst and raising his eyes to Heaven, said solemnly,

' Let whoso put it in the bag be turned to stone ! '

Even as He spoke the hunchback was turned into stone.

6

THERE was another tavern, however, where the host was a different sort of man, and not only *said* he would take nothing when Jesus Christ and His disciples dined there, but really would never take anything; nor was it that by any miracle he had received advantages of another sort, but out of the respect and affection he bore the Master he deemed himself sufficiently paid by the honour of being allowed to minister to Him.

One day when Jesus Christ and His disciples were going away on a journey, St. Peter went to this host and said, ' You have been very liberal to us all this time : if you were to ask for some gift, now, you would be sure to get it.'

' I don't know that there is anything that I want,' said the host. ' I have a thriving trade, which you see not only supplies all my wants, but leaves me the means of being liberal also; I have no wife to provide for, and no children to leave an inheritance to : so what should I ask for ? There is one thing, to be sure, I should like. My only amusement is playing at cards : if He would give me the faculty of always winning, I should like that; it isn't that I care for what one wins, it is that it is nice to win. Do you think I might ask *that ?* '

' I don't know,' said St. Peter, gravely. ' Still you might ask ; He is very kind.'

The host did ask, and Jesus Christ granted his desire. When St. Peter saw how easily He granted it, he said, ' If I were you, I should ask something more.'

' I really don't know what else I have to ask,' replied the host, ' unless it be that I have a fig-tree which bears excellent figs, but I never can get one of them for myself; they are always stolen before I get them. I wish He would order that whoever goes up to steal them might get stuck to the tree till I tell him he may come down.'

' Well,' said St. Peter, ' it is an odd sort of thing to ask, but you might try ; He is very kind.'

The host did ask, and Jesus Christ granted his request. When St. Peter saw that He granted it so easily, he said, ' If I were you I should ask something more.'

' Do you really think I might?' answered the host. ' There is one thing I have wanted to ask all along, only I didn't dare. But you encourage me, and He seems to take a pleasure in giving. I have always had a great wish to live four hundred years.'

'That is certainly a great deal to ask,' said St. Peter, 'but you might try; He is very kind.'

The host did ask, and Jesus Christ granted his petition, and then went His way with His disciples. St. Peter remained last, and said to the host, 'Now run after him, and ask for the salvation of your soul.' ('St. Peter always told them all to ask that,' added the narrator in a confidential tone.)

'Oh, I can't ask anything more, I have asked so much,' said the host.

'But that is just the best thing of all, and what He grants the most willingly,' insisted St. Peter. 'Really?' said the host; and he ran after Jesus Christ, and said, 'Lord! who hast so largely shown me Thy bounty, grant me further the salvation of my soul.'

'Let it be granted!' said Jesus Christ; and continued His journey.

All the things the host had asked he received, and life, passed away very pleasantly, but still even four hundred years come to an end at last, and with the end of it came Death.

'What! is that you, Mrs. Death,[10] come already?' said the host.

'Why, it's time I should come, I think; it's not often I leave people in peace for four hundred years.'

'All right, but don't be in a hurry. I have such a fancy for the figs of that fig-tree of mine there: I wish you would just have the kindness to go up and pluck a good provision of them to take with me, and by that time I'll be ready to go with you.'

'I've no objection to oblige you so far,' said Mrs. Death; 'only you must mind and be quite ready by the time I do come back.'

'Never fear,' said the host; and Mrs. Death climbed up the fig-tree.

'Now stick there!' said the host, and for all her struggling Mrs. Death could by no means extricate herself any more.

'I can't stay here, so take off your spell; I have my business to attend to,' said she.

'So have I,' answered the host; 'and if you want to go about your business, you must promise me, on your honour, you will leave me to attend to mine.'

'I can't do it, my man! What are you asking? It's more than my place is worth. Every man alive has to pass through my hands. I can't let any of them off.'

'Well, at all events, leave me alone another four hundred years, and then I'll come with you. If you'll promise that, I'll let you out of the fig-tree.'

'I don't mind another four hundred years, if you so particularly wish for them; but mind you give me your word of honour you come then, without giving me all this trouble again.'

'Yes! and here's my hand upon it,' said the host, as he handed Mrs. Death down from the fig-tree.

And so he went on to live another four hundred years. ('For you know in those times men lived to a very great age,' was the running gloss of the narrator.)

The end of the second four hundred years came too, and then Mrs. Death appeared again. 'Remember your promise,' she said, 'and don't try any trick on me this time.'

'Oh, yes! I always keep my word,' said the host, and without more ado he went along with her.

As she was carrying him up to Paradise, they passed the way which led down to Hell, and at the opening sat the Devil, receiving souls which his ministers brought to him from all parts. He was marshalling them into ranks, and ticketing them ready to send off in batches to the distinct place for each.

'You seem to have got plenty of souls there, Mr.

Devil,' said the host.   'Suppose we sit down and play for
them?'

'I've no objection,' said the Devil.   'Your soul against
one of these.   If I win, you go with them ; if you win, one
of them goes with you.'

'That's it,' said the host, and picking out a nice-looking soul, he set him for the Devil's stake.

Of course the host won, and the nice-looking soul was
passed round to his side of the table.

'Shall we have another game?' said the host, quite
cock-a-hoop.

The Devil hesitated for a moment, but finally he
yielded.   The host picked out a soul that took his fancy,
for the Devil's stake, and they sat down to play again,
with the same result.

So they went on and on till the host had won fifteen
thousand souls of the Devil.   'Come,' said Death when
they had got as far as this, 'I really can't wait any
longer.   I never had to do with anyone who took up so
much time as you.   Come along!'

So the host bowed excuses to the Devil for having had
all the luck, and went cheerfully the way Mrs. Death
led, with all his fifteen thousand souls behind him.   Thus
they arrived at the gate of Paradise.   There wasn't so
much business going on there as at the other place, and
they had to ring before anyone appeared to open the door.

'Who's there?' said St. Peter.

'He of the four hundred years!'

'And what is all that rabble behind?' asked St. Peter.

'Souls that I have won of the Devil for Paradise,'
answered the host.

'Oh, that won't do at all, here!' said St. Peter.

'Be kind enough to carry the message up to your
Master,' responded the host.

St. Peter went up to Jesus Christ.   'Here is he to
whom you gave four hundred years of life,' he said;

*and he has brought fifteen thousand other souls, who have no title at all to Paradise, with him.'

' Tell him he may come in himself,' said Jesus Christ, ' but he has nothing to do to meddle with the others.'

' Tell Him to be pleased to remember that when He came to my eating-shop I never made any difficulty how many soever He brought with Him, and if He had brought an army I should have said nothing,' answered the host; and St. Peter took up that message too.

' That is true ! that is right ! ' answered Jesus Christ. ' Let them all in ! let them all in ! '

7

PRET' OLIVO.[11]

WHEN Jesus Christ was on earth, He lodged one night at a priest's house, and when He went away in the morning He offered to give His host, in reward for his hospitality, whatever he asked. What Pret' Olivo (for that was his host's name) asked for was that he should live a hundred years, and that when Death came to fetch him he should be able to give her what orders he pleased, and that she must obey him.

' Let it be granted ! ' said Jesus Christ.

A hundred years passed away, and then, one morning early, Death came.

' Pret' Olivo ! Pret Olivo ! ' cried Death, ' are you ready ? I'm come for you at last.'

' Let me say my mass first,' said Pret' Olivo; ' that's all.'

' Well, I don't mind that,' answered Death; ' only mind it isn't a long one, because I've got so many people to fetch to-day.'

' A mass is a mass,' answered Pret' Olivo; ' it will be neither longer nor shorter.'

As he went out, however, he told his servant to heap up a lot of wood on the hearth and set fire to it. Death went to sit down on a bench in the far corner of the chimney, and by-and-by the wood blazed up and she couldn't get away any more. In vain she called to the servant to come and moderate the fire. 'Master told me to heap it up, not to moderate it,' answered the servant; and so there was no help. Death continued calling in desperation, and nobody came. It was impossible with her dry bones to pass the blaze, so there she had to stay.

'Oh, dear! oh, dear! what can I do?' she kept saying; 'all this time everybody is stopped dying! Pret' Olivo! Pret' Olivo! come here.'

At last Pret' Olivo came in.

'What do you mean by keeping me here like this?' said Death; 'I told you I had so much to do.'

'Oh, you want to go, do you?' said Pret' Olivo, quietly.

'Of course I do. Tell some one to clear away those burning logs, and let me out.'

'Will you promise me to leave me alone for another hundred years if I do?'

'Yes, yes; anything you like. I shall be very glad to keep away from this place for a hundred years.'

Then he let her go, and she set off running with those long thin legs of hers.

The second hundred years came to an end.

'Are you ready, Pret' Olivo?' said Death one morning, putting her head in at the door.

'Pretty nearly,' answered Pret' Olivo. 'Meantime, just take that basket, and gather me a couple of figs to eat before I go.'

As she went away he said, 'Stick to the tree' (but not so that she could hear it); for you remember he had power given him to make her do what he liked. She had therefore to stick to the tree.

'Well, Lady Death, are you never going to bring those figs?' cried Pret' Olivo after a time.

'How can I bring them, when you know I can't get down from this tree? Instead of making game of me, come and take me down.'

'Will you leave me alone another hundred years if I do?'

'Yes, yes; anything you like. Only make haste and let me go.'

The third hundred years came to an end, and Death appeared again. 'Are you ready this time, Pret' Olivo?' she cried out as she approached.

'Yes, this time I'll come with you,' answered Pret' Olivo. Then he vested himself in the Church vestments, and put a cope on, and took a pack of cards in his hand, and said to Death, 'Now take me to the gate of Hell, for I want to play a game of cards with the Devil.'

'Nonsense!' answered Death. 'I'm not going to waste my time like that. I've got orders to take you to Paradise, and to Paradise you must go.'

'You know you've got orders to obey whatever I tell you,' answered Pret' Olivo; and Death knew that was true, so she lost no more time in disputing, but took him all the way round by the gate of Hell.

At the gate of Hell they knocked.

'Who's there?' said the Devil.

'Pret' Olivo,' replied Death.

'Out with you, ugly priest!' said the Devil. 'I'm surprised at you, Death, making game of me like that; you know that's not the sort of ware for my market.'[12]

'Silence, and open the door, ugly Pluto![13] I'm not come to stay. I only want to have a game of cards with you. Here's my soul for stake on my side, against the last comer on your side,' interposed Pret' Olivo.

Pret' Olivo won the game, and hung the soul on to his cope.

'We must have another game,' said the Devil.

'With all my heart!' replied Pret' Olivo; and he won

another soul. Another and another he won, and his cope was covered all over with the souls clinging to it.

Meantime, Death thought it was going on rather too long, so she looked through the keyhole, and, finding they were just beginning another game, she cried out loudly;

' It's no use playing any more, for I'm not going to be bothered to carry all those souls all the way up to Heaven —a likely matter, indeed !'

But Pret' Olivo went on playing without taking any notice of her; and he hung them on to his beretta, till at last you could hardly see him at all for the number of souls he had clinging to him. There was no place for any more, so at last he stopped playing.

' I'm not going to take all those other souls,' said Death when he came out; ' I've only got orders to take you.'

' Then take me,' answered Pret' Olivo.

Death saw that the souls were all hung on so that she could not take him without taking all the rest; so away she went with the lot of them, without disputing any more.

At last they arrived at the Gate of Paradise. St. Peter opened the door when they knocked; but when he saw who was there he shut the door again.

' Make haste !' said Death ; ' I've no time to waste.'

' Why did you waste your time in bringing up souls that were not properly consigned to you ? ' answered St. Peter.

' It wasn't I brought them, it was Pret' Olivo. And your Master charged me I was to do whatever he told me.'

' My Master ! Oh, then, I'm out of it,' said St. Peter. ' Only wait a minute, while I just go and ask Him whether it is so.' St. Peter ran to ask; and receiving an affirmative answer, came back and opened the gate, and they all got in.

8

DOMINE QUO VADIS.

'You know, of course, about St. Peter, when they put him in the prisons here; he found a way of escaping through the "catacomboli," and just as he had got out into the open road again he met Jesus Christ coming towards him carrying His cross. And St. Peter asked Him what he was doing going into the "catacomboli." But Jesus Christ answered, "I am not going into the 'catacomboli' to stay; I am going back by the way you came to be crucified over again, since you refuse to die for the flock." Then St. Peter turned and went all the way back, and was crucified with his head downwards, for he said he was not worthy to die in the same way as his Master.'

[Counterparts of these stories abound in the collections of all countries; in the Norse, and Gaelic, and Russian, more of the pagan element seems to stick to them. In Grimm's are some with both much and little of it. From Tirol I have given two, which are literally free from it, in 'Household Stories from the Land of Hofer;' and I have one or two picked up for me by a friend in Brittany, of which the same may be said. On the other hand, we meet them again in another form in that large group of strange compounds, of which 'Il Rè Moro,' p. 97, &c., are the Roman representatives, and 'Marienkind,' pp. 7–12, 'Grimm Kinder und Hausmährchen,' ed. 1870, the link between them. In the minds of the Roman narrators, however, I am quite clear no such connexion exists. See also p. 207 *infra*.

One of the quaintest legends of this class is given in Scheible's 'Schaltjahr.' It is meant for a charm to drive away wolves.]

> 'Lord Jesus Christ and St. Peter went in the morning out.
> As our Lady went on before she said (turning about),
> " Ah, dear Lord! whither must we go in and out?
> We must over hill and dale (roundabout).
> May God guard the while my flock (devout).
> Let not St. Peter go his keys without;
> But take them and lock up the wild dogs' * snout,
> That they no bone of them all may flout."'

---

* 'Holzhund,' I suppose, is used for wild dog.

[1] The Holy Babe.

[2] 'Date mi un po' d'allogio ;' *lit.*, Give me a small quantity of lodging —a humble mode of expression.

[3] 'Chi è ?' ('Who's there'); but the humour of the expression here lies in its being the invariable Roman custom to sing out 'Chi è ?' and wait till 'Amici !' is answered, before any door is opened.

[4] Comp. with Legend of the Marmolata in 'Household Stories from the land of Hofer.'

[5] 'Un pagnotto di polenta' was the expression used, meaning a great coarse loaf of Indian corn. The Roman poor have much the same contempt for inferior bread that we meet with in the same class at home, none eat 'seconds' who can possibly avoid it; but the pagnotto di polenta is only eaten by the poorest peasants.

[6] 'Strutto,' lard, enters into the composition of almost every Roman popular dish.

[7] 'Che bolliva,' constantly applied in Roman parlance to solids as well as liquids.

[8] The narrator was an admirable reciter, and as she uttered this 'Vi sia concessa,' in a solemn and majestic manner, she raised her hand and made the sign of the cross with a rapid and facile gesture, just as she might have seen the Pope do as he drove through Rome.

[9] 'Trattoria,' can only be translated by 'tavern,' but unfortunately the English word represents quite a different idea from the Roman. 'Tavern' suggests noise and riot, but a 'trattoria' is a place where a poor Roman will take his family to dine quietly with him on a festa as a treat.

[10] 'Death,' being feminine in Italian, has to be personified as a woman. The same occurs in a Spanish counterpart of this story which I have given under the title of 'Starving John the Doctor' in 'Patrañas.' The Spanish counterpart of the rest of the story will be found in 'Where one can dine two can dine' ('Un Convidado invida a ciento') in the same series.

[11] 'Olive the priest.' 'When we were children,' said the narrator, 'my father used to tell us such a lot of stories of an evening, but of them all the two we used to ask for most, again and again, and the only two I remember, were " Mi butto," and "Pret' Olivo." Do you know "Mi butto"? We used to shudder at it, and yet we used to ask for it.' I incautiously admitted I did know it, instead of acquiring a fresh version. 'Then here is "Pret' Olivo." I don't suppose I was more than seven then, and now I am thirty-five, and I have never heard it since, but I'll make the best I can of it. Of course it is not a true story ; we knew that it *couldn't* be true, as anyone can see; but it used to interest us children.'

[12] 'Vaene brutto prete ! Questa non è roba per me.'

[13] 'Brutto Plutone !' The traditional application of the name will not have escaped the reader.

PIETRO BAILLIARDO.[1]

1

WHAT! Never heard of Pietro Bailliardo! Surely you must, if you ever heard anything at all. Why, everybody knows about Pietro Bailliardo! Why, he was here and there and everywhere in Rome; and turned everybody's head, and they have his books now, that they took away from him, locked up in the Holy Office.[2]

Pietro Bailliardo was a scholar boy, and went to school like other boys. One day he found at a bookstall a book of divination;[3] with this he was able to do whatever he would, and wherever he was, there the Devil was in command.

He fell in love with a girl, and she would have nothing to do with him; and one day afterwards they found her on Mont Cavallo with a great fire burning round her, and everyone who passed had to stir the fire whether he would or not.

Whatever he wanted he ordered to come and it came to him, and nobody could resist him.

As to putting him in prison it was no manner of use. One day when they had put him in prison he took a piece of charcoal and drew a boat on the white prison wall, then he jumped into it, and said to all the other prisoners, ' Get in too,' and they got in, and he rowed away, and next morning they were all loose about Rome. But there was an old man asleep in a corner of the prison, and the guards came to him and said, ' Where are all the prisoners gone?' And he told them about Pietro Bailliardo drawing the boat on the prison wall with the charcoal and their all getting away in it. ' And why didn't you go too?' asked the guards. ' Because I was asleep so comfortably I did not want to move,' said he. ('But then, how did he see it all unless Pietro Bailliardo had him put under a spell on purpose that he might tell the authorities how he had defied them ?' added the narrator.)

Another time again they shut him up in prison, and the next morning when they came to look for him they found nothing but an ass's head in his place, which he had left there just to show his contempt for them.

One day a zealous friar met him and warned him to repent. 'What have I to repent of?' said he. 'I can hear mass better than you, for I can hear mass in three places at once.' Then he went away and made the Devil take him to Constantinople and Paris to hear mass at each while all at one and the same time he was hearing one at Rome too! Then he came and told the friar what a grand thing he had done. But the friar told him it was worse than not hearing mass at all to attempt to use diabolical arts in that way.

After that one day he was going up past the church of SS. John and Paul⁴ when the Devil met him.

'Now,' said the Devil, 'you have had your swing long enough; I have come to fetch you!'

When Pietro Bailliardo, who had set all the world at defiance all his life, saw the Devil and heard him say he had come to fetch him, he was seized with such terror that he began to repent, and ran inside the church. The Devil durst not follow him thither, but waited outside thinking he would soon be turned out.

But Pietro Bailliardo took up a great stone and went and kneeled down before the crucifix and smote his bare breast with the big stone, saying the while, 'Behold! merciful Lord, I beat my breast with this stone till Thou bow Thy head in token that Thou forgive me.'

And he went on beating his breast till the blood ran down, and at last our Lord had compassion on him and bowed His head from the cross to him, and he died there. So the Devil did not get him.

2

'You have told me so many stories, why have you never told me anything about Pietro Bailliardo—don't you know about him?'

'Of course I know about him. Who in Rome doesn't know about him? but I can't remember it all. I know he had the book of divination, and could make the Devil do whatever he chose by its means. And then one day, I don't remember by what circumstance, he was led to do penance; but he would do it in his own way, not in the right way, and he made a vow to the Madonna that he would pay a visit to some shrine in Rome and to S. Giacomo di Galizia,[5] and to the *Santa Casa di Loreto* all in the same night. As devils can fly through the air at a wonderful pace he called upon a devil by his divining book and told him what he wanted; then he got on the back of the devil and rode away through the air and actually visited all three in one night.

'But that sort of penance was no penance at all. After that he did penance in right earnest at some church, I forget which.'

'Was it SS. John and Paul?' I asked.

'Yes, to be sure; SS. John and Paul. And you knew it all the time, and yet have been asking me!'

3

'Do you want to know about Pietro Bailliardo too?' said the old man who had given me No. 2 of San Giovanni *Bocca d'oro.* 'Oh, yes; I did know a deal about him. This is what I can remember.

'Pietro Bailliardo had a bond [6] with the Devil, by which he was as rich as he could be, and had whatever he wanted; but the day came when the compact came to an end, and Pietro Bailliardo quailed as that day approached, for he knew that after that time the Devil could take him and he could not resist.

'Before noon on that day, therefore, he set out to go to St. Paul's.'

'To SS. John and Paul?' asked I, full of the former versions.

'No, no! to the great St. Paul's outside the walls, where the monks of St. Benedict are; and he waited there all day, for before the time was out the Devil couldn't take him. At last evening came on, and the chierico [7] wanted to shut the church up; so he told Pietro Bailliardo he must go, and showed him to the door. But when he came to the door, he found the Devil there waiting for him dressed like a paino.[8] When he saw that, no power of the chierico could make him go; so the chierico was obliged to call the Father Abbot.

'To the Father Abbot Pietro Bailliardo told his whole story, and the Father Abbot said, "If that is so, come with me to the Inquisition, and tell your story there and receive absolution." Then he sent for a carriage, and said to the driver, "Be of good heart, for I have many relics of saints with me, and whatever strange thing you may see or hear by the way, have no fear, it shall not harm you."

'The Devil saw all this, and was in a great fury, for he has no power to alter future events, and so he couldn't help Pietro Bailliardo going into the church for sanctuary before the time was up. He got a number of devils together, therefore, and made unearthly and terrible noises all the way. But the driver had confidence in the word of the Abbot, and drove on without heeding. Only when they got to the bridge of St. Angelo the noise was so tremendous he got quite bewildered; moreover the bridge heaved and rocked as though it were going to break in twain.

'"Fear nothing, fear nothing! Nothing will harm you," said the Father Abbot; and the driver, having confidence in his words, drove on without heeding, and they arrived safely at the Palace of the Inquisition.

'The Father Abbot now delivered Pietro Bailliardo over to the Penitentiary, to whom, moreover, he made confession of his terrible crimes, and begged to remain to perform his penance and obtain reconciliation with God.

'But as Pietro Bailliardo had been used to follow his own strange ways all his life, he must needs now perform his penance too in his own strange way. Therefore he made a vow that he would perform such a penance as man never performed before ; and this penance was to visit, all in one night, the SS. Crocifisso in the Chapel of the Holy Office, S. Giacomo di Galizia, and the sanctuary of Cirollo. All in one night!'

'Stop! S. Giacomo di Galizia I know; we call it S. James of Compostella ; but the sanctuary of Cirollo! I never heard of that ; where is it?'

'Oh, Cirollo is all the same as if you said Loreto; the Madonna di Loreto ; it is all one.'

I appealed to one sitting there who, I knew, had been brought up at Loreto.

'Yes, yes,' she said. 'That is all right; Cirollo is just a walk from Loreto. *Noi altri* when living at Loreto often go there, but those who come from far, most often don't ; so we have a saying, " Who goes to Loreto and not to Cirollo, he sees the mother, but not the son." [9] 'It is a saying, and nothing more.'

'*Basta !*' interposed the old man, who, like other old people, was apt to forget the thread of his story if interrupted. '*Basta!* it doesn't matter: they were anyhow three places very far apart.[10] So Pietro Bailliardo, who couldn't get out of his habit of commanding the devils, called up a number of them, and said, " Which of all you fiends can go the fastest?" and the devils, accustomed to obey him, answered the one before the other, some one way some another, each anxious to content him : " I, like lightning," said one ; " I, like the wind," said another ; but " I —I can go as fast as thought," [11] said another. " Ho! Here!

O

You fiend. You, who can travel as fast as thought. You come here, and take me to-night to St. James of Compostella, and to the sanctuary of Cirollo, and bring me back here to the Chapel of the Holy Office before morning breaks."

'He spoke imperiously, and sprang on to the devil's back, and all was done so quickly the devil had no time for thought or hesitation.

'Away flew the devil, and Pietro Bailliardo on his back, all the way to St. James of Compostella, and, whr-r-r-r all the way to the sanctuary of Cirollo, fast, fast as thought. Then suddenly the devil stopped midway. An idea had struck him. "What had a devil to do with going about visiting shrines in this way; no harm had been done to the sacred place; not a stone had been injured;[12] why then had they gone to S. Giacomo; why were they going to Cirollo?"

'"Tell me, Ser Bailliardo," said he, "on whose account am I sweating like this? is it for your private account, or for my master's; because I only obey you so long as you command in his name, and how can it serve him to be doing pilgrim's work?"

'"Go on, ugly monster! don't prate,"[13] answered Pietro Bailliardo, and gave him at the same time a kick in each flank; and such was his empire over him that the devil durst say no more, and completed the strange pilgrimage even as he had commanded.[14]

'Thus even in his penitence Pietro Bailliardo had the devils subject to him. But after that he did penance in right good earnest, only he chose a strange way of his own again.

'He knelt before the Crucifix in the Chapel of the Inquisition, and he took a great stone and beat his breast with it and said, "Lord, behold my repentance; I smite my breast thus till Thou forgive me." And when the blood flowed down the Lord had compassion on him and bowed His head upon the cross and said, " I have forgiven thee ! "

' After that he died in peace.'

[1] Unquestionably a very exaggerated tradition of the aberrations and final submission to the Church of Abelard (Pietro Abelardo in Italian), some of whose writings were publicly burnt in Rome by the Inquisition in 1140.

[2] The Office of the Inquisition behind the Colonnade of St. Peter's.

[3] ' Libro di comando.' A book of divination.

[4] St. John and Paul. The Church of the Passionists on the Cœlian.

[5] I.e. St. Iago di Compostella.

[6] ' Scrittura,' a written compact.

[7] ' Chierico ' of course means a cleric, but in common parlance it is reserved for the boy who, though lay, wears a clerical dress for the time he is serving mass, or attending to the church generally. In the present instance it would probably be a youth in minor orders.

[8] ' Paino ' and ' paina ' mean one, who, according to his or her condition, ought to be dressed in the national style, but who does affect to dress like a gentleman or lady.

[9]
'Chi va a Loreto
E non va a Cirollo,
Vede la Madre
E non vede il figliuolo.'

[10] I took another opportunity of asking the one who was familiar with Loreto, about Cirollo, and she explained its introduction into the story to mean that he was not to pay a hasty visit, but a thorough one, even though it was done so rapidly. ' Cirollo,' she said, ' is a poor village with few houses, but the church is fine, and the Crucifix is reckoned *miracolosissimo.*' In Murray's map it is marked as Sirollo, close by the sea, without even a pathway from Loreto, about five miles to the north ; and he does not mention the place at all in his text.

Subsequently I was talking with another who called herself a Marchegiana, i.e. from the March of Ancona, in which Loreto is situated, and boasted of having been born at Sinigallia, the birthplace of Pio Nono. ' Have you ever been to Loreto?' I asked by way of beginning inquiry about Cirollo.

' Yes ; six times I have made the pilgrimage from Sinigallia, and always on foot,' she replied with something of enthusiasm. ' And you who have travelled so far, you have been there too, of course ? '

' Not yet,' I replied ; ' but I mean to go one day ;' and just as I was coming to my question about Cirollo, she added of her own accord :

' Mind you do, and mind when you go you go to Sirollo too (she pronounced it Sirollo like the spelling in the map). ' Everyone who goes to Loreto ought to go to Sirollo. There is a Crucifix there which is *miracolosissimo.*'

[11] ' Quanto la mente dell' uomo.'

[12] ' Dispetto,' an affront, rather than an injury.

[13] ' Tira via, brutta bestia,' literally ' fire away '—is used in all senses the same as in English.

[14] The question of night flights through the air, and more, whether in the body or out of the body, than whether they were ever effected at all, was one of the most hotly contested questions of demonographers. Tartarotti, lib. I. cap. viii. § vi., winds up a long account of the subject with the following :—' . . . So divided was opinion on the subject, not only of Catholics as against heterodox, but between Catholics and Catholics, that after reading in Delrio ' qui hæc asserunt somnia esse et ludibrio certe peccant contra reverentiam Ecclesiæ matri debitam,' and ' Hæc opinio (somnia hæc esse) tanquam hæretica est reprobanda ;' and in Bartolomeo Spina, ' Negare quod diabolus possit portare homines de loco in locum est hæreticum ;' you may see in Emmanuel Rodriguez, a great theologian and canonist, ' Peccat mortaliter qui credit veneficos aut veneficas vel striges corporaliter per aëra vehi ad diversa loca, ut illi existimant ;' while Navarro mildly says, ' Credere quod aliquando, licet raro, dæmon aliquis de loco in locum, Deo permittente, transportet non est peccatum.'

Tartarotti supplies a long list of writers who, in the course of the sixteenth and two following centuries, took the opposite sides on this question, and quotes from Dr. John Weir, (Protestant) physician to the Duke of Cleves (In Apol. sec. iv. p. 582), that the Protestants were most numerous on the side which maintained that it was an actual and corporeal and not a mental or imaginative transaction. Cesare Cantù has likewise given an exposition of the treatment of the question in ' Gli Eretici d'Italia,' discorso xxxiii., and ' Storia Universale,' epoca xv. cap. 14, p. 488. In note 1 he gives a list of a dozen of the most celebrated Protestant writers who upheld the actuality of the witches' congress.

S. GIOVANNI BOCCA D'ORO.

1

St. John of the Golden Mouth was another famous penitent we had here in Rome. He had treated a number of young girls shamefully, and then killed them.

But one day the grace of God touched him, and he went out into the Campagna, to a solitary place, and there, with a wattle of rushes, he made himself a hut, and lived there doing penance far, far away from any human habitation.

One day a king, and his wife, and his sons, and his daughter all went out to hunt. They got overtaken by a storm, and separated ; some hasted home in one direction, and some in another, but the daughter they could not find anywhere, and when they had searched everywhere for many days and could not find her, they gave her up for lost.

But she, as she was running, had seen the hut of St. John of the Golden Mouth, and knocked at the door.

'Begone !' shouted the penitent, thinking it was the Devil come to tempt him.

But she continued knocking.

'Begone ! Out into the wild ! nor disturb my peace, Evil One !' shouted he again.

'I am not the Evil One,' answered the princess ; 'I am only a woman ; I have lost my way, and crave shelter from the storm.'

When he heard that, he got up and let her in ; but when he saw her, he could not resist treating her as he had treated the other maidens. Then he killed her, and threw her body into a well.

But the next day, when he came to think of what he had done, he said to himself,

'How is it possible that I, who have come here to do penance for my crimes, should out here, even in my penitential hut, commit the same crime again? I must go further from temptation, and do deeper penance yet.'

So he left the shelter of his hut, and all his clothes, and went into the wild country and lived with the wild beasts, and became like one of them. After many years he grew quite accustomed to go on all fours, and his body was all covered with hair like a lion's, and he lost the use of speech.

Then, one day the same king went out hunting. Suddenly there was a great cry of the dogs. They had found an animal of which the huntsmen had never seen the like before. So strange was it, that they said, we must not kill it, but must bring it to the king. With much difficulty they whipped the dogs off, and they brought it to the king, so like a four-footed creature had San Giovanni Bocca d'oro grown.

Neither could the king make out what kind of creature it was; so he told the huntsmen to put a chain on it, and bring it to the palace.

When they got home to the palace, everyone was astonished at the appearance of the creature the huntsmen had with them, and they called out with such loud exclamations that the queen, who was ill in bed, heard them, and she asked what it was about. When they told her, she was seized with a violent desire to see the creature. But they said she must by no means see it, being ill; but the more they opposed her wish, the more vehement she was to see it, till, at last, the nurses said it would do more harm to continue refusing her than to let her see it.

So they led the creature by the chain into her room, and placed him by her bedside.

When the queen saw him, she said, 'This is no four-footed beast, but a man, like one of you.' And she spoke to him, and asked him to say who he was; but he had lost the use of speech, and could not answer her.

Then the baby that was lying on the pillow by her side, just born, raised its head, and said out loud, so that all could hear, in a voice plain and clear—

'GIOVANNI BOCCA D'ORO, GOD HATH FORGIVEN THEE THY SINS AND INIQUITIES.'

The queen was yet more astonished when she heard her new-born babe speak thus, and she asked St. John what it could mean. When she saw he could not answer her, she ordered that they should give him pen and paper.

Then, though they gave him a common pen, all he wrote appeared in letters of shining gold, and he wrote down all that I have told you. Moreover, he bid them send to the well where he had thrown the body of the princess, and fetch her back.

When they had done so, they found her whole and sound, and only a little cicatriced wound in her throat. Then they asked her in astonishment how she had lived in that dark, damp well all these years.

But she answered, 'Every day there came to me a beautiful Roman matron in shining apparel, and she brought me food and consoled me, and after she had been there the well was bright, and sweet, and perfumed.' And they knew that it must have been the Madonna.

As soon as she was thus restored to her parents, and had declared these things, San Giovanni Bocca d'oro died in peace, for God had forgiven him.

2

'Ah! I knew so many of those things once, but now they are all gone, all gone.' This was said by a fine old man, who boasted of having the same number of years and the same name as the Pope.

'I dare say you can tell me something about San Giovanni Bocca d'oro, however,' I said.

'San Giovanni Bocca d'oro! Of course. Everybody in Rome knows about San Giovanni Bocca d'oro. Do you want to know about him? That's not a story; that's a fact.'

'Yes, all you know about him I want to hear.'

'It's a long story—too long to remember.'

'Never mind, tell me all you can recall.'

'San Giovanni Bocca d'oro lived in a village—'

'Not in Rome, then!' interposed I.

'Yes, yes, one of the villages about Rome; I don't remember now which, if I ever knew, but about Rome of course. One day he saw a beautiful peasant girl, and fell in love with her. But he behaved very ill to her and never married her, and afterwards killed her and threw her body into a well.

'Afterwards a great sorrow came upon him for what he had done, and he was so ashamed of his sin that he said he would remain no more to pollute other Christians with his presence, but went out into the Campagna and lived like a four-footed beast; and made a vow that he would remain with his face towards the earth[1] until such time as God should be pleased to let him know, by the mouth of a little child, that His wrath was appeased.

'Many years passed, and San Giovanni continued his penance without wearying, always on all fours.

'One day, the nurse of some emperor or king was out with the little child she had charge of when a storm came on, and they ran and lost their way. Thus running, they came upon San Giovanni in his penance. He looked so wild and strange the nurse would have run away from him, but the child held out its arms towards him without being at all frightened, and, although so young that it had never spoken, cried aloud, "Giovanni, get up, God hath forgiven thee!"

'At this voice all the people gathered round, and they took him back to the village; and he went straight to the well and blessed it, and there rose out of it, all whole and fresh, the maiden whom he had killed.

'Then he sent for pen and tablet, for he had lost the use of speech, and wrote down all that had befallen him; and as he wrote all the letters became gold. That is why he is called San Giovanni Bocca d'oro.

'And when he had written all these things he died in peace.'

3

In another version he was living an ordinary life in his 'villa,' not in a penitential cell, when the king's daughter lost her way at the hunt. After the crime he was seized with compunction, and went out into the Campagna, living only on the herbs he could gather with his mouth, like an animal, and vowing that he would never again raise his head to Heaven till God gave him some token that He had forgiven him.

After eight years the king found him when out hunting, and, taking him for some kind of beast, put him in the stables. The little prince who was just born was taken by to the church to be baptised about this time; and, as they carried him back past the stables, he said aloud, 'Rise, Giovanni, for God hath forgiven thy sins.' Every one was very much astonished to hear him speak, and they sent for Giovanni and asked him to explain what it meant.

The rest as in the other versions.

[1] 'Bocca a terra.'

[I have repeatedly come across this story, but without any material variation from one or other of the versions already given. It would be curious to trace how St. John Chrysostom's name ever became connected with it. Though famous for his penitential life as much as for his eloquence, and though the four years he passed in the cells of the Antiochian cenobites were austere enough, yet his memory is stained by no sort of crime. So far from it, he was most carefully brought up by a widowed mother, whose exemplary virtues are said to have occasioned the exclamation from the Saint's master, 'What wonderful women have these Christians!'—Butler's 'Lives.' There is something like its termination in that of 'The Fiddler in Hell.'—Ralston's 'Russian Folk Tales,' pp. 299, 300. The years of voluntary silence, and the finding of the silent person by a king out hunting, enter into many tales otherwise of another class, as in 'Die Zwölf Brüder' (the Twelve Brothers), Grimm, p. 37, and 'Die Sechs Schwäne' (the Six Swans), p. 191.]

DON GIOVANNI.

WE had another Giovanni who had done worse things
even than these, and who never became a penitent at all.
Don Giovanni he was called.   Everybody in Rome knew
him by the name of Don Giovanni.

Among the other bad things he did, he killed a great
man who was called the Commendatore; and though he
had the crime of murder on his conscience he took no
account of it, but swaggered about with an air of bravado
as if he cared for no one.

One day when he was walking out in the Campagna
he saw a great white skeleton coming to meet him.   It
was the skeleton of the commendatore whom he had killed.

'How dy'e do?' said Don Giovanni, with effrontery.
'There's an Accademia[1] to-night at my house, I shall be
very happy to see you at it;' and he took off his hat with
mock gravity.

'I will certainly come,' replied the commendatore in
a sepulchral voice; but Don Giovanni burst out laughing.

In the midst of the Accademia some one knocked.
'All the guests are arrived,' said the servant, 'yet some
one knocks.'

'Never mind, open!' replied Don Giovanni, carelessly.
'Let him in whoever it is.'

The servant went to open, and came running back to
say he could not let the new guest in because he was only
the miller, who had come in his white coat all over flour.

All soon saw, however, that the guest was not the miller,
though he looked so white.   For it was the white skeleton
of the commendatore; and it followed the servant into
the room.   Then fear seized on all and they ran away to
hide themselves; some behind the door, some behind
the curtains, and some under the table.

Don Giovanni stood alone in the middle of the room

with his usual effrontery, and held out his hand to the skeleton.

'Repent thee!'[2] said the White Skeleton, solemnly.

'A cavalier like me doesn't repent like common beggars!' replied Don Giovanni, scornfully.

'Repent!' again repeated the White Skeleton, with more awful emphasis.

'I have something much more amusing to do!' replied Don Giovanni, with a laugh.

'Don Giovanni!' cried the White Skeleton, the third time yet more solemnly. 'Though you took away my life yet am I come to save your soul, if I may, and therefore I say again, Repent! or beware of what is to follow.'

'Well done, old fellow! very generous of you!' said Don Giovanni, with a mocking laugh, and again holding out his hand.

They were his last words. The next minute he gave an awful yell which might have been heard all over Rome. The White Skeleton had disappeared, and the Devil had come in his place, and had taken Don Giovanni by his extended hand and dragged him off.

[1] 'Accademia' used here for 'Conversazione.'
[2] 'Pentiti!'

[Tullio Dandolo, 'Monachismo e Leggende' p. 314-5, quotes a similar legend from Passavanti, ' Specchio della vera Penitenza.' The story of Don Giovanni's misdeeds brought up in the narrator's mind those of Pepe (Giuseppe) Mastrilo, famous in the annals of both Spanish and Italian bandits. It was, however, only a story of violence and crime without point.]

THE PENANCE OF SAN GIULIANO.

'CAN you tell me the story of San Giovanni Bocca d'oro?'

'Of course I know about San Giovanni Bocca d'oro, that is, I know he was a great penitent, but I couldn't re-

member anything, not to tell you about him. But I
know about another great penitent. Do you know about
the Penitence of San Giuliano? *That* is a story you'll
like if you don't know it already; but it's not a *favola*,
mind.'

'I know there are seven or eight saints at least of the
name of Julian, but I don't know the acts of them all; so
pray tell me your story.'

'Here it is then.

'San Giuliano was the only son of his parents, who
lived at Albano. In his youth he was rather wild,[1]
and gave his parents some anxiety; but what gave them
more anxiety still on his account was that an astrologer
had predicted that when he grew up he should kill both
his parents.

'"It is not only for our lives," said the parents, "that
we should be concerned—that is no such great matter;
but we must put him out of the way of committing so
great a crime."

'Therefore they gave him a horse, and his portion of
money, and told him to ride forth and make himself a
home in another place. So San Giuliano went forth; and
thirty years passed, and his parents heard no more of
him. Thirty years is a long time; many things pass
out of mind in thirty years. Thus the astrologer's pre-
diction passed out of their minds; but what never passes
out of the mind of a mother is the love of her child, and
the mother of San Giuliano yearned to see him after thirty
years as though he had gone away but yesterday.

'One day when they were walking in the woods about
Albano they saw a little boy come and climb into a tree
and take a bird's nest; and presently, after the little boy
was gone away with the nest, the parent birds came back
and fluttered all about, and uttered piercing cries for the
loss of their young.

'"See!" said San Giuliano's mother, taking occasion

by this example, "how these unreasoning creatures care for the loss of their young, and we live away from our only son and are content."

' "By no means are we content," replied the father; " let us therefore rise now and go seek him."

' So they put on pilgrims' weeds, and wandered forth to seek their son. On and on they went till they came to a place, a city called Galizia; [2] and there, as they walk along weary, they meet a gentle lady, who looks upon them mildly and compassionately, and says, "Whence do you come, poor pilgrims? what a long way you must have travelled!" [3]

' And they, cheered by her mode of address and sympathy, make answer, "We have wandered over mountains and plains. We come from the mountain town of Albano. We go about seeking our son Giuliano." [4]

' "Giuliano!" exclaimed the lady, "is the name of my husband. Just now he is out hunting, but come in with me and receive my hospitality for love of his name." She took them home and washed their feet, and refreshed them, and set food before them, and ultimately gave them her own bed to sleep in.

' But the Devil came to Giuliano out hunting, and tempted him with jealous thoughts about his wife, and tormented him with all manner of calumnious insinuations, so that his mind was filled with fury. Coming home hunting-knife in hand, he rushed into the bedroom, and seeing two forms in bed, without waiting to know who they were, he plunged his knife into them, and killed them.

' Thus, without knowing it, he had killed both his father and his mother.

' Coming out of the room he met his wife, who came to seek him to welcome him.

' "What, you here!" he cried. "Who then are those in the bed, whom I have killed?"

' "Killed !" replied the wife, " they were a pilgrim couple to whom I gave hospitality for love of you, because they wandered seeking a son named Giuliano." Then Giuliano knew what he had done, and was seized with penitence for his hasty yielding to suspicion and anger. So stricken with sorrow was he, he was as one dead, nor could anyone move him to speak. Then his wife came to him and said, " We will do penance together ; we will lay aside ease and riches, and will devote ourselves to the poor and needy."

' And he embraced her and said, " It is well spoken."

' Near where they lived was a rapid river, and no bridge, and many were drowned in attempting to cross it, and many had a weary way to walk to find a bridge. Said Giuliano, " We will build a bridge over the river." And many pilgrims came to Galizia who had not where to rest. Said Giuliano, " We will build a hospice for poor pilgrims, where they may be received and be tended according to their needs, till God forgives me."

' So they set forth, Giuliano and his wife, to go to Rome to find workmen.⁵ But as they went, a troop met them, and came round them, and said to them, " Where are you going ? "

' " We go to Rome," answered Giuliano, " to find workmen to build a bridge."

' " We are your men, we are your men ; for we have built many bridges ere now."⁶

' Then Giuliano took them back with him, and all in two days they built the bridge.

' " How can this be ? " said Giuliano's wife ; " here is something that is not right," for she was so holy that she discerned the Evil One was in it.

' " Be sure, Giuliano," she said, " there is some snare here. Take, therefore, a cheese, hard and round, and roll it along the bridge,⁷ and send our dog after it ; if they get across, well and good."

'Giuliano, always prone to accept his wife's prudent counsel, did as she bid him, and rolled the cheese along the bridge, and sent the dog after it; and, see! no sooner were they in the middle of the bridge than the bridge sank in; and they knew that the Devil had built it, and that it was no bridge for Christians to go over.

'Then said Giuliano, "God has not forgiven me yet. Now, let us build the hospice."

'They set out, therefore, to go to Rome to find workmen to build the hospice; and when the troop of demons came round them, saying, "We are your workmen, we are your workmen!" they paid them no heed, but went on to Rome, and fetched workmen thence, and the hospice was built; and all the pilgrims who came they received, and gave them hospitality, and the whole house was full of pilgrims.

'Then, when the house was full, quite full of pilgrims, there came an old man, and begged admission. "Good man," said Giuliano's wife, "it grieves my heart to say so, but there is not a bed, nor so much as an empty corner left;" and the old man said:

'"If ye cannot receive me, it is because ye have done so much charity to me already; therefore take this staff:" so he gave them his pilgrim's staff, and went his way.

'But it was Jesus Christ who came in the semblance of that old man; and when Giuliano took the staff, behold three flowers blossomed on it, and he said:

'"See! God has forgiven me!"'

---

[1] 'Discolo,' 'wild,' 'fast.'

[2] The shrine of S. Iago di Compostella being traditionally known to the Roman poor as 'S. Giacomo di Galizia,' Galizia was not very unnaturally supposed by the narrator to be the name of a town.

[3]   'Dovene siete, poveri pellegrini,
        Quanti son' lunghi i vostri cammini?'

[4]   'Avemo camminati monti e piani,
        E siamo di Castello mont' Albano,
        Andiamo cercando un figlio Giuliano.'

A walled village, whether it had an actual castle or not, had the name of 'Castello;' and 'Castello' is the common name to the present day in Rome for the villages in the neighbourhood.

⁵ 'Mastri.'

⁶　　　　　'Noi siamo i mastri! noi siamo i mastri!
　　　　　Chè tanti ponti abbiamo fatti.'

⁷ 'Arruzzicatelo' was the word used. Ruzzica is a game played by rolling circles of wood of a certain thickness along a smooth alley. She tells him to roll the cheese in this way as an inducement to the dog to go over to try the strength of the bridge.

[Now I see this story in type I am inclined to think it is not strictly traditional, like the rest; but that the narrator had acquired it from one of the rimed legends mentioned at p. vii..]

THE PILGRIMS.

THERE was a husband and wife, who had been married two or three years, and had no children. At last, they made a vow to S. Giacomo di Galizia that if they only had two children, one boy and one girl, even if no more than that, they would be so grateful that they would go a pilgrimage to his shrine, all the way to Galizia.

In due time two children were born to them, a boy and a girl, who were twins; and they were full of gladness and rejoicing, and devoted themselves to the care of their children, but they forgot all about their vow. When many years were passed, and the children were, it maybe, fifteen or sixteen years old, they dreamed a dream, both husband and wife in one night, that St. James appeared, and said:

'You made a vow to visit my shrine if you had two children. Two children have been born to you, and you have not kept your vow; most certainly evil will overtake you for your broken word. Behold, time is given you; but if now you fulfil not your vow, both your children will die.'

In the morning the wife told the dream to the husband, and the husband told the dream to the wife, and they said to each other, ' This is no common dream; we must look to it.' So they bought pilgrims' dresses, and went to 'Galizia,' the husband, and wife, and the son; but concerning the daughter they said, ' The maiden is of too tender years for this journey, let her stay with her nurse; ' and they left her in the charge of the nurse and the parish priest. But that priest was a bad man—for it will happen that a priest may be bad sometimes; and, instead of leading her right, he wanted her to do many bad things, and when she would not listen to him, he wrote false letters to her parents about her, and gave a report of her conduct to shock her parents. When the brother saw these letters of the priest concerning his sister, he was indignant with her, and, without waiting for his parents' advice, went back home quickly, and killed her with his dagger, and threw her body into a ditch. But he went back to the shrine of St. James to live in penance.

Not long had her body lain in the ditch when a king's son came by hunting, and the dogs scented the blood of a Christian lying in the ditch, and bayed over it till the huntsmen came and took out the body; when they saw it was the body of a fair maiden, yet warm, they showed it to the prince, and the prince when he saw the maiden, loved her, and took her to a convent to be healed of her wound, and afterwards married her; and when his father died, he was king and she became a queen.

But her father and mother, hearing only that her brother had killed her and thrown her body in the ditch, and supposing she was dead, said one to the other, ' Why should we go back home, seeing that our daughter is dead? What have we to go home for? There is nothing but sorrow for us there.' So they remained at the shrine of St. James, and built a hospice for poor pilgrims, and tended them.

P

Meantime the daughter, who had become a queen, she also had two children, a boy and a girl, and her husband rejoiced in them and in her. But troubled times came, and her husband had to go forth to battle, and while she was left without him in the palace, the viceroy came to her and wanted her to do wrong, and when she would not listen to him, he took her two children and killed them before her eyes. ' What do I here,' said she, ' seeing my two children are dead?' And she took the bodies of her children and went forth. When she had wandered long by solitary places, she came one day to a mountain, and at the foot of the mountain sat a dwarf,[1] and the dwarf had compassion when he saw how she was worn with crying, and he said to her, ' Go up the mountain and be consoled.' Thus she went up the mountain till she saw a majestic woman, with an infant in her arms; and this was the Madonna, you must know.[2]

When she saw a woman like herself, with a child too, for all that she looked so bright and majestic, she was consoled; and she poured all her story into her ear. ' And I would go to S. Giacomo di Galizia to ask that my husband's love may be restored to me, for I know the viceroy will calumniate me to him; but how can I leave these children?' Then the lady said, ' Leave your children with me, and they shall be with my child, and go you to Galizia as you have said, and be consoled.' So she put on pilgrim's weeds, and went to Galizia.

Meantime the king came back from battle, and the viceroy told him evil about the queen: and his mother, who also believed the viceroy, said, ' Did I not tell you a woman picked up is never good for anything?'[3] But the king was grieved, for he had loved the queen dearly, and he took a pilgrim's dress and went to Galizia, to the shrine of S. Giacomo, to pray that she might be forgiven. Then the viceroy, he too was seized with compunction, and, unknown to the king, he too became a pilgrim, and went to do penance at the same shrine.

Thus it happened that they all met together, without knowing each other, in the hospice that that husband and wife had built at Galizia; and when they had paid their devotions at the shrine, and all sat together in the hospice in the evening, all told some tale of what he had seen and what he had heard. But there sat one who told nothing. Then said the king to this one, ' And you, good man, why do you tell no story?' for he knew not that it was the queen, nor that it was even a woman.

Thus appealed to, however, she rose and told a tale of how there had been a husband and wife who had made a vow that if they had children, they would go a pilgrimage to S. Giacomo di Galizia; ' and,' said she, ' they were just two people such as you might be,' and she pointed to the two who were founders of the hospice. And that when they were absent, and left their daughter behind, the parish priest calumniated her, so that her brother came back and stabbed her, and threw her body in a ditch. ' And he was just such a young man, strong and ardent, as you may have been,' and she pointed to the son of the founders. ' But that maiden was not dead,' she went on, ' and a king found her, and married her, and she had two children, and lived happily with him till he went to the wars, then the viceroy calumniated her till she ran away out of the palace; and the viceroy was just such a one, strong and dark, as you may be,' and she pointed to the viceroy, who sat trembling in a corner; ' and when the king came back, he told him evil of her; but that king was noble and pious as you may be,' and she pointed to the king, ' and in his heart he believed no evil of his wife, but went to S. Giacomo di Galizia to pray that the truth might be made plain.'

As she spoke, one after another they all arose, and said, ' How comes this peasant to know all the story of my life; and who has sent him to declare it here!' and they were all strangely moved, and called upon the peasant to tell them who had shown him these things. But the supposed peasant answered, 'My old grandfather, as we sat on the hearth together.'⁴ 'That cannot be,' said they, 'for to every one of us you have told his own life; and now you must tell us more, for we will not rest till we have righted her who has thus suffered.' When she found them so earnest and so determined to do right, she said further, 'That queen am I!' and she took off her hood, and they knew her, and all fell round and embraced her. Then said the king, ' And on this viceroy, on whose account you have suffered so sadly, what vengeance will you have on him?' But she said, 'I will have no vengeance; but now that he has come to the shrine of Galizia, God will forgive him; and may he find peace!'

Thus all were restored and united; and when she had embraced her parents and her brother, and spent some days with them, she went home with her husband and reigned in his kingdom.

[The story seemed to be ended, and I hoped it was, for the way in which the children were left seemed a poetic way of describing their death; but·to make sure, I said, 'And the children, they remained with the Madonna?'

'No, no! I forgot. It's well you reminded me. No; by their way home they went back to the mountain, and they found their children well cared for by that "Majestic Lady," and playing with her Bambino; she gave the children back, and blessed them, and then went up to heaven; and they built a chapel in the place where she had been.']

---

¹ 'Uomicino,' a little man. As the narrator had come to the borders of Wonderland, this must, I think, be taken to be.one of those dwarfs—little men of the mountains, 'Bergmänlein,' who have so large a place in German, especially in Tirolean mythology, but are so rarely to be met in that of Rome.

² 'Una donna maestosa con un bambino in braccia; e questa era la Madonna, capisce.' This use of the verb *capire* to express 'you see,' &c., is a favourite Romanism; in Tuscany they use the verb *intendere*.

³ 'Donna trovata non fu mai buona.'

⁴ 'Il nonno accanto al fuoco.' Giving to understand that it was an old traditionary tale.

SANTA VERDANA.

THERE was a man with a general shop who had an excellent girl for a servant, and she was so honest as well as diligent that he left her to attend to the shop besides doing the work. All he gave her to do she did well, and his business flourished without his having any trouble about it.

But some envious people came to him and said that the girl had given away all his substance, and there was nothing left; so he watched, and he saw it was indeed so. To every poor person who came she gave whatever they asked for the love of God, and all the stores and presses were empty. Yet, as there seemed no lack of anything either, and when customers came she always continued to supply them, he hesitated to interfere.

So it might have gone on, only people went on whispering doubts. And one said one day, ' Suppose she should die, where would you be then?' That is true, he thought to himself, and upon that he went and asked her where all the things were gone. She never made any reply, but knelt down and prayed, and as she prayed all the presses and stores became full again with all kinds of merchandise as at the first. But she went away from him after that, and built herself a cell, walled up all round, next to the church of St. Anthony, where she lived in continual prayer, and she took a brick out of the wall to make a hole through which she heard mass. At last one day came when they saw her no more at the hole hearing mass, and they opened her cell and found her lying on the floor with her hands crossed on her breast, and the cell was filled with a beautiful perfume, for she had been sanctified there, and her soul had gone thence to God.

SAN SIDORO.

[THIS seems very like another version of the foregoing.]

St. Isidor was the steward of a rich man, and as he was filled with holy piety and compassion, he could never turn away from any that begged of him, but gave to all liberally ; to one Indian corn meal, to another beans, to another lentils.

At last men with envious tongues came to his master and said : ' This steward of yours of whom you think so much is wasting all your substance, and he has given away so much to the poor that there can be nothing left in any of your barns and storehouses ; you had better look to it.' The master, after hearing this, came down to St. Isidor very angry, and bade him bring the keys and open all the barns and storehouses. St. Isidor did as he was bid without an angry word, and behold they were all so full of grain and beans, and every species of good gift of God, that you could not go into them, they were full to the very doors. After that the master let him give away as much as he would.

[I have heard the same at Siena told of San Gherardo, or Gheraldo as the people call him, under the character of a Franciscan laybrother. He seemed to give away all the provisions people gave him in alms for the convent, but when the Superior, warned by envious tongues, chid him, he showed that there remained over more than sufficient for the needs of the community.]

THE FISHPOND OF ST. FRANCIS.[1]

ST. FRANCIS had a little fishpond, where he kept some gold and silver fish as a pastime.

Some bad people wanted to vex him, and they went and caught these poor little fish and fried them, and sent them up to him for dinner.

But St. Francis when he saw them knew that they were his gold fish, and made the sign of the cross over them, and blessed them, and soon they became alive again, and he took them and put them back into the fishpond, and no one durst touch them again after that.

[1] La Pescheria di San Francesco.' Pescheria, see p. 45. Many Italian convents are provided with such.

ST. ANTHONY.[1]

St. Anthony's father was accused of murder, and as facts seemed against him, he was condemned to be executed.

St. Anthony was preaching in the pulpit as his father was taken to the scaffold. 'Allow me to stop for a minute to take breath,' he said, and he made a minute's pause in the midst of his discourse, and then went on again.

But in that minute's pause, though no one in church had lost sight of him, he had gone on to the scaffold.

'What are you doing to that man?' he asked.

'He has committed a murder, and is going to be executed.'

'He has murdered no one. Bring hither the dead man.'

No one knew who it was that spoke, but they felt impelled to obey him nevertheless.

When the dead man's body was brought, St. Anthony said to him:—

'Is this the man who killed you? say!'

The dead man opened his eyes and looked at the accused.

'Oh, no; that's not the man at all!' he said.

'And you, where are you?' continued St. Anthony.

'I should be in Paradise, but that there is a ground of excommunication on me, therefore am I in Purgatory,' answered the dead man. Then St. Anthony put his ear down, and bid him tell him the matter of the excommunication; and, when he had confessed it, he released him from the bond, and he went straight to Paradise. The father of St. Anthony, too, was pronounced innocent, and set free.

And all the while no one had missed St. Anthony from the pulpit!

2

SANT' ANTONIO E SORA[1] CASTITRE.

I too know a story about St. Anthony.

St. Anthony was a fair youth, as you will always see in his portraits. As he went about preaching there was a young woman who began to admire him very much, and her name was Sora Castitre. Whenever she could find out in which direction he was going she would put herself in his way and try to speak to him. St. Anthony at first kept his eyes fixed on the ground, and took no notice of her; then he tried to make her desist by rebuking her, but she ceased not to follow him.

Then he thought to himself, with all a saint's compunction, ' It is not she who is to blame, and who is worthy of rebuke, but I, who have been the occasion of sin to her. God grant that sin be not imputed to her through loving me.'

The next time she met him, it was in a deserted part of the Campagna.

' Brother Antonio, come along with me down this path. No one will see us there,' said Sora Castitre.

Much to her surprise, instead of pursuing the severe tone he had always adopted towards her, St. Anthony greeted her and smiled with a smile which filled her with a joy different from anything she had known before. What was more, he seemed to follow her, and she led on.

But as she went the way seemed quite changed. She knew well the retired path by which she had meant to lead him, but now everything around looked different; not one landmark was the same. Yet 'how could it be different?' she said within herself; and she led on.

What was her astonishment, when, instead of finding it terminate in a rocky gorge as she had found before, there rose before her presently an austere building surrounded with walls and gates!

St. Anthony stepped forward as they reached the gate. A nun opened to them, and St. Anthony asked for the mother abbess. 'I have brought you a maiden,' he said, 'whom I recommend to your affectionate and tender care.' The mother abbess promised to make her her special charge, and St. Anthony went his way, first calling the maiden aside and charging her with this one petition he would have her make:

'I have sinned; have mercy on me.'

Then St. Anthony went back to his convent and called all the brethren together, and asked them all to pray very earnestly all through the night, and in the morning tell him what manifestation they had had.

The brethren promised to comply; and in the morning they all told him they had seen a little spark of light shining in the darkness.

'It suffices not, my brethren!' said St. Anthony; 'continue your charity and pray on instantly this night also.'

The brethren promised compliance; and in the morning they all told him they had seen a pale streak of light stealing away towards heaven.

'It suffices not, my brethren!' said St. Anthony; 'of your charity pray on yet again this night also.'

The brethren promised compliance; and in the morning they told him they had all seen a blaze of light, and in the midst of it a bed on which lay a most beautiful maiden, white² as a lily, carried up to heaven, borne by four shining angels.

'It is well, my brethren!' replied St. Anthony; 'your prayers have rendered a soul to the celestial quires.'

Afterwards he went to the convent where he had left Sora Castitre, and learnt from the mother abbess that, spending three penitential days saying only, ' I have sinned ; have mercy on me,' she had rendered up her soul to God in simplicity and fervour.

3

THE legend of St. Anthony preaching to the fishes is well known from paintings, and I do not reproduce it because it was told me with no variation from the usual form.   But another legend, which early pictures have rendered equally familiar, I received with an anachronistic addition which is worth putting down.

4

ST. ANTHONY AND THE HOLY CHILD.[3]

ST. ANTHONY had been sent a long way off to preach ; [4] by the way fatigue overtook him, and he found hospitality for a few days in a monastery by the way.   Later in the evening came a Protestant [5] and asked hospitality, and he also was received, because you know there are many Protestants who are very good; and, besides that, if the man needed hospitality the monks would give it, whoever he might be.

The monks were all in their cells by an early hour in the evening, but the Protestant walked up and down the corridors smoking.

Suddenly through the cracks and the keyhole and all round the lintel of the door he saw a bright light issue where anon all was dark ; it seemed as if the cell was on fire.   ' One of the good monks has set fire to his bed-clothes!' he said, and looked through the keyhole.   What did he see ? on the open book from which a father who was kneeling before it had been taking his meditations stood a beautiful Child whom it filled you with love to look at, and from Whom shone a light too bright to bear.

Anxious to obtain a better view of the glorious sight the Protestant knocked at the door; St. Anthony, for it was he, called to him to come in; but instantly the vision vanished.

' Who was that Child who was talking to you? ' asked the Protestant.

' The Divine Infant! ' answered St. Anthony with the greatest simplicity.

The next night the Protestant, curious to know if the Child would appear again, again walked up and down the corridor smoking, keeping his eye on the door of St. Anthony's cell; nor was it long before the same sight met his eye, but this time he was led to prolong his converse with the saint. The next night there was the same prodigy, and that night they sat up all night talking.

When morning came he told the father abbot he wished to make his adjuration and join the order, and he finally took the habit in that monastery.

5

THEY say there was once a poor man who had paid what he owed for his ground. You know the way is, that when a man has gathered in his harvest and turned a little money then he pays off what he owes. This man paid for his ground as soon as he had made something by his harvest, but the seller did not give him any receipt. Soon after the owner died, and his son came to ask for the money over again. ' But I paid your father,' said the poor man. ' Then show your receipt,' said the son. ' But he didn't give me one,' answered the poor man. ' Then you must pay me,' insisted the new proprietor.

' What shall I do! what shall I do! ' exclaimed the poor man in despair. ' St. Anthony, help me! ' He had hardly said the words when he saw a friar⁶ coming towards him.

' What's the matter, good man?' said the friar, 'that you are so distressed: tell me.' And the poor man told him all the story of his distress.

' Shall I tell you how to get the receipt?' asked the friar.

' Indeed, indeed!'⁷ exclaimed the poor man, 'that would be the making of me; but it's more than you can do—the man is dead!'

' Never mind that. You do what I tell you,' said the monk. ' Go straight along that path;' and the man saw that where he pointed was a path that had never been there before. 'Follow that path,' said the monk, 'and you will come to a casino with great iron gates which shut and open of themselves continually. You must watch the moment when they are open and go boldly in. Inside you will see a big room and a man sitting at a table writing ceaselessly and casting accounts. That is your landlord·; ask him for the receipt and he won't dare withhold it now. But mind one thing. Don't touch a single article in the room, whatever you do.'

The poor man went along the path, and found all as the monk had told him.

' How did you get here?' exclaimed the landlord, as soon as he recognised him; and the poor man told him how he had been sent and why he was come. The landlord sat at his desk writing with the greatest expedition, as if some one was whipping him on, and knitting his brows over his sums as if they were more than his brain could calculate; nevertheless, he took a piece of paper and wrote the receipt, and moreover he wrote two or three lines more on another piece of paper, which he bade him give to his son.

The poor man promised to deliver it, and turned to go; but as he went could not forbear putting his hand over the polished surface of a table he had to pass, unmindful of the charge the monk had given him not to touch anything. His hand was no sooner in contact with the table than the whole skin was burnt off, and he understood that he was in Hell. With all expedition he watched the turn of the door opening, and hastened out.

'What have you got about your hand?' asked St. Anthony when the man came back, for the friar was none other than St. Anthony.

'I touched one of the tables in that house,' he answered, 'forgetting what you told me, and burnt my hand so badly I had to dip this cloth in a river as I came by and tie it up. But I have the receipt, thanks to you.' So St. Anthony touched his hand and healed it, and he saw him no more.

Then the man took the letter to the old lord's son. 'Why, this is my father's writing!' he exclaimed; 'and my father is dead. How did you come by it?' And he told him. And the letter said: 'Behold, I am in Hell! But you, mend your ways; give money to the poor; compensate this man for the trouble he has had; and be just to all, lest you also come hither.'

Then the old landlord's son gave the man a large sum of money to compensate him for his anxieties, and sent him away consoled.

---

[1] 'Sora' in this place does not mean 'sister'; it is an expression in Roman vernacular for which we have no equivalent, and is applied to respectable persons of the lower class who do not aspire to be called 'Signora,' 'Mrs.,' or 'Miss,' as with us. 'Sor' or 'Ser' is the masculine equivalent; we had it in use at p. 194.

[2] The word used was 'candida,' and not 'bianca,' as expressive of purest white.

[3] 'Sant' Antonio ed il Santo Bambino.'

[4] I believe St. Anthony was never in Rome; but his genial winning character made him so popular that the people speak of him as one of themselves.

[5] St. Anthony's date is 1195–1231; so the idea of making his observer a Protestant, and a smoker to boot, is very quaint, and is an instance of how chronological order gets confused by tradition.

[6] 'Fraticello'; 'good little friar.' An affectionate way of speaking of Franciscans often used.

[7] 'Magàri!' a very strong form of 'indeed.'

ST. MARGARET OF CORTONA.

ST. MARGARET wasn't always a saint, you must know: in her youth she was very much the reverse. She had a very cruel stepmother, who worried her to death,[1] and gave her work she was unequal to do.

One day her stepmother had sent her out to tie up bundles of hay. As she was so engaged a Count came by, and he stopped to look at her, for she was rarely beautiful.[2]

'What hard work for such pretty little hands,' he began by saying; and after many tender words had been exchanged he proposed that she should go home with him, where her life would be the reverse of the suffering existence she had now to endure.

Margaret consented at once, for her stepmother, besides working her hard, had neglected to form her to proper sentiments of virtue.

The count took her to his villa at a place called Monte Porciana, a good way from Cortona. Here her life was indeed a contrast to what it had been at home at Cortona. Instead of having to work, she had plenty of servants to wait upon her; her dress and her food were all in the greatest luxury, and she was supplied with everything she wished for. Sometimes as she went to the theatre, decked out in her gay attire, and knowing that she was a scandal to all, she would say in mirth and wantonness, 'Who knows whether one day I may not be stuck up there on high in the churches, like some of those saints? As strange things have happened ere now!' But she only said it in wantonness. So she went on enjoying life, and when their son was born there was nothing more she desired.

In the midst of this gay existence, word was brought her one evening that the Count, who had gone out that morning full of health and spirits to the hunt, had been overtaken and assassinated, and as all had been afraid to pursue the murderers, they knew not where his body was.

Margaret was thrown into a frenzy[3] at the news ; her fine clothing and her rich fare gave her little pleasure now. All amusement and frivolity were put out of sight ; and she sat on her sofa and stared before her, for she had no heart to turn to anything that could distract her thoughts from her great loss. Then one day—it might have been three days after—a favourite dog belonging to the count came limping and whining up to her. Margaret rose immediately ; she knew that the dog would take her to the count's body, and she rose up and motioned to him to go : and the dog, all glad to return to his master, ran on before. All the household were too much afraid of the assassins to venture in their way, so Margaret went forth alone. It was a long rough way ; but the dog ran on, and Margaret kept on as well as her broken strength would admit. At last they came to a brake where the dog stopped, and now whined no longer but howled piteously.

Margaret knew that they had reached the object of their search, and it was indeed here the assassins had hidden the body. Moving away with her own hands the leaves and branches with which they had covered it over, the fearful sight of her lover's mangled body lay before her. The condition into which the wounds and the lapse of time had brought it was more than she could bear to look at, and she swooned away on the spot.

When she came to herself all the course of her thoughts was changed. She saw what her life had been ; the sense of the scandal she had given was more to her even than her own distracting grief. As the most terrible penance she could think of, she resolved to go back to her stepmother and endure her hard treatment, sharpened by the invectives with which she knew it would now be seasoned.

Taking with her her son, she went to her, therefore, and with the greatest submission of manner entreated to be readmitted. But not even this would the stepmother grant her, but drove her away from the door. She then turned to her father, but he was bound to say the same as his wife. She now saw there was one misery worse than harsh treatment, and that was penury—starvation, not only for herself, but her child.

Little she cared what became of her, but for the child something must be done. What did she do? She went and put on a sackcloth dress,[4] tied about the waist with a rope, and she went to the church at the high mass time; and when mass was over she stood on the altar step, and told all the people she was Margaret of Cortona, who had given so much scandal, and now was come to show her contrition for it.

Her sufferings had gone up before God. As she spoke her confession so humbly before all the people, the count's mother rose from her seat, and, coming up to her, threw her handkerchief over her head[5]—for she was bareheaded—and led her away to her home.

She would only accept her hospitality on condition of being allowed to live in a little room apart, with no more furniture than a nun's cell. Here she lived twelve years of penance, till her boy was old enough to choose his state in life. He elected to be a Dominican, and afterwards became a Preacher of the Apostolic Palace; and she entered a Franciscan convent, where she spent ten more years of penance, till God took her to Himself.

She cut off all her long hair when she went to live in her cell at the house of the count's mother, that she might not again be an occasion of sin to anyone. And after that, when she found she was still a subject of human admiration, she cut off her lips, that no one might admire her again.[6]

¹ 'La strapazzava,' a word particularly applied to overworking a horse.

² 'Di una rara bellezza.'

³ 'Era disperata.'

⁴ 'Un sacco crudo,' a loose garment made of harsh sackcloth that had not been dressed.

⁵ Handkerchiefs are used so habitually for tying up parcels in Rome, that the narrator thought it worth while to specify that this one was a 'fazzaletto di naso.'

⁶ The life is thus given in Butler:—'Margaret was a native of Alviano in Tuscany. The harshness of a stepmother and her own indulged propension to vice cast her headlong into the greatest disorders. The sight of the carcase of a man, half-putrefied, who had been her gallant, struck her with so great a fear of the Divine judgments, and with so deep a sense of the treachery of the world, that she in a moment became a perfect penitent. The first thing she did was to throw herself at her father's feet, bathed in tears, to beg his pardon for her contempt of his authority and fatherly admonitions. She spent the days and nights in tears; and to repair the scandal she had given by her crimes, she went to the parish church of Alviano with a rope about her neck, and there asked public pardon for them. After this she repaired to Cortona and made her most penitent confession to a father of the Order of S. Francis, who admired the great sentiments of compunction with which she was filled, and prescribed her austerities and practices suitable to her fervour. Her conversion happened in the year 1274, the twenty-fifth of her age. . . . This model of true penitents, after twenty-three years spent in severe penance, twenty of them in the religious habit, being worn out by austerities and consumed by the fire of divine love, died on the 22nd of February 1297.'

ST. THEODORA.¹

WHEN Santa Teodora was young she was married, and lived very happily with her husband, for they were both very fond of each other.

But there was a count who saw her and fell in love with her, and tried his utmost to get an opportunity of telling her his affection, but she was so prudent that he could not approach her. So what did he do? he went to a bad old woman¹ and told her that he would give her ever so much money if she would get him the opportunity of meeting her. The old wretch accepted the commission willingly, and put all her bad arts in requisition to make Theodora forget her duty. For a long time Theodora refused to listen to her and sent her away, but she went on finding excuses to come to her, and again and again urged her persuasions and excited her curiosity so that finally she consented that he might just come and see her, and the witchwoman assured her that was all he asked. But what he wanted was the opportunity of speaking his own story into her ear, and when that was given him he pushed his suit so successfully that it wasn't only once he came, but many times.

Yet it was not a very long time before a day came when Theodora saw how wrong she had been, and then, seized with compunction, she determined to go away and hide herself where she would never be heard of more. Before her husband came home she cut off all her hair, and putting on a coarse dress she went to a Capuchin monastery and asked admission.

'What is your name?' asked the Superior.

'Theodore,' she replied.

'You seem too young for our severe rule,' he continued; 'you seem a mere boy;' but she expressed such sincere sentiments of contrition as showed him she was worthy to embrace their life of penance.

The Devil was very much vexed to see what a perfect penitent she made, and he stirred up the other monks to suspect her of all manner of things; but they could find no fault against her, nor did they ever suspect that she was a woman.

One day when she was sent with another brother to beg for the convent a storm overtook them in a wood, and they were obliged to seek the shelter of a cottage there was on the borders of the wood where they were belated. 'There is room in the stable for one of you,' said the peasant who lived there; 'but that other one who looks so young and so delicate' (he meant Theodora) 'must sleep indoors, and the only place is the loft where my daughter sleeps; but it can't be helped.' Theodora, therefore, slept in the loft and the monk in the stable, and in the morning when the weather was fair they went back to their convent. Months passed away, and the incident was almost forgotten, when one day the peasant came to the monastery and rang the bell in a great fury, and he laid down at the entrance a bundle in which was a baby. ' That young monk of yours is the father of this child,' he said, ' and you ought to turn him out of the convent.' Then the Superior sent for ' Theodore,' and repeated what the peasant had said.

' Surely God has sent me this new penance because the life I lead here is not severe enough,' she said. ' He has sent me this further punishment that all the community should think me guilty.' Therefore she would not justify herself, but accepted the accusation and took the baby and went away. Her only way of living now was to get a night's lodging how she could, and come every day to the convent gate with the child and live on the dole that was distributed there to the poor. What a life for her who had been brought up delicately in her own palace !

She was not allowed to rest, however, even so, for people took offence because she was permitted to remain so near the monastery, and the monks had to send her away. So she went to seek the shelter of a wood, and to labour to find the means of living for herself and the child in the roots and herbs she could pick up. But one of the monks one day found her there, and saw her so emaciated that he told the Superior, and he let her come back to receive the dole.

At last she died, and when they came to bury her they found she had in one hand a written paper so tightly clasped that no one had the strength to unclose it; and there she lay on her bier in the church looking so sad and worn, yet as sweetly fair as she had looked in life, and with the written paper tightly grasped in her closed hand.

Now when her husband found that she had left his palace the night she went away he left no means untried to discover where she was; and when he had made inquiries and sent everywhere, and could learn no tidings whatever, he put on pilgrim's weeds and went out to seek for her everywhere himself.

It so happened that he came into the city where she died just as she was thus laid on her bier in the church. In spite of her male attire he knew her; in the midst of his grief he noticed the written paper she held. To *his* touch her hand opened instantly, and in the scroll was found recorded all she had done and all she had suffered.

[1] 'Vecchiaccia'; the addition *accia* implies that she was bad: probably a witch was intended.

NUN BEATRICE.[1]

NUN BEATRICE had not altogether the true spirit of a religious: she was somewhat given to vanity;[2] though but for this she was a good nun, and full of excellent dispositions. She held the office of portress;[3] and, as she determined to go away out of her convent and return into the world, this seemed to afford her a favourable opportunity for carrying out her design. Accordingly, one day when the house was very quiet, and there seemed no danger of being observed, having previously contrived to secrete some secular clothes such as passed through her hands to keep in store for giving to the poor, she let herself out and went away.

In the parlour was a kneeling-desk with a picture of Our Lady hanging over it, where she had been wont to kneel and hold converse with Our Lady in prayer whenever she had a moment to spare. On this desk she laid the keys before she went, thinking it was a safe place for the Superior to find them; and she commended them to the care of Our Lady, whose picture hung above, and said, ' Keep thou the keys, and let no harm come to this good house and my dear sisters.'

As she said the words Our Lady looked at her with a glance of reproach, enough to have melted her heart and made her return to a better mood had she seen it; but she was too full of her own thoughts and the excitement of her undertaking to notice anything. No sooner was she gone out, however, than Our Lady, walking out of the canvas, assumed the dress that she had laid aside, and, tying the keys to her girdle, assumed the office of portress.

With the habit of the portress Our Lady also assumed her semblance; so that no one noticed the exchange, except that all remarked how humble, how modest, how edifying Beatrice had become.

After a time the nuns began to say it was a pity so perfect a nun should be left in so subordinate a position, and they made her therefore Mistress of the Novices. This office she exercised with as great perfection, according to its requirements, as she had the other; and so sweetly did she train the young nuns entrusted to her direction that all the novices became saints.

Beatrice meantime had gone to live in the world as a secular; and though she often repented of what she had done, she had not the courage to go back and tell all. She prayed for courage, but she went on delaying. While she was in this mind it so happened one day that the factor⁴ of the convent came to the house where she was living. What strange and moving memories of her peaceful home filled her mind as she saw his well-known form, though he did not recognise her in her secular dress! What an opportunity too, she thought, to learn what was the feeling of the community towards her, and what had been said of her escape!

'I hope all your nuns are well,' she said. 'I used to live in their neighbourhood once, and there was one of them I used to know, Suora⁵ Beatrice. How is she now?'

'Sister Beatrice!' said the factor. 'She is the model of perfection, the example of the whole house. Everybody is ready to worship her. With all respect to the Church, which never canonizes the living, no one doubts she is a saint indeed.'

'It cannot be the same,' answered Beatrice. 'The one I knew was anything but a saint, though I loved her well, and should like to have news of her.' And she hardly knew how to conceal the astonishment with which she was seized at hearing him speak thus; for the event on which she expected him to enlarge at once was the extraordinary fact of her escape. But he pursued in the same quiet way as before. 'Oh yes, it must be the same. There has never been but one of the name since I have known the convent. She was portress some time ago; but latterly she has been made Mistress of the Novices.'

There was nothing more to be learnt from him; so she pursued her inquiries no further. But he had no sooner had start enough to put him at a safe distance, than she set out to go to the convent and see this Sister Beatrice who so strangely represented her.

Arrived at the convent door, she asked to see Sister Beatrice, and in a very few minutes the Mistress of the Novices entered the parlour.

The presence of the new Mistress of the Novices filled Beatrice with an awe she could not account for; and, without waiting to ask herself why, she fell on her knees before her.

'It is well you have come back, my child,' said Our Lady; 'resume your dress, which I have worn for you; go in to the convent again, and do penance, and keep up the good name I have earned for you.'

With that Our Lady returned to the canvas; Beatrice

resumed her habit, and strove so earnestly to form herself by the model of perfection Our Lady had set while wearing it, that in a few months she became a saint.

¹ 'La Monica Beatrice.' 'Monica,' provincialism or vulgarism for 'monaca,' a nun.

² 'Albagia,' self-esteem, vanity.

³ 'Rotara,' equivalent to portress; it alludes to her having charge of the 'ruota,' or 'turniquet,' through which things are passed in and out and messages conveyed through a convent-wall, without the nun having to present herself at the door.

⁴ 'Fattore,' an agent employed by most convents to attend to their secular affairs.

⁵ 'Suora' is the received word for a 'Sister' in a convent. 'Sister,' the natural relationship, is 'Sorella.'

[Mr. Ralston gives a Russian story (pp. 249–50), in which St. Nicholas comes in person and serves a man who has been devout to his picture.]

PADRE FILIPPO.

[St. Philip Neri is a giant indeed in the household memories of the Roman poor. His acts have become travestied and magnified among them in the most portentous way, and they always talk of him with the most patriotic enthusiasm. 'He was a Roman !— a Roman indeed !' they will say. And yet he was not a born Roman, but was made 'Protector of Rome' by the Church.

'Padre Filippo' is their favourite way of naming him, and sometimes 'il buon Filippo' and 'Pippo buono.']

1

There was in Padre Filippo's time a cardinal who was Prefect of the provisions,¹ who let everything go wrong and attended to nothing, and the poor were all suffering because provisions got so dear.

Padre Filippo went to the Pope—Papa Medici[2] it was—and told him how badly off the poor were; so the Pope called the Cardinal to account, and went on making him attend to it till Padre Filippo told him that things were on a better footing.

But the Cardinal came to Padre Filippo and said:

'Why do you vex me by going and making mischief to the Pope?'

But Padre Filippo, instead of being frightened at his anger, rose up and said:

'Come here and I will show you what is the fate of those who oppress and neglect the poor. Come here Eminentissimo, and look,' and he took him to the window and asked him what he saw.

The Cardinal looked, and he saw a great fire of Hell, and the souls writhing in it. The Cardinal said no more and went away, but not long after he gave up being a cardinal and became a simple brother under Padre Filippo.

[Who this cardinal may have been I do not know, but the story was told me another time in this form :—]

1A

THERE was a cardinal — Gastaldi was his name — who went a good deal into society to the neglect of more important duties. One evening, when he was at a conversazione, Padre Filippo came to the house where he was and had him called out to him in an empty room.

'Your Eminence ! come to this window, I have something to show you.'

The Cardinal came to the window and looked out, and instead of the houses he saw Hell opened and all the souls[3] in the flames; a great serpent was wriggling in and out among them and biting them, and in the midst was a gilt cardinalitial chair.

'Who is that seat for?' inquired the Cardinal.

'It is placed there for your Eminence,' replied St. Philip.

'What must I do to escape it?' exclaimed the Cardinal, horrified and self-convicted.

Padre Filippo read him a lecture on penitence and amendment of life, and for the practical part of his advice warned him to devote to good works moneys he had been too fond of heaping up. The Cardinal after this became very devout, and the poor were great gainers by St. Philip's instructions to him, and the two churches you see at the end of the Corso and Babbuino in Piazza del Popolo were also built by him with the money Padre Filippo had warned him to spend aright, and you may see his arms up there any day for yourself.[4]

2

SOME of their stories of him are jocose. There was a young married lady who was a friend of the Order, and had done it much good. She was very much afraid of the idea of her confinement as the time approached and said she could never endure it. Padre Filippo knew how good she was and felt great compassion for her.

'Never mind, my child,' said the 'good Philip'; 'I will take all your pain on myself.'

Time passed away, and one night the community was very much surprised to hear 'good Philip' raving and shouting with pain; he who voluntarily submitted to every penance without a word, and whom they had often seen so patient in illness. That same night the lady's child was born and she felt no pain at all.

Early next morning she sent to tell him that her child was born, and to ask how he was.

'Tell her I am getting a little better now,' said 'good Philip,' 'but I never suffered anything like it before. Next time, mind, she must manage her affairs for herself. For never will *I* interfere[5] with anything of *that* sort again.'

3

ANOTHER who had no child was very anxious to have one, and came to Padre Filippo to ask him to pray for her that she might have one. Padre Filippo promised to pray for her ; but instead of a child there was only a shapeless thing. She sent for Padre Filippo once more, therefore, and said :

'There ! that's all your prayers have brought !'

'Oh never mind !' said Padre Filippo ; and he took it and shaped it (the narrator twisted up a large towel and showed how he formed first one leg then the other, then the arms, then the head, as if she had seen him do it). Then he knelt down by the side and prayed while he told them to keep silence, and it opened its eyes and cried, and the mother was content.

[His winning and practical ways of dealing with his penitents afford an endless theme of anecdote, but some have grown to most extravagant proportions. The following shows how, as in all legends, mysteries are made to wear a material form. The fact that on some occasions he satisfied some, whom no one else could satisfy, of the boundless mercy of God, is brought to proof in such a tangible way as to provoke the denial it was invented to silence.]

4

THERE was a man who was dying, and would not have a priest near him. He said he had so many sins on him it was impossible God could forgive him, so it was no use bothering himself about confessing. His wife and his children begged and entreated him to let them send for a priest, but he would not listen to them.

So they sent for Padre Filippo, and as he was a friend he said :

'If he comes as a visitor he may come in, but not as a priest.'

Good Philip sat down by his side and said:

' A visitor may ask a question. Why won't you let me come as a priest ? '

The sick man gave the same answer as before.

' Now you're quite mistaken,' said St. Philip, ' and I'll show you something.'

Then he called for paper and pen and wrote a note.

' Padre Eterne ! ' he wrote. ' Can a man's sins be forgiven ? ' and he folded it, and away it went of itself right up to heaven.

An hour later, as they were all sitting there, another note came back all by itself, written in shining letters of gold, and it said :—

' Padre Eterne forgives and receives everyone who is penitent.'

The sick man resisted no longer after that ; he made his confession and received the sacrament, and died consoled in ' good Philip's ' arms.

5

PADRE FILIPPO was walking one day through the streets of Rome when he saw a great crowd very much excited. ' What's the matter ? ' asked ' good Philip.'

' There's a man in that house up there beating his wife fit to kill her, and for nothing at all, for she's an angel of goodness. Nothing at all, but because she's so ugly.'

Padre Filippo waited till the husband was tired of beating her and had gone out, and all the crowd had dispersed. Then he went up to the room where the poor woman lived, and knocked at the door. ' Who's there ? ' said the woman.

' Padre Filippo ! ' answered ' good Philip,' and the woman opened quickly enough when she heard it was Padre Filippo who knocked.

But good Philip himself started back with horror when he saw her, she was so ugly. However, he said nothing, but made the sign of the cross over her, and prayed, and immediately she became as beautiful as she had been ugly ; but she knew nothing, of course, of the change.

'Your husband won't beat you any more,' said good Philip, as he turned to go ; 'only if he asks you who has been here send him to me.'

When the husband came home and found his wife had become so beautiful, he kissed her, and was beside himself for joy ; and she could not imagine what had made him so different towards her. 'Who has been here?' he asked.

'Only Padre Filippo,' answered the wife ; 'and he said that if you asked I was to tell you to go to him ;' the husband ran off to him to thank him, and to say how sorry he was for having beaten her.

But there lived opposite a woman who was also in everything the opposite of this one. She was very handsome, but as bad in conduct as the other was good. However, when she saw the ugly wife become so handsome, she said to herself, 'If good Philip would only make me a little handsomer than I am, it would be a good thing for me ;' and she went to Padre Filippo and asked him to make her handsomer.

Padre Filippo looked at her, and he knew what sort of woman she was, and he raised his hand and made the sign of the cross over her, and prayed, and she became ugly ; uglier even than the other woman had been !

'Why have you treated me differently from the other woman?' exclaimed the woman, for she had brought a glass with her to be able to contemplate the improvement she expected him to make in her appearance.

'Because beauty was of use to her in her state of life,' answered Padre Philippo. 'But you have only used the beauty God gave you as an occasion of sin ; therefore a stumbling-block have I now removed out of your way.'

And he said well, didn't he ?

6

ONE Easter there came to him a young man of good family to confession, and Padre Filippo knew that every one had tried in vain to make him give up his mistress, and that to argue with him about it was quite useless. So he tried another tack. 'I know it is such a habit with you to go to see her you *can't* give it up, so I'm not going to ask you to. You shall go and see her as often as you like, only will you do something to please me?'

The young man was very fond of good Philip, and there was nothing he would have not done for him except to give up his mistress ; so as he knew that was not in question, he answered 'yes' very readily.

'You promise me to do what I say, punctually?' asked the saint.

'Oh, yes, father, punctually.'

'Very well, then ; all I ask is that though you go to her as often as you like, you just pass by this way and come up and pull my bell every time you go ; nothing more than that.'

The young man did not think it was a very hard injunction, but when it came to performing it he felt its effect. At first he used to go three times a day, but he was so ashamed of ringing the saint's bell so often, that very soon he went no more than once a day. That dropped to two or three times a week, then once a week, and long before next Easter he had given her up and had become all his parents could wish him to be.

7

'THERE was another such case ; just such another, only this man had a wife too, but he was so infatuated with the other, he would have it she loved him the better of the two.'

'Yes ; and the other was a miniature-painter,' broke in

corroboratively a kind of charwoman who had come in to tidy the place while we were talking.

'Yes, she was a miniature-painter,' continued the narrator; 'but it's I who am telling the story.'

'Padre Filippo said, "How much do you allow her?"'

'Twenty pauls a day,' broke in the charwoman.

'Forty scudi a month,' said the narrator positively.

'There's not much difference,' interposed I, fearing I should lose the story between them. 'Twenty pauls a day is sixty scudi a month. It doesn't matter.'

'Well, then, Padre Filippo said,' continued the narrator, "Now just to try whether she cares so much about you, you give her thirty scudi a month."'

'Fifteen pauls a day,' interposed the charwoman.

'Thirty scudi a month!' reiterated the narrator.

'Never mind,' said I. 'Whatever it was, it was to be reduced.'

'Yes; that's it,' pursued the narrator; 'and he made him go on and on diminishing it. She took it very well at first, suspecting he was trying her, and thinking he would make it up to her afterwards.'

'But when she found he didn't,' said the charwoman,

'She turned him out,' said the narrator, putting her down with a frown. 'He was so infatuated, however, that even now he was not satisfied, and said that in stopping the money he had been unfair, and she was in the right. So good Philip, who was patience itself, said, "Go and pay her up, and we'll try her another way. You go and kill a dog, and put it in a bag, and go to her with your hands covered with blood, and let her think you have got into trouble for hurting some one, and ask her to hide you." So the man went and killed a dog.'

'It was a cat he killed, because he couldn't find a dog handy,' said the irrepressible charwoman.

'Nonsense; of course it was a dog,' asseverated the narrator. 'But when he went to her house and pretended

to be in a bad way, and asked her to have pity on him,
she only answered: " Not I, indeed! I'm not going to
get myself into a scrape[6] with the law, for *him!* " and
drove him away. And he came and told Padre Filippo.

' " Now," said good Philip, " go to your wife whom you
have abandoned so long. Go to her with the same story,
and see what she does for you."

' The man took the dead dog in the bag, and ran to the
lodging where his wife was, and knocked stealthily at her
door. " It is I," he whispered.

' " Come in, husband," exclaimed the wife, throwing
open the door.

' " Stop! hush! take care! don't touch me!" said the
husband. "There's blood upon me. Save me! hide me!
put me somewhere!"

' " It's so long since you've been here, no one will think
of coming after you here, so you will be quite safe. Sit
down and be composed," said the wife soothingly; and she
poured him out wine to drink.

' But the police were nearer than he fancied. He had
thought to finish up the affair in five minutes by explain-
ing all to her. But " the other," not satisfied with refusing
him shelter, had gone and set the police on his track;
and here they were after him.

' The wife's quick ears heard them on the stairs. " Get
into this cupboard quick, and leave me to manage them,"
she said.

' The husband safely stowed away, she opened the door
without hesitation, as if she had nothing to hide. " How
can you think he is here?" she said when they asked for
him. " Ask any of the neighbours how long it is since he
has been here."

' " Oh, three years," " four years," " five," said various
voices of people who had come round at hearing the police
arrive.

' " You see you must have come to the wrong place,"

she said. And the husband smiled as he heard her standing out for him so bravely.

'Her determined manner had satisfied the police; and
they were just turning to go when one of them saw tell-
tale spots of blood on the floor that had dropped from the
dead dog. The track was followed to the cupboard, and
the man dragged to prison. It was in vain that he assured
them he had killed nothing but a dog.

'"Ha! that will be the faithful dog of the murdered
man," said the police. "We shan't be long before we find
the body of the man himself!"

'The wife was distracted at finding her husband, who
had but so lately come back to her, was to be taken away
again; and he could discern how real was her distress.

'"Go to Padre Filippo, and he will set all right," said
the husband as they carried him away. The woman went
to Padre Filippo, and he explained all, amid the laughter
of the Court. But the husband went back to his wife, and
never left her any more after that.'

[The story was told me another time with this variation, that
the penitent was a peasant[7] who came up to Rome with his ass,
and tied it to a pillar set up for the purpose outside the church,
while he went in to confess. The first time he went, St.
Philip told him he must have nothing more to do with the occasion of sin, who in this case was a spinner instead of a miniature-
painter. The peasant was so angry with the advice that he
stayed away from confession a whole year. At the end of the
year he came back. St. Philip received him with open arms,
saying he had been praying ever since for his return to a better
mind. The sum that formed the sliding-scale that was to open
his eyes to the mercenary nature of the affection he had so
much prized, was calculated at a lower rate than the other;
but the rest of the story was the same.]

8

'Ah, there's plenty to be said about Padre Filippo,'
said the charwoman; and I should have liked to put her

under examination, but that it would have been a breach
of hospitality, as the other evidently did not like the interruption; so I was obliged to be satisfied with the testimony
she had already afforded of the popularity of the saint.
'Ha, good Padre Filippo, he was content to eat "black
bread" like us'; and she took a hunch out of her pocket
to show me; (it was only like our 'brown bread.')

'There was no lack where he was. Once I know, with
half a rubbio[8] of corn, he made enough to last all the community ten years,' she, however, ran on to say before she
could be dismissed.

9

ONE day Padre Filippo was going over Ponte S.
Angelo, when he met two little boys who seemed to attract
his notice. 'Forty-two years hence you will be made a
cardinal,' he said to one, as he gave him a friendly tap
with his walking-stick. 'And that other one,' he added,
turning to his companion, 'will be dead in two years.'

And so it came true exactly.

10

THERE was another peasant who, when he came into Rome
on a Sunday morning, always went to the church where
St. Philip was.[9] 'You quite weary[10] one with your continual preaching about the Blessed Sacrament. I'm so
tired of hearing about it, that I declare to you I don't
care so much about it as my mule does about a sack of
corn.' Padre Filippo preferred convincing people in some
practical way to going into angry discussions with them;
so he did not say very much in answer to the countryman's
remarks, but asked him the name of his village. Not
long after he went down to this village to preach; and
had a pretty little altar erected on a hill-side, and set
up the Blessed Sacrament in Exposition. Then he went
and found out the same countryman, and said, 'Now bring

R

a sack of corn near where the altar is, and let's see what the mule does.' The countryman placed a sack of corn near the altar, and drove the mule by to see what it would do.

The mule kicked aside the sack of corn, and fell down on its knees before the altar; and the man, seeing the token, went to confession to St. Philip, and never said anything profane any more.

11

THERE were two other fellows [11] who were more profane still, and who said one to the other, 'They make such a fuss about Padre Filippo and his miracles, I warrant it's all nonsense. Let's watch till he passes, and one of us pretend to be dead and see if he finds it out.'

So said so done. 'What is your companion lying on the ground for?' said St. Philip as he passed. 'He's dead! Father,' replied the other. 'Dead, is he?' said Padre Filippo; 'then you must go for a bier for him.' He had no sooner passed on than the man burst out laughing, expecting his companion to join his mirth. But his companion didn't move. 'Why don't you get up?' he said, and gave him a kick; but he made no sign. When he bent down to look at him he found he was really dead; and he had to go for the bier.

---

[1] 'Grascia e annòna' are two old words meaning all kinds of meat and vegetable (including grain) food. It was the title of one department of the local administration. There was a great dearth in Rome in the year 1590–1, mentioned in the histories of the times. It is probable the people would ascribe to the head of the department the fault of the calamity.

[2] These people generally call the popes by their family names. This 'Papa Medici' would be Pius IV., who reigned from 1559 to 1566.

[3] 'Brutte anime,' 'ugly souls.'

[4] All legends have doubtless some foundation in fact; but unfortunately for the detail of this one, the arms up in the façade of the said Churches, 'Dei Miracoli' and 'di Monte Santo'—are the arms of a Cardinal Gastaldi or Castaldi, who rebuilt them about a hundred years later than St. Philip's time. Alexander VII. having rebuilt the Flaminian Gate, or Porta del Popolo, the insignificance of these two churches became more noticeable than before; but

he did not survive to carry out his intention of rebuilding them. This was subsequently performed by Cardinal Gastaldi.—Maroni, xii. 147, xxviii. 185 ; Panciroli, 169 ; Melchiorri, 254 and 420.

⁵ 'Impicciare,' 'entangle myself with,' 'interfere with'—a very favourite Romanism.

⁶ 'Impicciare,' again here.

⁷ 'Campagnola,' a peasant of the Campagna near Rome.

⁸ A *rubbio* is between four and five acres,

⁹ St. Philip lived and taught for thirty-three years at the Church of S. Girolamo della Carità, not very far from the vegetable market in Campo de' Fiori, all the streets about containing shops much frequented by the country people when they come up to Rome with their vegetables.

¹⁰ 'Scocciare,' to persevere to weariness ; to din.

¹¹ 'Vassalli,' in the older dictionaries 'vassallo' is only defined as a vassal ; but in modern Roman parlance it means a scamp, a vagabond.

[Cancellieri has collected some curious incidents ('Morcato,' p. 210–12, Appendix N. xxii.) concerning an attempt which was made by Princess Anne Colònna to obtain from Urban VIII. the authority to remove a part of the Saint's body to her chapel at Naples. The Fathers of the Oratory and the people were greatly averse to dividing it, as it was very well preserved in its entirety. By a fatality, which the people readily believed to be providential, Monsig. Moraldo, who was charged to bring the matter under the Pope's notice, forgot it every time he was in attendance on the Pope, though it was the most important thing he had to say. At last he put the Bull concerning it out on his desk that he might be sure to remember it, though otherwise he would have kept it concealed, for it bore the endorsement, 'Per levare (to remove) parte del corpo di S. Filippo Neri.' While he was talking about it to one of the papal secretaries standing near the window, a priest, who had come about other matters, was shown in, and thus happened to pass by the side of the table when the endorsement of the Bull caught his eye. With all a Roman's desire to preserve the body to Rome intact, he immediately gave notice at the Oratory, and two courageous young fathers took upon themselves to hide the body. When the prelates, therefore, came shortly after to claim the fulfilment of the Bull, the Rector opened the shrine in good faith, but the body was not there, and the report ran among the vulgar that it had been miraculously removed. Subsequently the Rector gave them the heart, and drew a tooth of the Saint, which was a verbal compliance with the terms of the Bull, being certainly 'a part of the body.' Some years after, the body was restored to its shrine, and in 1743 Prince Chigi provided it with velvets and brocades to the value of 1,000 scudi.]

THE PARDON OF ASISI.[1]

ST. FELIX,[2] St. Vincent,[3] and St. Philip went together once upon a time to the Pardon of Asisi.

As they were three great saints, the Pope sent for them as soon as they came back, saying he had a question to ask them. It was Innocent IX. or X., I am not sure which; but I know it was an Innocent.[4] He took them one by one, separately, and began with St. Felix.

'Were there a great many people at the Pardon?' said the Pope.

'Oh yes, an immense number,' answered simple St. Felix; 'I had not thought the whole world contained such a number.'

'Then a vast number of sins must have been remitted that day?' said the Pope.

St. Felix only sighed in reply.

'Why do you sigh?' asked the Pope.

St. Felix hesitated to reply, but the Pope bade him tell him what was in his mind.

'There were but few who gained the indulgence in all that multitude,' replied the Saint; 'for among them all were few who came with the contrition required.'

'How many were there who did receive it?' again asked the Pope.

Once more St. Felix hesitated till the Pope ordered him to speak.

'There were only four,' he then said.

' Only four ! ' exclaimed the Pope. ' And who were they ?'

St. Felix showed even more reluctance to answer this question than the others ; but the Pope made it a matter of obedience, and then he said,

' The four were Father Philip, Father Vincent, one old man, and one other.' [5]

The Pope next called for Father Vincent, and went through nearly the same dialogue with him, and his list was

' Father Philip, Father Felix, one old man, and one other.'

Then the Pope sent for St. Philip, and held the same discourse with him, and his list was

' Father Vincent, Father Felix, one old man, and one other.'

And the Pope saw that their testimony agreed together, and that each out of humility had abstained from naming that he was one of the four.

But when the people heard the story, they all began demanding that the three fathers should be canonized.

[1] ' Il Perdon di Asisi.' The indulgences attached to visiting the Church of S. Maria degli Angeli near Asisi (otherwise called the Porziuncula), received this name on occasion of its consecration on the 1st and 2nd August, 1225. The visit on the anniversary became one of the most popular of Italian pilgrimages.

[2] San Felice di Cantaliccio, 1513-87, is a very popular saint among the Romans, for one reason because he was born of poor parentage. Though of low origin, and only a lay brother in his convent, he was frequently consulted by important people on account of his piety and prudence. St. Charles Borromeo took great note of his advice. He was a contemporary of St. Philip.

[3] St. Vincent Ferrer, who is so popular a saint among the Romans, so continually coupled with St. Philip and his acts, and always spoken of as if he had all his life been an inhabitant of Rome, lived just two centuries earlier. (1351-1419) than the 'Apostle of Rome.' Though he went about preaching and reforming all over Europe, and even in England and Ireland at the invitation of Henry IV., he was yet never in Rome at all, though much at Avignon under the so-called Benedict XIII., his countryman, with whom he used all his influence to make him put an end to the schism.

⁴ Innocent IX., who reigned 1590-1, took a great deal of notice of St. Philip. It is curious the narrator should have been so far out concerning St. Vincent and so correct about this.

⁵ 'Un vecchietto e un' altro.'

[Concerning St. Philip's devotion to the Portiuncula, Cancel-lieri, 'Mercato,' § xxi. note 7, records that he never missed attending it every August at the little Church of S. Salvatore, in Onda, near Ponte Sisto, now a hospice for infirm priests (he gives a curious inscription in note * * *), then in the hands of the Franciscans for many years, while he lived in the neighbouring Palazzo Caccia.]

PADRE VINCENZO.

1

THERE was Padre Vincenzo too, who wasn't much less than Good Philip himself. He was a miracle of obedience. One day when he was ill the Father-General sent him a codfish. Padre Vincenzo sent back word to thank him, but said he couldn't eat it. 'Nonsense!' answered the Father-General, who thought he spoke out of regard to his love of abstinence. 'Nonsense! tell him he is to eat it all.' The message was given to Padre Vincenzo, who was really too ill to eat anything; but in his simplicity thinking he ought to obey, he ate the whole fish, head, tail, bones, and all.

By-and-by the Father-General came to see him. He seemed almost at the last gasp, suffocated by the effort he had made, and his throat all lacerated with swallowing the fish-bones. The Father-General praised the simplicity of his obedience, but told the brother who took the message that he ought to have explained it better.

But Padre Vincenzo did not lose anything by his obedience, for that same evening he was cured of his illness altogether, and was quite well again.

2

PADRE VINCENZO worked so many miracles that all Rome was talking about him, and the Father-General thought he would get vain, so he told him not to work any more miracles. Padre Vincenzo therefore worked no more miracles; but one day as he was walking along the street, he passed under a high scaffolding of a house that was being built. Just as he came by, a labourer missed his footing and fell over from the top. 'Padre Vincenzo, save me!' cried the man, for everybody knew Padre Vincenzo, and he had just seen him turn into the street. 'Stop there!' said Padre Vincenzo; 'I mustn't save you, as the Padre-Generale says I'm not to work miracles; but wait there, and I'll go and ask if I may.' Then he left him suspended in the air while he ran breathless to ask permission of the Father-General to work the miracle of saving him.

3

ONE morning Padre Vincenzo had to pass through the Rotonda [1] on business of his community. A temptation of the throat [2] took him as he saw a pair of fine plump pigeons such as you, perhaps, cannot see anywhere out of the Rotonda hanging up for sale. Padre Vincenzo bought the pigeons, and took them home secretly under his cloak. In his cell he plucked the pigeons, and cooked them over a little fire. The unwonted smell of roast pigeon soon perfumed the corridor, and two or three brothers, having peeped through the keyhole and seen what was going on in Padre Vincenzo's cell, ran off to say to the Father-General,

'What do you think Padre Vincenzo, whom we all reckon such a saint, is doing now! He is cooking pigeons privately in his cell.'

'It's a calumny! I can't believe it of him,' answered the Father-General indignantly.

The spying brothers bid him come and see.

' I am certain if I do, it will be to cover you with confusion in some way or other for telling tales ! ' replied the
Father-General as he went with them.

As they passed along the corridor there was the smell
of roast pigeon most undeniably ; but when the Father-
General opened the cell door what did they see ?

Padre Vincenzo was on his knees, praying for forgiveness in a tone of earnest contrition ; round his throat were
tied the two pigeons, burning hot, as he had taken them
from the fire. A spirit of compunction had seized him as
he was about to accomplish the unmortified act of eating
in his cell in contravention of his rule, and he had adopted
this penance for yielding in intention to the temptation.

---

[1] ' Rotonda,' the vulgar name of the Pantheon, gives its appellation to
the market which is held in the ' Salita de' Cresconzi ' and other adjoining
streets.

[2] ' Gola,' the throat ; used for ' gluttony.'

PADRE FONTANAROSA.

1

THERE was Padre Fontanarosa too. Did you never
hear of him ? He was a good friend to the poor ; and all
Rome loved him. He was a Jesuit ; but somehow there
were some Jesuits who didn't like him. Papa Braschi[1] was
very fond of him, and used to make him come every day
and tell him all that went on in Rome, for he was very
good to the people, and that way the Pope heard what the
people wanted ; and many things that were wrong got set
right when Padre Fontanarosa explained to the Pope the
real state of the case.

One day Padre Fontanarosa said to the Pope, ' People
say I have been talking too freely, and call it telling tales ;
but I have only obeyed the wishes of Your Holiness. If
I have done wrong send me away.' But Papa Braschi

answered, 'You have done me good service. Fear nothing.'

The next day after that Padre Fontanarosa did not come to the Vatican, or the next, or the next.

Then Papa Braschi called for his carriage, and said, 'Drive to the Gesù!' Arrived at the Gesù, he said, 'I want Padre Fontanarosa; where is he?'

They answered, 'In his cell.'

But he had been confined in his cell on bread and water for chattering.

'Then let him be brought out of his cell; for I want him!' answered Papa Braschi.

That time he took Padre Fontanarosa away in his carriage, and no one durst say anything to him any more.

2

FATHER FONTANAROSA was very simple in his habits himself; and he thought the best way to keep the Order simple was to keep it poor. Whenever anyone wanted to leave money to it, instead of encouraging them, he used to tell them of some other good work to which they might leave it.

One day there was a penitent of his who was very devoted to the Jesuits, a very rich nobleman, who came to die, and, as he was making his will, he would have Padre Fontanarosa and the notary present together. 'I leave all of which I die possessed to the Church of the Gesù,' dictated the rich nobleman.

'What! do you leave all to the Son and nothing to the Mother!' said Padre Fontanarosa, who knew he was too weak to argue with him as to whether the Order was better without the money or not, and therefore adopted this mode of avoiding the snare, without damaging the good purpose of the testator.

'Ah! you are right,' answered the dying man. 'Thank you for reminding me. Make a codicil,' he said to the notary, 'and say I meant it for Gesù *and* Maria.'

The notary wrote just what he was bid, and the dying man and the witnesses signed all duly. But the money had to go, not to 'the Gesù' at all, but to the church of 'Gesù e Maria'—you know where, at the end of the Corso, which doesn't belong to the Jesuits at all, but to the Augustinians.

3

OTHERS give him not quite such a good character, and tell the following story of him :—

The reason why the Jesuits did not look favourably on Father Fontanarosa was that they thought he went too often to the house of a certain lady. He perceived that they had found out that he visited her, but he went on all the same, only he said to her, 'If anything happens that the fathers send after me, and anyone comes into the room suddenly; fall down on your knees before the crucifix, and I will speak so that I may seem to be here to give you a penitential warning.'

There happened to be a handsome crucifix, kept more for ornament than devotion, on a slab in her boudoir, and she promised to heed his caution.

One day, when they were together, they heard a ring at the outer door; then a whispering in the passage; then footsteps in the adjoining room. Padre Fontanarosa looked at the lady, and the lady looked at Padre Fontanarosa. Each understood that they were under surveillance. She fell down on her knees before the crucifix, and he exhorted her to take a pattern from the Magdalen; and, as she knelt clasping the foot of the cross, with her beautiful hair all loose over her shoulders, she really looked like a living picture of the Magdalen. Still no one came into the room. But they felt they were being watched; so it was necessary to keep up the deception. Padre Fontanarosa had to speak loudly and fervently in order to make his words resound well in the adjoining room; the lady had to sob to show she was attending to them. Still no one came in; and Padre Fontanarosa had to continue his discourse till, partly through fear lest his courage should fail, and partly lest he should be discovered, he forced himself to forget present circumstances, and to throw himself into his exhortation to such an extent that he preached with a force and eloquence he had never exercised in his life before.

At last those who had been listening felt satisfied of his sincerity, and went back to the General and told him there was no fault to be found in him.

But so effectually had he preached, and so salutary had been his warnings, that the next day the lady entered a convent, to be a penitent all her days.

¹ Pius VI., who reigned 1775–1799.

S. GIUSEPPE LABRE.¹

1

' THERE was Giuseppe Labre too, and many wonderful things he did; he was a great saint, as all the people in the Monti ² knew. I don't know if they've put all about him in books yet; if so, you may have read it; but I can't read.'

' I know a Life of him has been published; but tell me what you have heard about him all the same.'

Giuseppe Labre, you know, passed much of his time in meditation in the Coliseum ; the arch behind the picture of the Second Station,³ that's where he used to be all day, and where he slept most nights, too. There was a butcher in the Via de' Serpenti who knew him, and kept a little room for him, where he made him come and sleep when the nights were bad and cold, or stormy. These people were very good to him, and, though not well off themselves, were ready to give him a great deal more than he in his love for poverty would consent to accept.

One great affliction this butcher had; his wife was bedridden with an incurable disorder. One night there was a terrible storm, it was a burning hot night in summer, and Giuseppe Labre came to sleep at the butcher's. He was lying on his bed in the little room, which was up a step or two higher than the butcher's own room, where his wife lay, just as it might be where that cupboard is there. Presently the butcher's wife heard him call her, saying,

'Sora Angela, bring me a cup of water for the love of God!'

'My friend, you know how gladly I would do anything to help you, but my husband is not come up, and I have no one to send, and you know I cannot move.'

Nevertheless Giuseppe called again, 'Sora Angela, bring me a cup of water for the love of God!'

'Don't call so, good friend,' replied she; 'it distresses me; you know how gladly I would come if I could only move.'

Yet still the third time Giuseppe Labre said,

'Sora Angela, hear me! Bring me a cup of water for the love of God!' And he spoke the words so authoritatively that the good woman felt as if she was bound to obey him, she made the effort to rise, and, can you believe it! she got up as if there was nothing the matter with her; and from that time forward she was cured.

2

THERE was a poor cobbler who always had a kind word for Giuseppe too. One day Giuseppe Labre came to him, and said he wanted him to lend him a pair of shoes as he was going a pilgrimage to Loreto. The cobbler knew what a way it was from Rome to Loreto, and that there would not be much left of a pair of shoes after they had done the way there and back. Had Labre asked him to *give* them, his regard for him would have prompted him to assent however ill he could afford it ; but to talk of lending shoes to walk to Loreto and back seemed like making game of him, and he didn't like it. Nevertheless he couldn't find it in his heart to refuse, and he gave him a pretty tidy pair which he had patched up strong to sell, but without expecting ever to see them again.

Giuseppe Labre took the shoes and went to Loreto, and when he came back his first call was at the cobbler's shed ; and sure enough he brought the shoes none the worse for all the wear they had had. So perfectly uninjured were they that the cobbler would have thought they were another pair had it not been that he recognised the patches of his own clumsy work.

3

ANOTHER more matter-of-fact account of this story was that he did not wear the shoes on the journey, as he did that barefoot, i.e. with wooden sandals, and only borrowed the shoes to be decent and reverent in visiting the Sanctuary. In this case the story was told me to illustrate his conscientiousness both in punctually returning the shoes and in taking so much care of his trust.

[1] S. Joseph Labre was born at Boulogne, of parents of the lower middle class, in 1749, and died 1783. He came to Rome on a pilgrimage when young, and remained here the rest of his days, passing his time in prayer and contemplation in the various shrines of Rome. He every year made the pilgrimage to Loreto on foot. He was supported entirely by the alms of the people.

[2] In the Rione Monti are the streets chiefly inhabited by the poor and working classes of Rome. Joseph Labre passed his life in their midst, and they always speak of him with affection, as a hero of their own order. It only needs to go to the Church of the Madonna de' Monti on the day of his ' Patrocinio ' to see how popular he is.

[3] The stations of the ' Way of the Cross' are arranged round the interior of the Coliseum.; and until out-of-door devotions were forbidden by the new Government, the Via Crucis was constantly performed here, led by a Capuchin and by various confraternities, and always well attended.

THE TWELVE WORDS OF TRUTH.[1]

THIS is a 'ritornella,' the whole being repeated over as each new sentence is added. I remember, years ago, meeting the same in Wiltshire, and then there was this additional refrain to be repeated:

> 'When want is all the go;
> And it evermore shall be so.'

Then it went on:

> 'I'll sing you three O;
> Three O are rivo.'

If I remember right, there were no numbers before three-*o*. Four, were the four Evangelists, and nine, the nine orders of angels, as in the text; but the seventh line was 'seven are the seven bright stars in the sky,' and this, taken in connexion with the text, establishes a curious link in popular mythology between the mysterious Seven-branch Candlestick and the Pleïades. Subjoined is a translation of the text.

'One, and first, is the Lord God, ever ready to help us.' ('Domeniddio' is a popular way of naming God, like the French 'le bon Dieu,' identical with the German 'unser Herrgott.')[2]

'Two stands for the keys of heaven. There is gold.' (This would be the literal rendering of this line, but it has manifestly been lamed by bad memory.)[3]

'Three stands for three patriarchs, &c.'[4]

'Four stands for the four columns which support the world, &c.'[5]

'Five stands for the five wounds of Jesus Christ.'[6]

'Six stands for the six cocks which crowed in Galilee.'[7]

'Seven are the seven tapers that burnt in Jerusalem.' ('Cantorno' for cantarono, a vulgar transposition, like 'hunderd,' and 'childern,' in English; 'ardorno' similarly,

instead of ' arderono,' though ' arsero ' would be the correct form.) [8]

' Eight' stands for the octave of Christ. (Probably in
allusion to the ' octave,' or eight days' festival, of Christ-
mas.) [9]

' Nine ' stands for the nine quires of angels. [10]

' Ten ' stands for the ten years of Christ. (*What* ' ten
years ' it is not easy to see.) [11]

' Eleven ' stands for the crowning with thorns. (St.
Bridget or Sœur Emmerich, in their minute meditations
or ' Revelations ' on the Passion, have fixed a number for
the thorns in our Lord's crown, but I do not remember what
they make it; there *may* be a tradition that it was
eleven.) [12]

' Twelve ' stands for the Twelve Apostles. [13]

[1] Le dodici Parole della Verità.

[2] ' Uno e primo è Domeniddio, che sempre c'aiuta.'

[3] ' Due sono le chiavi del cielo, c'è l'oro.'

[4] ' Tre sono tre Patriarchi Abramme, Giacobbe, e Isaache.'

[5] ' Quattro sono le quattro colonne che il mondo mantiene; Luca,
Giovanni, Marco, e Matteo.'

[6] ' Cinque sono le piaghe de Gesù Cristo.'

[7] ' Sei sono i sei galli che cantorno in Galilea.'

[8] ' Sette sono i sette cerini ch' ardorno in Gerusalemme.'

[9] ' Otto è l'ottava di Cristo.'

[10] ' Nove sono i nove cori degli angeli.'

[11] ' Dieci è la diecenna di Cristo.'

[12] ' Undici è la coronazione di spine.'

[13] ' Dodici sono i dodici Apostoli.'

GHOST AND TREASURE STORIES AND

FAMILY AND LOCAL TRADITIONS.

THERE was a parcel of young fellows once who were a nuisance to everybody in Rome, for they were always at some mischievous tricks when it was nothing worse. But there was one of them who was not altogether so bad as the rest. For one thing, there was one practice of devotion he had never forgotten from the days when his mother taught him, and that was, to say a De Profundis whenever he saw a dead body carried past to burial. But what concerned his companions, was the fear lest he should some day perhaps take it into his head to reform, and in that case it was not impossible he might be led to give information against them.

At last they agreed that the best thing they could do was to put him out of the way. Quietly as their conspiracy was conducted, he saw there was something plotting, and determined to be out of reach of their murderous intentions; so he got up early one morning, and rode out of Rome.

On, on, on,[2] he went till he had left Rome many miles behind, and then he saw hanging in an oak-tree the body of a man all in pieces, among the branches.

For a moment he was overcome with horror at the sight; but, nevertheless, he did not forget his good practice of saying a De Profundis.

No sooner had he completed the psalm, than one by one the pieces came down from the tree and put themselves together, till a dead man stood before him, all complete. Gladly would he have spurred his horse on and got away from the horrible sight, but he was riveted to the spot, and durst not move, or scarcely take breath. But worse was in store, for now the dreadful apparition took hold of his bridle.

'Fear nothing, young man!' said the corpse, in a tone, which though meant to be kind, was so sepulchral that it thrilled the ear. 'Only change places with me for a little space; you get up in the oak-tree, and lend your horse to me.'

The youth mechanically got off his horse, and climbed up into the tree, while the mangled corpse got on to the horse, and rode away back towards Rome. He had not been gone five minutes when he heard four shots [3] fired.

Looking from his elevation in the direction of the sound, he saw his four evil companions, who had just fired their pieces into the corpse which rode his horse, without making it sit a bit less erect than before. Then he saw them go stealthily up to the figure and look at it, and then run away, wild with terror.

As soon as they had turned their backs, the corpse turned the horse's head round, and trotted back to the oak-tree.

'Now, my son,' said the corpse, alighting from the horse, 'I have done you this good turn because you said a De Profundis for me; but such interpositions don't befall a man every day. Turn over a new leaf, before a worse thing happens.'

Having said this, the dead body, piece by piece, replaced itself amid the branches of the oak-tree, where it had hung before.

The young man got on his horse again, penitent and thoughtful, and rode to a friary, [4] where, after spending an edifying life, he died a holy death.

---

[1] 'Il Morto della Quercia.'

[2] 'Camminò, camminò, camminò;' see note 6, p. 13.

[3] 'Quattro arquebuzate.'

[4] 'Frateria,' a popular word for a monastery.

THE DEAD MAN'S LETTER.[1]

THERE was a rich man, I cannot tell you how rich he was, who died and left all his great fortune to his son, palaces and houses, and farms and vineyards. The son entered into possession of all, and became a great man ; but he never thought of having a mass said for the soul of his father, from whom he had received all.

There was also, about the same time, a poor man, who had hardly enough to keep body and soul together, and he went into a church to pray that he might have wherewithal to feed his children. So poor was he, that he said within himself, 'None poorer than I can there be.' As he said that, his eye lighted on the box where alms were gathered, that masses might be offered for the souls in Purgatory. 'Yes,' he said, then, 'these are poorer than I,' and he felt in his pocket for his single *baiocco*, and he put it in the alms box for the holy souls.[2]

As he came out, he saw a *painone*[3] standing before the door, as if in waiting for him ; but as he was well-dressed, and looked rich, the poor man knew he could have no acquaintance with him, and would have passed on.

'You have done me so much good, and now you don't speak to me,' said the stranger.

'When did I thee much good?' said the poor man bewildered.

'Even now,' said the stranger ; for in reality he was no *painone*, but one of the holy souls who had taken that form, and he alluded to the poor man's last coin, of which he had deprived himself in charity.

'I cannot think to what your Excellency[4] alludes,' replied the poor man.

'Nevertheless it is true,' returned the *painone* ; 'and now I will ask you to do me another favour. Will you take this letter to such and such a palace ?' and he gave him the exact address. ‘ When you get there, you must insist on giving it into the hands of the master of the house himself. Never mind how many times you are refused, do not go away till you have given it to the master himself.’

‘ Never fear, your Excellency,’ answered the poor man, ‘ I’ll deliver it right.’

When he reached the palace, it was just as the *painone* had seemed to expect it would be. First the porter came forward with his cocked hat and his gilt knobbed stick, with the coloured cord twisted over it all the way down, and asked him whither he was going.

‘ To Count so-and-so,’ answered the poor man.

‘ All right ! give it here,’ said the splendid porter.

‘ By no means, my orders were to consign it to the count himself.’

‘ Go in and try,’ answered the porter. ‘ But you may as well save yourself the stairs ; they won’t let such as you in to the count.’

‘ I must follow orders,’ said the poor man, and passed on.

At the door of the apartment a liveried servant came to open.

‘ What do you want up here? if you have brought anything, why didn’t you leave it with the porter ? ’

‘ Because my orders are to give this letter into the count’s own hands,’ answered the poor man.

‘ A likely matter I shall call the “ Signor Conte ” out, and to such as you ! Give here, and don’t talk nonsense.’

‘ No ! into the count’s own hands must I give it.’

‘ Don’t be afraid ; I’ve lived here these thirty years, and no message for the “ Signor Conte ” ever went wrong that passed through my hands. Yours isn’t more precious than the rest, I suppose.’

‘ I know nothing about that, but I must follow orders.’

'And so must I, and I know my place too well to call out the "Signor Conte" to the like of you.'

The altercation brought out the valet.

'This fellow expects the "Signor Conte" to come to the door to take in his letters himself,' said the lackey, laughing disdainfully. 'What's to be done with the poor animal?'

'Give here, good man,' said the valet, patronisingly not paying much heed to the remarks of the servant; 'I am the "Signor Conte's" own body servant, and giving it to me is the same as giving it to himself.'

'Maybe,' answered the poor man, 'but I'm too simple to understand how one man can be the same as another. My orders are to give it to the count alone, and to the count alone I must give it.'

'Take it from him, and turn him out,' said the valet, with supreme disdain, and the lackey was not slow to take advantage of the permission. The poor man, however, would not yield his trust, and the scuffle that ensued brought the count himself out to learn the reason of so much noise.

The letter was now soon delivered. The count started when he saw the handwriting, and was impelled to tear the letter open at once, so much did its appearance seem to surprise him.

'Who gave you the letter?' he exclaimed, in an excited manner, as soon as he had rapidly devoured its contents.

'I cannot tell, I never saw the person before,' replied the poor man.

'Would you know him again?' inquired the count.

'Oh, most undoubtedly!' answered the poor man; 'he said such strange things to me that I looked hard at him.'

'Then come this way,' said the count; and he led him into a large hall, round which were hung many portraits in frames. 'Do you see one among these portraits that at all resembles him?' he said, when he had given him time to look round the walls.

'Yes, that is he!' said the poor man, unhesitatingly, pointing to the portrait of the count's father, from whom he had inherited such great wealth, and for whom he had never given the alms of a single mass.

'Then there is no doubt it was himself,' said the count. 'In this letter he tells me that you of your poverty have done for him what I with all my wealth have never done,' he added in a tone of compunction. 'For you have given alms for the repose of his soul, which I never have; therefore he bids me now take you and all your family into the palace to live with me, and to share all I have with you.'

After that he made the man and all his family come to live in the palace, as his father directed, and he was abundantly provided for the rest of his life.

¹ 'La Lettera del Morto.'
² 'Bussola,' a box for alms, &c.
³ 'Painone,' 'Paino'; a sneering way of naming a well-dressed person. 'Painone,' augmentative of the same.
⁴ 'Sua Eccellenza.' The cant form of address of the Roman beggar.

['I know one of that kind,' interposed one sitting by. 'Will you hear it? But mine is true, mine is a real fact, and happened no longer ago than last October;' and he told me the very names and address of the people concerned with the greatest particularity; this was in January 1873.]

THE WHITE SOUL.¹

THE people he had named were a husband and wife, shop-keepers, with a good business. They had taken in a woman, a widow, as they thought, to board with them for life.²

The first night after she came the wife suddenly woke up the husband, saying :—

' What is it that kneels at the foot of the bed ? surely it is a white soul.'

' I see nothing,' said the husband ; ' go to sleep ! '

The wife said no more, but the next night it was the same thing, and the next, and the next; and she described so sincerely what she saw, and with so much earnestness, that the husband could have no doubt that what she said was true. And as he saw it disturbed her rest, and made her ill, he said :—

' If it comes again, to-night, we will conjure it.'

It had been going on almost a month (I told you it happened in October), and it was just the night of All Souls' day [3] that he happened to say this.

That night, again, the wife woke him with a start—

' There it is,' she said, ' the white soul ; it kneels at the foot of the bed.'

The husband said nothing, but following the direction of his wife's hand, he solemnly bid the apparition depart, in the name of the Most Holy Trinity and the Madonna.

Though he had seen nothing, he, too, now heard a voice, and the voice said that it was her father whom the wife had seen ; that it was not well that they should have in the house the woman whom they had taken in to board, for that it was on her account he was now suffering penance. ' Think of this,' he said, finally, ' for I cannot stay to tell you more ; for it is the hour of prayer.' [4]

The lighting up of a masked ball could not be compared to the brightness [5] which filled the room as the spirit disappeared. And this the husband saw well, though he had not seen the soul.

The husband and wife thought a good deal of what they had heard ; they had never known before of the father's intimacy with this woman, but they inquired, and found it was even so.

Then the man took into his head to go to one of these new people, what do they call it? *spiritismo, magnetismo,* [6] or whatever it is. He made them call up the spirit of his wife's father, and he asked if it was he who had appeared at night in the bedroom all the month through, and he said, 'yes, that it was.' And he asked him about all the particulars, and he confirmed them all. 'Then,' he said, 'if indeed it was you, give me some sign to-night;' and he said he would.

There was a ruler in the chest of drawers in the bed-room, and all through the night there were knocks; now on the ceiling, now on the floor, now on the walls, as if given with that ruler, and we know those '*spiritismo*' people say the spirits make themselves understood by knocking.

After that, they sent away their boarder, though at considerable pecuniary loss.

---

[1] ' L'Anima Bianca.'

[2] ' A vitalizia' is an agreement by which persons pay a sum down and are taken in to board for the rest of their lives.

[3] ' La Festa dei Morti,' November 2.

[4] ' Chè è ora dell' orazione.' I give this very quaint idea in the words in which it was told to me.

[5] ' Era altro che un festino, il chiarore.' The lighting up of a theatre for a public masqued ball would naturally be the highest impression of brightness for a poor man in Rome. 'Altro che' is his favourite word in the sense of 'no comparison.' 'Altro!' alone stands for 'I should think so!' 'Isn't it indeed!' &c.

[6] Since the invasion of September 1870, Rome has been placarded with announcements of mediums who may be consulted on every possible occasion. I give the whole story as it was told me, but I have, of course, no means of knowing how the *séance* was conducted, and there is every likelihood the man would be so full of the strange occurrence that he would begin by letting out all on which he came to it to seek confirmation. The introduction of these mediums has been welcomed as supplying the means of gratifying that craving after the supernatural which was denied them under the former administration. 'Witchcraft was forbidden by the former law, therefore we may suppose it was wrong,' reason the less intelligent and those who wish to be deceived; '*spiritismo* is allowed by the law which rules us to-day, therefore we may suppose it is right;' and thus we are beginning to see here what Cantù had written of other parts of Italy and Europe: 'But who will feel the courage to contemn the follies of another age when he sees the absurd credulity of our own, which upon similar manifes-

tations founds other theories. . . . Recent writers on the subject (see in particular, Allan Kardec, ' Le Spiritisme à sa plus simple expression,' ' Le Livre des esprits,' &c.), themselves acknowledge that the oracles and pythonesses of old, and the genii, sorcerers, and magicians of later ages, were the predecessors of these mediums. We have therefore come back to that which we ridicule in our ancestors.'

[' I know a story like that,' said the first man, ' and a true one too; it happened in 1848 or 1849.']

THE WHITE SERPENT.[1]

MY story is also of a husband and wife, but they were peasants, and lived outside the gates.

'It is so cold to-night,' said the husband to the wife, as they went to bed, ' we shall freeze if we have another night like it. We must contrive to wake before it is light, and go and get some wood somewhere before we go to work, to make a fire to-morrow night.'

So they woke very early, before it was light, and went out to get wood.[2] The husband stood up in the tree, and the wife down below in a ditch, or hole. As she stood there she saw a great white serpent glide past her. ' Look, look!' she cried to her husband; ' see that great white serpent; surely there is something unnatural about it!'

' A white serpent!' answered her husband; ' what nonsense! Who ever heard of such a thing as a white serpent!'

' There it goes, then,' said the wife; ' you can see it for yourself.'

' I see nothing of the kind,' said the husband. ' There are no serpents about Rome this many a long year; and as for a white one, such a thing doesn't exist.'

While he spoke the serpent went through a hole in the ground. As the husband was so positive, the wife said no more, but they gathered up the wood and went home.

In the night, however, the wife had a dream. She

saw an Augustinian friar, long since dead, standing before her, who said ' Angela ! (that was indeed her name) if you would do me a favour listen to me. Did you see a white serpent this morning ? '

' Yes,' she answered; 'that I did, though my husband said there was no such thing as a white serpent in existence.'

' Well, if you would do me a pleasure, go back to the place where you saw the white serpent go in—not where he came out, but where you saw him go into the earth. Dig about that place, and, when you have dug a pretty good hole, a dead man will start up; [3] but don't be afraid, he can't hurt you, and won't want to hurt you. Take no notice of him, and go on digging, and no harm will come to you; you have nothing to be afraid of. If you dig on you will come to a heap of money. Take some of the biggest pieces of gold and carry them to St. Peter's, and take some of the smaller pieces and carry them to S. Agostino,[4] and let masses be said for that dead man. But you must tell no one alive anything about it.'

The woman was much too frightened to do what the friar had said, but she managed to keep the story to herself, though it made her look so anxious her husband could not help noticing something.

The next night the friar came again, and said the same words, only he added : 'If you are so frightened, Angela, you may take with you for company a little boy, but he must not be over seven, nor under six; and what you do you must tell no one. But you have nothing to fear, for if you do as I have said no one can harm you.'

For all his assurances, however, she could not make up her mind to go, nor this day could she even keep the story from her husband, for it weighed upon her mind. When he heard the story he said, ' I'll go with you.'

' Ah ! if you'll go, then I don't mind,' she said. ' But how will it be ? The friar was so particular that I should tell no one, evil may happen if I take another with me.'

'If there is nothing in the story, there's nothing to fear,' said the husband; 'and, if the story is true, there is a heap of money to reward one for a little fear; so let's go. Besides, if you think any harm will happen to you for taking me, I can stand on the top of the bank while you go down to the hole, and it can't be said properly that I'm there, while I shall yet be by to give you courage and help you if anything happens.'

'That way, I don't mind it,' answered the wife; and they went out together to the place, the husband, as he had said, standing by on a bank, and the wife creeping down into a hole. They took also two donkeys with them to bring away the treasure.

At the first stroke of the woman's spade there came such lugubrious cries that she was frightened into running away.

'Don't be afraid,' said the husband; 'cries don't hurt!' So the woman began digging again, and then there came out cries again worse than before, and the noise of rattling of chains, dreadful to hear. So terrified was the woman that she swooned away.

The husband then went down into the hole with what water he could find to bring her to herself, but the moment he got into the hole the spirits set upon him and beat him so that he had great livid marks all over.

After that neither of them had the heart to go back to try it again.

But the woman was in the habit of going to confession to one of the Augustinian fathers, and she told him all. The fathers sent and had the place dug up all about, and thought they had proved there was nothing there; but for all that, it generally happens that when a thing like that has to be done, it must be done by the person who is sent, and anybody else but that person trying it proves nothing at all.

One thing is certain, that when those horrid assassins [5] hide a heap of money they put a dead man's body at the entrance of the hole where they hide it, and say to it, ' Thou be on guard till one of such a name, be it Teresa, be it Angela, be it Pietro, comes;' and no one else going can be of any use, for it may be a hundred years before the coincidence can happen of a person just of the right name lighting on the spot—perhaps never.

' Yes, yes! that's a fact; that is not old wives' nonsense,' [6] was the chorus which greeted this enunciation.

---

[1] 'La serpe bianca;' 'serpe' is of both genders, but is most commonly used in the feminine as in the common saying 'allevarsi la serpe in seno,' to nurture a serpent in one's bosom.

[2] 'Per far legna.' 'Fare' is brought in on all occasions. Bazzarini gives 59 closely printed columns of instances of its various uses; here it means to cut wood for burning; 'legno' is wood; 'legna,' wood for burning.

[3] 'S'alzerà un morto.'

[4] S. Agostino is the favourite with the people of all the churches of Rome.

[5] 'Brutti assassini.' In a country where the cultus of ' il bello ' has been so well understood, ' ugly' has naturally come to be used as a term of deepest reproach.

[6] 'Si, si, questo è positivo, non è *donnicciolara*, è positivo.'

[7] This kind of spell seems analogous to one of which a curious account is preserved by Menghi (Compendio dell' Arte Essorcista, lib. ii. cap. xl.), which I quote, because it has a local connexion with Rome, and there are not many such. An inhabitant of Dachono in Bohemia, he says, brought his son, a priest, to Rome in the Pontificate of Pius II. (1458–64) to be exorcised, as all relief failed in his own country ; a woman whom he had reproved for her bad life had bewitched him, adding, 'that the spell (*maldicio*) was imposed on him by her under a certain tree, and if it was not removed in the same way, he could not otherwise be set free ; and she would not reveal under what tree it was.' The spell acted upon him only at such times as he was about to exercise his sacred ministry, and then it impeded his actions, forced him to put his tongue out at the cross, &c. &c. ' The more earnest the devotion with which I strive to give myself to prayer,' he said, ' so much the more cruelly the devil rends me ' (*mi lacera*). In St. Peter's, the narrator goes on to say, is a column brought from the Temple of Solomon, by means of which many possessed persons have been liberated, because our Lord had leant against it when teaching there, and it

was thought that this might be sufficiently potent to represent the fatal tree. He was brought to it, however, in vain. Being tied to it, and asked to point out the spot where Christ had touched it, the spirit which possessed him replied by making him bite it on a certain spot with his teeth and say, 'Qui stette, qui stette,' (here He stood) in Italian, although he did not know a word of the language, and was obliged to inquire what the words he had uttered meant. But the spell, nevertheless, was not got rid of thus. It was then understood that the spirit must be of that kind of which Christ had said 'he goeth not out except by prayer and fasting;' and a pious and venerable bishop, taking compassion on the man, devoted himself to prayer and fasting for him all through Lent; and thus he was delivered and sent back to his own country rejoicing.

['I, too, know a fact of that kind which most certainly happened, for I know Maria Grazia to whom it happened well, before she went to live at Velletri,' said one of them.]

THE PROCESSION OF VELLETRI.

MARIA GRAZIA lived in a convent of nuns at Velletri, and did their errands for them. One night one of the nuns who was ill got much worse towards night, and the factor[1] not being there, the Superior called up Maria Grazia and said to her,—'Maria Grazia, Sister Maria such a one[2] is so very bad that I must get you to go and call the provost to her. I'm sorry to send you out so late, but I fear she won't last till morning.'

Maria Grazia couldn't say nay to such an errand, and off she set by a clear moonlight to go to the house of the provost, which was a good step off and out of the town. All went well till Maria Grazia had left the houses behind her, but she was no sooner in the open country than she saw a great procession of white-robed priests and acolytes bearing torches coming towards her, chanting solemnly. 'What a fine procession!' thought Maria Grazia; 'I must hasten on to see it. But what can it be for at this time of night?'

Still she never doubted it was a real procession till she

got quite close, and then, to her surprise, the procession parted in two to let her go through the midst, which a real procession would never have done.

You may believe that she was frightened as she passed right through the midst of those beings who must have belonged to the other world, dazed as she was with the unearthly light of the flaring torches; it seemed as if it would last for ever. But it did come to an end at last, and then she was so frightened she didn't know what to do. Her legs trembled too much to carry her on further from home, and if she turned back there would be that dreadful procession again. Curiosity prompted her to turn her head, in spite of her fears; and what gave her almost more alarm than seeing the procession was the fact that it was no longer to be seen. What could have become of it in the midst of the open field? Then the fear of the good nun dying without the sacraments through her faint-heartedness stirred her, but in vain she tried to pluck up courage. 'Oh!' she thought, 'if there were only some one going the same road, then I shouldn't mind!'

She had hardly formed the wish when she saw a peasant coming along over the very spot where the procession had passed out of sight. 'Now it's all right,' she said; for by the light of the moon he seemed a very respectable steady-looking peasant.

'What did you think of that procession, good man,' said Maria Grazia; 'for it must have passed close by you, too?'

The peasant continued coming towards her, but said nothing.

'Didn't it frighten you? It did me; and I don't think I could have moved from the spot if you hadn't come up. I've got to go to the provost's house, to fetch him to a dying nun; it's only a step off this road, will you mind walking with me till I get there?'

The peasant continued walking towards her, but answered nothing.

'Maybe you're afraid of me, as I was of the procession, that you don't speak,' continued Maria Grazia; 'but I am not a spirit. I am Maria Grazia, servant in such and such a convent at Velletri.'

But still the peasant said nothing.

'What a very odd man!' thought Maria Grazia. 'But as he seems to be going my way he'll answer the purpose of company whether he speaks or not.' And she walked on without fear till she came to the provost's house, the peasant always keeping beside her but never speaking. Arrived at the provost's gate she turned round to salute and thank him, and he was nowhere to be seen. He too had disappeared! he too was a spirit!

When the archpriest came he had his nephew and his servant to go with him, and they carried torches of straw,[3] for it seems in that part of the country they use straw torches; so she went back in good company.

And Maria Grazia told me that herself.

[1] 'Fattore,' an agent; a man who attends to the business and pecuniary affairs of a convent.

[2] 'Suora Maria tale.' Mary being such a favourite name, it has to be generally qualified by a second name being appended to it by way of distinction.

[3] 'Fiaccole di paglia.'

SMALLER GHOST AND TREASURE STORIES AND FAMILY AND LOCAL TRADITIONS.

1

BUT the belief in ghosts, though it exists, as we have seen by the above specimens, is by no means generally diffused. 'No!' I don't believe such things,' is the general reply I have received when inquiring for them. I could not, indeed, help being annoyed with the strongmindedness of an old woman one day, who asserted her contempt for the idea so persistently that she quite 'shut up' two others who were inclined to be communicative of their experiences.

'I've often slept in a room where it was said the ghost of a woman who was killed there, walked about with her head under her arm; but I never saw her,' said I, to set the thing going.

'Oh! I wouldn't have done that for the world!' exclaimed Nos. 2 and 3 together.

'And why not?' said No. 1. 'There was nothing to be seen, of course. There are no such things as ghosts!'[2]

'Ah! Some see them and some don't see them, and you're one of those who don't see them. *That's* where it is,' said No. 2.

'Yes,' added No. 3; 'I know lots of people who *have* seen them,' and she was going on to give examples, but No. 1 put her down.

'Did you ever see one yourself?' interposed I, to keep the ball rolling.

'Well, yes . . . so far that . . .' she began, hesitatingly; but No. 1 broke in again with her vehement iteration that there are no ghosts.

'I *know* there *are*, though,' persisted No. 2; 'for my mother has told me there is a house . . .'

'Here in Rome?' asked I.

'Yes, here in Rome, where she used to work, where there was a ghost[3] that used to pull the bedclothes off anyone who slept in that particular room, and leave him uncovered. As fast as you pulled them over you, the spirit pulled them off again;' and she imitated the movement with her hands.

2

'Oibo!' interposed No. 1. '*I*'ll tell you what ghosts are. Ghosts are most often robbers, who get people to think they are ghosts, in order to be able to rob in peace. There was a famous one, I remember well, about the year 1830, who used to be called the Ghost of St. John's,[4] because he used to make himself heard in the houses about St. John Lateran. There were several robberies in the same neighbourhood just at the same time, but no one thought of connecting the two things, till at last one bethought him of it, and he laid in wait, pistol in hand, till the ghost came by.

'By it came; and "pop!" went the pistol. And there, on the spot, lay the body of one whom the police didn't see for the first time.

'That's what ghosts are!'

'That may have been,' replied Nos. 2 and 3; 'but that doesn't prove that there are no ghosts for all that.'

3

'Ghosts! ghosts! are all in silly people's own heads!' exclaimed No. 1. 'I can tell you of one there was in an old palace at Foligno. No one would sleep there because of the ghosts, and the palace became quite deserted. At last a sportsman,[5] who was a relation of mine, said *he* wasn't afraid; he would go up there one night, and give an account of it. He went there, pistol in hand. At the time for the ghosts to appear, in through a hole over the window *did* come a great thing with wings. The sportsman, nothing daunted, fired at it; and, lo and behold, a large hawk [6] fell dead on the floor; then another, and another, up to five of them.

'That's what ghosts are, I tell you!'

[The following is from another narrator.]

4

SOME friars were going round begging for their convent, when night overtook them in a wood.

'What shall we do if any wolves come? I don't believe there is any habitation in these parts, and there will be no place to run to and no one to help us. We must commend ourselves to the Madonna, and wait the event.'

They had scarcely done so when one of them saw a light sparkling through the trees. They thought it came from some woodman's cottage, and followed its leading; but instead of a cottage they came to a handsome inn. As the door stood invitingly open they went in: a fire blazed on the hearth; a repast was spread on the table;

a number of maidens, attired in pure and shining white, flitted about and brought all they wanted. When they had well supped, these led them to a room where was a bed apiece, and in the morning again they gave them breakfast.

Before they started again, the friars asked the maidens to take them to offer their thanks to the mistress of the house, and they led them into a room where was a most beautiful lady, who inquired kindly if they had been well served and wished them a good journey. Moreover, as they went she gave them a folded paper.

The friars, unused to be so entertained, were much bewildered, and wondered what lady it could be who lived all alone with her maidens in that wild wood; and they turned back to look at the inn that they might know it again, but it had entirely disappeared, nor was there a vestige of it to be found.

Then they opened the folded paper the lady had given them, and by the shining letters within they knew it was the Madonna herself had entertained them.

5

Another, who didn't believe there were ghosts to be seen— 'she had heard plenty of such stories, but she didn't give her mind to such things,'—yet told me, she believed there were treasures hid in countless places,[7] but people could seldom get at them ; there was always a hailstorm, or an earthquake, or something, which happened to stop them ; the Devil wouldn't let people get at them.

6

Another, whose belief in ghosts was doubtful, reckoned she *knew* various cases to be facts, in which men hid treasures under a spell, that could be removed if a person could devise the counterspell, by hitting, even accidentally, on what the original spell had been.[8]

7

‘ If you want ghost-stories, I can tell them as well as another ; but mind I don't believe such things,’ said another.

‘ Tell me what you've heard, then.’

‘ WELL, I have heard say that there was a woman in the Monti,[9] and not so long ago either, who was always finding money about the house, and that too, in places where she knew no one could have put it. The first thing in the morning when she got up she would find it on the floor all about the room. Or if she got up from her work in the middle of the day, though she knew no one had come in, there it would be.

‘ One day she saw three silver *papetti* [10] on the floor. It wasn't that there was no silver money ever to be seen, and nothing but dirty paper notes, and half of them false, as it is now o' days. It was in the time of the Pope, and there was plenty of silver for those who had money at all, but still, to see three silver *papetti* lying on the floor all of a sudden was a sight for anyone.

‘ It looked so strange that she hesitated before she picked it up. But at last she made up her mind and took it. No sooner had she done so than a spirit appeared before her, and said, “ Come down with me into the cellar and I'll show you something.”

‘ “ No, thank you, sir,” said the woman, not knowing what to do for fear.

‘ “ Nonsense ! come down, you shan't be hurt,” said the spirit.

‘ “ I'd *rather* not, sir, thank you,” was all the woman could stammer out.

‘ “ You must come ! I'll give you something to make you rich for good and all,” persisted the spirit ; and, somehow, she didn't know how, she felt herself obliged to follow him.

‘ Down in the cellar was another spirit awaiting her,

and the moment she got down they took her, the one by the head and the other by the feet, and laid her into a coffin [11] which stood there all ready on a bier.[12]　One at each end, they took it up, with the woman in it, and walked round and round the cellar with it, chaunting the " Miserere," and she was too frightened to call out, much more to attempt to move.

' By-and-by they set the bier down, and as she heard nothing more she concluded the spirits were gone ; still she durst not move till some few rays of daylight began to peep through ; then she summoned up courage to get out of the coffin.

' When she did so she saw it was all of solid gold, as well as the bier.　There was gold enough to have made her rich to the end of her days, but she was so frightened that she wasn't able to enjoy it, but died at the end of a month ; for riches that are got in ways that are not straightforward never profit anyone.

' That's the story as it's told ; but I don't believe those things, mind you.'

8

' Ah ! I remember, too, when I was quite a girl and lived with my father and mother in a house near Piazza Barberini, I remember one day my little sister Ghisa coming running up out of the cellar crying out there was a spirit which had stood waving its hand, and beckoning to her.

' And when the others went down to see what it was all about, they did find some human bones in a corner of the cellar, and no one knew how they got there.　But that didn't prove that the child had actually seen a ghost.'

9

[The above story of the golden coffin, it will be observed, was told as of a particular district in Rome.　Another time, it was

told me of a village in the Campagna; the narrator said she
knew the name well, but could not recollect it at the moment.
In other respects, there were few differences of detail; but the
countrywoman was more robust and courageous than the town
woman, and this is how she got on.]

'She was always finding half-pence about the ground
where she worked. One day she found a silver piece; as
she went to pick it up she saw "One" standing by.
"Come with me!" he said; and the countrywoman, not
at all afraid, went with him. He led her by solitary
ways till he came to a lone empty cottage, when he left
her. Quite undaunted, she walked in. There was a large
empty room in the midst, all lighted up with ever so
many lights.

' "Don't touch, don't touch!" screamed an anxious
voice. "Touch! touch!" shouted a more gloomy voice.
At last she did touch.'

['Touched *what*?' asked I; 'the lights, or the floor, or
what?'
The narrator was posed by the question.
'Oh, I don't know *what* she touched. It must be supposed
she touched *something*.']

'Instantly all the lights went out, and she stood in
the strange place in the dark. Still she was not frightened.
She had the courage to strike a light. By its means she
saw there was now a large coffin in the midst of the room.
She went straight up to it and opened it. It was *full* of
money! Waiting till daylight, she took home with her
as much as ever she could carry. But she kept her own
counsel, and never told anyone, and when she wanted
money she went back there and took it.

' But if she never told anyone, how did anyone know
the story?'

10

' This one now is quite true, for Sora Maria (you know who I mean) told me of it, and she knew the woman as well as her own sister.

' This woman lived near the church of S. Spirito de Napoletani—you know it ? '

' Yes, in Via Giulia.'

' Exactly. Well, she used to take in washing to make a little for herself more than what her husband gave her. But he didn't like her doing it, and was very angry whenever he saw her at it. But as he was out all day at his work, she used to manage to get through with it in his absence pretty well.

' One day the water would not boil, all she could do. First she got excited, then she got angry. " It isn't that I care," she said ; " but if my husband comes home and sees what I am doing he'll be so angry ! What *will* he say ! What *shall* I do ! I would give my soul to the devil only to get it boiling in time ! "

' Scarcely had she said the words when *blu, blu, blu !* the water began to bubble up in the pot, boiling furiously all of a sudden, and though it was now so short a time before her husband came back, all the work was done and out of sight, and he perceived nothing.

' In the night came a *paino*,[13] and stood in the doorway of the bedroom and beckoned to her ; and as she looked she saw that every now and then flames and sparks flew about, out of him.

' At last she could stand it no longer, and she woke her husband and told him all. The husband could see nothing, and tried to quiet her, but she kept crying out, now, " Here he is, here ! " and now, " There he is, there ! " till at last he was obliged to call the friars of S. Spirito de' Napolitani to her to exorcise the spirit ; and it was very difficult, because she had promised to give her soul to the devil ;

but it had been thoughtlessly done, and in the end the apparition was got rid of.'

[It so happens, however, that the church of S. Spirito de' Napolitani is served by secular priests, and not friars.]

11

' Here's another thing I have heard that will do for you.

' There were two who took a peasant and carried him into the Campagna.'

' What ! two ghosts ? '

' No, no ! two fellows who had more money than they knew what to do with. They took him into the Campagna and made an omelette very good, with plenty of sweet-scented herbs in it, and made him eat it.

' Then they took a barrel and measured him against it, and then another, till they found one to fit, and killed him and filled it up with money, and made a hole in the earth and buried it.

' And they said over it, " No one may disturb you till one comes who makes an omelette with just the same sweet-scented herbs as we have used, and makes it just on the top of this hole. Then, come out and say, ' This gold is yours.' "

' And, of course, in the ordinary course of things, no one would have thought of making an omelette with just those same herbs, just on the top of that hole. But there was one who knew the other two, and suspected something of what they were going to do, and he went up and hid himself in a tree, and watched all that was done, and heard the words.

' As soon as they were gone he came down and took some nice fresh eggs, and just the same sweet-scented herbs the others had used, and made an omelette just over the hole where he had seen them bury the barrel with the money and the man in it.

' He had no sooner done so than the man came out all whole and well, and said: "Oh, how many years have I been shut up in that dark place" (though he hàdn't been there half-an-hour) "till you came to deliver me! Therefore all the gold is yours."

' Such things can't be true, so I don't believe them; but that's what they tell.'

12

' And don't they tell other stories about there being treasures hid about Rome?'

' Oh, yes; and some of *them are* true. It is quite certain that —— ' (and she named a very rich Roman prince) ' found all the money that makes him so rich bricked up in a wall. They were altering a wall, and they came upon some gold. It was all behind a great wall, as big as the side of a room—all full, full of gold. When they came and told him he pretended not to be at all surprised, and said: " Oh, yes; it's some money I put away there; it's nothing; leave it alone." But in the night he went down secretly and fetched it away,[14] and that's how he became so rich; for his father was a money-changer, who had a table where he changed money in the open street, and my father knew him quite well.'

13

' Then there's the —— ' (another rich family). ' They got their money by confiscation of another[15] family, generations ago. That's why they're so charitable. What they give away in charity to the poor is immense; but it is because they know how the money came into the family, and they want to make amends for their ancestors.'

---

[1] ' Ma che! ' is a very strong and indignant form of ' No! ' about equivalent to ' What are you thinking of?' ' How can you?' In Tuscany they say, ' Che! Che!'

[2] ' Fantasimi,' for ' fantasmi,' apparitions.

[3] ' Spirito.'

[4] ' Il fantasimo di S. Giovanni.'

[5] ' Cacciatore ' is a huntsman or sportsman of any kind; but in Rome it designates especially a man of a roving and adventurous class whose occupation in life is to shoot game for the market according to the various seasons, as there are large tracts of country where game is not preserved.

[6] ' Falcaccio,' a horrid, great hawk.

[7] Cancellieri (Mercato, § xvi.) mentions the actual finding of such a treasure; or at least of ' thousands of pieces of gold money, in a hole leading to a drain of the fountain in Piazza Madama, on May 30, 1652, by a boy who had accidentally dropped a toy into this hole.' One such fact would afford substance to a multitude of such fictions: though they doubtless had their origin in the discovery of mineral wealth.

[8] See conversation at the end of the ' Serpe bianca.' Further details of a similar nature were given me in connection with a number of brigand stories which I have in MS.

[9] ' Monti,' Rione Monti, the most populous district in Rome.

[10] ' Papetto,' equal to two pauls; about three halfpence more than a (silver) lira or franc. In use in Rome until the monetary convention with France in 1868.

[11] ' Cataletto,' a kind of large roomy coffin, with a hollow wagonheaded lid, in which dead or wounded persons are carried.

[12] ' Barretta ' or ' bara,' is the bier on which the ' cataletto ' is carried; but it is most often made all in one, and either word is used for either, as also ' feretro.' ' Aver la bocca sulla bara,' is ' to have one foot in the grave.'

[13] ' Paino,' see n. 3, p. 264.

[14] It must be a very quaint condition of mind which can imagine that a fortune of something like three millions sterling can be quietly removed in secret in gold coin from a cellar to a bedroom in the small hours of the night. But then to persons like the narrator a few pieces of gold seem a fortune.

[15] I do not give the names because, though the tradition is probably true enough of somebody, the particular names introduced were decidedly incorrect historically.

[These treasure stories are common everywhere. In Tirol, especially, they abound, and are of two kinds. First, concerning treasure hidden in the earth, arising out of the metal mines that were formerly worked there, and the carbuncles which are still found; and the second, precisely like these, of money walled-up in old houses and castles. A countryman, who saw me sketching the old ruin of Monte Rufiano, on a height not far from the banks of Lake Thrasimene, told me a story about it, just like a Tirolese story, of treasure hidden ever so deep under it, and guarded by twelve spectres, who went about, carrying torches in procession, on a Good Friday.

Senhor de Saraiva tells me there is a great variety of such stories in Portugal, where the treasures are generally said to have been hidden by the Moors, and are supposed to be buried under a gigantic depth of rock. A place was once pointed out to him, where there were said to be two enormous jars, one full of gold, and the other of boiling pitch. If, in digging, a man came upon the right one, he would be rich enough to buy up the whole world; but if, by ill luck, his spade first reached the other, the pitch would overflow and destroy everyone on the face of the earth; so that no one dared to make the attempt. The people believe that such localities may be revealed to them in dreams. But they must dream the same dream three nights running, and not tell it to anyone. If they tell it, they will find the money all turned to charcoal. Brick boxes of charcoal have frequently been found buried under Roman boundary stones in Portugal, and in this, he thinks, lies the origin of this latter fancy.

It is remarkable how many odds and ends of history remain laid up in the memories of the Roman people, like the majolica vases and point-lace in their houses. A great favourite with them is the story of Beatrice Cenci, which they tell, under the name of ' La bella Cenci,' with more or less exaggeration of detail.

' Do you know the story of " Sciarra Colonna ? " ' said an old woman, who seemed scarcely a person likely to know much about such matters.]

1

SCIARRA COLONNA.

THERE were two of the Colonna. One was Sciarra; I don't know the name of the other. They were always fighting against the pope of their time.[1] At last they took him and shut him up in a tower in the Campagna, and kept him there till they had starved him to death; and when the people found him afterwards, what do you think?—in his extremity he had gnawed off all the tips of his fingers.

When these two Colonna found they had actually

killed a Pope, they got so frightened that they ran away to hide themselves. They ran away to France, to Paris, and at last, when all the money they were able to carry with them was spent, they were obliged to take a place as stablemen in the king's palace, and they washed the carriages and cleaned down the horses like common men. But they couldn't hide that they were great lords; the people saw there was something different from themselves about them, and they watched them, and saw that they waited on each other alternately every day at table, and you could see what great ceremony they were used to. Then other things were seen, I forget what now, but little by little, and by one thing and another, people suspected at last who they really were.

Then some one went and told the king of France, and he had them called up before him.

They came just as they were, in their stable clothes, wooden shoes [2] and all.

The king sat to receive them in a raised seat hung all round with cloth of gold, and he said :

'Now, I know one thing. You two are hiding from justice. Who you are I don't know exactly for certain. I believe you are the Colonna. If you confess you are the Colonna, I will make the affair straight for you; but, if you will not say, then I will have you shut up in prison till I find out who you are, and what you have done.'

Then they owned that they were the Colonna,[3] and the king sent an ambassador to the Pope that then was, and the thing was arranged, and after a time they came back to Rome.

---

[1] Litta, 'Storia delle Famiglie italiane,' traces that from the beginning the Colonna family was always Ghibeline. The present representatives of the house, however, are reckoned Papalini.

[2] 'Zoccolo,' a wooden sandal kept on the foot by a leather strap over the instep. It is worn by certain 'scalsi' or 'barefooted' friars, hence called by the people 'zoccolanti.' The street near Ponte Sisto in Rome, called Via delle Zoccolette, received its name from a convent of nuns there who also wore 'zoccoli.'

¹ That Sciarra Colonna headed a band of 'spadassini' against Boniface VIII., and made himself the tool of Philippe le Bel, is of course true to history, as also that he held him imprisoned for a time at Anagni. The Pontiff's biographer, Tosti, mentions however only to refute them, ' le favole Ferretiane,' to which Sismondi, ' Storia delle Republiche italiane,' gives currency, and which embody the floating tradition in the text. 'Ferreto da Vicenza,' writes Tosti, ' narrates that a kind of poison was administered to this great Pontiff, which put him in a state of phrenzy; the servant who waited on him, also, was sent away, and being left alone in the room he is supposed to have gnawed at a stick (in another allusion to the same fable— at page 293—he says, ' his fingers' as in the text), and struck his head against the wall so desperately that his white hairs were all stained with blood; finally, that he suffocated himself under the counterpane invoking Beelzebub. But when we think how Boniface arrived at extreme old age, enfeebled with reverses; how, shut up in a room alone, there was no one to be witness to the alleged gnawing and knocking and Satanic invocations, and how that the manner of his death was quite differently related by eye-witnesses, I do not know for whom Sismondi could have thought he was writing when he marred his history by inserting such a fable. What certainly happened, and it is certified by Cardinal Stefaneschi, who was present, and by the Report afterwards drawn up of the acts of Boniface—was, that ' he was lodged in the Vatican at the time of his death, and breathed his last tranquilly. The bed of the dying Pontiff was surrounded by eight cardinals and by other distinguished persons (Process. Bonif. p. 37, p. 15), to whom, according to the custom of his predecessors, he made confession of faith, affirming, however enfeebled his voice, that he had lived in that faith, and wished to die in it, a Catholic. Consoled with the Viaticum of the Sacraments he gave up his soul to God, weary with the prolonged struggle he had sustained for the rights of the Church, . . . thirty-five days after his imprisonment at Anagni' (vol. ii. p. 286-7). Platina goes into less detail, but also records that he died in Rome (Le vite de' Pontefici, Venice, 1674, p. 344). The magnanimous stedfastness evinced by Boniface when attacked by Colonna and Nogaret, all abandoned as he was by human aid (detailed by Tosti, p. 276, *et seq.*), could not but have been succeeded by a grander closing scene than that imagined by Ferreto. Maroni (vi. 17-18) not only narrates that he survived the Anagni affair to return to Rome, but that with great Christian charity he ordered Nogaret, who had been taken prisoner by the Romans in the meantime, to be released from confinement; and [xiv. 283] that he could have had no poison administered to him at Anagni, for all the time he was imprisoned he would eat nothing but eggs on purpose to be proof against it.' The best disproof of the story, however, is that given by Tosti (p. 296-7). In the clearing for the rebuilding of the nave of St. Peter's, 302 years after the death of Boniface, his sepulchre was opened and the grave then revealed the truth. It so happened that his body had scarcely undergone any change, and those who stood by could hence depose that both his head and his hands were quite perfect;

there were no marks or blows on the former, and so far from his finger-tips being gnawed, they noticed that the nails even were particularly long. The face also wore a peculiarly placid expression.

Several contemporary writers cited by Tosti tell, however, that Benedict XI., Boniface's successor, died of poison believed to have been administered by Sciarra Colonna at the instigation of Philippe le Bel. But unfortunately for the tradition in the text Moroni [xiv. 283], who also mentions this, adds that Sciarra Colonna died in exile as he deserved. The two Cardinals Colonna, however, who had been exiled with the rest of the family, were reinstated by Benedict XI., and Clement V. in 1305 restored the other members of it to their possessions in the Roman States, where they made themselves obnoxious enough during the Papal residence at Avignon, and were as hostile to Rienzi as they had ever been to the Popes.

2

DONNA OLIMPIA.

THE vices of the rich are never forgotten by the people, and the traditions that still are current in Rome about Donna Olimpia [1] are such that I have had to refuse to listen to them. But I feel bound to mention them here, because it is curious that they should so live on for more than two hundred years (the traditions of Sciarra Colonna, however, are six hundred years old). They have, doubtless, rather gained than lost in transmission. Cardinal Camillo Pamfili, Donna Olimpia's son, presents one of those rare instances of which history has only five or six in all to record, in which, for the sake of keeping up the succession to a noble or royal house, it has been permitted [2] to leave the ecclesiastical state for married life.[3] The singularity of this incident has impressed it in the memory of the people, and her promotion of it has contributed to magnify, not only the fantastic element in their narratives, but also the popular feeling against her; thus she is accused of having had a second object in promoting it, namely, to get the place in the pontifical household thus vacated filled by a very simple[4] nephew, and thus increase her own importance at the papal court. The pasquinades written about her in her own age were such that Cancellieri[5] tells us ' spies were set, dressed in silk attire, to discover the authors of such lampoons (*motti vituperosi*).'

[1] Donna Olimpia Pamfili, nata Maidalchini, wife of the brother of Innocent X.

[2] Cancellieri Mercato, § ix. note 7.

[3] He had not, however, been originally intended for the Church ; had been General of the Pontifical forces before he was Cardinal, and was only in Deacon's orders.

[4] His simplicity was the subject of many contemporary *mots* and anecdotes ; e.g. at the time of his elevation to the purple the Pasquin statue had been temporarily lost to view by a hoarding put up for the erection of a neighbouring palace ; 'Marforio' was supposed to express his condolence for the eclipse of his rival in the following distich :

> ' Non piangere Pasquino
> Chè sarà tuo compagno Maidalchino.'

His want of capacity seems however to have been compensated by his goodness of heart.

[5] Cancellieri Mercato, § viii. As I have been desirous to put nothing in the text but what has reached myself by verbal tradition, I will add some no less interesting details collected by Cancellieri, in this place.

It was at her house in Piazza Navona that Bernini was rehabilitated in his character of first sculptor and architect of his time. 'Papa Pamfili,' though only the son of a tailor,[1] was yet a patron of art. Highly famed under Urban VIII. the preceding Pontiff, Bernini had been misrepresented by his rivals to Innocent. In an unpublished Diary of Giacinto Gigli, Cancellieri finds that he was taken so seriously ill on St. Peter's Day, 1641 [2] that his life was for some time despaired of, in consequence of his Campanile—a specimen one of two he had designed for St. Peter's—being disapproved by the Pope and ordered to be taken down. Another cognate tradition he gives from a MS. Diary of Valerio is, that in digging the foundations for this tower a 'canale d'acqua' was discovered deeper than the bed of the Tiber and wide enough to go on it in a boat; Mgr. Costaguti, maggiordomo of his Holiness, told me about it himself, and he had had him-

[1] A certain Niccolo Caferri was much ridiculed for the spirit of adulation with which he pretended to trace up Innocent X.'s genealogy to Pamphilus, king of Doris, 300 years before the birth of Rome. But the Pope himself was so little ashamed of his origin that Cancellieri tells us he took a piece of cloth for one of his armorial bearings in memory of it.

[2] This date, however, must be incorrect, as Innocent X. only began to reign in 1644. This grandiose Campanile is described at length, and a plate of it given in Fontana, 'Descrizione del tempio Vaticano,' p. 262, *et seq.* It was 360 ft. in height.

self let down to see it. As it had a sandy bottom, it washed away the foundations of the tower, and rendered it impossible to leave it standing. The water
came from Anguillara' (on Lake Bracciano, about 28 miles) 'and the Pope
had the old conduit reconstructed and used the water for many fountains
in imitation of Sixtus V.[1] He goes on to add an extraordinary account
of a Dragon quite of the legendary type, that was found in charge of this
water, and was killed, not by a hero or a knight, but, by the labourers
working at the conduit.

It was Innocent X.'s ambition to remove the great obelisk (since
called 'Obelisco Pamfilio') which lay in three pieces in the Circo di Mas-
senzio, near the Appian Way, and to set it up in Piazza Navona. Bernini
being, as I have said, in disfavour, other architects were commissioned to
offer designs for the work; but the Pope was not satisfied with any of them,
and the matter stood over. Meantime Piombino (Niccolò Ludovisi) who,
had married a niece of the Pope's, and who was a great friend of Bernini,
privately instructed him to send him a model of what he would suggest for
the purpose, saying he wanted it for his own satisfaction, lest Bernini should
refuse the unauthorised competition. Bernini then produced the elaborate
conception which has been so warmly extolled by some and so hastily blamed
by others, but which cannot be judged without a prolonged study of all the
poetical allegories and conceits it was his intention to embody.

The Pope went to the house of Donna Olimpia in Piazza Navona to
dine after the Procession to the Minerva on the Annunciation,[2] and she
placed the model in a room through which the Pope must pass after dinner.
It did not fail to arrest his notice, and he was so much struck with it that
he spent half an hour examining it in detail and listening to the explanation of its emblematical devices. At last he exclaimed, 'It can be by no
other hand than Bernini's! and he must be employed in spite of all that
may be said against him!' From that time Bernini was once more all
that he had been before in Rome (Mercato, § ix.). When Innocent saw
the great work completed, and the water of the four rivers for the first time
gushing from it, he declared to Bernini he had given him pleasure great
enough to add ten years to his life; and he sent over to Donna Olimpia for
a hundred 'Doppie'[3] to distribute among the workmen. Subsequently he
had a medal struck with the inscription AGONALIUM CRUORE ABLUTO AQUA
VERGINE, in allusion to the games of which Piazza Navona is supposed[4]
to have been the scene, and the 'Vergine' aqueduct from which the fountains were supplied. 'Papa Pamfili' also restored St. John Lateran, and

---

[1] He does not specify what pope, and the wording used seems to imply
Innocent X., but this aqueduct is always ascribed to Paul V., twenty years
earlier. and is called the *Acqua* Paola.

[2] Described in Cancellieri, 'Descrizione delle Cappelle Ponteficie,' cap. x.

[3] In Melchiorri's table of Roman moneys he gives the value (in 1758, a hundred years later) of a *doppio* as 4 scudi 40 bajocchi ; and of a *doppia* at 6 scudi,
42 bajocchi. It appears to be the latter the Pope sent for.

[4] Dyer says it was the *Stadium* of Domitian, and Becker, that there is no
proof it was ever a circus.

undertook many other works, but was somewhat hampered by the discontent of the people at the expense, expressed in the following pasquinades :

> ' Noi volemo altro che guglie e fontane :
> Pane volemo, pane! pane! pane!'

and

> ' Ut lapides isti panes fiant!'

To return to Donna Olimpia. One of the pasquinades on her preserved in Cancellieri from Gigli's diary, refers to an accusation against her, that she had been very liberal both to religious communities and to the people until her brother-in-law[1] was made Pope, and that when that object was attained she ceased her bounty. Pasquin wrote upon this, ' Donna Olimpia ' fuerat olim pia, nunc impia.'

Another declared that the said brother-in-law ' Olympiam potius quam Olympum respicere videbatur,' an accusation he declares to have been invented solely for the sake of punning, and without any truth, on faith of the character given him by his biographers, and of the fact that he was more than seventy-one when raised to the Papacy, and so deformed and ugly that Guido put his portrait under the feet of the archangel in his famous picture of St. Michael. (Mercato, Appendix, n. 4 to N. x.) She was, however, sometimes inexcusable in her haughty caprices, as, for instance, when she invited five and twenty Roman ladies to see a pageant, and then asked only eight of them to sit down to table with her, leaving the remainder 'mortificate alle finestre ; ' and frequently more free than choice in her *mots.* Her grandchildren seem to have inherited this freedom of speech; Gigli (quoted by Cancellieri, Mercato § xvi. and xx.) records in his Diary that the eldest of them, Giambattista, being asked one day by the Pope, who took great notice of him, if he had seen St. Agnese in Piazza Navona, which he was then building, replied (though only seven years old), ' I have not seen it yet ; but you, if you don't make haste, won't live to see it completed.' It would seem to have been a popular prophecy which the child had caught up, and it so happens that the event bore it out.

There is nothing, however, which shows the heartless character of Donna Olimpia more glaringly than her refusal to pay a farthing to bury the Pope, alleging she was ' only a poor widow! ' and this, though the Pope had not only ' favoured her so much as to endanger his reputation,'[2] but had handed to her all his disposable property on his deathbed. Donna Olimpia so utterly abandoned his body that it was carried down into a lumber-room where workmen kept their tools, and one poor labourer had the charity to buy a tallow candle to burn beside it, and another paid some one to watch it, to keep the mice off which abounded there. Finally, a Mgr.

---

[1] Cancellieri calls Innocent her *cognato,* and *cognato* in common conversation now is used for a cousin. Bazzarini explains it as ' any relationship by marriage.'

[2] MS. life of his successor Alex. VII. by Card. Pallavicini, quoted by Novaes : Storia de' Sommi Pontefici, x. 61.

Scotti, his maggiordomo, paid for a coffin of 'albuccio,'[1] and a former maggiordomo, whom he had dispossessed, gave five scudi (returning good for evil) to pay the expenses of burying him. It was not till twelve years later that he had a fitting funeral in S. Maria dell' Anima.

When a few months after Innocent's death Donna Olimpia endeavoured to put herself on her old footing at the Vatican Court, by sending a valuable present of some gold vases to Alexander VII., that Pope testified his appreciation of her by returning her offering ; adding the message that she was not to take the trouble to visit his palace, as it was no place for women.[2] There was subsequently some angry correspondence between her and this Pope concerning the delays occasioned by her parsimony in completing the church in Piazza Navona, and the consequent obstruction of the Piazza, a great inconvenience to the public on account of its use as a market-place. Finally he banished her from Rome, fixing her residence at Orvieto, where she fell a victim to the plague two years after.

Her palace in Piazza Navona became in 1695 the residence of Lord Castlemaine, ambassador of James II. to the Holy See. He had an ox roasted whole before it, and other bounties distributed to the people on occasion of the birth of 'The Pretender.'

THE MUNIFICENCE OF PRINCE BORGHESE.

[If the Romans remember the vices of their princely families, they are proud of storing up the memory of their virtues too ; and the following narrative was told me with great enthusiasm.]

LIBERALITY is a distinguishing characteristic of the Borghese family. It was always a matter of emulation who should get taken into their service, and no one who was once placed there ever let himself be sent away again, it was too good a thing to lose.

There was a man-servant, however, once who gave the Prince, I think it was the father of this one, an insolent answer, and he turned him off.

No one would take that man. Wherever he applied, when they asked him, 'Where have you lived?' and he answered, '*in casa Borghese*,' everyone answered, ' Oh, if you couldn't live with Borghese, I'm sure I've nothing

---

[1] Nothing better than deal, I believe.
[2] Mercato, § xxi.

better to offer you!' and the door was shut in his face.
It wasn't in one place or two, but *everywhere*, Borghese's
character is so well known in Rome.   As he couldn't get
a place, however, he was reduced to near starvation, and
he had a wife and six children, all with nothing to eat.
Every article of furniture went to the Monte di Pietà,
and almost every article of clothing; and yet hunger
stared them in the face.

Then the man got desperate, and he went out one
night and waited for Borghese in a lonely street in the
dark, with a knife in his hand, and said, ' Your purse!'

Borghese thought he had a gang behind him, round
the corner, and handed him his purse.   But the man only
took out three pauls and gave it back, and he looked so
thin and haggard that Borghese could not but notice it,
dark as it was, though he had forgotten his face.

'That is not a thief, he is some poor fellow who
wants relief,' said Borghese to his servant.   'Go after
him and see what he does, but take care not to be seen,'
and he walked home alone.   In less than half an hour
the servant came back.   He had seen him spend the three
pauls in food; had seen him take it home to his family;
had seen them scarcely covered with rags; had seen the
room denuded of furniture; had heard the man say, as he
put the food on the table, ' Here is wherewith to keep
you alive another day, and to-morrow I die in sin, for I
had to steal it.'

Then Borghese called up the steward (Maestro di
Casa), and told him to go to the house and find out who
the man was, and leave them what was wanted for the
night.

The steward did as he was told, and left a scudo that
the man might get a supper without eating stolen food,
but without saying who sent him, for he had learnt by his
inquiries that he was the servant whom Borghese had sent
away.

The next day Borghese sent and clothed all the family ; furnished their place again for them ; put the children to schools, and gave the parents ten scudi a month. He wouldn't take the man back, having once had to send him away—for that was his rule—but he gave him a pension for the rest of his life.

'POPE JOAN.'

' You know, of course, that there was once a Papessa ? They have put *that* in the books, I suppose ? '

' I know there is such a story, but learned writers have proved it was a mere invention.

' Well, I daresay it isn't true; but there's no one in Rome who has not heard of it. And what makes them believe it is this.[1] Outside of St. Peter's somewhere there's a statue of her all among the apostles and saints ; and they say it's because a Pope must have a statue, and they didn't dare to put *hers inside* the church, so they put it up *outside*. And if it isn't a Papessa, what is a woman's statue doing there, for it wasn't the Madonna, that's certain ? '

' Oh ! that's a statue of Religion, or the Church.[2] There never was a woman-pope.'

' Ah, well ! you read books. I dare say you know best ; but, anyhow, that's what they say. And, after all, who knows ! '

[1] An argument worthy to take rank beside the famous one of ' Mrs. Brown ' concerning Noah's Ark.

[2] I said this, really thinking at the moment there was such a statue surmounting the apex of the pediment of the façade ; but it afterwards came to mind and I have since verified it on the spot, that the statues on the pediment represent the twelve Apostles with Christ in the centre, and there is no female figure there. Among the numerous statues of saints surmounting the colonnade, are a small proportion of female saints, but no *one* at all prominent.

GIACINTA MARESCOTTI.

THERE was a prince Marescotti,[1] who had two daughters, Cecilia and Giacinta. From her childhood Cecilia had always been gentle and pious, and everyone said, ' When she grows up she will be a nun.' Giacenta was proud, handsome, and passionate, and everyone said, ' She will be a leader of society, and woe betide whoso offends her.'

But their father, good man,[2] knew them better, and one day he announced to them the choice of a state of life which he had made for them; for the pious, gentle Cecilia there was a great lord coming from abroad to make her his wife; but the proud, passionate Giacinta was to enter a convent.

The one was as dismayed as the other at the time, though the event showed he had chosen right. Cecilia, who loved quiet and repose, tenderly entreated her father to let her off the anxieties and responsibilities of becoming the head of a great family, while Giacinta made a great noise[3] at the idea of her beauty and talents being laid up hidden in a nun's cell. Nevertheless, in those days long gone by, girls were used to obey.[4] Cecilia married and proved herself an exemplary wife and mother, and carried respect for religion wherever she went.

Giacinta, on the other hand, took all her worldly state into her convent with her; her cell was furnished like the drawing-room of a palace, and she insisted on having her maids to wait on her; the other nuns she scarcely spoke to, and treated as the dust under her feet.

One day the bishop came to visit the convent. ' What a smell!'[5] he said, as he passed the cell of Giacinta Marescotti.

' A smell, indeed! In my cell which is not only the sweetest in the convent, but which is the only one fit to go into!' exclaimed poor Giacinta in deep indignation. ' What can you possibly mean by " a smell!"'

'A smell of sin!' responded the bishop; and it was observed that for a wonder Giacinta made no retort.

'A smell of sin,' said Giacinta to herself, as she sat alone in her elegant and luxurious cell that night. The words had touched her soul and awakened a train of thoughts latent and undisturbed till then. Always hitherto she had ambitioned the loftiest, most refined objects of research, and thought she knew the secret of attaining them. The bishop's words spoke to her of there being 'a more excellent way' yet. They cast a light upon a higher path than that which she was treading, and revealed to her that those who walked along it, lowly as they might seem, could afford to look down upon hers.

She saw that those who despised distinctions were grander than those who courted them, to become, in the end, their slaves; that those who aspired to celestial joys were nobler than those who surrounded themselves with the most exquisite luxuries of earth.[6]

From that day, little by little,[7] Giacinta's cell grew nearer and nearer to the pattern of the House of Nazareth. The mirror, the cosmetics, and the easy couch made way for the crucifix, the discipline, and the penitential chain.[8] From having been shunned as a type of worldliness, she became to her whole order a model of humility and mortification.[9]

[1] The Marescotti were a noble family of Bologna, the second city of the Pontifical Dominions; there were two cardinals of the name.

[2] 'Il buon uomo di loro padre.'

[3] 'Faceva il diavolo,' lit. 'raised the devil.'

[4] 'In quei tempi antichi ubbedirono le figlie, capisce.' 'Capisce,' lit. understand,' equivalent to 'you see.'

[5] 'Puzza—puzza di peccato!' Lit. 'It stinks—it stinks of sin.' (See n. 5, p. 13.)

[6] I give the story, as near as possible, in the words which the pious faith of the narrator prompted her to use. The success of the final results of a measure may prove that what seemed tyranny was really prudent foresight; the contemporary views of parental responsibility must also be taken into account. But it is impossible for the modern English mind to sympathise readily with so violent an interference with natural instincts.

⁷ ' A mano, a mano.'

⁸ ' Catenella,' lit. ' little chain,' an instrument of penance worn by some persons on the arm or waist.

⁹ The following are briefly the authentic particulars of her life from Moroni, xxx. 194. She was daughter of Marc Antonio Mariscotti and Ottavia Orsini, born in 1585, and baptised by the name of Clarice. Although brought up in the fear of God and led to appreciate holiness, her youth was passed in worldliness and vanity. Her younger sister having been asked in marriage before her, she was so much vexed and annoyed that she became insupportable at home, on which account her father proposed to her to become a nun in the convent of S. Bernardino at Viterbo, where she had been educated, and she adapted herself to his counsel, though without any personal inclination for it. At the end of her noviciate she made her father arrange that she should have a room of her own magnificently furnished. Sister Giacinta lived ten years thus a religious in name but not in mind. Nevertheless she was not without virtue, for she was always obedient to her superior as she had been to her parents ; and her modesty, purity, and respect for holy things was observed by all. A serious illness was to her the call of grace ; having given up to the abbess of the convent all the things that had been brought in for her use by special privilege, she devoted herself to severe penance and continual meditation. On occasion of a contagious disease with which Viterbo was afflicted, she gave abundant proof of her charity towards her neighbour, for she founded two societies, the object of one of which was to collect assistance for the convalescent and those who had fallen into reduced circumstances ; the other to support a hospital built to receive the sick. These two societies, which she called ' Oblates of Mary,' still continue (the date of Moroni's work is 1845) in full activity.

PASQUINO.

1

' No, I can't say I remember any pasquinades, not to repeat ; but I know what happened once when they tried to stop them.

' There had been so many one time that the Government put a guard all round about Pasquino to watch and see who did it, but for a long time they saw no one.

' One night, at last, a clownish countryman came by with a bundle of hay on his back, drivelling and half silly. "Let me sit here a bit to rest ; I'm so weary with carrying this load I can't go any farther ; but I won't do any harm."

' The guards laughed at the poor idiot's simplicity in fancying they could expect such as he to be the author of the witty, pungent sort of wares they were on the search for, and said with contemptuous pity, " Yes, yes; *you* may sit there ! " And the stupid old countryman sat down at the foot of the statue.

' " Heaven reward you for your kindness ! " he said, when he got up after half-an-hour's rest.

' " Don't mention it ; go in peace ! " returned the guards, and the man passed out of sight.

' Next morning, high over head of Pasquino floated a gay paper balloon.

' " The balloon ! the balloon ! " screamed the street urchins.

' " The balloon ! the balloon ! " shouted a number of men, assembled by preconcerted arrangement, though seemingly passers-by attracted by the noise.

' The clumsy clodhopper of overnight was an adroit fellow disguised, and he had attached the string of the balloon to the statue.

' To seize the string, pull down the balloon, and burst it was quick work ; but out of it floated three hundred and sixty-six stinging pasquinades, which were eagerly gathered up.'

2

' MANY a time a simple exterior is a useful weapon ; but when a man who is really simple pretends to be clever he is soon found out. For another time there had been a pasquinade which so vexed the Government that the Pope declared whoever would acknowledge himself the author of it should have his life spared and five hundred scudi reward.

' One day a simple-looking rustic came to the Vatican, and said he was come to own himself the author of the pasquinade. As such he was shown in to the Pope.

' " So you are the author of this pasquinade, are you, good man ? "

' " Yes, Your Holiness, I wrote it," answered the fellow.

' " You are quite sure you wrote it ? "

' " Oh, yes, Your Holiness, quite sure."

' " Take him and give him the five hundred scudi," said the Pope.

' An acute Monsignore, who felt convinced the man could not be the author of the clever satire, could not refrain from interposing officially when he found the Pope really seemed to be taken in.

' " They have their orders," said the Pope, who was no less discerning than he.

' A chamberlain took the man into a room where five hundred scudi lay counted on the table, and at the same time put on a pair of handcuffs. .

' " Halloa now! What is this? It was announced that the man who owned himself the author of the Pasquinade should have his life free and five hundred scudi."

' " All right ; no one is going to touch your life, and there are the five hundred scudi. But you couldn't imagine that the man who wrote that satire would be allowed to go free about Rome. That was self-evident—there was no need to say it."

' " Oh, but I never wrote a word of it, upon my honour," exclaimed the countryman.

' " I thought not," said the Pope, who had come in to amuse himself with the fellow's confusion. " Now go, and another time don't pretend to any worse sins than your own." '

---

[1] The statue called by this name was not originally found in its present situation. The shop of the tailor Pasquino was in the Via in Parione, a turning out of the Via del Governo Vecchio, some little distance off, nor was it discovered at all till after Pasquino's death. At his time it was buried unperceived in the pavement of the street, and the inequalities of its outline afforded stepping-stones by means of which passengers picked their way through the puddles! Cancellieri (Mercato, appendix, N. iii.)

quotes a passage from a certain Tibaldeo di Ferrara, quoted in a book, his dissertation concerning the author of which is too long to quote. This Tibaldeo, however, says, ' as the street was being repaired, and I had the shop that was Pasquino's made level, the trunk of a statue, probably of a gladiator, was found, and the people immediately gave it his name.' He, however, quotes from other writers mention of other sites for its discovery mostly somewhat nearer to the present situation. The site of the present Palazzo Braschi was then occupied by the so-called Torre Orsini, a building of a very different ground-plan. Cancellieri quotes from more than one MS. diary that at the time the Marquis de Créquy came to Rome as ambassador of Louis XIII. in 1633, the Palazzo de' Orsini, where he was lodged, was designated as 'sopra Pasquino.' And again from another MS. diary, that in 1728, when the palace was bought by the Duca di Bracciano-Odo-scalchi, the same designation remained in use. In the Diary of Cracas, under date March 19, 1791, is an entry detailing the care with which the Pasquino statue was removed to a pedestal prepared for it in front of Palazzo Pamfili during the completion of the contiguous portion of the Palazzo Braschi, and its restoration is duly entered on the 14th March of the same year.[1]

It was Adrian VI. (not Alexander VI. as Murray has it), who proposed to throw it into the Tiber. Adrian VI. was a victim of pasquinades for two reasons,—the first, because born at Utrecht and tutor of Charles V., and afterwards viceroy in Spain, during all Charles' absence in Germany Rome feared at his election that he would set up the Papal See in Spain; and it is not altogether impossible that the popular satires may have had some influence in deciding him on the contrary to repair immediately to Rome,—the second, because he was an energetic and unsparing reformer; and those who were touched by his measures were just those who could afford to pay the hire of the tongues of popular wags.

Nor was it only during his life that he was the subject of such criticisms. When his rigorous reign was suddenly brought to a close after he had worn the tiara but twenty months, on the door of his physician was posted this satire, ' Liberatori Patriæ S.P.Q.R.'[2]; and his tomb in St. Peter's, between that of Pius II. and Pius III., was disgraced with this epitaph: ' *Hic jacet impius inter Pios*,' till some years later, when his body was removed to a worthier monument in S. Maria del Anima.

---

[1] There is clearly a typographical error about one of these dates, which could doubtless be corrected by reference to ' Notizie delle due famose statue di un fiume e di Patroclo dette volgarmente di Marforio e di Pasquino,' by the same author, Rome, 1789, which I have not been able to see. Moroni, vi. 99, gives 1791 as the year in which it was bought by Duke Braschi, the nephew of Pius VI. while the Pope was in exile in France, and the completion by the re-building must, therefore, have been some years later.

The date of its discovery is told in the following inscription by the cardinal inhabiting Torre Orsini at the time, and who saved it from destruction :—

> Oliverii Caraffa
> Beneficio hic sum
> Anno Salvati Mundi—MDI.

[2] Giovio; Vit. Hadr. VI.

[The ' Pasquino ' statue was not only the receptacle of the invectives of the vulgar, it often served also to mark the triumphs of the great. The first time it was put to this use was in 1571, on occasion of the triumph of M. A. Colonna, when the parts wanting were restored, and it was clad in shining armour. On various occasions, as a new pope went in procession from the Vatican to perform the ceremony called ' taking possession ' of St. John Lateran, it was similarly *risanato del suo stroppio ordinario* (healed of the usual lameness of its members), and made to bear a sword, a balance, a cornucopia, and other emblematical devices, which are given at great length by Cancellieri.

The opinions of Winkelman, and others, concerning the great artistic merits both of this statue and that called ' Marforio,' do not belong to our present aspect of it. Sprenger, ' Roma nuova,' says that besides these two there was another statue which used to take part in this satirical converse, namely, that of the Water-seller, with his barrel (commemorative of a well-known, though humble character), opposite the Church of S. Marcello, in the Corso, which the present rulers, ignorant of Roman traditions, removed. The Romans, however, clamoured against its destruction, and it is now replaced round the corner, up the Via Lata.]

CÈCINGÙLO.

' THERE was one who would have done much better for you than Pasquino; that was Cècingùlo,[1] at least that's the nickname people gave him. There was no end to the number of stories *he* could tell.

' In days gone by,[2] he used to sit in Piazza Navona of an evening when people had left work and had time to listen, and he would pour them out by the hour. Now and then he stopped, and went round with his hat, and there were few who did not spare him a bajocco.'

' Did you ever hear him yourself?'

' No; it was before my time, but my father has heard

him many's the time, and many of the stories I have told you are the tales of Cècingùlo. How often I have said to him, "Tell me one of Cècingùlo's tales, papa!"" [3]

[1] I have not been able to make out the origin of this name. It is possibly, a mere combination of Cecco, short for Francesco, and a family name, or the name of the village of which he was native which I do not recognise

[2] 'Nei tempi di prima.'

[3] It is very likely Cècingùlo was some generations older even than the narrator's 'papa.' I have thought it worth while to put this much about him on record, as he was doubtless one of those who have given the local colouring to these very tales. The old women whose heads are their storehouse, as they repeat them over the spinning-wheel, say them with no further alteration than want of memory or want of apprehension necessarily occasions. It is the professional wag who, sitting in the midst of the vegetable market amid a peasant audience, will ascribe to a *cicoriaro* the acts of a paladin, and insert 'a casino in the Campagna' in the place of an oriental palace. I have met various people who had heard as much as the above about Cècingùlo, but no more.

THE WOOING OF CASSANDRO.[1]

'DID you ever hear of Sor Cassandro?'

'No, never.'

'Do you know where Panìco is?'

'I know the Via di Panìco [2] which leads down to Ponte S. Angelo.'

'Very well; at the end of Panìco [3] there is a frying-shop,[4] which, many years ago, was kept by an old man with a comely daughter. Both were well known all over the Rione.

'One day there came an old gentleman, with a wig and tights, and a comical old-fashioned dress altogether, and said to the shopkeeper—

'"I've observed that daughter of yours many days as I have passed by, and should like to make her my wife."

'"It's a great honour for me, Sor Cassandro, that you

should talk of such a thing," answered the old man ; and he said " Sor Cassandro " like that because everybody knew old Sor Cassandro with his wig, and his gold-knobbed stick, and his tights, and his old-fashioned gait. " But," he added, as a knowing way of getting out of it, " you see it wouldn't do for a *friggitora* to marry a gentleman ; a *friggitora* must marry a *friggitore*."

' " I don't know that that need be a bar," replied Sor Cassandro.

' " You don't understand me, Sor Cassandro," pursued the man.

' " Yes, I understand perfectly," answered the other. " You mean that if she must marry a *friggitore*, I must become a *friggitore*."

' " You a *friggitore*, Sor Cassandro ! That would never do. How could you so demean yourself ? "

' " Love makes all sweet," responded Sor Cassandro. " You've only to show me what to do and I'll do it as well as anyone."

' The *friggitore* was something of a wag, and the idea of the prim little Sor Cassandro turned into a journeyman *friggitore* tickled his fancy, and he let him follow his bent.

' The next morning Sor Cassandro was at Panìco as soon as the shop was open. They gave him a white jacket and a large white apron, and put a white cap on his head, with a carnation stuck in it. And the whole neighbour-hood gathered round the shop to see Sor Cassandro turned into a *friggitore*. The work of the shop was in-creased tenfold, and it was well there was an extra hand to help at it.

' Sor Cassandro was very patient, and adapted himself to his work surprisingly well, and though the master fryer took a pleasure in ordering him about, he submitted to all with good grace, and not only did he make him do the frying and serving out to perfection, but he even taught him to clip his words and leave off using any expression that seemed inappropriate to his new station.[5]

'There was no denying that Sor Cassandro had become a perfect *friggitore*, and no exception could be taken to him on that score. As soon as he felt himself perfect he did not fail to renew his suit.

'The father was puzzled what objection to make next. He knew, however, that Sor Cassandro was very miserly, so he said, " You've made yourself a *friggitore* to please me, now you must do something to please the girl. Suppose you bring her some trinkets, if you can spare the price of them."

' " Oh, anything for love ! " answered Sor Cassandro ; and the next day he brought a pair of earrings.

' " How did she like my earrings ? " he whispered next night to her father.

' " Oh, pretty well ! " replied the father. " You might try something more in that style."

'The next day he brought her a necklace, the next day a shawl, and after that he brought fifty scudi to buy clothes such as a girl should have when she's going to be married.

' After all this he asked for the girl herself.

' " You must take her," said the father, and Sor Cassandro went to take her. But she was a sprightly, impulsive girl, and the moment he came near her she screamed out—

' " Get away, horrid old man ! " [5] and wouldn't let him approach her.

' " Leave her alone to-night, and try to-morrow. I'll try to bring her round in the meantime."

'Sor Cassandro came next day ; but the girl was more violent than ever, and would say nothing but " Get away, horrid old man ! "

'Finding this went on day after day without amendment, Sor Cassandro indignantly asked for his presents back.

' " You shall have them!" cried the girl, and the clothes she tore up to rags, and the trinkets she broke to atoms and threw them all at him.

' But for the rest of his life, wherever he went, the boys cried after him, " *Sor Cassandro, la friggitora! Sor Cassandro, la friggitora!* " '

¹ ' Lo Sposalizio di Sor Cassandro.' For 'Sor' see p. 194.

² The 'Via di Panico' is so called, according to Rufini, because on a bit of ancient sculpture built into the wall of one of the houses where it had been dug up as is so commonly done in Rome, the people thought they saw the likeness of some ears of millet, *panico*, and birds pecking them.

³ Just as at Oxford, men say ' the High ' and ' the Corn,' &c., it is very common in Rome to use the name of a street omitting the word Via.

⁴ 'Friggitoria,' an open shop where all manner of fried dishes very popular among the lower classes, and varying according to the time of year, are made and sold ; three or four or more enormous pans of oil and of lard are kept boiling, and at one season fish, at another rice-balls, at another artichokes, &c. &c., always previously dipped into light batter, are cooked therein to a bright gold colour. On St. Joseph's Day, as it always falls in Lent, a meagre festa-dish is made of balls of batter fried in oil, in as universal request as our pancakes on Shrove Tuesday. A writer in the ' Giovedì ' mentions two popular traditions on the connexion between the ' frittelle ' or ' frittatelli ' and St. Joseph. One is that St. Joseph was wont to make such a dish for his meal by frying them with the shavings from his bench, in the same dangerous way that you may see those of his trade heating their glue in any carpenter's shop in Rome. The other, that on occasion of the Visitation, the B. Virgin and St. Elizabeth remained so long in ecstatic conversation that the dinner was forgotten, and St. Joseph took the liberty allowed to so near a relation of possessing himself of a frying-pan and preparing a dish of ' frittelle.'

The writer already quoted narrates in another paper that the ' friggitori ' formerly plied their trade in the open air, but one day a cat escaping from the attentions of an admirer she did not choose to encourage, sprang from a low roof adjoining, right into the frying-pan of a ' friggittore ' full as it was of boiling oil and spluttering ' frittelle '; the cat overturned the frying-pan, setting herself on fire, and carrying a panic together with a stream of flaming oil into the midst of the crowd in waiting for their ' frittelle.' Since that day the ' friggitore ' fries under cover, though still in open shops.

⁴ Great part of the fun of the story consisted of jokes upon these technicalities which it would be too tedious to reproduce and explain.

⁵ ' Brutto vecchiaccio ! ' ugly, horrid old man.

I COCORNI.

THIS story of Sor Cassandro led to others of the same
nature, but without sufficient interest in the detail
to put in print, though they seemed to illustrate the
fact that an imaginative people will rapidly turn the
most ordinary circumstances into a myth. For instance,
one concerned a family named Cocorni, who seem to have
been nothing more than successful grocers, the Twinings
of Rome, and here is a specimen of the language used
about them :—' When his daughter was old enough to
marry, Cocorno would hear of no proposal for her. "No,"
said he ; "no one marries my daughter but he who comes
in a carriage and four to fetch her." And it really did
happen that one came in a carriage and four and took her
away ;' as if it were such a great matter that it implied
something supernatural.

THE BEAUTIFUL ENGLISHWOMAN.

THERE was a beautiful Englishwoman here once, beautiful
and rich as the sun.[1] Heads without number were turned
by her : but she would have nothing to say to anyone who
wanted to marry her. Some defect she found in all. She
was very accomplished, as well as rich and beautiful, and
she drew a picture, and said ' When one comes who is
like this I will marry him ; but no one else.' Some time
after a friend came to her, and said :

' There is So-and-so, he is exactly like the portrait you
have drawn, and is dying to see you.'

' Is he *really* like it ?' she inquired.

' To me he seems exactly like it ; and I don't see he
has any defect at all, except that he has one tooth a little
green.'

'Then I won't have anything to say to him.'

'But, if he is exactly like the portrait you have drawn?'

'He can't be, or he wouldn't have any defect.'

'But he *is* exactly like it, and so you must see him; if it's only for curiosity.'

'Well, for curiosity, then, I'll see him; but don't let him build any hopes upon it.'

The friend arranged that they should meet at a ball, and the one was as well pleased as the other; but not wishing to seem to yield too soon, she said:

'Do you know, I don't like that green tooth you've got.'

And he, not to appear too easy either, answered:

'And, do you know, I don't like that patch² you have on your face.'

The next time they met, neither he had a green tooth, nor had she a patch; for, you know, a patch can be put on and taken off at pleasure, and this happened a long long while ago, in the days when they wore such things.

She then said:

'If you've put in a false tooth I'll have nothing to say to you.'

'No,' answered he; 'you have taken off your patch, and I've taken off my green tooth.'

'How could you do that?' she asked.

'Oh! it was only a leaf I put on to see if you were really as particular as you seemed to be.'

As they were desperately in love with each other, the next thing was to arrange the marriage secretly. His father had a great title, and would never have consented to his marrying her, because she had none. But she had money enough for both; so they contrived a secret marriage. And then they bought a villa some way off, and lived there.

For thirteen years they lived devoted to each other, and

full of happiness; and two children were born to them, a boy and a girl. It was only after thirteen years that the father discovered where the son was, and when he did, he sent for an assassin,[3] and giving him plenty of money, told him to go and by some device or other to bring him to him and get through the affair. The assassin took a carriage and dressed like a man of some importance, and said that some chief man or other in the Government had sent for him to speak to him. The husband suspected nothing, and went with him. As it was night he could not see which way they drove, and thus he delivered his son to his father, who kept him shut up in his palace.

The assassin went back to the villa, and by giving each of the servants fifty scudi apiece, got access to the wife, and murdered her, and then took the children to the grandfather's palace.

'Papa, that man killed mama,' said the little boy, as soon as he saw his father.

The husband seized the man, and made him confess it.

'Then now you must kill him who hired you to do it,' he exclaimed. 'As you have done the one, you must do the other. He who ordered my wife to be killed is no father to me.'

So the assassin went in and killed the father, but when he came out the husband was ready for him, and he said :

'Now your turn has come,' and he shot him dead.

[1] 'Bella e ricca quanto il sole.'
[2] 'Mosca' and 'neo' both mean either a mole or a patch.
[3] 'Sicario,' hired assassin.

[I have not had the opportunity of sifting this story, but it manifestly contains the usual popular exaggerations.]

THE ENGLISHMAN.

[That a rich Englishman should fall in love with a beautiful but poor Roman girl, and marry her, is no impossible incident, and may have happened more than once ; but it is very curious to watch how it has passed into the mythology of the people.

The idea of a ' Gran Signore ' coming on a visit from a land where all are rich is the first fantastic element of the tradition. The idea that *all* English people are rich is very common among the Roman lower classes, and is not an unnatural fancy for people to take up who have seen no specimens of the creature but such as *are* rich. There is one old woman whom I have never been able to disabuse of the idea. I shall never forget the blank astonishment with which she repeated my words the first time I broke it to her that there were poor people in England, and she has never thoroughly grasped it.

' Io pensava che in Inghilterra tutti erano ricchi—*tutti* ricchi—' (I thought everyone—*everyone* in England was rich) she always says, as if in spite of me she thought so still.

That such an one should be won by the charms of a beautiful Roman girl, and should carry her off to that unknown land bright with gold but devoid of sun, and that in the end the fogs and the Protestantism should prove unendurable to the child of the South, are not bad materials for a fairy story.

I have met with such stories several times.

One old woman assured me, that when she was a child her father had let an apartment to the very man, and that he took the room for a month, and though he spontaneously offered ten times as high a price as the owner could ever have asked, he never slept there. He had secretly married a Roman girl who was imprisoned for breaking the law by marrying a Protestant, and he opened her prison doors with his ' *wand*,' that is, he bribed the jailer to admit him to pass all his time in prison with her ; ultimately he carried her off to England, but she soon died there.

Another pointed out to me a shop where in former days had been a butcher, whose daughter had charmed a rich Englishman, who carried her off to his own country, and married her there.

But this was a very *tetra* (sad, gloomy) story, for after many years she came back looking like the ghost of herself. She had gone away a blooming girl, the pride and the admiration of the whole neighbourhood; she came back prematurely grey, hollow-eyed, and thin as a skeleton.

She said it was the climate had disagreed with her, and further than that she would say nothing. But who knows what she may not have had to go through !

Bresciani has made the same tradition the groundwork of one of his most interesting romances.]

THE MARRIAGE OF SIGNOR CAJUSSE.[1]

THERE was a rich farmer[2] who had one only daughter, and she was to be his heiress. She fell in love with a count who had no money—at least only ten scudi a month. When he went to the farmer to ask her in marriage he would not hear of the alliance, and sent him away.

But the girl and he were bent on the marriage, and this is how they brought it about. The girl had a thousand scudi of her own; half of this she gave to him, and said: ' Go over a certain tract of the Campagna and visit all the peasants about, and give five piastres to one and ten to another according to their degree, that they may say when they are asked that they all belong to Signor Cajusse. Then take papa round to hear what they say, and he will think you are a great proprietor, and will let us marry.'

Signor Cajusse, for such was his name, took the money and did as she told him, and then hired a carriage and came to her father, and said: ' You are quite mistaken in thinking I'm too poor to marry your daughter ; come and take a drive with me, and I will show you what a great man I am.'

So the farmer got into his carriage, and he drove

him round to all the peasants he had bribed. First they
stopped at a farm.[3]

' Good morning, Signor Cajusse,' said the tenant, who
had been duly primed, bowing down to the ground ; and
then he began to tell him about his crops, as if he had
been really proprietor.

After this he proposed to walk a little way, and all the
labourers left their work and flocked after him, crying,
' Good day, Signor Cajusse ; health to you and long life,
and may God prosper you !' and they tried to kiss his hand.

Further along they came to a villa where Cajusse had
ascertained that the real proprietor would not come that
day.   Here he went straight up to the casino, where the
servant in charge, who had been also duly bribed, received
him with all the honours due to a master.

' Welcome, Signor Cajusse,' he said, and opened the
doors and shutters and set the chairs.

' Bring a little of that fine eight-year-old wine,' ordered
Cajusse ; ' we have brought a packet of biscuits, and will
have some luncheon.'[4]

' Very good, Signor Cajusse,' replied the servant re-
spectfully, and shortly after brought in a bottle of wine
handed to him for the purpose by Cajusse the day before.
When they had drunk they took a stroll round the place,
and wherever they turned the labourers all had a greeting
and a blessing for Signor Cajusse.

When the merchant saw all this he hardly knew how
to forgive himself for having run the risk of losing such a
son-in-law.   He was all smiles and civility as they drove
home, and the next day was as anxious to hurry on the
match as he had been before to put it off.   As all were
equally in a hurry to have it, of course it was not long before
it was celebrated.   With the girl's remaining five hundred
scudi a handsome apartment was hired to satisfy appear-
ances before the parents, and for a few days they lived on
what was left over.

They sat counting their last two or three scudi. 'What is to be done now?' said Cajusse; 'that will soon be spent, and then how are we to live?'

'I'll set it right,' answered the bride. 'Now we're married that's all that signifies. Now it's done they can't help it.'

So she went to her mother and told her all, and the good woman, knowing the thing could not be altered, talked over the father; and he gave them something to live upon and found a place for Cajusse, and they were very happy.

[1] 'I Matrimonio del Signor Cajusse.' This story, it will be seen, is altogether disconnected with the other of the same name at p. 158–69, and it is curious so similar a title should be appended to so dissimilar a story. It has not half the humour of Mr. Campbell's 'Baillie Lunnain,' No. xvii. b. Vol. i., but is sufficiently like to pair off against it. It is also observable for representing exactly the proceeding of the 'Marquis di Carabas' in 'Puss in Boots.'

[2] 'Mercante di Campagna,' see n. 2, p. 154.

[3] 'Tenuta,' a farm; a holding.

[4] 'Merenda,' see n. 7, p. 155.

THE DAUGHTER OF COUNT LATTANZIO.[1]

COUNT LATTANZIO had a daughter who was in love with a lawyer, but the count was not at all inclined to let her marry beneath her station, and he took all the pains imaginable to prevent them from meeting; so much so that he scarcely left her out of his sight. One day he was obliged to go to his vineyard outside the gates, and before he left he gave strict injunctions to his servant to let no one in till he came back at 21 o'clock.[2]

It was an hour before 21 o'clock, and there was a knock at the door.

'Is the Count Lattanzio in?'

'No, he won't be in just yet.'

'Ah, I know, he won't be in till 21 o'clock; he said I was to wait. I'm come to measure him for a pair of new boots.'

'If he told you to wait I suppose you must,' said the servant; 'otherwise he had told me not to let anyone in.' And as he showed him in he thought he was a rather gentlemanly bootmaker.

Soon after there was another knock.

'Is the Count Lattanzio in?'

'No, he won't be in for some time yet.'

'Ah, never mind; he said I was to wait if he hadn't come in. I'm the tailor, come to measure him for a new suit.'

'If he said you were to wait I suppose you must,' answered the servant; 'but it's very odd he should have told you so, as he particularly told me to let no one in.' However, he showed him in also. Directly after there came another knock.

'Is the Count Lattanzio at home?'

'No, he won't be in for some time yet.'

'Never mind; I'm the lawyer engaged in his cause before the courts. He said I was to wait if he wasn't in.'

But the servant began to get alarmed at having to disobey orders so many times, and he thought he would make a stand.

'I'm very sorry,' he said, 'but master said I wasn't to show anyone in.'

'What! when I've come here with my two clerks, on particular business of the greatest importance to your master, do you suppose I'm going away again like that, fellow?'

The servant was so amazed by his imperative manner that he let him in, too.

Twenty-one o'clock came at last, and with it Count Lattanzio. Having given orders that no one should be let ·

in, of course he expected to find no one. What was his astonishment, therefore, when, as he opened the drawing-room door, a loud cry of ' Long live Count Lattanzio ! ' [4] uttered by several voices, met his ear.

The shoemaker was the bridegroom, the tailor the best man, the lawyer and his two clerks were the notary and his witnesses. The marriage articles had been duly drawn up and signed, and as the parties were of age there was no rescinding the contract.

Count Lattanzio sent away the servant for not attending to orders ; but that made no difference—the deed was done.

[1] This story, again, is perhaps more curious for the sake of the repetition of the name of Lattanzio, in so different a story as that at p. 155, than for its contents. There is doubtless a reason why this name should come into this sort of use as with that of 'Cajusse,' but I have not as yet been able to meet with it.

[2] '21 o'clock,' three hours before the Ave.

[3] 'Gisbuse' are high boots of unblackened leather reaching up to the thighs, worn by sportsmen about Rome.

[4] 'Viva !' or 'Evviva !' is a not very uncommon, though rather old-fashioned, mode of hearty greeting.

BELLACUCCIA.

THERE was once a pleader[1] who sat writing in his room all day whenever he was not in court.

One day as he so sat there came in at the window a large monkey, and began whisking about the room. The lawyer, pleased with the antics of the monkey, called it *scimmia bellacuccia*,[2] and caressed and fed it. By-and-by he had to go out on his business, and though he was in some fear of the pranks the monkey might be up to in his absence, he had taken such a fancy to it that he did not like to send it away, and at last left it alone in his apartment.

When he came home, instead of the monkey having been at any mischievous pranks, the whole suite of rooms was put in beautiful order, and out of very scanty materials in the cupboard an excellent dinner was cooked and laid ready.

'*Scimmia bellacuccia!* is this your doing!' said the lawyer, and the monkey nodded assent.

'Then you are a precious monkey, indeed,' he replied, and he called it to him and fed it, and gave it part of the dinner.

The next day the monkey did the work of the house, and the lawyer sent away his servant because he had no further need for one, the monkey did all much better and in a more intelligent way.

All went well for a time, when one day the lawyer had occasion to visit a friar he knew at St. Nicolò da Tolentino, for in those days there were friars [3] there instead of nuns as now. He did not fail to tell him of the treasure he had found in his *bellacuccia,* as he called his monkey.

'Don't let yourself be deceived, friend!' exclaimed the friar. 'This is no monkey; it is not in the nature of a monkey to do thus.'

'Come and see it yourself,' said the lawyer. 'You will find I have over-stated nothing of what it can do and does every day.'

Some days after this the friar came, having taken care to provide himself with his stole and a stoup of holy water. Directly he came into the lawyer's apartment he put on his stole and sprinkled the holy water.

The monkey no sooner saw the shadow of his habit than it took to flight, and, after scrambling all round the room to get away from the sight of him, finally hid itself under the bed.

'You see!' said the friar to the lawyer.

But the lawyer cried, 'Here *bellacuccia*; come here!' and as the monkey was by habit very docile and obedient, when he had said '*bellacuccia*' a great many times, it at last forced itself to come to him, but stealthily and warily, showing great fear of the monk.

When it had got quite close to the lawyer, and he was holding it, the friar once more put on his stole, sprinkled it with holy water and exorcised it.

Instantly *bellacuccia* burst away from the lawyer, and, clambering up to the window, broke away through the upper panes and disappeared, leaving a smoke and a smell of brimstone behind. But it was really a man who had been put under a spell by evil arts,[4] and when thus released by the monk's exorcism he went and became a monk, I forget in what order, but I know it was one of those who dress in white.

[1] 'Curiale,' a lawyer, a pleader.

[2] 'Scimmia,' a monkey. In England we usually speak of a cat as of feminine gender, and in Germany the custom is so strong that the well-known riddle pronounces the 'Kater' (tom cat) 'keine Katze' (no cat), while in France, Spain and Italy the normal cat is masculine. In Italian, on the other hand, the monkey is always spoken of in the feminine gender; it becomes noteworthy in this instance when we consider the termination of the story. 'Bellacuccia,' 'dear little pretty one.'

[3] I do not know at what period the transfer took place, but in the edition of 1725, of Panciroli's book on Rome, the church is named as built and served by the 'Eremiti scalsi di S. Agostino,' corroborating this part of the story.

[4] 'Fatato.'

THE SATYR.

1

THERE was once a great king who had one only little daughter, and this daughter was always entreating him to take her out hunting.

'It is not proper for little girls to go out hunting,' he used to say ; but it was no use. She went on begging all the same, and at last her importunity gained the day, and

he took her with him. But in the forest she got separated
from him and lost herself, and he, full of the ardour of
the chase, forgot the care of her, and, when he came
to think of her, she could no more be found.

She wandered about the forest crying for her father,
but her father came not; and instead of her father a
selvaggio[1] found her, and fell in love with her, and took
her to his den and married her, and she had two children.

When ten years had passed, and there were no tidings
of her, the queen, her mother, died of a broken heart.[2]

But the *selvaggio* loved her dearly, and did everything
in his power to give her pleasure. When he found she
could not eat the raw game which he brought her, he
would go into the towns and steal cooked food and bring
it to her, and when he could not get that he would go ever
so far to find fruits and roots. Everything, he did to please
her, but it was no use, she could not love him.

At last, however, after so many years were passed, he
thought she was at least used to the way of life with him,
and he no longer watched her so closely. One day when
he was gone to a long distance she wandered on to a cliff
that overhung the sea, and looked till she saw a ship, then
she called to it and made signs to it to come and pick
her up.

The captain took compassion on her distress, and
made for the land, and took her on board and wrapped
her in a cloak,[3] and she told him who she was and he
promised to take her home. He gave her a white kerchief
to put on her head and another to hold in her hand.

They had not got far out to sea when the *selvaggio*
found out what had happened, and came running to the
same cliff where she had stood, and made signs entreating
her to come back; but she shook the handkerchief she
held in token of refusal.

Then what did he do? He ran back to the den and
fetched one of the children and held it up, appealing to

her mother's instincts; but she always continued waving the handkerchief in token of refusal. When he saw that this prevailed not, he ran back to the den and fetched the other child, and held them both up to plead with her to come back. But she always, and always, went on waving the handkerchief in token of refusal. Then what did he do? He took out his knife and plunged it into the one child, as signifying that if she did not come back he would kill the other also. But even for that she was not moved, but went on waving the handkerchief in token of refusal. Then with his knife he killed the other child, for he had no hope left; but she could not go back to that life with him, and went on waving the handkerchief in token of refusal.

Then with his claw [4] he tore open his breast, and tore out his heart, and died for the love he bore her.

But the sailors took her home, and they were richly rewarded, and there was great rejoicing.

2

THE SATYRS.

They say there was a queen whose husband was dead, and she had one only son. Imagine how devoted she was to him, her only child, soon to be the king of vast dominions.

One day a lady, unknown to her, came and asked if she might put a horse of hers in her stable.

'No,' said the queen; 'I cannot have the horses of anyone else mixed up there.'

The lady turned to go; but as she went, she met the prince coming in from hunting, surrounded by all his suite. The lady was a fairy, and in her indignation at the queen's refusal of her demand, she turned the prince and all those following him into *salvatichi*. [5]

Imagine the horror and the cries of the queen when

she saw what had happened. What was to be done? Much as she adored her son, it was impossible to keep him in the palace now.

'You must put him in the stables,' said the cruel fairy, who had waited to enjoy her revenge, and now preserved her coolness amid the confusion and excitement of those around. 'You must put him in the stables, and all the others too now. Your stables will be full enough, indeed!'

But the queen's grief was too deep to waste itself in a strife of words with her.

'There is only one mode of redemption for him. If he can find a maiden to consent to marry him as he is, without knowing he is a prince, I will come and remove the spell.'

The queen had seen the proof of her relentless spirit, and knew it would be vain if she should humble herself to entreat her to alter her sentence. So she said nothing, and the fairy went away.

To find a maiden who should consent to marry such a monster as her son now was, and who should yet be meet to be his wife when restored to his due estate, was a hopeless task indeed; but what will not a mother's love attempt? With endless fatigue and continued mortifications she made the fruitless effort in every quarter. When this had utterly failed, she condescended to maidens of lower estate, and tried daughters of merchants and tradesmen, and even peasants, to whom the elevation of rank might in some measure compensate the ill-conditioned union. But it was all in vain, there were only fresh repulses and deeper mortifications.

It happened that adjoining the paddock in which the stables lay, were the grounds of a duke. One day the duke's daughter was walking in her garden, and the prince immediately turned his head and saw her, and began beckoning to her, for he had the head and arms and body of a man from the waist upwards still, and the rest of him was like the hindquarters of a goat, only he stood upright, like a man. The duke's daughter was perplexed, however, at the sight of such a monster, and ran away.

Nevertheless the next day she came. back, and the prince beckoned to her again, and all his suite, who were satyrs like himself, beckoned to her too, till at last she came near.

'Do you wish me well?' [6] he asked.

'No!' exclaimed the duke's daughter with disgust, because she could not say that she loved him: and she ran away. Every day it was the same thing; and when she told her mother what had happened, she bid her keep away, and beware of going near such a monster.

For a whole month, therefore, she kept away; but curiosity overcame her at last, and she went down into the garden as before. All the satyrs began beckoning as usual, and she went up to them.

'If you will say you wish me well, you will give me endless happiness,' [7] said the prince; 'and if not, I will dash my head against this wall, and put an end to my life.'

He was so much in earnest, and the tears were in his eyes, and his sighs and entreaties were so moving, that she almost forgot his monstrous form. The prince observed that her face betrayed signs of interest, and he redoubled his sighs, and all the other satyrs [8] made signs and gesticulations to her that she should consent.

'Say you wish me well! Let me just have the happiness of once hearing you say so!' continued the prince.

'Poor fellow, he seems so sad, and so anxious I should just say it once. There can't be much harm in saying just once that I wish him well,' said the maiden to herself.

'Say, say just once, that you wish me well!' persisted the prince; and the maiden in her compassion said:

'Yes! I wish you well.'

Immediately the fairy appeared and took the spell from off the prince, and from off all his suite.

When the duke's daughter found to what a fine hand-some prince she was promised, she saw her compassion was well rewarded.

[1] 'You know what a "selvaggio" is, I suppose?' asked the narrator. 'Yes; a wild man,' I answered, thinking of the German myths. 'No, they weren't altogether men, they were those creatures there used to be in old times, half men with legs like goats, but they walked on two legs, and had heads and arms like men.' After this description, I thought I might take the license of adopting the title for a word incidentally used by the narrator in telling the story. The shepherds and goatherds about Rome with their goatskin leggings covering leg and thigh, readily suggest to the eye how the idea of a satyr may have first arisen.

[2] 'Appassionata,' 'of a broken heart.'

[3] 'Ferraiuola,' the light cloak with a shoulderpiece which priests wear out of doors in Rome in summer. It was formerly worn by others besides priests.

[4] Sgramfia, or granfa or gramfia, is a claw of a beast, or of a bird of prey, most often used for the latter. I hardly know how this came to be ascribed to a satyr, unless she meant simply that his nails were rather strongly developed.

[5] Bazzarini gives 'salvatico' as synonymous with 'satiro.'

[6] 'Mi volete bene,' literally, only 'do you wish me well?' but the accepted form of saying, 'do you love me?' when therefore the girl says the words at last she is supposed to make a sort of compromise by means of which she saves the prince and her own good taste at the same time.

AMADEA.

AMADEA was a beautiful queen who fell in love with a king not of her own country; he loved her too, and married her, and took her home. But the king her father, and the prince her brother, were very wroth that she should go away with the stranger.

When Amadea heard that her brother was preparing to prevent her going away with her husband, she turned upon him and killed him, and then cut his body in pieces, and threw the mangled limbs in her father's way, to show him what he might expect if he followed after her too. And when she found that he was not deterred by the sight, she turned and killed him in like manner.

Only fancy what a woman she must have been !

When her husband, who had liked her before, saw this, he began to be afraid of her ; nevertheless, they lived for some time happily together, and had two beautiful children. But after that again, her husband's love cooled towards her when he thought of the horrors she had committed, and he took their two children and went away and left her.

After a time Amadea not only found out where he was, but found out that she had a rival. Then she made her way to the place, and demanded to see her rival ; but knowing of what she was capable, this her husband would by no means allow. Then she prepared a most beautiful necklace of pearls, and sent it as a present to her rival. But she had poisoned it by her arts, for she was a sort of witch, and when her rival put it on she died.

Meantime she had sent a message to her husband, saying, 'If I may not come to your court, at least let me see my children for one hour, and then I will go away, and molest you no more for ever.'

' *That* I will grant you,' was his answer ; and the children were brought to her.

When she saw her children, she wept, and embraced them, and wept again, and said :

' Now, my children, I must kill you.'

' And why must you kill us ? ' asked the little boy.

' Because of the too great love I bear you,' she replied, and drew out her dagger.

At that instant her husband came into the room, and she stabbed the children before his eyes. After that she stabbed herself, and he died of grief.

[It was about the time that Prince Amadeo gave up his attempt to hold the throne of Spain that I was visiting a poor person who had before given me some of the stories of this collection. The abdication of Prince Amadeo being the subject of the hour, we, of course, talked about that; when she said: 'Ah, you who are so fond of *favola*, do you know the *favola* of Queen Amadea, for one name brings up another?' I told her I did not; for I expected she meant some legend of the House of Savoy; she then told me the story of Medeia in the text. It is very rare, however, to meet remnants of classical traditions in such direct form.]

THE KING OF PORTUGAL.

THEY say that once there was a king of Portugal who had a beautiful daughter, and there came a prince to marry her. When the prince saw how old and feeble the king was, he seized him, and shut him up in prison, and ordered him to be fed on only bread and water, that he might die without killing him. 'And then,' he said, 'I shall take the government.'

Then he would send and ask, 'How does he look to-day? Does he grow lean and pale? Does he look like to die?'

But the answer ever was, 'Nay, prince, he looks hale and stout. Every day his face is fresher and fatter. Every day he seems stronger and firmer.'

Then the prince grew in despair of ever accomplishing his design, and he said, 'It cannot be as you say, unless there is treachery,' and he changed the guards, and set a watch upon them; but the same thing happened, and the old king continued to grow stouter and stronger. He made them search the princess, too, when she went to see her father, and they assured themselves that she took nothing to him. Then he bade them watch her, and they saw that she placed her breast against the prison bars, and fed him with her own milk.

For it had been thus, that when she learnt what was the design of the prince, she was filled with earnest desire to save her father's life, and prayed so hard that she might have wherewith to support him, that, young girl as she was, the means was afforded her, and thus by her devotion she preserved him in life and health.

When the prince heard what she did, he was seized with compunction, and sent and released the king, and restored him to his throne, and went his way in shame. But the king sent for him back, and forgave him : he gave him his daughter also, and when he died he left him the succession to the kingdom.   .

['I have no "favole" for you to-day,' was one day my greeting from an old lady who had given me many, 'but there has just come to mind a " bell' fatto " (a grand deed), which is better than a " favola " for it is historic truth.' Then she told me the story in the text, and I was surprised to find she was positive it was a king of Portugal and that she never seemed to have heard of the ' Carità Romana.' It is odd that while so many legends get localised any should get dis-localised.]

CIARPE.

Two friars once went out on a journey, that is to say, a friar and a lay brother.[2]   One day of their journey, when they were far from their convent, the friar said to the lay brother : ' We fare poorly enough all the days of our life in our convent, let us, for one day of our lives, taste the good things of this world which others enjoy every day.'

' You know better than I, who am only a poor simple lay brother,' answered the other, 'whether such a thing may be done.   I don't mean to say I should not like to have a jolly good dinner for once ; but there is the uneasiness of conscience to spoil the feast, and the penance afterwards.   I think we had better leave it alone.'

They journeyed on, therefore, and said no more about it that day, but the next, when they were very hungry after a long walk through the cold mountain air, the scent of the viands preparing in the inn as they drew near brought the subject of yesterday's conversation to their minds again, and the friar said to the lay brother : ' You know even our rule says that when we are journeying we cannot live as we do in our convent ; we must eat and drink whatever we find in the places to which we are sent; moreover, some relaxation is allowed for the restoration of the body under the fatigues of the journey.   Now, if we come, as it has often happened to us, to a poor little mountain village, where scarcely a wholesome crust of bread is to be found, to be washed down with a glass of sour wine, we have to take it for all our dinner, and eat it with thanksgiving.   Therefore why, now, when we come to a place where the fare is less scanty, even as by the odours we perceive is the case here, should we not also take what is found ready, and eat it with thanksgiving?'

'What you say seems right and just enough,' said the lay brother, not at all sorry to have his scruples so speciously explained away. 'But there is one thing you have not thought of. It is all very well to say we will eat and drink this and that, but how are we poor friars, who possess nothing, to command the delicacies which are smoking round the fire, and which have to be paid for by well-stored purses?'

'Oh! that is not the difficulty,' replied the friar; 'leave that to me.'

By this time they had reached the threshold of the inn, and, taking his companion's last feeble resistance for consent, the friar strutted into the eating-room with so bold an air that the lay brother hardly knew him for the humble religious he had been accompanying anon.

'Ho! here! John, Peter, Francis, whatever you are called!'

'Francesco, to your service,' replied the host humbly, thinking by his commanding tone he must be some son of a great family.

'Francesco *guercino*,[3] then,' continued the friar in the same high-sounding voice, 'take away this foul table-cloth, and bring the cleanest and finest in your house; remove these cloudy glasses and bring out the bright ones you have there locked up in the glass case, and replace these bone spoons and forks[4] with the silver ones out of your strong box.'

'Your Excellency is served!'[5] said the host, who, as well as his wife and son, had bustled so fast to do what he was so peremptorily ordered that all was done as soon as spoken.

'Now then Francesco *guercino*, what have you got to put before a hungry gentleman in this poor little place of yours?'

'Excellenza! when you have tasted the cooking of my poor little house,' said the host, 'you will not, I am sure, be displeased; all unworthy as it is of your Excellency's palate. For what we have ready, we have beef for our boiled meat, good brains for our fried, the plumpest poultry for our grilled, and the freshest eggs for our omelette; or, if your Excellency prefers it, we have hashed turkey, with crisp watercresses; and as for our soup,[6] there is not an inn in the whole province can beat us, I know. And for dessert we have cheese and fruits, and '——

'Well done, Francesco *guercino*,' said the friar interrupting him. 'You know how to cry your own wares, at all events. Bring us the best of what you have; it is not for poor friars to complain of what is set before us.'

The last sentence gave the host a high idea of the piety of his guest just as the hectoring tone he had assumed had convinced him he must be high-born, and in a trice the best of everything in the house was made ready for the table of the friar. All other guests had to wait, or go away unserved; the host was intent only on serving the friar.

Every dish he took to the table himself, and as he did so each time the friar, fixing on him a look of sanctity, exclaimed,—

'Blessed Francesco! Blessed Francesco!'[7]

At the close of the meal, as he was hovering about the table, nervously wiping away a crumb, or polishing a plate, he said, with trembling:

'Excellenza! Permit a poor man to put one question. What is there you see about me that makes you look at me as though you saw happiness in store, and exclaim with so much unction as quite to fill me with joy, "Blessed Francesco!"?'

'True, something I see wherefore I call thee blessed,' replied the friar; 'but I cannot tell it thee now. To-morrow, perhaps, I may find it easier. Impossible now, friend. Now, pray thee, show us our rooms.'

It needed not to add any injunctions concerning the rooms; of course, the cleanest and the best were appointed by Francesco spontaneously for such honoured guests.

'How do you think we are getting on?' said the friar to the lay brother when they were alone.

'Excellently well so far,' replied the other; 'things have passed my lips this night which never have they tasted before, nor ever may again. But the reckoning, the reckoning; that is what puzzles me: when it comes to paying the bill, what'll you do then?'

'Leave it all to me,' returned the friar; 'I'm quite satisfied with the man we have to deal with. It will all come right, never fear.'

The next morning the two brothers were astir betimes, but Francesco was on the look-out to serve them.

'Excellenza! you will not leave without breakfast, Excellenza!'

'Yes, Francesco; poor friars must not mind going without breakfast.'

'Never, from my house, Excellenza!' responded Francesco. 'I have the table ready with a bottle of wine freshly drawn from the cellar, eggs that were born [8] since daylight, only waiting your appearance to be boiled, rolls this moment drawn from the oven, and my wife is at the stove preparing a fried dish [9] fit for a king.'

'Too much, too much, Francesco! You spoil us; we are not used to such things,' said the lay brother as they sat down; but Francesco had flown into the kitchen, and returned with the dish.

'Blessed Francesco!' said the friar as he set it on the table.

'I will not disturb your Excellency now,' said Francesco; 'but, after you have breakfasted, I crave your remembrance of your promise of last night, that you would reveal to me this morning wherefore you say with such enthusiasm " Blessed Francesco ! " '

' It is not time to speak of it now,' said the friar; ' first we have our reckoning to make.'

The lay brother hid his face in his table-napkin in terror, and seemed to be seized with a distressing fit of coughing.

' Oh, don't speak of the reckoning, Excellenza ; that is as nothing.'

' Nay,' said the friar ; 'that must not be;' and he made a gesture as if he would have drawn out a purse, while under the table he had to press his feet against those of the lay brother to silence his rising remonstrance for his persistence.

' I couldn't think of taking anything from your Excellenza,' persisted the host, putting his hands behind him that no money might be forced upon him.

The more stedfastly he refused the more perseveringly the friar continued to press the payment, till, with his companion, he had gained the threshold of the door.

As they were passing out, however, the host once more exclaimed, ' But the explanation your Excellency was to give me of why you said " Blessed Francesco ! " '

' Impossible, friend ; I cannot tell it here. Wait till I have gained the height of yonder mound, while you stand at its foot, and I will tell it you from thence.'

With this they parted.

When the friar and his companion had reached the height he had pointed out, and were at a sufficient distance to be saved the fear of pursuit, he turned to the host, who stood gaping at the bottom, and said:

' Lucky for you, Francesco, that when you come to die you will only have the trouble of shutting one eye, instead of two, like other men.' [10]

¹ Though I believe there is no rule or ground for the distinction, in conversational language, 'fratello' is used for ' brother,' and ' frate' for

'monk' (as 'sorella' usually means any sister and 'suora' a nun). 'Frate,' again, is usually, though not by any rule, or exclusively, reserved for the mendicant Franciscans. A Capuchin is called 'padre cappucino,' and a Dominican, generally, a 'padre domenicano.'

² 'Laico.'

³ 'Guercino.' There is no very definitely expressed distinction in Italian in the way of saying weak-sighted, or one-eyed, or squinting; 'guercio' is used to express all. The termination 'ino' here is not an actual diminutive, but means 'he who is one-eyed,' or 'he who is weak-sighted,' or 'he who squints,' with an implied expression of sympathy (see Note 5, p. 379). In this case the conclusion shows that 'one-eyed' was intended.

⁴ 'Posate,' plural of 'posata,' knife, fork, and spoon.

⁵ 'Ecco servito, Excellenza.' 'It is all done as you desire.'

⁶ The poor, badly fed themselves, delight to dilate on a description of good living, just as dreaming of eating is said to arise from a condition of hunger. I have not added a word here in the text to those of the narrator of the story, and her enumeration is a very fair rendering of the usual repertory of a Roman innkeeper. Broth or thin soup ('minestra'); a dish of boiled meat ('lesso'), of 'arrosto,' that is, grilled or baked, and of 'fritto' (fried) is the regular course: 'gallinaccio spezzato' is a turkey cut up in joints and served with various sauces, and is much more esteemed than if cooked whole, a rather unusual dish; 'frittata,' omelette; 'crescione,' watercresses.

⁷ 'Beato a te, Francesco.'

⁸ 'Born,' an Italianism for 'laid.'

⁹ 'Fritto dorato.' Romans, though not eminent in the culinary art, fry admirably. They always succeed in making their fried dishes a rich golden colour, and they ordinarily express a fried dish by the two words together, 'fritto dorato.'

¹⁰
   'Beato a te, Francesco,
   Che quando morirai
   Un occhio serrerai
   E l'altro no!'

[Such a story at the expense of a single unworthy monk contains no implied taunt at the religious orders, who are deeply honoured in Rome, and none more than the mendicant Franciscans, most of whom are themselves of the very people. Ever since the invasion of September 20, 1870, every effort has been used to stir up the people against them, but with little effect. At the last Carneval the most elaborate car was got up with the purpose of ridiculing them, but it met with no approval, except from members of the clubs. The narrator of the story was herself not only a devoted member of the Church, but had a relative in the order of St. Francis, nor did she tell it without an edifying exordium on the goodness of the *frati* in general, though there must be unworthy members of all professions. *Facetiæ* of this class are much rarer in Rome than in Spain.]

THE PREFACE OF A FRANCISCAN.

A FRANCISCAN friar was travelling on business of his order when he was overtaken by three brigands, who stole from him his ass, his saddle, and his doubloons. Moreover, they told him that if he informed any man of what they had done they would certainly come after him again and take his life; for they could only sell the ass and the saddle that were known to be his by representing that he had sold them to them, otherwise no one would have bought them.

The friar told no man what had happened to him, for fear of losing his life; yet he knew that if he could only let his parishioners know what had occurred, they would soon retake for him all that he had lost.

So he hit on the following expedient: next Sunday, as he was saying Mass, when he came to the place in the Preface where special additions commemorative of the particular festivals are inserted, after the enumeration of the praises of God, he added the words, ' Nevertheless, me, Thy poor servant, evil men have robbed of my ass and her saddle, and all my doubloons; but to no man have I declared the thing, save unto Thee only, Omnipotent Father, who knowest all things, and helpest the poor;' and then he went on, ' et ideò cum angelis et arch-angelis,' &c.[1]

The parishioners were no sooner thus informed of what had occurred, than they went after the brigands and made them give up all they had taken. The next time, there-fore, the father was out in the Campagna, the brigands came after him and said:

'Now, we take your life; last time we let you off, saying we would spare you if you told no man what we had done; but you cannot keep your own counsel, so you must die like the rest.'

But the good monk showed them that he had not spoken to man of the thing, but had only lamented his loss before God, which every man was free to do. And the brigands, when they heard that, could say nothing, and they let him go by uninjured, him and his beast.

¹ The merit of this story consists much in the mode of telling. The narrator should be able to imitate the peculiar tone to which the ' Preface ' is sung, and to supply the corresponding notes for the additional insertion. It was very effectively done by the person who told it to me.

[Such stories are the result of a household familiarity with sacred matters, and are told with genuine fun without the least infusion of irreverence. Just as out of the fulness of the heart the mouth speaks, even so we make jokes on whatever subject we are most occupied with. Religious offices are so much a part of the daily life of the Catholic poor that it would be impossible to banish the language of them from their simple jokes. I have had numbers of such told me without the least expression that could be called scoffing in the teller; but I forbear to give more than the two or three in the text by way of specimens, lest the spirit of them should be misjudged.]

THE LENTEN PREACHER.

A FRIAR came to preach the Lenten sermons in a country place. The wife of a rich peasant sat under the pulpit, and thought all the time what a nice-looking man he was, instead of listening to his exhortations to penance.

When the sermon was over she went home and took out half-a-dozen nice fine pocket-handkerchiefs, and sent them to him by her maid, with a very civil note to beg him to come and see her.

As the maid was going out, the husband met her.

' Where are you going ? ' said he.

The maid, who did not at all like her errand, promised if he would not be angry with her, and would not let her mistress know it, she would tell him all.

The husband promised to hold her harmless, and she gave him the handkerchiefs and the note.

' Come here,' said the husband ; and he took her into his room and wrote a note as if from the friar, saying he was much obliged by her presents, and would like to see the lady very much, but that it was impossible they could meet, so she must not think of it. This note the maid took back to her mistress as if from the friar.

A few days after this the husband gave out that he would have to go to a fair, and would be away two or three days. Immediately the wife took a pound of the best snuff and sent it as a present to the friar by the same maid with another note, saying the husband was going away on such an evening, and if he then came to see her at an hour after the Ave he would find the door open. This also the maid took to her master ; the husband took the snuff and wrote an answer, as if from the friar, to say he would keep the appointment. In the evening he said good-bye to his wife, and went away. But he went to the butcher and bought a stout beef sinew, and at the hour appointed for the friar, he came back dressed as a friar, and beat her with the beef sinew till she was half dead. Then he went down in the kitchen and sent the servant up to heal her, and went away for three days. When he came back the wife was still doubled up, and suffering from the beating.

' What is the matter ? ' he said, sympathisingly.

' Oh ! I fell down the cellar stairs.'

' What do you mean by leaving your mistress to go down to the cellar ? ' he cried out to the servant, with great solicitude. 'How can you allow her to do such things? What's the use of you?'

'Don't scold the servant,' answered the wife; 'it wasn't her fault. I shall be all right soon.' And she made as light of her ailment as she could, to keep him from asking her any more questions. But he was discreet enough to say no more.

Only when she was well again he sent to the friar and asked him to come home to dine with them.

'My wife is subject to odd fancies sometimes,' he said, as they walked home. 'If she should do anything extravagant, don't you mind; I shall be there to call her to order.'

Then he told the servant to bring in the soup and the boiled meat without waiting for orders, but to keep the grill back till he came to the kitchen door to call her.

At the time for the grill, therefore, he got up from table to go and call her, and thus left his wife and the friar alone together. They were no sooner alone than she got up, and calling him a horrid friar, gave him a sound drubbing. The husband came back in time to prevent mischief, and to make excuses; and finding she was cured of her affection, said no more of the affair.

ASS OR PIG.[1]

A COUNTRYMAN was going along driving a pig before him. 'Let's have a bit of fun with that fellow,' said the brother porter of a monastery to the father guardian,[2] as they saw him coming along the road. 'I'll call his pig an ass, and of course he'll say it's a pig; then I shall laugh at him for not knowing better, and he will grow angry. Then I'll say, "Well, will you have the father guardian to settle the dispute? and if he decides I'm right I shall keep the beast for myself." Then you come and say it is an ass, and we'll keep it.'

The father guardian agreed, with a hearty laugh; and as soon as the countryman came up the brother porter did all as he had arranged.

The countryman was so sure of his case that he willingly submitted to the arbitration of the father guardian; but great was his dismay when the father guardian decided against him, and he had to go home without his pig.

But what did the countryman do ? He dressed himself up as a poor girl, and about nightfall, and a storm coming on, he rang at the bell of the monastery and entreated the charity of shelter for the night.

' Impossible ! ' said the brother porter; ' we can't have any womenkind in here.'

' But the dark, and the storm ! ' clamoured the pretended girl; ' think of that. You can't leave me out here all alone.'

' I'm very sorry,' said the porter, ' but the thing's impossible. I can't do it.'

The good father guardian, hearing the dispute at that unusual hour, put his head out of the window and asked what it was all about.

' It is a difficult case, brother porter,' he said when he had heard the girl's request. ' If we take her in we infringe our rule in one way; if we leave her exposed to every kind of peril we sin against its spirit in another direction. I only see one way out of it. I can't send her into any of your cells; but I will let her pass the night in mine, provided she is content not to undress, and will consent to sit up in a chair.'

This was exactly what the countryman wanted, therefore he gave a ready assent, and the father guardian took him up into his cell. The pretended girl sat up in a chair quietly enough through the dark of the night, but when morning began to dawn, out came a stick that had been hidden under the petticoats, and whack, whack [3]—a

fine drubbing the poor father guardian got, to the tune of
—'So you think I don't know a pig from an ass, do you?'

When he had well bruised him all over, the countryman made the best of his way downstairs, and off and away
he was before anyone could catch him.

The next day what did he do? He dressed up like a
doctor, and came round asking if anyone had any ailments
to cure.

'That's just the thing for us,' said the brother porter
to himself as he saw him come by. 'The father guardian
was afraid to let the doctor of the neighbourhood attend
him, for fear of the scandal of all the story coming out ;
the strange doctor will just do, as there is no need to tell
him anything.'

The countryman in his new disguise, therefore, was
taken up to the father guardian's cell.

'There's nothing very much the matter,' he said when
he had examined the wounds and bruises; 'it might all
be set right in a day by a certain herb,' which he named.

The herb was a difficult one to find, but as it was so
important to get the father guardian cured immediately,
before any inquiry should be raised as to the cause of his
sufferings, the whole community set out to wander over
the Campagna in search of it.

As soon as they were a good way off, the pretended
doctor took out a thick stick which he held concealed
under his long robe, and whack, whack—belaboured the
poor father guardian more terribly even than before, to
the tune of—'So you think I don't know an ass from a
pig, do you?'

How far soever the brothers were gone, his cries were
so piteous that they recalled them, but not till the countryman had made good his escape.

'We have sinned, my brethren,' said the father guardian when they were all gathered round him; 'and I have
suffered justly for it. We had no right to take the man's

pig, even for a joke. Let it now, therefore, be restored to him, and in amends let there be given him along with it an ass also.'

So the countryman got his pig back, and a donkey into the bargain.

¹ 'Asino o porco.'
² 'Padre Guardiano' is the ordinary title of the Superior in Franciscan convents.
³ 'Zicherte! Zacherte!'

THE SEVEN CLODHOPPERS.¹

SEVEN clodhoppers went to confession.

'Father, I stole something,' said the first.

'What was it you stole?' asked the priest.

'Some *mistuanza*,² because I was starving,' replied the country bumpkin.

That the poor fellow, who really looked as if he might have been starving, should have stolen some herbs did not seem such a very grave offence; so with due advice to keep his hands from picking and stealing, and a psalm to say for his penance, the priest sent him to communion.

Then came the second, and there was the same dialogue. Then the third and the fourth, till all the seven had been up.

At last the priest began to think it was a very odd circumstance that such a number of full-grown men should all of a sudden have taken into their heads to go stealing salad herbs; and when the seventh had had his say he rejoined,—

'But what do you mean by *mistuanza*?'

'Oh, any mixture of things,' replied the countryman.

'Nay; that's not the way we use the word,' responded the priest; 'so tell me *what* " things " you mean.'

'Oh, some cow, some pig, and some fowl.'³

'You men of the *mistuanza!*' shouted the priest in righteous indignation, starting out of the confessional; 'Come back! come back! you can't go to communion like that.'

The seven clodhoppers, finding themselves discovered, began to fear the rigour of justice, and decamped as fast as they could.

¹ 'I sette Villani.'

² 'Un po' di mistuanza.' 'Mistuanza' is a word in use among the poor for a mixture of herbs of which they make a kind of poor salad.

³ 'Un po' di bove, un po' di porchi, un po' di galline.'

'Un po' (un poco) a little. The effect of the story depended a good deal on the tones of voice in which it was told. The deprecatory tone of the penitent as he says, 'un po' di bove,' &c., and the horror of the priest as he cries out, 'Signori della *mistuanza!*'

This same story in quite another dress was told me one evening in Aldershot Camp; and as it is a very curious instance of the migration of myths, I give the home version.

'It would seem that in Aldershot lingo, or in the lingo of a certain regiment once stationed there, to 'kill a fox' means to get drunk. Possibly the expression was acquired during the Peninsular war, as 'tomar una zorrilla' has an equivalent meaning in Spanish. The story was this. Once during the brief holiday of the chaplain of the regiment, a French priest who knew a little English took his place. At confession the chief fault of which, according to the story, the men accused themselves was that they had 'killed a fox,' an expression perfectly well understood by their own pastor. The good French priest, however, instead of being shocked at finding how often men got drunk, was highly edified at the angelic simplicity of these Angles, who showed so much contrition for having indulged in the innocent pastime—in France, not even an offence among sportsmen—of having killed a fox.

At last there came one of a more humorous turn of mind than the rest, and the *surnois* air with which he pronounced the expression revealed to the good Frenchman that the words meant something more than they said.

'Vat mean you ven you say, "kill de fox?"' now inquired the Frenchman of his penitent with fear and trembling. And the blunt soldier had no sooner expounded the slang than the bewildered foreigner threw open the front wicket of the confessional and cried aloud:

'Come back! all you dat have killed de foxes! Come back! come back!'

[Next to gossiping jokes on subjects kindred to religion are jokes about domestic disputes, the greater blame being generally ascribed to the wife.]

THE LITTLE BIRD.[1]

THERE was an old couple who earned a poor living by working hard all day in the fields.

'See how hard we work all day,' said the wife; 'and it all comes of the foolish curiosity of Adam and Eve. If it had not been for that we should have been living now in a beautiful garden, with nothing to do all day long.'

'Yes,' said the husband; 'if you and I had been there, instead of Adam and Eve, all the human race had been in Paradise still.'

The count, their master, overheard them talking in this way, and he came to them and said: 'How would you like it if I took you up into my palazzo there, to live and gave you servants to wait on you, and plenty to eat and drink?'

'Oh, that would be delightful indeed! That would be as good as Paradise itself!' answered husband and wife together.

'Well, you may come up there if you think so. Only remember, in Paradise there was one tree that was not to be touched; so at my table there will be one dish not to be touched. You mustn't mind that,' said the count.

'Oh, of course not,' replied the old peasant; 'that's just what I say: when Eve had all the fruits in the garden, what did she want with just that one that was forbidden? And if we, who are used to the scantiest victuals, are supplied with enough to live well, what does it matter to us whether there is an extra dish or not on the table?'

'Very well reasoned,' said the count. 'We quite understand each other, then?'

'Perfectly,' replied both husband and wife.

'You come to live at my palace, and have everything you can want there, so long as you don't open one dish'

which there will be in the middle of the table. If you
open that you go back to your former way of life.'

' We quite understand,' answered the peasants.

The count went in and called his servant, and told him
to give the peasants an apartment to themselves, with
everything they could want, and a sumptuous dinner,
only in the middle of the table was to be an earthen dish,
into which he was to put a little bird alive, so that if one
lifted the cover the bird would fly out. He was to stay
in the room and wait on them, and report to him what
happened.

The old people sat down to dinner, and praised everything they saw, so delightful it all seemed.

' Look ! that's the dish we're not to touch,' said the wife.

' No ; better *not* look at it,' said the husband.

' Pshaw ! there's no danger of wanting to open it, when
we have such a lot of dishes to eat our fill out of,' returned
the wife.

So they set to, and made such a repast as they had
never dreamed of before. By degrees, however, as the
novelty of the thing wore off, they grew more and more
desirous for something newer and newer still. Though
when they at first sat down it had seemed that two dishes
would be ample to satisfy them, they had now had seven
or eight and they were wishing there might be others
coming. There is an end to all things human, and no
other came ; there only remained the earthen dish in the
middle of the table.

' We might just lift the lid up a little wee bit,' said
the wife.

' No ; dont talk about it,' said the husband.

The wife sat still for five minutes, and then she said :
' If one just lifted up one corner of the lid it could scarcely
be called opening it, you know.'

' Better leave it alone altogether, and not think about
it at all,' said the husband.

The wife sat still another five minutes, and then she said : ' If one peeped in just the least in the world it would not be any harm, surely ; and I *should* so like to know what there can possibly be. Now, what *can* the count have put in that dish ? '

' I'm sure I can't guess in the least,' said the husband ; ' and I must say I can't see what it can signify to him if we did look at it.'

' No ; that's what I think. And besides, how would he know if we peeped ? it wouldn't hurt him,' said the wife.

' No ; as you say, one could just take a look,' said the husband.

The wife didn't want more encouragement than that. But when she lifted one side of the lid the least mite she could see nothing. She opened it the least mite more, and the bird flew out. The servant ran and told his master, and the count came down and drove them out, bidding them never complain of Adam and Eve any more.

¹ ' L'uccelletto,' the little bird.

² ' Terrino,' a high earthen dish with a cover, probably the origin of our ' tureen,' almost the only kind of Italian dish that ever has a cover.

THE DEVIL WHO TOOK TO HIMSELF A WIFE.¹

LISTEN, and I will tell you what the devil did who took to himself a wife.

Ages and ages ago, in the days when the devil was loose—for now he is chained and can't go about like that any more—the head devil ² called the others, and said, ' Whichever of you proves himself the boldest and cleverest, I will give him his release, and set him free from Inferno.'

So they all set to work and did all manner of wild and terrible things, and the one who pleased the head devil best was set free.

This devil being set free, went upon earth, and thought he would live like the children of men. So he took a wife, and, of course, he chose one who was handsome and fashionable, but he didn't think about anything else, and he soon found that she was no housewife, was never satisfied unless she was gadding out somewhere, would not take a word of reproof, and, what was more, she spent all his money.

Every day there were furious quarrels; it was bad enough while the money lasted—and he had brought a good provision with him—but when the money came to an end it was much worse; he was ever reproaching her with extravagance, and she him with stinginess and deception.

At last he said to her one day, ' It's no use making a piece of work; I'm quite tired of this sort of life; I shall go back to Hell, which is a much quieter place than a house where you are. But I don't mind doing you a good turn first. I'll go and possess myself of a certain queen. You dress up like a doctor, and say you will heal her, and all you will have to do will be to pretend to use some ointments⁴ for two or three days, on which I will go out of her. Then they will be so delighted with you for healing her that they will give you a lot of money, on which you can live for the rest of your days, and I will go back to Hell.' But though he said this, it was only to get rid of her. As soon as he had provided her with the price for casting him out once, he meant to go and amuse himself on earth in other ways; he had no real intention of going back to Hell. Then he instructed her in the means by which she was to find out the queen of whom he was to possess himself, and went his way.

The wife, by following the direction he gave, soon found him, and, dressed as a doctor, effected the cure; that is, she made herself known to him in applying the ointments, and he went away as he had agreed.

When the king and the court saw what a wonderful

cure had been effected, they gave the woman a sackfull of scudi, but all the people went on talking of her success.

The devil meantime had possessed himself of another sovereign, a king this time, and everybody in the kingdom was very desirous to have him cured, and went inquiring everywhere for a remedy. Thus they heard of the fame of the last cure by the devil's wife. Then they immediately sent for her and insisted that she should cure this king too. But she, not sure whether he would go out a second time at her bidding, refused as long as she could; but they took her, and said, 'Unless you cure him we shall kill you!'

'Then,' she said, 'you must shut me up alone with this king, and I will try what I can do.'

So she was shut up alone with him.

'What! you here again!' said the devil as soon as he perceived her. 'No; that won't do this time. I am very comfortable inside this old king, and I mean to stay here.'

'But they threaten to kill me if I don't make you go; so what am I to do?' answered the wife.

'I can't help that,' he replied; 'you must get out of the scrape the best way you can.'

At this she got in a passion, and, as she used to do in the days when they were living together, rated him so fiercely that at last he was fain to go to escape her scolding.

Once more she received a high price for the cure, and her fame got the more bruited abroad.

But the devil went into another queen, and possessed himself of her. The fame of the two cures had spread so far that the wife was soon called in to try her powers again.

'I really can't,' she pleaded; but the people said:

'What you did for the other two you can do for this one; and, if you don't, we will cut off your head.'

To save her head, therefore, she said, 'Then you must shut me up in a room alone with the queen.'

So she was shut up in the room with her.

'What! you here again!' exclaimed the devil as soon as he perceived her. 'No; I positively won't go this time; I couldn't be better off than inside this old queen, and till you came I was perfectly happy.'

'They threaten to take my head if I don't make you go; so what am I to do?'

'Then let them take your head, and let that be an end of it,' replied the devil testily.

'You are a pretty husband, indeed, to say such a speech to a wife!' answered she in a high-pitched voice, which he knew was the foretaste of one of those terrible storms he could never resist.

Basta! she stormed so loud that she sickened him of her for good and all, and this time, to escape her, instead of possessing himself of any more kings and queens, he went straight off to Hell, and never came forth any more for fear of meeting her.

[1] 'Il Diavolo che prese Moglie.'
[2] 'Il Capo diavolo.'
[3] 'Il più bravo.'
[4] Witches were generally accused of communicating with the Devil, going to midnight meetings with him, &c., by means of ointments. See 'Del Rio,' lib. ii. Q. xvi. p. 81, col. 1, C., and lib. iii. P. 1, 2, ii. p. 155, col. 1, B., &c., &c.

[For variants of this *Ciarpa*, see Ralston's 'Russian Folk Tales,' pp. 37–43; 'The Ill-tempered Princess' in 'Patrañas,' &c.]

THE ROOT.

THERE was a rich count who married an extravagant wife. As he had plenty of money he let her spend whatever she liked. But he had no idea what a woman could spend, and very much surprised was he when he found that dressmakers, and milliners, and hairdressers, and shoemakers had made such a hole in his fortune that there was very little left. He saw it was high time to look after it, and he ventured to tender some words of remonstrance; but the moment he began to speak about it she went into hysterics. There was such a dreadful scene that he feared to approach the subject again, but the matter became so serious that at last he was obliged to do so. The least allusion, however, brought on another fit of hysterics.

What was he to do? To go on at this extravagant rate was impossible; equally impossible was it to endure the terrible scenes which ensued when he attempted to make her more careful.

At last he went to a doctor whom he knew, and asked him if he could give him any remedy for hysterics, telling him the whole story of what he wanted it for.

'Oh, yes!' replied the doctor; 'I have an infallible cure. It is a certain root which must be applied very sharply to the back of the neck. If it doesn't succeed with the first half-dozen applications, you must go on till it does. It never fails in the end.' So saying, he gave him a stout root, as thick as a walking stick, with a knobbed end.

Strong with the promised remedy, the husband went home, and sent word to all the dressmakers, milliners, hairdressers, and shoemakers that he would pay for nothing more except what he ordered himself. Indeed he met the shoemaker on the step of the door, who had just come to take the measure for a pair of velvet slippers.

'Don't bring them,' he said: 'she has seven or eight pairs already, and that is quite enough.'

Then he went up to his wife, and told her what he had done. Such a scene of hysterics as he had never imagined before awaited him now, but he, full of confidence in his remedy, took no notice further than to go up to her and apply the root very smartly to the back of her neck as he had been directed.

'But to me it seems that was all one with beating her with a stick,' exclaimed another old woman who was sitting in the room knitting.

'Of course! That's just the fun of it!' replied the narrator. 'And the beauty of it was that he was so simple that he thought it was some virtue in the root that was to effect the cure.'

The hysterics stopped, and he ran off to the doctor to thank him for the capital remedy. The wife ran off, too, and went to her friends crying with terrible complaints that her husband would not allow her a single thing to put on, and, moreover, had even been beating her.

When the count got back from the doctor, he found the father and half the family there ready to abuse him for making his wife go about with nothing on, and beating her into the bargain.

'It is all a mistake,' said the count. 'I will allow her everything that is right, only I will order myself what I pay for; and, as to beating her, I only applied this root which I got from the doctor to cure hysterics; nothing more.'

'Oh! it's a case of hysterics is it!' said the father; 'then it is all quite right,' and he and the rest went away; and the count and his wife got on very well after that, and he never had to make use of the doctor's root again.

THE QUEEN AND THE TRIPE-SELLER.[1]

THEY say there was a queen who had such a bad temper that she made everybody about her miserable. Whatever her husband might do to please her, she was always discontented, and as for her maids she was always slapping their faces.

There was a fairy who saw all this, and she said to herself, 'This must not be allowed to go on;' so she went and called another fairy, and said, 'What shall we do to teach this naughty queen to behave herself?' and they could not imagine what to do with her; so they agreed to think it over, and meet again another day.

When they met again, the first fairy said to the other, 'Well, have you found any plan for correcting this naughty queen?'

'Yes,' replied the second fairy; 'I have found an excellent plan. I have been up and all over the whole town, and in a little dirty back lane [2] I have found a tripe-seller as like to this queen as two peas.' [3]

'Excellent!' exclaimed the first fairy. 'I see what you mean to do. One of us will take some of the queen's clothes and dress up the tripe-seller, and the other will take some of the tripe-seller's clothes and dress up the queen in them, and then we will exchange them till the queen learns better manners.'

'That's the plan,' replied the second fairy. 'You have said it exactly. When shall we begin?'

'This very night,' said the first fairy.

'Agreed!' said the second fairy; and that very night, while everyone else was gone quietly to bed they went, one into the palace and fetched some of the queen's clothes, and, bringing them to the tripe-seller's room, placed them by the side of her bed; and the other went to the tripe-seller's room and fetched her clothes, and took them and put them by the side of the queen's bed. They also woke them very early, and when each got up she put on the things that were by the side of the bed, thinking they were the things she had left there the night before. Thus the queen was dressed like a tripe-seller, and the tripe-seller like a queen.

Then one fairy took the queen, dressed like a tripe-seller, and put her down in the tripe-seller's shop, and the other fairy took the tripe-seller, dressed like a queen, and placed her in the palace, and both of them did their work so swiftly that neither the queen nor the tripe-seller perceived the flight at all.

The queen was very much astonished at finding herself in a tripe-shop, and began staring about, wondering how she got there.

'Here! Don't stand gaping about like that!' cried the tripe-man,' who was a very hot-tempered fellow; 'Why, you haven't boiled the coffee!'

'Boiled the coffee!' repeated the queen, hardly apprehending what he meant.

'Yes; you haven't boiled the coffee!' said the tripe-man. 'Don't repeat my words, but do your work!' and he took her by the shoulders, put the coffee-pot in her hand, and stood over her looking so fierce that she was frightened into doing what she had never done or seen done in all her life before.

Presently the coffee began to boil over.

'There! Don't waste all the coffee like that!' cried the tripe-man, and he got up and gave her a slap, which made the tears come in her eyes.

'Don't blubber!' said the tripe-man; 'but bring the coffee here and pour it out.'

The queen did as she was told; but when she began to drink it, though she had made it herself, it was so nasty she didn't know how to drink it. It was very different stuff from what she got at the palace; but the tripe-man had his eye on her, and she didn't dare not to drink it.

'A halfp'th of cat's-meat!'⁵ sang out a small boy in the shop.

'Why don't you go and serve the customer?' said the tripe-man, knocking the cup out of the queen's hand.

Fearing another slap, she rose hastily to give the boy what he wanted, but not knowing one thing in the shop from another, she gave him a large piece of the best tripe fit for a prince.

'Oh, what fine tripe to-day!' cried the small boy, and ran away as fast as he could.

It was in vain the tripe-man hallooed after him, he was in too great a hurry to secure his prize to think of returning.

'Look what you've done!' cried the tripe-man, giving the queen another slap; 'you've given that boy for a penny a bunch of tripe worth a shilling.' Luckily, other customers came in and diverted the man's attention.

Presently all the tripe hanging up had been sold, and more customers kept coming in.

'What has come to you, to-day!' roared the tripe-man, as the queen stood not knowing what to do with herself. 'Do you mean to say you haven't washed that other lot of tripe!' and this time he gave her a kick.

To escape his fury, the queen turned to do her best with washing the other tripe, but she did it so awkwardly that she got a volley of abuse and blows too.

Then came dinner-time, and nothing prepared, or even bought to prepare, for dinner. Another stormy scene ensued at the discovery, and the tripe-man went to dine at the inn, leaving her to go without any dinner at all, in punishment for having neglected to prepare it.

While he was gone she helped all the customers to the wrong things, and, when he came home, got another scolding and more blows for her stupidity. And all through the afternoon it was the same story.

But the tripe-seller, when she found herself all in a palace, with half-a-dozen maids waiting to attend her, was equally bewildered. When they kept asking her if there was nothing she pleased to want, she kept answering, 'No thank you,' in such a gentle tone, the maids began to think that a reign of peace had come to them at last.

By-and-by, when the ladies came, instead of saying, as

the queen had been wont, 'What an ugly dress you have got; go and take it off!' she said, 'How nice you look; how tasteful your dress is!'

Afterwards the king came in, bringing her a rare nosegay. Instead of throwing it on one side to vex him, as the queen had been wont, she showed so much delight, and expressed her thanks so many times, that he was quite overcome.

The change that had come over the queen soon became the talk of the whole palace, and everyone congratulated himself on an improvement which made them all happy. The king was no less pleased than all the rest, and for the first time for many years he said he would drive out with the queen; for on account of her bad temper he had long given up driving with her. So the carriage came round with four prancing horses, and an escort of cavalry to ride before and behind it. The tripe-seller hardly could believe she was to drive in this splendid carriage, but the king handed her in before she knew where she was. Then, as he was so pleased with her gentle and grateful ways, he further asked her to say which way she would like to drive.

The tripe-seller, partly because she was too much frightened to think of any other place, and partly because she thought it would be nice to drive in state through her own neighbourhood, named the broader street out of which turned the lane in which she lived, for the royal carriage could hardly have turned down the lane itself. The king repeated the order, and away drove the royal cortége.

The circumstance of the king and queen driving out together was sufficient to excite the attention of the whole population, and wherever they passed the people crowded into the streets; thus a volley of shouts and comments ran before the carriage towards the lane of the tripe-man. The tripe-man was at the moment engaged in administering a severe chastisement to the queen for her latest mistake, and the roar of the people's voices afforded a happy pretext for breaking away from him.

She ran with the rest to the opening of the lane just as the royal carriage was passing.

'My husband! my husband!' she screamed as the king drove by, and plaintive as was her voice, and different from her usual imperious tone, he heard it and turned his head towards her.

'My husband! my royal husband!' pleaded the humbled queen.

The king, in amazement, stopped the carriage and gazed from the queen in the gutter to the tripe-seller in royal array by his side, unable to solve the problem.

'This is certainly my wife!' he said at last, as he extended his hand to the queen. 'Who then can you be?' he added, addressing the tripe-seller.

'I will tell the truth,' replied the good tripe-seller. 'I am no queen; I am the poor wife of the tripe-seller down the lane there; but how I came into the palace is more than I can say.'

'And how come you here?' said the king, addressing the real queen.

'That, neither can I tell; I thought you had sent me hither to punish me for my bad temper; but if you will only take me back I will never be bad-tempered again; only take me away from this dreadful tripe-man, who has been beating me all day.'

Then the king made answer: 'Of course you must come back with me, for you are my wife. But,' he said to the tripe-seller; 'what shall I do with you? After you have been living in luxury in the palace, you will feel it hard to go back to sell tripe.'

'It's true I have not many luxuries at home,' answered the tripe-seller; 'but yet I had rather be with my husband than in any palace in the world;' and she descended from the carriage, while the queen got in.

A A

'Stop!' said the king. 'This day's transformation, howsoever it was brought about, has been a good day, and you have been so well behaved, and so truth-spoken, I don't like your going back to be beaten by the tripe-man.'

'Oh, never mind that,' said the good wife; 'he never beats me unless I do something very stupid. And, after all, he's my husband, and that's enough for me.'

'Well, if you're satisfied, I won't interfere any further,' said the king; 'except to give you some mark of my royal favour.'

So he bestowed on the tripe-man and his wife a beautiful villa, with a nice casino outside the gates, on condition that he never beat her any more.

The tripe-man was so pleased with the gifts which had come to him through his wife's good conduct, that he kept his word, and was always thereafter very kind to her. And the queen was so frightened at the thought that she might find herself suddenly transformed into a tripe-seller again, that she kept a strict guard over her temper, and became the delight of her husband and the whole court.

---

[1] 'La Regina e la Triparola;' 'Triparola,' female tripe-seller.

[2] 'Vicolo,' a narrow dirty street.

[3] 'Due gocciette d'acqua,' two little drops of water, the Roman equivalent for 'as like as two peas.'

[4] 'Triparolo,' a male tripe-seller.

[5] 'Un bajocco di tripa-gatto,' the worst part of the tripe, sold for cats' and dogs' meat.

THE BAD-TEMPERED QUEEN.[1]

THEY say there was a queen who was so bad-tempered that no one who could help it would come near her. All the servants ran away when she came out of her apartment, for fear she should scold and maltreat them; all the people ran away when she drove out, for fear she should vex them with some tyrannical order.

As she was rich and beautiful, and ruled over vast dominions, many princes—who in their distant kingdoms had heard nothing of her failing—came to sue for her hand, but she sent them all away and would have nothing to say to any of them. She used to say she did not want to have anyone to be her master; she had rather live and govern by herself, and have everything her own way.

As time went on, however, the council of state grew dissatisfied with this resolution. They insisted that she must marry, that there might be a family of princes to carry on the succession to the throne without dispute. When the queen found that she could not help it she agreed she would marry; but she was determined she would not marry any of the princes who had come to court her, because, as they were equal to herself in birth and state, they would want to rule over her and expect obedience from her. She declared she would marry no one but a certain duke, who, as she had observed in the council and in the state banquets and balls, was always very quiet and hardly ever spoke at all. She thought he would make a nice quiet manageable sort of husband, and she would have him if she must have one at all.

The duke was as silent as usual when he was spoken to about it; but as he made no objection he was reckoned to have consented, and the marriage was duly solemnised.

As soon as the marriage was over the queen went on making her arrangements and ordering matters in the palace just as if nothing had happened, and she were still her own mistress. In particular she issued invitations for the grandest ball she had ever given, asking to it all the ministers and their families, and all the nobility of the kingdom.

The husband said nothing to all this, only a few hours before the time appointed for the banquet he called to the queen, saying: ' Put on your travelling dress, and make haste; the carriage will be round directly.'

' I'm not going to put on my travelling dress,' answered the queen scornfully ; ' I am just seeing about my
evening dress for the banquet this evening.'

' If you are not ready in your travelling dress in five
minutes, when the carriage comes round, it will be worse
for you. Mind I have warned you.'

And he looked so determined that she quailed before
him.

' How can we be going into the country, when I have
invited half the kingdom to a banquet ? ' exclaimed the
queen.

' *I* have invited no one,' answered the husband quietly.
' Don't stand hesitating when I tell you to do a thing; go
and get ready directly ! we are going into the country ! '
he added in his most positive voice, and, though she shed
many secret tears over the loss of the banquet, she ventured to oppose nothing more to his orders, but went up
and dressed, and when the carriage came round she was
nearly ready. In about five minutes she came down.

' I won't say anything this time about your keeping
me waiting,' he said when she appeared; ' but mind it
does not happen again, or you will be sorry for it.'

The queen had a favourite little dog, which she fondled
and talked to all the way, to show she was offended with
her husband and independent of his conversation.

Watching an opportunity when she was silent, the
husband said to the little dog, ' Jump on to my lap.'

' He's not going to obey you,' said the queen contemp-
tuously ; ' he's *my* dog ! '

' I keep no one about me who does not obey me,' said
her husband quietly; and he took out his pistol and shot
the dog through the head.

The queen began to understand that the husband she
had chosen was not a person to be trifled with, nor did
she venture even to utter a complaint.

When they arrived at the villa, as the queen was going

to her apartment to undress, her husband called her to him into his room and bade her pull off his boots.

The queen's first impulse was to utter a haughty refusal; but by this time she had learnt that, as she would certainly have to give in to him in the end, it was better to do his bidding with a good grace at the first. So she said nothing, but knelt down and pulled off his boots.

When she had done this he got up and said: 'Now sit down in this armchair and I will take off your shoes; for my way is that one should help the other. If you behave to me as wife should, you need never fear but that I shall behave to you as a husband should.'

By the time their visit to the country was at an end, and when they returned to the capital, everybody found their naughty queen had become the most angelic being imaginable.

¹ 'La Regina Cattiva.'

[After people's bad tempers, their follies form the most prolific subject of the *Ciarpe.*]

THE SIMPLE WIFE.¹

THERE was a man and his wife who had a young daughter to marry; and there was a man who was seeking a wife. So the man who was seeking a wife came to the man who had a daughter to marry, and said, 'Give me your daughter for a wife.'

'Yes,' said the man who had a daughter to marry;² 'you'll do very well; you're just about the sort of son-in-law I want.' And then he added: 'If our daughter is to be betrothed to-day, it is the occasion for a feast.' So to the wife he said, 'Prepare the table;' and to the daughter he said, 'Draw the wine.'

The daughter went down into the cellar to draw the

wine. But as she drew the wine she began to cry, saying:
' If I am to be married I shall have a child, and the child
will be a son, and the son will be a priest, and the priest
will be a bishop, and the bishop will be a cardinal, and
the cardinal will be a pope.' And she cried and cried,
and the wine was running all the time, so that the bottle[3]
she was filling ran over, and went on running over.

Then said the father and mother: ' What can the girl
be doing down in the cellar so long?' But the mother
said : ' I must go and see.'

So the mother went down to see why she was so long,
but the moment she came into the cellar she, too, began
to cry ; so that the wine still went on running over.

Then the father said: 'What can the girl and her
mother both be doing so long down in the cellar? I must
go and see.'

So the father went down into the cellar; but the
moment he got into the cellar he, too, began to cry, and
could do nothing for crying ; so the wine still went on
running over.

Then he who had come to seek a wife said: ' What
can these people all be doing so long down in the cellar?'
So he, too, went down to see, and found them all crying
in the cellar and the wine running over. Only when the
wine was all run out they left off crying and came upstairs
again.

Then the betrothal and the marriage were happily
celebrated.

One day after they were married the husband went
into the market to buy meat, and he bought a large provision because he had invited a friend to dinner. When
the wife saw him buy such a quantity of meat she
began to cry, saying : ' What can we do with such a lot
of meat?'

' Oh, never mind, don't make a misery of it,' said the
husband ; ' put it behind you.'[4]

The simple wife took the meat and went home, saying to her parents,[5] and crying the while: 'My husband says I am to put all this meat behind me! Do tell me what *can* I do?'

'You can't put the whole lot of it behind you, that's certain,' replied the equally simple mother; 'but we can manage it between us.'

Then she took the meat and put all the hard, bony part on one chair, where she made the father sit down on it; all the fat, skinny part she put on another chair, and made the wife sit down on it; and the fleshy, meaty part she put on another chair, and sat down on that herself.

Presently the husband came with his friend, ready for dinner, knocking at the door. None of the three dared to move, however, that they might not cease to be fulfilling his injunctions. Then he looked through the keyhole, and, seeing them all sitting down without moving when he knocked, he thought they must all be dead; so he ran and fetched a locksmith, who opened the door for him.

'What on earth are you all doing there,' exclaimed the hungry husband, 'instead of getting dinner ready?'

'You told me to put the meat behind me, and I have done so,' answered the simple wife.

Then he saw they were sitting on the meat. Out of all patience with such idiocy, he exclaimed: 'This is the last you'll ever see of me. At least I promise you not to come back till I have met three other people as idiotic as you, and that's hardly likely to occur.'

With that he took his friend to a tavern to dine, and then put on a pilgrim's dress and went wandering over the country.

In the first city he came to there was great public rejoicing going on. The princess had just been married, and the court was keeping high festival. As he came up to the palace the bride and bridegroom were just come back from church. The bride wore one of those very high round headdresses that they used to wear in olden time, with a long veil hanging from it. It was so very high that she could not by any means get in at the door, and there she stuck, not knowing what to do. Then she began to cry, saying : ' What shall I do? what shall I do ? '

' Shall I tell you what to do ? ' said the pilgrim-husband, drawing near.

' Oh, pray do, if you can ; I will give you a hundred scudi if you will only show me how to get in.'

So he went and made her go a few steps backward, and then bow her head very low, and so she could pass under the door.

' Really, I have found one woman as simple as my people at home,' said the pilgrim-husband, as he sat down to the banquet at the special invitation of the princess, in reward for his services. Afterwards she counted out a hundred scudi to him, and he went further.

Further along the road he came to a farm, with barns and cattle and plenty of stock about, and a large well at which a woman was drawing water. Instead of dipping in the pail, she had got the well-rope knotted into a huge knot, which she kept dipping into the water and squeezing out into the pail, and she kept crying as she did so: ' Oh, how long shall I be filling the pail! The pail will never be full ! '

' Shall I show you how to fill it ? ' asked the pilgrim-husband, drawing near.

' Oh, yes, do show me if you can. I will give you a hundred scudi if you will only show me.'

Then he took all the knots out of the rope and let down the pail by it, and filled it in a minute.

' Here's a second woman as stupid as my people at home,' said the pilgrim-husband, as the farmer's wife asked him in to dinner in reward for his great services; ' if I go on at this rate I shall have to return to her at last, in spite of my protestations.'

After that the farmer's wife counted out the hundred scudi of the promised reward, and he went on further, having first packed six eggs into his hollow staff as provision for the journey.

Towards nightfall he arrived at a lone cottage. Here he knocked and asked a bed for his night's lodging.

' I can't give you that,' said a voice from the inside; ' for I am a lone widow. I can't take a man in to sleep here.'

' But I am a pilgrim,' replied he; ' let me in at least to cook a bit of supper.'

' *That* I don't mind doing,' said the good wife, and she opened the door.

' Thanks, good friend!' said the pilgrim-husband as he sat down by the stove; 'now add to your charity a couple of eggs in a pan.' [6]

So she gave him a pan and two eggs, and a bit of butter to cook them in; but he took the six eggs out of his staff and broke them into the pan, too.

Presently, when the good wife turned her head his way again, and saw eight eggs swimming in the pan instead of two, she said: ' Lack-a-day! you must surely be some strange being from the other world. Do you know so-and-so there' (naming her dead husband)?

' Oh, yes,' said the pilgrim-husband, enjoying the joke; ' I know him very well; he lives just next to me.'

' Only to think of that!' replied the poor woman. ' And do tell me, how do you get on in the other world? What sort of a life is it?'

' Oh, not so very bad; it depends what sort of a place you get. The part where we are is not very bad, except that we get very little to eat. Your husband, for instance, is nearly starved.'

' No, really!' cried the good wife, clasping her hands; ' only fancy! my good husband starving out there; so fond as he was of a good dinner, too!' Then she added, coaxingly: ' As you know him so well, perhaps you wouldn't mind doing him the charity of taking him a little somewhat to give him a treat. There are such lots of things I could easily send him.'

' O, dear no, not at all; I'll do it with great pleasure,' answered he; ' but I'm not going back till to-morrow; and if I don't sleep here I must go on further, and then I shan't come by this way.'

' That's true,' replied the widow. ' Ah, well, I mustn't mind what the folks say, for such an opportunity as this may never occur again. You must sleep in my bed, and I must sleep on the hearth; and in the morning I'll load a donkey with provisions for my poor dear husband.'

' Oh, no,' replied the pilgrim; ' you shan't be disturbed in your bed; only let me sleep on the hearth, that will do for me; and as I'm an early riser I can be gone before anyone's astir, so folks won't have anything to say.'

So it was done, and an hour before sunrise the woman was up loading the donkey with the best of her stores. There were ham, and maccaroni, and flour, and cheese, and wine. All this she committed to the pilgrim, saying: ' You'll send the donkey back, won't you ? '

' Of course I would send him back; he'd be no use to us out there : but I shan't get out again myself for another hundred years or so, and I fear he won't find his way back alone, for it's no easy way to find.'

' To be sure not; I ought to have thought of that,' replied the widow. ' Ah, well, so as my poor husband gets a good meal never mind the donkey.'

So the pretended pilgrim from the other world went his way. He hadn't gone a hundred yards before the widow called him back.

' Ah, she's beginning to think better of it ! ' said he to himself; and he continued his way, pretending not to hear.

' Good pilgrim ! ' shouted the widow; ' I forgot one thing. Would any money be of use to my poor dear husband ? '

'Oh dear yes, all the use in the world,' replied the pilgrim; 'you can always get anything for money everywhere.'

'Oh, do come back then, and I'll trouble you with a hundred scudi for him.'

The pretended pilgrim came back willingly for the hundred scudi, and the widow counted them out to him.

'There is no help for it,' soliloquised he as he went his way; 'I must go back to those at home. I have actually found three women each more stupid than they.'

So he went home to live, and complained no more of the simplicity of his wife.

---

¹ 'La Sposa Cece,' the simple wife. 'Cece' among the common people seems to mean pretty nearly the same as 'tonto,' 'silly,' 'idiotic;' in this place more exactly 'simple' or 'half-witted.'

² It is a characteristic of the Roman people that as a rule they never call people by their names; the 'casato' or married name, and the 'cognome' or family name, are used indifferently when such a name is called in request at all, by married people. If they must give a name to a stranger it is always the Christian name that comes first to their lips; among themselves, however, it is seldom the genuine name that is used. They have some 'sopranome' or nick-name for everybody, or at least a shortening of the Christian name, as 'Checca' and 'Checco' for Francesca and Francesco; 'Pippo' for Filippo; 'Pepe' for Giuseppe; 'Cola' for Niccola; 'Maso' for Tomaso; 'Teta' for Teresa; 'Lalla' for Adelaide; 'Lina' for Carolina; 'Tuta' for Geltrude; the abbreviations for Giovanni are innumerable.

But what they most love to designate people by is a description of their persons. When you come home from your walk, your servant does not tell you Mr. and Mrs. So-and-so have called, but it will be 'Quel signore vecchio ingobbato' (that old hump-backed kind of gentleman), if he be the least grey and high-shouldered, however young he may be; or 'Quel bel giovane alto' (that tall, handsome, young gentleman), whatever his age, if he be only *bien conservé*. Then 'Quella signora alta, secca, che veste di lutto' (that tall thin lady dressed in mourning). 'Quella signora bella bionda, giovane' (that lady, pretty, fair, young). Or 'Quello che porta il brillante' (he who wears a brilliant), because the same friend happened to have a diamond stud in his cravat one day; or 'Quella contessa che veste di cilestro,' because the lady happened once to wear a blue dress, and so on, with all manner of signs and tokens which it may take you half-an-hour to recognise a person by, if you ever make it out at all. Or, if there is no distinctive mark of the kind to seize upon, it will be

' Quel signore,' or ' quella signora di Palazzo,' or ' Via,' or ' Piazza' So-and-so. And this not from the difficulty of catching a foreign name, because it is still more in vogue when designating their own people ; if you are asking for the address of a servant, a tailor, a dressmaker, &c., it is in vain you try to make them out by the name, you must do your best to describe them, and then they will break out with an exclamation hitting it off for themselves : ' Ah ! si, quel scimunito' (that silly-looking fellow); 'quel gobbo' (that high-shouldered fellow—lit. ' hunchbacked'); 'quella strega' (that ugly old woman, cunning woman—lit.' witch') ; 'quella bella giovane alta' (that tall handsome girl); 'quella donna bassetta' (that short little woman), for with their descriptions as with their names they must super-add a diminutive or a qualification, and ' basso' (short) is pretty sure to be rendered by 'bassetto,' 'piccola' (little) by ' piccinina,' 'vecchio' (old) by 'vecchietto.' ' Quella scimia' or 'scimietta' (that old woman, or that little old woman who looks like a monkey). ' Quella donna anziana' (that respectable old woman). ' Quella donniciuola' (that nasty little old woman, contemptible old woman). ' Quel ragazzino, tanto carino, tanto caruccio ' (that nice boy, that very nice boy). ' Quel vecchietto ' (that nice old man); and in this way the hero of this story is designated as ' The man who has a daughter to marry.'

³ ' Boccione,' a large coarse glass bottle commonly used in Rome for carrying wine. When it is covered with twisted rushes—like the oil-flasks that come to England—it is called a ' damigiana,' a young lady, a little lady.

⁴ 'Mettetevelo addietro.' Lit. ' Put it behind you,' a way of saying 'Never mind it,' 'don't care about it.' But the woman is supposed to be so foolish that she understands it literally.

⁵ The Italian custom of the newly married couples continuing to live with the parents of one or other of them is here brought in.

⁶ 'Tegame,' a flat earthen pan much in vogue in Roman kitchens; ' ova in tegame' is a favourite and not a bad dish. A little fresh butter is oiled, and the eggs are dropped into it as for poaching, and very slowly cooked in it ; when scarcely set they are reckoned done.

[We have the German of this story in ' Die Klugen Leute,' Grimm, p. 407, and again the beginning of it in ' Die Kluge Else ' (Clever Lizzie), Grimm, p. 137 (which ends with the despera-tion of the wife as the second Roman version ends with the death of the husband); in some variants given in the ' Russian Folk Tales,' pp. 53–4 ; in an Italian-Tirolese tale, ' Le donne matte ' (the title resembling that of the next Roman version); and the ending, in the Norse ' Not a pin to choose between them.' Senhor de Saraiva told me the following Portuguese story entitled ' Pedro da Malas Artes' (Tricky Peter), which embodies these incidents, but opens with a different purport.

TRICKY PETER was a knowing blade; so he went out on his travels to set all the world straight; and he found plenty to do.

In the very first town he came to there was a great commotion. A bride had come to church to be married, and there she stuck at the church door, mounted on her mule, while the people deliberated whether they should facilitate her ingress by cutting off some of her head or some of the mule's legs.

'Let her alight and walk in,' said Tricky Peter; 'and the door will be high enough.' And all the people applauded his wisdom.

At the next town he found the people all full of discontent, because one of them had to sit up by turns to tell the others when the sun rose.

'I'll give you a bird to perform that office,' said Tricky Peter; and he went home and fetched a cock, and then they could all rest comfortably.

After this the story has no more silly people to deal with; but Peter fools a giant, and overcomes his strength with craft. He does not seem, either, to get paid for his services, as do the heroes of 'La Sposa Cese,' and all the others.

I have also another Roman story (too long to print here) of a man who sets out with a different purpose again, who meets with three sets of people afflicted with similar follies, and who also makes a good deal of money by his counsel; together with various stories in which men go to fetch their wives back from the devil's kingdom, get three commissions of a similar nature by the way, for executing which they get richly paid on their return.

There is a story in the 5th Tantra given as 'Le Brahme aux vains projets' in Abbé Dubois' translation of the 'Pantcha-Tantra,' which has an analogous opening to that of 'La Sposa Cece.' There is another among the 'Contes Indiens' published at the end of it, in which four Brahmans have a great dispute as to which of them can claim to be the greatest idiot—a strife only second in folly to that of the 'Three Indolent Boys' in Grimm, p. 551—and they each narrate such proof of having acted with consummate folly that the decision given is that there is not a pin to choose between them.

In a somewhat analogous story, which he calls 'Aventures du

Gourou Paramarta,' one of the disciples commits the counting mistake ' of the well-known Irishman,' in omitting to reckon himself in his computation, also found in the Russian ' Folk Tales,' p. 54, and they go to buy a foal's egg, just as do certain peasants of the Trentino in an Italian-Tirolese *' storiella da rider'* [1] (laughable story).]

LA SPOSA CECE.

2

Another version of this story was told me, or rather an entirely different story embodying the same purport, which, though full of fun, turned on the double meanings of common words of household use too homely for the most part, and some too coarse to please the English reader. The husband, among other things, tells his wife to prepare dinner for a friend and to mind she has ' brocoli strascinati' and ' uovi spersi,' [2] as they are his favourite dishes. 'Strascinare' is to drag anything along, but is technically used to express brocoli chopped up and fried, the commonest Roman dish. 'Spergere' is to scatter, but the word is used among common people to express eggs poached in broth, a favourite delicacy; (eggs poached as in England are called ' uova in bianco'). The wife, taking the words literally, drags the brocoli all over the house and all over the yard, till it is so nasty it cannot be eaten, instead of frying it, and scatters the eggs all about the place instead of poaching them, and so on through a number of other absurdities difficult to explain in detail. In the end the husband falls ill, partly from her bad cooking and partly from annoyance; a doctor is called in, who tells her (among other directions which she similarly misunderstands), that he must have nothing but ' brodo,' [3] but she is to make it 'alto, alto.' 'Alto' is literally ' high,' but he uses it for ' good,' ' strong; ' she, however, understands him to mean her to make it in a high place, and goes up on the roof to make it. When the husband asks for it she says she cannot get it for him then as it is up on the roof.

Ultimately the husband dies of vexation.

There is a very familiar German story which everyone who has any acquaintance with the people must have met, of a lady who complains to her servant that the tea has not ' drawn,' and the simple girl answers, ' It is not my fault, I have *drawn* it all about the place enough I'm sure ' (Ich hab' es genug umherge-zogen).

[1] Such notions are not altogether so impossible as they seem. I myself heard a very intelligent little boy one day say to his mother, 'Mama, I should so like to see a horse's egg.' 'A horse's egg, my dear—there are no such things,' was the reply of course. 'Oh yes, there *must* be,' rejoined the child, ' because I've heard Pa several times talk about finding a mare's nest.'

[2] 'Uovo,' by the way, is a word with which great liberties are taken. The correct singular is ' uovo ' and the plural ' uova,' but it is very common to make the plural in 'i' and also to say 'uova' for the singular, and 'uove' for plural, while the initial ' u ' is most usually dropped out.

[3] 'Brodo' is beef-tea or clear broth with nothing in it; broth with ver-micelli or anything else in it is 'minestra;' 'zuppa,' which sounds most like 'soup,' is rather 'sop,' and when applied to broth, means strictly only broth with bread in it, from 'inzuppare,' to steep, soak, or sop; but it is also used for broth with anything else in it besides bread, but never with-out anything in it.

THE FOOLISH WOMAN.[1]

THERE was once a couple well-to-do in the world, who had one only daughter.

The son of a neighbour came to ask her in marriage, and as the father thought he would do, the father asked him to dinner, and sent the daughter down into the cellar to draw the wine.

' If I am married,' said the girl to herself, and began to cry as she drew the wine, ' I shall have a child, and the child will be a boy, and the boy will be called Petrillo, and by-and-by he will die, and I shall be left to lament him, and to cry all day long " Petrillo! Petrillo! where are you!"' and she went on crying, and the wine went on running over.

Then the mother went down to see what kept her so

long, and she repeated the story all over to her, and the mother answered, 'Right you are, my girl!' and she, too, began to cry, and the wine was all the time running over.

Then the father went down, and they repeated the story to him, and he, too, said, 'Right you are!' and he, too, began to cry, and the wine all the time went on running all over the floor.

Then the young man also goes down to see what is the matter, and stops the wine running, and makes them all come up.

'But,' he says, 'I'll not marry the girl till I have wandered over the world and found other three as simple as you.' He dines with them, and sets out on his search.

The first night he goes to bed in an inn, and in the morning he hears in the room next him such lamenting and complaining that he goes in to see what is the matter. A man is sitting by the side of the bed lamenting because he cannot get his stockings on.

The young man says, 'Take hold of one side this way, and the other side that way, and pull them up.'

'Ah, to be sure!' cries the man, and gives him a hundred scudi for the benefit he has done him.

'There's one of my three simpletons, at all events,' says the young man, and journeys on.

The next day, at the inn where he spends the night, he hears a noise *bru, bru!* goes in to see, and finds a man fruitlessly trying to put walnuts into a sack by sticking a fork into them.

'You'll never do it that way,' says the young man; and he shows him how to scoop them up with both his hands and so pour them in.

'Ah, to be sure!' answers the man, and gives him a hundred scudi for the favour he has done him.

'There is my second simpleton,' says the young man, and goes further.

The third day——Ah! I can't remember what he meets the third day; but it is something equally stupid, and he gets another hundred scudi, and goes back and marries the girl as he had promised.

When they had been married some time, he goes out for two or three days to shoot.

'I'll come with you,' says the wife.

'Well, it's not quite the thing,' answered he; 'but perhaps it's better than leaving you at home; but mind you pull the door after you.'

'Oh yes, of course,' answers the simple wife, and pulls it so effectually that she lifts it off its hinges and carries it along with her.

When they had gone some way he looks back and sees her carrying the door.

'What on earth are you bringing the door along for!' he cries.

'You told me to pull it after me,' answers she.

'Of course, I only meant you to pull it to, to make the house secure,' he says.

'If merely pulling it to, made the house secure, how much securer it must be when I pull it all this way!' answers she.

He finds it useless to reason with her, and they go on. At night they climb up into a tree to sleep, the woman still carrying the door with her. A band of robbers come and count their gains under the tree; the woman from sheer weariness, and though she believes it will rouse the robbers to come and kill them, drops the door upon them. They take it for an earthquake and run away. The man and his wife then gather up the money, and are rich for the rest of their lives.

---

[1] 'La Donna Mattarella.' 'Matto' is simply 'mad,' with the diminutive 'ella' it comes to mean 'slightly mad,' 'simple.'

2

[A version from Sinigaglia was very like the last. It only took up the story, however, after the husband and wife are married. The first silly thing the wife does is the feat of the 'brocoli strascinati,' as in 'La Sposa Cece,' No. 2. Some variety is always thrown in in the way of telling. This wife was represented as having a very sweet voice, and saying, 'Si, si, marito mio!' in the gentlest and tenderest way in the world, to everything her husband tells her, though she mismanages everything so. After the brocoli affair he tells her to cook some beans for dinner. 'Si, si, marito mio,' she says in her sweet tone, but takes four beans only and boils them in a pot of water. When he comes in and asks if the beans are done, she says, 'Si, si. marito mio!' She says she has cooked two beans apiece, but one has boiled away, so she will only take one for her share.

He finds it impossible to live with her, and goes away, but she in her simplicity says if he goes away she will go with him! When he finds he can't prevent this he tells her to pull the door after her, and the story has the same ending as the last.]

After tales of simple wives come similar tales cf simple boys. Compare 'Russian Folktales,' pp. 10 and 49. An analogous incident to the selling of the linen to a statue in the following is told of a grown-up peasant in Grimm's 'Der gute Handel,' p. 30, which story is not unlike one called 'How the poorest became the richest' I have given from the German-Tirolese province of Vorarlberg at the end of 'Household Stories from the Land of Höfer,' a close counterpart of which I have met in a Roman periodical, told as collected at Modena. The Italian-Tirolese counterpart bears the name of 'Turlulù,' and resembles the Roman very closely. There is a place in German Tirol where they not only tell the story, but point out the *Bildstocklein* (the wayside image), to which the simple boy sold his linen; I cannot recall the place now, though I remember having occasion to mention it in 'Traditions of Tirol' in the 'Monthly Packet.' In the German there is also 'Der gescheidte Hans,' which is somewhat different in structure; but Scheible, 'Schaltjahr,' i. 493, gives a story which contains both ways of telling.]

THE BOOBY.[1]

THEY say there was once a widow woman who had a very simple son. Whatever she set him to do he muddled in some way or other.

' What am I to do?' said the poor mother to a neighbour one day. ' The boy eats and drinks, and has to be clothed; what am I to do if I am to make no profit of him?'

' You have kept him at home long enough;' answered the neighbour. ' Try sending him out, now; maybe that will answer better.'

The mother took the advice, and the next time she had got a piece of linen spun she called her boy, and said to him:

' If I send you out to sell this piece of linen, do you think you can manage to do it without committing any folly?'

' Yes, mama,' answered the booby.

' You always say "yes mama," but you do contrive to muddle everything all the same,' replied the mother. ' Now, listen attentively to all I say. Walk straight along the road without turning to right or left; don't take less than such and such a price for it. Don't have anything to say to women who chatter; whether you sell it to anyone you meet by the way, or carry it into the market, offer it only to some quiet sort of body whom you may see standing apart, and not gossiping and prating, for such as they will persuade you to take some sort of a price that won't suit me at all.'

The booby promised to follow these directions very exactly, and started on his way.

On he walked, turning neither to the right hand nor to the left, thus passing the turnings which led to the villages, to one or other of which he ought to have gone. But his mother had only meant that he was not to turn off the pathway and lose himself.

Presently he met the wife of the syndic of the next town, who was driving out with her maids, but had got out to walk a little stretch of the way, as the day was fine. The syndic's wife was talking cheerfully with her maids, and when one of them caught sight of the simpleton, she said to her mistress:

'Here is the simple son of the poor widow by the brook.'

'What are you going to do, my good lad?' said the syndic's wife kindly.

'Not going to tell you, because you were chattering and gossiping,' replied the booby boorishly, and tried to pass on.

The syndic's wife forgave his boorishness, and added:

'I see your mother has sent you to sell this piece of linen. I will buy it of you, and that will save you walking further; put it in the carriage, and I'll give you so much for it.'

Though she had offered him twice as much as his mother had told him to get for it, he would only answer:

'Can't sell it to you, because you were chattering and gossiping.'

Nor could they prevail on him to stop a moment longer.

Further along he came to a statue by the roadside.

'Here's one who stands apart and doesn't chatter,' said the booby to himself. 'This is the one to sell the linen to.' Then aloud to the statue, 'Will you buy my linen, good friend?' Then to himself. 'She doesn't speak, so it's all right.' Then to the statue, 'The price is so-and-so; have the money ready against I come back, as I have to go on and buy some yarn for mother.'

On he went and bought the yarn, and then came back to the statue. Some one passing by meanwhile, and seeing the linen lie there had picked it up and walked off with it.

Finding it gone, the booby said to himself, 'It's all right, she's taken it.' Then to the statue, 'Where's the money I told you to have ready against I came back?' As the statue remained silent, the booby began to get uneasy. 'My mother *will* be finely angry if I go back without the linen or the money,' he said to himself. Then to the statue, 'If you don't give me the money directly I'll hit you on the head.'

The booby was as good as his word; lifting his thick rough walking-stick, he gave the statue such a blow that he knocked the head off.

But the statue was hollow, and filled with gold coin.

'That's where you keep your money, is it?' said the booby, 'all right, I can pay myself.' So he filled his pockets with money and went back to his mother.

'Look, mama! here's the price of the piece of linen.'

'All right!' said the mother out loud; but to herself she said, 'where can I ever hide all this lot of money? I have got no place to hide it but in this earthen jar, and if he knows how much it is worth, he will be letting out the secret to other people, and I shall be robbed.'

So she put the money in the earthen jar, and said to the boy:

'They've cheated you in making you think that was coin; it's nothing but a lot of rusty nails;' but never mind, you'll know better next time.' And she went out to her work.

While she was gone out to her work there came by an old rag-merchant.

'Ho! here, rag-merchant!' said the booby, who had acquired a taste for trading. 'What will you give me for this lot of rusty nails?' and he showed him the jar full of gold coin.

The rag-merchant saw that he had to do with an idiot, so he said:

'Well, old nails are not worth very much; but as I'm a good-natured old chap, I'll give you twelve pauls for them,' because he knew he must offer enough to seem a prize to the idiot.

'You may have them at that,' said the booby. And the rag-merchant poured the coin out into his sack, and gave the fool the twelve pauls.

'Look mama, look! I've sold that lot of old rusty worthless nails for twelve pauls. Isn't that a good bargain?'

'Sold them for twelve pauls!' cried the widow, tearing her hair, 'Why, it was a fortune all in gold coin.'

'Can't help it, mama,' replied the booby; 'you told me they were rusty nails.'

Another day she told him to shut the door of the cottage; but as he went to do it he lifted the door off its hinges. His mother called after him in an angry voice, which so frightened him that he ran. away, carrying the door on his back.

As he went along, some one to tease him, said, 'Where did you steal that door?' which frightened him still more, and he climbed up in a tree with it to hide it.

At night there came a band of robbers under the tree, and counted out all their gains in large bags of money. The booby was so frightened at the sight of so many fierce-looking robbers, that he began to tremble and let go of the door.

The door fell with a bang in the midst of the robbers, who thinking it must be that the police were upon them, decamped, leaving all their money behind.

The booby came down from the tree and carried the money home to his mother, and they became so rich that she was able to appoint a servant to attend to him, and keep him from doing any more mischief.

[1] 'Il Tonto.'
[2] 'Chiodacci;' 'chiodi,' nails; 'chiodacci,' old rusty nails.

[After the boys, the girls come in for their share of hard

jokes; here is one who figures both as a daughter and a wife. Grimm has the same, with a slight variation, as ' Rumpelstilzchen,' p. 219, and the Italian-Tirol Tales give it as ' Tarandandò; ' the incident on which these two hinge of a supernatural being giving his help on condition of the person he favours remembering his name, is of frequent occurrence. I have met it in two German-Tirolese stories, ' The Wilder Jäger and the Baroness,' and in ' Klein-Else ' in ' Household Stories,' and in a local tradition told me at Salzburg, which I have given in ' Traditions of Tirol,' No. XVI. in ' Monthly Packet,' each time the sprite gets a new name; in this one it was ' Hahnenzuckerl.' The supernatural helper delivering the girl from future as well as present labour occurs in the Spanish equivalent, ' What Ana saw in the Sunbeam,' in ' Patrañas,' but in favour of a good, instead of a lazy or greedy girl; and so with the girl in the Norse tale of ' The Three Aunts.' ' Die faule Spinnerin,' Grimm, p. 495, helps herself to the same end without supernatural aid.]

THE GLUTTONOUS GIRL.[1]

THERE was a poor woman who went out to work by the day. She had one idle, good-for-nothing daughter, who would never do any work, and cared for nothing but eating, always taking the best of everything for herself, and not caring how her mother fared.

One day the mother, when she went out to her work, left the girl some beans to cook for dinner, and some pieces of bacon-rind[2] to stew along with them. When the pieces of bacon-rind were nicely done, she took them out and eat them herself, and then found a pair of dirty old shoe-soles, which she pared in slices, and put them into the stew for her mother.

When the poor mother came home, not only were there no pieces of bacon which she could eat, but the beans themselves were rendered so nasty by the shoe-soles that she could not eat them either. Determined to give her daughter a good lesson, once for all, on this occasion, she took her outside her cottage door, and beat her well with a stick.

Just as she was administering this chastisement, a farmer [3] came by.

'What are you beating this pretty lass for?' asked the man.

'Because she *will* work so hard at her household duties that she works on Sundays and holidays the same as common days,' answered the mother, who, bad as her daughter was, yet had not the heart to give her a bad character.

'That is the first time I ever heard of a mother beating her child for doing too much work; the general complaint is that they do too little. Will you let me have her for a wife? I should like such a wife as that.'

'Impossible!' replied the mother, in order to enhance her daughter's value; 'she does all the work of the house, I can't spare her; what shall I do without her?'

'I must give you something to make up for the loss,' replied the merchant; 'but such a notable wife as this I have long been in search of, and I must not miss the chance.'

'But I cannot spare such a notable daughter, either,' persisted the mother.

'What do you say if I give you five hundred scudi?'

'If I let her go, it is not because of the five hundred scudi,' said the mother; 'it is because you seem a husband, who will really appreciate her; though I don't say five hundred scudi will not be a help to a poor lone widow.'

'Let it be agreed then. I am going now to the fair; when I come back let the girl be ready, and I'll take her back with me.'

Accordingly, when the farmer returned from the fair, he fetched the girl away.

When he got home his mother came out to ask how his affairs had prospered at the fair.

'Middling well, at the fair,' replied the man; 'but, by the way, I found a treasure, and I have brought her home to make her my wife. She is so hardworking that she can't be kept from working, even on Sundays.'

'She doesn't look as if there was much work in her,' observed the mother dryly; 'but if you're satisfied that's enough.'

All went well enough the first week, because she was not expected to do much just at first, but at the end of that time the husband had to go to a distant fair which would keep him absent three weeks. Before he went he took his new wife up into the store-room, and said, ' Here are provisions of all sorts, and you will have all you like to eat and drink; and here is a quantity of hemp, which you can amuse yourself with spinning and weaving if you want more employment than merely keeping the place in order.'

Then he gave her a set of rooms to herself, next the store-chamber, that there might be no cause of quarrel with the mother-in-law, who, he knew, was inclined to be jealous of her, and said good-bye.

Left to herself, she did no more work than she could help; all the nice things she found she cooked and ate, and that was all the work she did. As to the hemp, she never touched it; nor did she even clean up the place, or attempt to put it tidy.

When the husband had been gone a fortnight, the mother-in-law came up to see how she was going on, and when she saw the hemp untouched, and the place in disorder, she said, 'So this is how you go on when your husband is away!'

'You mind your affairs, and I'll mind mine,' answered the wife, and the mother-in-law went away offended.

Nevertheless, it was true that in eight days the husband would be back, and might expect to see something done, so she took up a lot of hemp and began trying to spin it; but, as she had no idea of how to do it, she went on in the most absurd way imaginable with it.

As she stood on the top of the outside staircase, twisting it this way and that, there passed three deformed fairies. One was lame, and one squinted,[5] and one had her head all on one side, because she had a fish-bone stuck in her throat.

The three fairies called out to ask what she was doing, and when she said 'spinning,' the one who squinted laughed so much that her eyes came quite right, and the one who had a bone stuck in her throat laughed so much that the bone came out, and her head became straight again like other people's, and when the lame one saw the others laughing so much, she ran so fast to see what it was that her lameness was cured.

Then the three fairies said:

'Since she has cured us of our ailments, we must go in and do her a good turn.'

So they went in and took the hemp and span it, and wove it, and did as much in the six remaining days as any human being could have done in twenty years; moreover, they cleaned up everything, and made everything look spick-and-span new.

Then they gave her a bag of walnuts, saying, 'in half an hour your husband will be home; go to bed and put this bag of walnuts under your back. When he comes in say you have worked so hard that all your bones are out of joint; then move the bag of walnuts and they will make a noise, *c-r-r-r-r*, and he will think it is your bones which are loosened, and will say you must never work again.'

When the husband came home his mother went out to meet him, saying—

'I told you I did not think there was much work in your "treasure." When you go up you'll see what a fine mess the place is all in; and as to the hemp, you had better have left it locked up, for a fine mess she has made of that.'

But the husband went up and found the place all in shining order, and so much hemp spun and woven as could scarcely be got through in twenty years. But the wife was laid up in bed.

When the husband came near the bed she moved the bag of walnuts and they went *c-r-r-r-r.*

'You have done a lot of work indeed!' said the husband.

' Yes,' replied the wife ; ' but I have put all my bones out of joint ; only hear how they rumble !' and she moved the walnuts again, and they went *c-r-r-r-r.* ' It will be sometime before I am about again.'

' Oh, dear ! oh, dear !' said the husband ; ' only think of such a treasure of a wife being laid up by such marvellous diligence.'

And to his mother he said : ' A mother-in-law has never a good word for her daughter-in-law ; what you told me was all pure invention.'

But to the wife he said : 'Mind I will never have you do any work again as long as you live.'

So from that day forth she had no work to do, but ate and drank and amused herself from morning till night.

---

[1] 'La Ragazza Golosa;' 'goloso' means, in particular, greedy of nice things.

[2] 'Codiche di presciúto.'

[3] 'Mercante di Campagna.' See Note 2, p. 154.

[4] 'Voi pensate a voi ed io penso a me!' 'Pensare' is much used in Rome in the sense of ' to attend to,' ' to provide for.'

[5] 'Guèrcia,' see Note 3 to 'The Two Friars;' in this case squinting seems intended.

2

THE GREEDY DAUGHTER.[1]

THERE was a mother who had a daughter so greedy that she did not know what to do with her. Everything in the house she would eat up. When the poor mother came home from work there was nothing left.

But the girl had a godfather-wolf.[2] The wolf had a frying-pan, and the girl's mother was too poor to possess such an article; whenever she wanted to fry anything she sent her daughter to the wolf to borrow his frying-pan, and he always sent a nice omelette in it by way of not sending it empty. But the girl was so greedy and so selfish that she not only always ate the omelette by the way, but when she took the frying-pan back she filled it with all manner of nasty things.

At last the wolf got hurt at this way of going on, and he came to the house to inquire into the matter.

Godfather-wolf met the mother on the step of the door, returning from work.

' How do you like my omelettes ? ' asked the wolf.

' I am sure they would be good if made by our god-father-wolf,' replied the poor woman; ' but I never had the honour of tasting them.'

' Never tasted them ! Why, how many times have you sent to borrow my frying-pan ? '

' I am ashamed to say how many times; a great many, certainly.'

' And every time I sent you an omelette in it.'

' Never one reached me.'

' Then that hussey of a girl must have eaten them by the way.'

The poor mother, anxious to screen her daughter, burst into all manner of excuses, but the wolf now saw how it all was. To make sure, however, he added: ' The omelettes would have been better had the frying-pan not always been full of such nasty things. I did my best always to clean it, but it was not easy.'

' Oh, godfather-wolf, you are joking! I always cleaned it, inside and out, as bright as silver, every time before I sent it back ! '

The wolf now knew all, and he said no more to the mother; but the next day, when she was out, he came back.

When the girl saw him coming she was so frightened and self-convicted that she ran under the bed to hide herself.

But to the wolf it was as easy to go under a bed as anywhere else; so under he went, and he dragged her out and devoured her. And that was the end of the Greedy Daughter.

¹ ' La Figlia Ghiotta.' ' Ghiotta' and ' golosa' have much the same meaning.

² ' Compare-lupo ' (lit. had a wolf for godfather); ' compare ' for ' compadre,' godfather, gossip. Lycanthropy had an important place in the mediæval as in the earlier mythologies; witches were often accused of turning people into wolves by the use of their ointments. Our ' Little Red Riding Hood' is connected with it, and several in the German and Tirolese Stories, but it is too wide a subject to enter upon here.'

[In the Italian-Tirolese tales is one very similar to this, called ' Catarinetta.'

After the faults of the young, the sins of the old have their share of mocking. In the ' Russian Folk Tales,' pp. 46–50, is a miser story, but, for a wonder, not the least trace of similarity.

In Scheible's ' Schaltjahr,' vol. i. pp. 169–71, is a very quaint miser story, bringing in also an instance of wolf-transformation, which is said to have happened ' in Italy,' to a certain Herr v. Schotenberg, on August 14, 1798. He had seized a poor peasant's only cow for a debt, and when, in punishment, all his own cows were struck dead, he accused the peasant's wife of bewitching them, and threatened to have her burnt. The peasant's wife answered that it was the judgment of God, not hers; and upon that he turned to the crucifix in the farmyard, saying : ' Oh, you did it, did you ? then you may go and eat the carrion you have made, with the dogs.' Then he took out his pistol, shot an arm off the crucifix, and flung it on to the heap of dead cows, saying, ' Now one piece of carrion lies with the rest!' ' Albeit it was only a wooden image,' says the account, ' yet it was of God in Heaven that he spoke, who punished him on the spot by turning him into a dog.' The portrait which accompanies the story is quaint, too, having a human face, with wolfish, erect ears, and the rest of the body like a dog. He wore at the time a fur cloak, of pale yellow with black spots, and that is how the dog's fur appeared ; and he had to eat carrion all his life, and follow his good wife about, wherever she went.]

THE OLD MISER.[1]

THEY say there was once an old man who had so much money he didn't know what to do with it. He had cellars and cellars, where all the floors were strewn with gold ; but the house was all tumbling down, because he would not spend a penny in repairing it ; and for all food he took nothing all day but a crust of bread and a glass of water.

He was always afraid lest some one should come to rob him of his wealth, so he seldom so much as spoke to anyone.

One day, however, a busy, talkative neighbour would have her say out with him, and among other things she said : ' How can you go on living in that ugly old house all alone now ? Why don't you take a wife ? '

' A wife !' replied the old miser ; ' how can *I* take a wife ? How am I to afford to keep a wife, I should like to know ? '

' Nonsense !' persisted the loquacious neighbour ; ' you've got plenty of money, you know. And how much better you'd be if you had a wife. Do you mean to tell me, now, you wouldn't be much better off with one ? Now answer me fairly.'

' Well, if I must speak the truth, as you are so urgent for an answer,' replied the old miser, ' I don't mean to say I haven't often thought I should like a wife ; but I am waiting till I find one who can live upon air.'[2]

' Well, maybe there might be such an one even as you say,' returned the busy neighbour; 'though she might not be easy to find.' And she said no more for that day.

She went, however, to a young woman who lived opposite, and said : ' If you want a rich husband I will find you one.'

' To be sure I should like a rich husband,' replied the young woman ; ' who would not ? '

' Very well, then,' continued the neighbour; ' I will tell you what to do. You have only, every day at dinner-time, to stand at the window and suck in the air, and move your lips as if you were eating. But eat no-thing; take nothing into your mouth but air. The old miser who lives opposite wants a wife who can live on air ; and if he thinks you can do this he will marry you. And when you are once installed it'll be odd if you don't find means, in the midst of so much money, to lay hold of enough to get a dinner every day without working for it.'

The young woman thanked her friend for the advice, and next day, when the bells rang at noon, she threw open the window and stood sucking in the air, and then moving her lips as if she was eating. This she did several days.

At last the old miser came across under the window, and said to her: ' What are you doing at the window there ? '

' Don't you see it's dinner-time, and I'm taking my dinner ? Don't interrupt me ! ' replied the young neigh-bour.

' But, excuse me,[3] I don't see you are eating anything, though your lips move.'

' O ! I live upon air ; I take nothing but air,' replied the young woman ; and she went on with her mock munching.

'You live upon air, do you? Then you're just the wife I'm looking for. Will you come down and marry me?'

As this was just what she wanted she did not keep him waiting, and soon they were married and she was installed in the miser's house.

But it was not so easy to get at the money as she had thought. At first the miser would not let her go near his cellars; but as he spent so much time down there she said she could not be deprived of his company for so long, she must come down too.

All the time she was down with him the miser held both her hands in his, as if he was full of affection for her; but in reality it was to make sure she did not touch any of his money.

She, however, bought some pitch, and put it on the soles of her shoes, and as she walked about in the gold plenty of it stuck to her shoes; and when she came up again she took the gold off her shoes, and sent her maid to the *trattoria*[4] for the most delicious dinners. Shut up in a room apart they fared sumptuously—she and her maid. But every day at midday she let the miser see her taking her fancied dinner of air.

This went on for long, because the miser had so much gold that he never missed the few pieces that stuck to her shoes every day.

But at last there came a Carneval Thursday,[5] when the maid had brought home an extra fine dinner; and as they were an extra length of time over this extra number of dishes and glasses, the old miser, always suspicious, began to guess there must be something wrong; and to find it out he instituted a scrutiny into every room in the crazy house. Thus he came at last to the room where his wife and her maid were dining sumptuously.

'This is how you live on air, is it?' he roared, red with fury.

'Oh, but on Carneval Thursday,' replied the wife, 'one may have a little extra indulgence!'

'Will you tell me you have not had a private dinner every day?' shouted the excited miser.

'If I have,' replied the wife, not liking to tell a direct falsehood, 'how do you know it is not with my own money? Tell me, have you missed any of yours?'

The miser was only the more angry at her way of putting the question, because he could not say he had actually missed the money; yet he was convinced it was his money she had been spending.

'How do I know it is not your money, do you ask?' he thundered; 'because if you had had any money of your own you would never have come to live here, you would not have married me.'

But weak as he was with his bread and water diet, the excitement was too much for him. As he said these words a convulsion seized him, and he fell down dead.

Thus all his riches came into possession of the wife.

[1] 'Il Vecchio Avaro.' (The Avaricious Old Man.)

[2] 'Che campasse d'aria,' who should subsist on air.

[3] 'Abbi pazienza,' have patience; equivalent to 'please,' 'pray excuse me,' &c.

[4] 'Trattoria,' an eating-house, but one where, as a rule, dinners are sent out.

[5] 'Giovedì grasso,' Thursday in Carneval week, a day of a little extra feasting.

THE MISERLY OLD WOMAN.[1]

THERE was an old woman who had three sons, and from her stinginess she could not bear that anyone should have anything to eat. One day the eldest son came to her and said he must take a wife.

'If you must, you must,' replied the miserly mother. 'But mind she is one who brings a great dowry, eats little, and can work all day long.'

The eldest son went his way and told the girl he was going to marry his mother's hard terms. As the girl loved him very much, she made no objection, and he married her, and brought her home.[2]

The first morning the mother-in-law came before it was light, and knocked at the door, and bid the bride get up and come down to her work.

'It is very hard for you,' said the young husband.

'Ah, well! I promised to submit to it before we married,' she replied. 'I won't break my promise.'

So she got up and went down and helped her mother-in-law to do the work of the house. By twelve o'clock she was very hungry; but the miserly mother-in-law only took out an apple and a halfpenny roll, and gave her half of each for all her food. She took it without a murmur; and so she went on every day, working hard, and eating little, and making no complaint.

By-and-by the second son came and told his mother that he was going to take a wife. The mother made the same conditions, and the wife submitted to them with equally good grace.

Then the third son came and said he too must take a wife. To him the old woman made the same terms; but he could not find a wife who would submit to them for his sake. The girl he wanted to marry, however, was very lively and spirited, and she said at last—

'Never mind the conditions; let's marry, and we'll get through the future somehow.'

Then they married. When her son brought home this wife, and the old woman found she had no dowry, she was in a great fury; but it was too late to help it.

The first morning, when she knocked at their door to wake her, she called out—

'Who's there?' though she knew well enough.

The mother-in-law answered, 'Time to get up!'

'*Oibo!*' exclaimed the young wife. 'Don't imagine

I'm going to get up in the middle of the night like this!
I shall get up when I please, and not before.' Then she
turned to her husband, and said, ' Just for her bothering
me like this I shan't get up till twelve o'clock.' Neither
did she.

The house was now filled with the old woman's
lamentations. ' This woman upsets everything! This
woman will be the ruin of us all!' she kept exclaiming.
But the third wife paid no heed, and dressed herself up
smart, and amused herself, and did no work at all.

When supper-time came the old woman took out her
apple and her halfpenny loaf, and cut them in four
quarters, serving a bit all round.

' What's that ?' said the third wife, stooping to look
at it, as if she could not make it out, and without taking
it in her hand.

' It's your supper,' replied the mother-in-law.

' My supper! do you think I've come to my second
childhood, to be helped to driblets like that!' and she
filliped it to the other end of the room.

Then she went to her husband and said—

' I'll tell you what we must do ; we must have false
keys made, and get into the store-closet[3] and take what
we want.'

Though the mother-in-law was so miserly, there was
good provision of everything in the store-closet ; and so
with the false keys she took flour and lard and ham, and
they had plenty of everything. One day she had made
a delicious cake of curdled sheep's milk,[4] and she gave a
woman a halfpenny to take it to the baker's to bake,
saying—

' Make haste, and bring it back, that we may get
through eating it while the old woman is at mass.'

She was not quick enough, however, and the mother-
in-law came in just about the same time that the cake
came back from the baker's. The third son's wife to hide

it from her caught it up and put it under her petticoats, but it burned her ankles, so that she was obliged to bring it out. Then the mother-in-law understood what had been going on, and went into such a fury, the house could not hold her.

Then the third son's wife sent the same woman to the chemist, saying, 'get me three pauls of quicksilver.' And she took the quicksilver, when the mother-in-law was asleep, and put it into her mouth and ears, so that she could not storm or scold any more. But after a time she died of vexation; and then they opened wide the store-room, and lived very comfortably.

[1] 'La Vecchia Avara.' This story was told in emulation of the last, otherwise it is hardly worth reproducing. The only merit of the story consisted in the liveliness of the pantomime with which the words of the third wife were rendered. To the poor, however, such a story is a treasure, as it tells of the condign punishment of an oppressor; and there are few of them who have not some experience of what it is to be trampled on.

[2] According to the local custom prevailing among all classes, of married sons and daughters continuing to live in the same house with their parents.

[3] 'Dispensa,' store-room.

[4] 'Pizza,' a cake; 'ricotta,' curds of sheep's milk.'

[Here may follow a couple of stories of mixed folly and craft.]

THE BEGGAR AND THE CHICK-PEA.[1]

THERE was once a poor man who went about from door to door begging his bread. He came to the cottage of a poor peasant and said : ' Give me something, for the love of God.'

The peasant's wife said, ' Good man, go away; I have nothing.'

But the poor man said, 'Leave me out something against I come again.'

The peasant's wife answered, ' The most I can give you is a single chick-pea.' [2]

' Very well ; that will do,' replied the poor man ; ' only mind the hen doesn't eat it.'

The peasant's wife was as good as her word, and put out a chick-pea on the dresser against the beggar came by next time. While her back was turned, however, the hen came in and gobbled it up. Presently after the beggar came by.

' Where's the chick-pea you promised me ? ' he asked.

' Ah ! I put it out for you, but the hen gobbled it up ! '

At this he assumed an air of terrible authority, and said : ' Did I not tell you to beware lest the hen should eat it ? Now, you must give me either the pea or the hen ! '

As it was impossible for the peasant's wife now to give him the pea, she was obliged to give him the hen.

The beggar, therefore, took the hen, and went to another cottage.

' Good woman,' he said to the peasant's wife ; ' can you be so good as to take care of this hen for me ? '

' Willingly enough ! ' said the peasant's wife.

' Here it is then,' said the beggar ; ' but mind the pig doesn't get it.'

' Never fear ! ' said the peasant's wife ; and the poor man went his way.

Next day the beggar came back and claimed his hen.

' Oh, dear me ! ' said the peasant's wife, ' while my back was turned, the pig gobbled it up ! '

Assuming an air of terrible authority, the man said : ' Didn't I warn you to beware lest the pig gobbled it up ? Now, you must give me either the hen or the pig.'

As the peasant's wife couldn't give him the hen, she was obliged to give him the pig. So the poor man took the pig and went his way.

He came now to another cottage, and said to the peasant's wife : ' Good woman, can you take care of this pig a little space for me ? '

'Willingly!' said the peasant's wife; 'put him in the yard.'

'Mind the calf doesn't get at him,' said the man.

'Never fear,' said the peasant's wife, and the beggar went his way.

The next day he came back and claimed his pig.

'Oh, dear!' answered the peasant's wife; 'while I wasn't looking, the calf got at the pig, and seized it by the throat, and killed it, and trampled it all to pieces.'

Assuming an air of terrible authority, the beggar said: 'Did I not warn you to beware lest the calf got at it? Now you must give me the pig or the calf.'

As the poor woman could not give him the pig, she was forced to give him the calf. The beggar took the calf and went away.

He went on to another cottage, and said to the peasant's wife: 'Good woman, can you take care of this calf for me?'

'Willingly!' said the peasant's wife; 'put it in the yard.'

The poor man put the calf in the yard; but he said: 'I see you have a sick daughter there in bed; mind she doesn't desire the calf.'

'Never fear!' said the peasant's wife; and the man went his way.

He was no sooner gone, however, than the sick daughter arose, and saying, 'Little heart! little heart!³ I must have you,' she went down into the yard and killed the calf, and took out its heart and ate it.

The next day the beggar man came back and claimed the calf.

'Oh, dear!' said the peasant's wife, 'while I wasn't looking, my sick daughter got up and killed the calf, and ate its heart.'

Assuming an air of terrible authority, the beggar said: 'Did not I warn you not to let the sick daughter get at the calf? Now, either calf or maiden I must have ; make haste with your choice ; calf or maiden, one or the other !' [4]

But the poor woman could not get back the calf, seeing it was dead, and she was resolved not to give up her daughter. So she said : ' I can't give you the calf, because it is dead. So I must give you my daughter, only if I went to take her now while she's awake, she would make such a fuss you would never get her along ; so leave me your sack, that while she's asleep I may put her in it, and then when you come back you can have her.'

So the beggar left his sack and went away. As soon as he was gone the peasant's wife took the sack and put some stones at the bottom, to make it heavy, and thrust in a ferocious mad dog ; then having made fast the mouth of the sack, she stood it up against the wall.

Next day the beggar came back and asked for his sack.

' There it is against the wall,' said the peasant's wife.

So the beggar put it on his shoulder and went away.

As soon as he got home, he opened the sack to take out the maiden ; but the ferocious mad dog rushed out upon him and killed him.

---

[1] ' Il Poverello del Cece.' The termination of the word ' Poverello' is one of those which determine the sentiment of the speaker in a way it is impossible to put into English. We use ' poor ' (*e.g.* joined to the name of a deceased friend) to express sympathy and endearment; if we put ' poor' in this sense before the expression 'povero,' 'a poor man,' 'poverello,' 'a *poor* poor man,' we have the nearest rendering. Dante calls St. Francis, apostle of voluntary poverty, 'Quel poverel' di Dio.' It is the common expression in Rome for a beggar. The ' Poverello' in this story, however, was not one that merited much compassion.

[2] ' Cece,' vetch, produces a very large pea in the south of Europe, and provides a staple article of food much liked among the lower orders. In Italy it is mostly eaten plain boiled, often cold, or else in soup and stews. All day long men go about the streets in Rome selling them (plain boiled) in wooden pails. Boys buy a handful as they would cherries, and eat them as they go along. In Spain, where it bears the name of ' garbanzo,' the favourite mode of cooking it is stewed in oil, with a large quantity of red pepper.

[3] ' Coratella,' nice little heart.

[4]   ' O la vitella,
   O la zitella.'

' Vitella,' a calf; ' zitella,' an unmarried person.

DOCTOR GRILLO.

DOCTOR GRILLO was a physician who had made himself a great name throughout his whole country, so that he was sent for and consulted from far and wide, and everybody looked up to him as a very wise man, whose word was final on any question of medicine. The discovery that 'no man is a hero to his valet' was made long before the idea so found expression in the seventeenth century; Doctor Grillo had a man-servant who chose to entertain a very different notion of his merits and powers from that of the rest of the world; and in time, from undervaluing his attainments, he came to conceive the belief that he could himself do just as well as his master.

One day, when the Doctor was out, this serving-man took into his head to roll up into a great bundle his doctor's gown and cap,[1] a number of prescriptions, and a quantity of bottles, and with these he stole away and betook himself to a far country, where he gave himself out for the famed Doctor Grillo.

Just at the time he arrived, the queen of the country was in great suffering, nor could any native professor of medicine succeed in benefiting her. Naturally the services of the great Doctor Grillo were put in request in her behalf, as soon as his cunning servant had given himself out as the owner of his world-wide reputation, and fortune favoured him in his two earliest attempts. Suffice it to say, he succeeded in satisfying her requirements by a kind of luck and from that day forward his fortune was made, justifying the Italian saying, 'An ounce of good fortune furthers one more than a pound of knowledge.'[2] Everywhere he was now called in, and though he prescribed his remedies all higgledypiggledy, without science or experience, not more of his patients died than those of other mediciners. The people were, therefore, quite satisfied that when Doctor Grillo had prescribed the best had been done that human skill could afford.

By-and-by it came to the ears of the real Doctor Grillo that a quack and impostor was wearing his laurels; nor did he sooner hear the news than he set out to confront him.

' Beware good people! What are you doing?' was his say. ' This man knows no more of medicine than one of yourselves; you will all die if you trust to him. He is no Doctor Grillo. I am Doctor Grillo.'

But all the people laughed in his face, filled as they were with the prepossession of their first impressions, and they began to drive him out of their midst; but he protested so loudly, ' I am Doctor Grillo,' that a wiseacre [3] in the crowd thought to win for himself a reputation for discernment by insisting that he should have a trial.

It happened that the daughter of the Chief Judge was at that time stricken with fever, and as he had observed in the language and manners of the new Doctor Grillo more traces of learning and refinement [4] than in the first arrived of the name, he willingly agreed that the case should be submitted to him for treatment. His wife had, however, just before sent for the false Doctor Grillo, so that both arrived in the sick-room at the same moment; and loud and long was the dispute between husband wife, master and servant, as to which doctor should approach the patient. By the time the husband had carried his point, and the real physician entered upon his functions, the fever had got such hold of the sufferer that no medicine more availed, and the girl succumbed to the consequences of the delay in administering the most ordinary remedies.

Nevertheless, it was in the hands of the real Doctor Grillo that she had died. The one proof of his identity which had been granted had gone against him, and the popular mind was quite satisfied that it was he was the impostor. As the pompous funeral of the Judge's daughter brought all the circumstances to the minds of the people, the feeling against him gathered and grew; and when at last one more mischievous and malicious than the rest proposed that he should be driven out of the community, the idea met with such a ready response that he would certainly not have escaped with his life from the yells and stone-throwing [5] of the infuriated populace, had not his retreat been protected by the more peaceably disposed citizens.

But the false Doctor Grillo remained thenceforward in undisturbed possession of the fame and fortune attaching to the name he had filched.

[1] ' Berretta,' (also written ' biretta ') is used for any kind of cap worn by men or boys. It would appear that no kind of head-covering except a hood to the cloak, enabling the wearer to cover the head, or leave it bare at pleasure, was in common use in Italy before the sixteenth century, though the ' berretta' is mentioned in documents as part of ecclesiastical, particularly of the pontifical, dress, as early as the tenth century. The round ' berretta' coming to be commonly used by the people, their superiors adopted the quadrated form, which, with some modifications, is that still adopted by the Catholic clergy. Graduates and doctors were privileged to wear it, hence its use by Doctor Grillo; and though monks generally are not, some of those engaged in preaching and teaching have a special permission to do so. The Superior of the Theatine Convent of Naples alone, among all superiors of nuns, has the privilege of wearing the ' berretta.' Orsola Benincasa, the founder, was called to Rome that the Pope (Gregory XIII., 1576) might examine whether the reputation she had acquired for learning and piety was well founded. Not only was the Pope well satisfied with her, but St. Philip Neri also gave her many tokens of approval, and, among others, in his playful way, put his ' berretta' on her head. This honour has been commemorated by her successors retaining its use.

[2] ' Vale più un oncia di fortuna che una libbra di sapere.'

[3] ' Un saccentuzze.'

[4] ' Garbatezza.'

[5] ' Sassata,' in Italian, has a more terrible significance than ' stone-throwing,' in English, conveys. The art of throwing and slinging stones with dexterity and accuracy of aim would seem to have been as favourite a pastime among the peasantry in Italy and Spain as archery among our own. For the purposes of the present volume, it needs only to allude to the Roman development of the practice. P. Bresciani, who has taken more pains than any writer of the present age in illustrating

the local customs of Rome, tells us the 'sassate' continued a favourite diversion of the youth of Rome almost down to our own day, and it was only by the most strenuous and vigorous measures that Cardinal Consalvi was enabled to put an end to it; being impelled thereto by the barbarous tone of feeling it engendered, and the frequent casualties resulting from it. The most idle and dissolute raggamuffins of the Monti and Trastevere quarters were among the most dexterous of marksmen. Whenever they aimed a throw, 'fosse di fionda o fosse di soprammano' (whether from a sling or from the hand) they were sure to hit the mark; so that any one of them might have written, like the Greek archer on his arrow, 'for the right eye of Philip,' on his 'ciotto.' ('Ciotto' is a stone such as would be used for throwing from a sling, and thus 'ciottolo' means equally a road made with rough stones and a 'sassata.' What is more to our present purpose is, that 'ciotto' means also 'lame,' suggesting how often persons may have been lamed by 'sassate'). It is said that in the Balearic islands, it was the custom for mothers to tie the meals of their children to a branch of a tree, and none got anything to eat till he had hit the string with a stone, and thus they were trained to 'fiondeggiare' (to throw from a sling) perfectly. The Roman raggamuffins, instead of their food, used to have for their mark the features of donna Lucrezia and Marforio, and they 'ciottolavanle' (pelted them) with stones from far and near. At other times their aim would be directed against a tuft of herbage dangling down from the arches of the aqueducts of Nero or Claudius, nor would they rest from their aiming till they had rooted it out with their stones. Their highest ambition was to direct a stone right through one of the small window-openings in the loftiest range at the Coliseum. After such practice, we may well believe the stones fell true when they had a living adversary before them.

'And as it is the evil custom of the sons of Adam to strive one against the other, and for the excitement of contention every village loves to keep up warfare with its next neighbouring village, so the "Rioni" of Rome delighted in trials of skill one against the other. Thus on every holiday a hundred or two of Montegiani and Trasteverini were to be found arrayed against each other, and all arranged in due order of battle, with its skirmishers and reconnoitring parties, its van-guard and rear-guard. One side would take the Aventine for its base of operations, and another the Palatine. . . . .' After describing very graphically the tactics in vogue, our author goes on to say, 'The adults of both factions stood by the while and backed up the boys, and often the strife which had begun as boys' pastime ended in serious maiming of grown-up men. Hence, not a holiday passed but some mother had to mourn over a son brought home to her with a broken head or an eye knocked out; or some wife over a husband riddled (sforacchiato) with wounds . . . .' Hence it was that Cardinal Consalvi, as we have seen, put an end to such rough play.

[This is probably a filtering of one of the many stories about Theophrastus Paracelsus. I think there was something very like it in a little book of popular legends about him given me at Salzburg, but I have not got it at hand to refer to. Zingerle, ' Sagen aus Tirol,' p. 417, tells a story of his servant prying into the wise man's penetralia, and getting a worse punishment for his pains than Gehazi.]

NINA.

THERE was a miller who got into difficulties, and could not pay his rent. The landlord sent to him a great many times to say that if he could not pay his rent he must go out; but as he paid no attention to the notice, the landlord went himself at last, and told him he must go. The miller pleaded that his difficulties were only temporary, and that if he would give him but a little time he would make it all straight. The landlord, however, was pitiless, and said he had waited long enough, and now he had come to put an end to it; adding, ' Mind, this is my last word : If you do not go out to-night peaceably, I shall send some one to-morrow to turn you out by force.'

As he turned to leave, after pronouncing this sentence, he met the miller's daughter coming back from the stream where she had been washing. ' Who is this buxom lass ?' inquired the landlord.

' That is my daughter Nina,' answered the miller.

' A fine girl she is too,' replied the landlord. ' And I tell you what, miller, listen to me; give Nina to me, and I will not only forgive you the debt, but will make over the mill and the homestead to you, to be your own property for ever.'

' Give me a proper document to that effect, duly signed by your own hand,' replied the miller, with a twinkle in his eye, ' and I will give you " Nina." '

The landlord went back into the house, and taking two sheets of paper drew up first a formal quittance of

the back rent, and then a conveyance of the mill and
homestead absolutely to the miller and to his heirs for
ever. These he handed to the miller ; and then he said,
' To-night, an hour before sundown, I will send for
" Nina." '

' All right,' said the miller ; ' you shall have " Nina," '
and so they parted.

An hour before sundown a servant came with a carriage to fetch " Nina " '

' Where's " Nina " ? ' said the servant. ' Master has
sent me to fetch " Nina." '

' In the stable—take her ! ' answered the miller.

In the stable was nothing to be seen but a very lean
old donkey.

' There's nothing here but an old donkey,' exclaimed
the servant.

' All right, that's " Nina," so take her,' replied the
miller.

' But this can't be what master meant me to fetch ! '
expostulated the servant.

' What have you got to say to it ? ' replied the miller.
' Your master told you to fetch " Nina ; " we always call
our donkey " Nina ; " so take her, and be off.'

The servant saw there was nothing to be gained by
disputing, so he took the donkey and went home. When
he got back, his master had got company with him, so he
did not know what to say about the donkey. But his
master seeing he was come back, took it for granted the
business was done ; and calling him to him privately said,
' Take " Nina " upstairs into the best bedroom and light
a fire, and give her some supper.'

' Take her ! upstairs into the best bedroom ! ' exclaimed the man.

' Yes ! do what you're told, and don't repeat my words.'

The servant could not venture to say any more ; so he
took the donkey up into the best bedroom, and lit a fire,

and put some supper there. As soon as his company was gone, the master called the servant—

'Is "Nina" upstairs?' asked he.

'Si, Signore; she's lying before the fire,' answered the servant.

'Did you take some supper up? I'll have my supper up there with "Nina."'

'Si, Signore,' replied the servant, and he turned away to laugh, for he thought his master had gone mad.

The landlord went upstairs; but it had now grown dark, so he groped his way to the fireplace, and there sure enough was 'Nina,' the donkey, lying down, and as he stroked her he said, 'What fine soft hair you've got, Nina!'

Presently the servant brought the lights; and when he saw the dirty old worn-out donkey, and understood what a trick the miller had played off on him, it may be imagined how furious he was.

The next day, as soon as the courts were opened, he went before the judge, and told all the tale. Then the miller came too, and told his; but the judge examined the documents, and pronounced that the miller was in the right; for his part of the contract was that he was to deliver over 'Nina,' and he had delivered over 'Nina.' There was no evidence that any other 'Nina' was intended but 'Nina' the donkey, and so the miller remained in undisputed possession of the mill.

And that is the truth, for it actually happened as I have told you.

---

[1] 'Quella,' in the original, lends itself better to the purposed misunderstanding of the story, meaning 'that one,' 'such an one as that!' in the feminine gender; and the master would think the servant said it in contempt because he spoke of a miller's daughter.

THE GOOD GRACE OF THE HUNCHBACK.[1]

A MOTHER and daughter lived alone in a cottage. The mother was old and came to die ; the daughter was turned out of house and home.[2] An ugly hunchback, who was a tailor, came by and said—

' What is your name, my pretty girl ? '

' They call me la Buona Grazia,'[3] answered the girl.

' Well, la Buona Grazia, I've got twenty scudi a month, will you come with me and be my wife ? '

The girl was starving, and didn't know where to set her foot, so she thought she could not afford to refuse : but she went along with a very bad grace, for she did not feel at all happy at the idea of marrying the ugly old hunchback.

When the hunchback saw how unhappy she was, he thought, ' This will never do. She's too young and too pretty to care for me. I must keep her locked up, and then when she sees no one else at all, she will at last be glad even of my company.' So he went all the errands himself, and never let her go out except to Mass, and then he took her to the church, and watched her all the time, and brought her back himself. The windows he whitened all over, so that she couldn't see out into the street, and there he kept her with the door locked on her, and she was very miserable.

So it went on for three years. But there was a dirty little window of a lumber room which, as it only gave a look out on to the court,[4] he had not whitened. As she happened to look out here one day a stranger stood leaning on the balcony of the court, for part of the house was an inn, and he had just arrived.

' What are you looking for, my pretty girl ? ' said the stranger.

' O ! nothing particular ; only I'm locked up here, and I just looked out for a change.'

'Locked up! who has locked you up?' asked the stranger.

'An old hunchback, who's going to marry me,' said the girl, almost crying.

'You don't seem much pleased at the idea of being married,' answered the stranger.

'It is not likely that I should, to such a husband!' returned the girl.

'Would you like to get away from him?' asked the stranger.

'Shouldn't I!' heartily exclaimed the girl; 'but it's impossible to manage that, as I'm locked in,' she added sorrowfully.

'It's not so difficult as you think,' rejoined the stranger. 'Most likely there's some picture or other on your wall.'

'Oh, yes! a great big one with the fair Giuditta just ready with her pouch[5] to put Lofferno's head in,' answered the girl.

'All right. You make a big hole behind the picture on your side, and when I hear by the sound where you are, I'll make one on mine. And when our two holes meet, you can come through.'

'Yes, that's a capital plan; but the hunchback will soon come after me.'

'Never mind, I will see to that; let's make the hole first?'

'Very well, I rely upon you, and will set to work immediately.'

'Tell me first how I am to call you?'

'They always call me Buona Grazia.'

'A very nice name. Good-bye, and we'll set to work.'

La Buona Grazia ran and unhooked the picture, and set to work to make a hole with all the available tools she could find; and the stranger, as soon as he had ascertained by the noise where she was at work, set to also. It turned out to be only a partition,[6] and not a regular wall, and the hole was soon cut.

'What fun!' said the girl, as she jumped through.
' Oh, how nice to be free! But,' she added, ' I can't travel
with you in these poor clothes.'

'No,' said the stranger. ' I'll have a travelling dress
made for you, by the hunchback himself.'

'Oh, take care!' cried the girl, earnestly.

' Don't be afraid,' answered the stranger; 'and above
all don't look frightened.'

Then he sent his servant to call the hunchback, and
when he came he said—

' I want a travelling dress made directly for my wife
here, so please take her measure.'

The hunchback started when he saw who it was he had
to measure.

'Why, she's exactly like my Buona Grazia!' exclaimed he.

' Very likely. I have always observed there was a sort
of likeness between the inhabitants of a town. She too is
a Roman, though I am a stranger. But make haste and
take the measure, I didn't call you here to make remarks.'

The hunchback got frightened at the stranger's authori-
tative tone, and took the measure without saying any
more; and the stranger then gave him something to go
and have a breakfast at the *caffè* to give the girl time to
get back and set the picture in its place again.

When he came up into the room all looked right, and
nothing seemed to have been moved.

' I've got to work hard to-day,' said the hunchback, ' to
get a travelling dress ready for the wife of a gentleman
staying in the inn, who is exactly like you.'

'Are they going to travel, then?' asked la Buona
Grazia.

'Yes, the gentleman said they should start as soon as
the dress is done.'

' Oh, do let me see them drive off!' said la Buona
Grazia, coaxingly. ' I should so like to see a lady who
looked like me wearing a dress you had made.'

' Nonsense, nonsense!' said the hunchback; 'get on with your work.'

And she did get on with her work, and stitched away, for she was anxious enough to help him to get the dress done; but she went on teazing him all the while to let her go to the window to see the gentleman and the lady, 'who looked so like her,' drive off, that at last the hunchback consented for that only day to take the whiting off the windows and let her look out.

The travelling dress was finished and taken home; and while the hunchback was taking it up by the stairs, la Bella Grazia was getting in by the hole behind the picture; but she had first made a great doll,[7] and dressed it just like herself, and stuck it in the window. The gobbo, who stood down below to see the gentry drive off, looked up and saw her, as he thought, at the window, and made signs for her not to stay there too long.

Presently the stranger and his lady came down; the hunchback was standing before the carriage door, as I have said, and two stablemen were standing by also.

' You give me your good grace?'[8] asked the stranger.

' Yes, yes!' readily responded the hunchback, delighted to find a rich gentleman so civil to him.

' You say it sincerely, with all your heart?' again asked the stranger.

' Yes, yes, yes! with all my heart,' answered the hunchback.

' Then give me your hand upon it.'

And the hunchback, more and more delighted, put out his hand, the two stablemen standing by looking on attentively all the time.

As soon as the carriage had driven away, the hunchback's first care was to look up at the window to see if the girl had gone in; but the doll was still there.

' Go in! go in!' he cried, waving his hand. But the figure remained unmoved. Indignant, he took a stick and ran up to punish the girl for her disobedience, and when the blows fell thick and fast and no cries came, he discovered the trick that had been played.

Without loss of time he ran off to the Court and laid a complaint before the judge, demanding that soldiers should be called out and sent after the fugitives ; but the stablemen had their orders, and were there before him, and deposed that they were witnesses to his having given ' his Good Grace ' up to the gentleman ' with all his heart,' and given him his hand upon the bargain.

' You see you have given her up of your own accord; there is nothing to be done!' said the judge. So he got no redress.

¹ 'La Buona Grazia del Gobbo.'

² 'In mezzo alla strada.'

³ ' Good Grace,' also the ' good favour,' the 'good graces.'

⁴ ' Cortile,' inner court of palaces and houses that are built in a quadrangle.

⁵ 'Saccoccia di polenta.' ' Polenta' is a porridge made of Indian corn meal, which makes a staple article of food of the Italian peasantry. It is, however, used for the meal of which the porridge is going to be made, though that is more usually called ' formentone,' or 'grano turco.' ' Saccroccia di polenta ' would be a large pouch in which poor country labourers carry a provision of meal, when going out to work in the Campagna. The girl takes Giuditta's bag in the picture for such a ' saccoccia ' as she had been used to see.

⁶ ' Tramezzo.'

⁷ ' Pupazza,' a doll, a stuffed figure.

⁸ 'Mi date la vostra buona grazia,' a common expression of no particular meaning ; a compliment, equivalent to, ' We part good friends,' ' Give me your good favour.'

THE VALUE OF SALT.

THEY say there was a king who had three daughters. He was very anxious to know which of them loved him most; he tried them in various ways, and it always seemed as if the youngest daughter came out best by the test. Yet he was never satisfied, because ⱨe ⱨas prepossessed with the idea that the elder ones loved him most.

One day he thought he would settle the matter once for all, by asking each separately how much she loved him. So he called the eldest by herself, and asked her how much she loved him.

' As much as the bread we eat,' ran her reply; and he said within himself, ' She must, as I thought, love me the most of all; for bread is the first necessary of our existence, without which we cannot live. She means, therefore, that she loves me so much she could not live without me.'

Then he called the second daughter by herself, and said to her, ' How much do you love me?'

And she answered, ' As much as wine!'

' That is a good answer too,' said the king to himself. ' It is true she does not seem to love me quite so much as the eldest; but still, scarcely can one live without wine,' so that there is not much difference.'

Then he called the youngest by herself, and said to her, ' And you, how much do you love me?'

And she answered, ' As much as salt!'

Then the king said, ' What a contemptible comparison! She only loves me as much as the cheapest and commonest thing that comes to table. This is as much as to say, she doesn't love me at all. I always thought it was so. I will never see her again.'

Then he ordered that a wing of the palace should be shut up from the rest, where she should be served with everything belonging to her condition in life, but where she should live by herself apart, and never come near him.

Here she lived, then, all alone. But though her father fancied she did not care for him, she pined so much at being kept away from him, that at last she was worn out,[2] and could bear it no longer.

The room that had been given her had no windows on to the street, that she might not have the amusement of seeing what was going on in the town, but they looked upon an inner court-yard. Here she sometimes saw the cook come out and wash vegetables at the fountain.

'Cook! cook!' she called one day, as she saw him pass thus under the window.

The cook looked up with a good-natured face, which gave her encouragement.

'Don't you think, cook, I must be very lonely and miserable up here all alone?'

'Yes, Signorina!' he replied; 'I often think I should like to help you to get out; but I dare not think of it, the king would be so angry.'

'No, I don't want you to do anything to disobey the king,' answered the princess; 'but would you really do me a favour, which would make me very grateful indeed?'

'O! yes, Signorina, anything which I can do without disobeying the king,' replied the faithful servant.

'Then this is it,' said the princess. 'Will you just oblige me so far as to cook papa's dinner to-day without any salt in anything? Not the least grain in anything at all. Let it be as good a dinner as you like, but no salt in anything. Will you do that?'

'I see!' replied the cook, with a knowing nod. 'Yes, depend on me, I will do it.'

That day at dinner the king had no salt in the soup, no salt in the boiled meat, no salt in the roast, no salt in the fried.

'What is the meaning of this?' said the king, as he pushed dish after dish away from him. 'There is not a single thing I can eat to-day. I don't know what they have done to everything, but there is not a single thing that has got the least taste. Let the cook be called.'

So the cook came before him.

'What have you done to the victuals to-day?' said the king, sternly. 'You have sent up a lot of dishes, and no one alive can tell one from another. They are all of them exactly alike, and there is not one of them can be eaten. Speak !'

The cook answered:

'Hearing your Majesty say that salt was the commonest thing that comes to table, and altogether so worthless and contemptible, I considered in my mind whether it was a thing that at all deserved to be served up to the table of the king; and judging that it was not worthy, I abolished it from the king's kitchen, and dressed all the meats without it. Barring this, the dishes are the same that are sent every day to the table of the king.'

Then the king understood the value of salt, and he comprehended how great was the love of his youngest child for him; so he sent and had her apartment opened, and called her to him, never to go away any more.

[1] In a wine country the idea of wine being almost a necessity of existence occurs more readily than in England, where, however general its use, it is still a luxury.

[2] 'Era stufa,' a way of saying, she was 'worn out,' 'wearied out.'

THE PRINCESS AND THE GENTLEMAN.

THERE was a princess whose mother had died of vexation because she was in love with a simple gentleman of the chamber, and would not hear of marrying anyone else, nor would she look at any prince who came to sue for her hand.

The king, not only vexed at her perversity, but still more at the loss of his wife, determined to devise a punishment to cure them both. He had two suites of apartments walled up, therefore; in one he had the princess imprisoned, and in the other the gentleman of the chamber with whom she was in love. The latter, he commanded, should see no one, thinking thereby to weary him out; the former he allowed only to see such persons as he should appoint, these persons being the princes one or other of whom he wished her to marry; for he thought that in her weariness at being so shut up, she would welcome the hand of anyone who would be her deliverer. It was not so, however. When the cook came in to the princess with her dinner, she begged him to give her a chicken that had been killed several days, and kept till it had a bad smell.

When her father now sent any prince to visit her she said, 'It is no use my father sending you here, the reason why I cannot marry anyone is that I have a great defect; my breath smells so bad that it is not pleasant for anyone to live with me.'

As the bad smell from the chicken was readily to be perceived in the room, they all believed her words and went away. There was one, indeed, who was so much pleased with her seeming candour that he thought he would excuse her defect, but on a second visit the smell of the dead chicken drove him away too.

The cooks in the kitchen talked together after the manner of cooks, and thus the cook who waited on the princess told what had happened to the cook who waited on the other prisoner, and thus it came round to his ears also, what the princess had done for love of him. Her stratagem then suggested another to him. Accordingly he sent to crave urgently an audience of the king.

When the king came in to him he said:

'Sire, closely as I have been confined and guarded, yet something of what goes on in the outer world has reached my ears, and the fact which has the greatest interest for me has naturally been told to me. I now learn that the reason why your daughter has refused the suit of all the princes is not as we thought, her love for me, but a certain personal defect, which in politeness I will not name more particularly. But that being so, my desire to marry her is, of course, cured like that of others; so if your majesty will give me my liberty I will go away to a far country, and your majesty would never hear of me any more.'

The king was delighted to get rid of him, for he believed that if he were at a distance the great obstacle to his daughter's happiness would be removed. As he knew nothing about the chicken, he thought that all the suitors had believed the princess's representations upon her simple word; and as he very well knew she had no defect, he thought the time would come when some prince should please her, whom she also should please. Therefore, he very willingly gave the gentleman his liberty, and bid him godspeed on his journey.

The gentleman, however, before setting out, went to his friend the cook, and, giving him three hundred scudi, begged him to house him for a few nights, while he dug out an underground passage between the garden and the apartment where the princess was imprisoned.

In the garden was a handsome terrace, all set out with life-sized statues; under one of these the gentleman worked his way, till he had reached the princess's chamber.

'You here!' exclaimed the princess in great astonishment, as soon as he had made his way through.

'Yes; I have come to fetch you,' he replied.

She did not wait for a second injunction to escape from prison, but gathering all the money and jewels she had at command, she followed him through the underground way he had made.

As soon as they had reached the free air, the gentleman replaced the statue, and no one could guess by which way they had passed. Then they went to a church to be married, and, after that, to a city a long way off, as the gentleman had promised the king he would.

For a long time they lived very happily on the money and jewels each had brought from home; but, by-and-by, these came to an end, and neither durst write for more, for fear of betraying where they were. So at last, having no means of living, they engaged themselves to a rich lady who had a large mansion;[1] the one as butler,[2] and the other as nurse.[3] Here they were well content to live at peace; and the lady was well content to have two such faithful and intelligent dependents, and they might have lived here till the end of their lives, but for a coincidence[4] which strangely disconcerted them, as you shall hear, as well as what came of it.

One day there came to visit the lady, their mistress, a nobleman belonging to the king's court. At dinner time the princess had to come to table along with the little daughter of the house, of whom she had the charge. Great was her terror when she recognised in the guest of the day one so familiar to herself and so near the sovereign. In conformity with the lowliness of the station she had assumed, she could escape actually talking to him, and she did her best to withdraw herself from his notice. She half hoped she had succeeded, when suddenly the butler had to come into the room to communicate an important despatch which had just arrived, to the mistress of the house. The princess could not restrain an anxious glance at the stranger, to see if he betrayed any sign of recognition; but he was used to courts, and therefore to dissemble; nor could she satisfy herself that he had discovered either of them. It was so likely that he should, however, that she was filled with fear, and he was no sooner gone than she held a long consultation with her husband as to what course they should pursue.

In the end, the difficulty of finding other employment decided them to remain, for the probability that they would be tracked seemed remote. After all, they reasoned, was it likely that the nobleman should think it worth while to observe two persons occupying such humble posts with sufficient attention to see who they were or who they were not?

The king meantime had been searching everywhere for his daughter, not being able by any means to divine how she could have escaped. Then one morning, all this time after, the nobleman comes down upon him with the news:

'I have found the princess. She is living as nurse to the Duchessa such a one, and her husband is the butler.'

The king could not rest a moment after he had heard the news; his travelling carriage was ordered round, and away he drove. It was just dinner-time when he arrived at the Duchessa's palace. If the princess had been terrified before, at being called to sit at table with a nobleman of the court, judge how much greater was her alarm when she saw her father himself seated at the board!

Great as had been his indignation, however, the joy of again meeting his child after the long separation blotted out all his anger, and after embracing her tenderly, he placed her by his side at the table. It was only when he came to take leave, and realised that she really belonged to another that his ire broke forth again. At this point the Duchessa put in a word. She highly extolled the excellent qualities of her butler, and declared he had been so skilful in the administration of her affairs, that he deserved to have a kingdom committed to him. In short, she softened the king's heart so completely that she brought him to own that, as he had now grown very old and feeble, he could not do better than recognise him for his son-in-law, and associate him with himself in the government.

And so he did,[5] and they all lived happily.

---

[1] 'Palazzo.'

[2] 'Credenziere,' confidential servant.

[3] 'Aia,' upper nurse, nursery governess.

[4] 'Combinazione.'

[5] 'E cosi fece' (and thus he did) is another of the expressions in universal use in Rome in tale-telling, forming a sort of refrain.

THE HAPPY COUPLE.[1]

I CAN tell you a story,[2] or two perhaps. What a number I used to know, to be sure! But what can I do? It is thirty years and more since anyone has asked me for them, and it's hard to put one's ideas together after such a time. You musn't mind if I put the wrong part of the story before, and have to go backwards and forwards a little.

I know there was one that ran thus :—

There was a married couple who lived so happy and content and fond of each other, that they never had a word of dispute about anything the live-long day, but only thought of helping and pleasing each other.

The Devil saw this, and determined to set them by the ears; but how was he to do it? Such love and peace reigned in their home, that he couldn't find any way into the place. After prowling and prowling about, and finding no means of entrance, what does he do? He went to an old woman,—she must have been one of those who dabble with things they have no business to touch,—and said to her:

' You must do this job for me ! '

' That's no great matter,' answered the old hag.[3] ' Give me ten scudi for my niece and a new pair of shoes for me, and I'll settle the matter.'

'Here are the ten scudi,' said the Devil; ' it will be time enough to talk about the shoes when we see how you do the business.'

The bad old woman set off accordingly with her niece and the ten scudi, instructing her by the way what she was to do.

This husband and wife lived in a place where there was a house on one side and a shop on the other, so that through a window in the house where they lived they could give an eye to anything that went on in the shop.

Choosing a moment when the man was alone in the shop, she sent the girl in with the ten scudi ; and the girl, who had been told what to do, selected a dress, and a handkerchief, and a number of fine things, and paid her ten scudi. Then she proceeded leisurely to put them on, and to walk up and down the shop in them. Meantime the bad old woman went up to the wife :—

'Poor woman!' she said. 'Poor woman! Such a good woman as you are, and to have such a hypocrite of a husband !'

'My husband a hypocrite!' answered the wife. 'What can you mean—he is the best man that ever was.'

'Ah! he makes you think so, poor simple soul. But the truth is, he is very different from what you think.'

So they went on conversing, and the bad old woman all the time watching what was going on in the shop till the right moment came. Just as the girl was flaunting about and showing herself off, she said :

'Look here, he has given all those things to that girl there.'

And though the wife did not believe a word, curiosity prompted her to look, and there she saw the girl bowing herself out with as many thanks and adieus as if the poor man had really given her the things she had bought.

'Perhaps you will believe that!' observed the bad old woman.

'Indeed, I cannot help believing it,' answered the wife, 'but never otherwise should I have thought it; and I owe you a great deal for opening my eyes;' and she gave her a whole cheese.⁴ 'I know what I shall do,' she continued, as she sobbed over her lost peace of mind; 'I shall show him I know his bad conduct by having no dinner ready for him when he comes up by-and-by.'

'That's right,' said the bad old woman. 'Do so, and show him you are not going to be trampled on for the sake of a drab of a girl like that;' and she tied her cheese up in a handkerchief, and went her way.

Down she went now to the husband, and plied him with suspicions of his wife, similar to those she had suggested to her against him. The husband was even less willing to listen to her than the wife had been, and when at last he drove her away, she said:

'You think she's busy all the morning preparing your dinner; but instead of that, she's talking to those you wouldn't like her to talk with. And you see now if to-day she hasn't been at this game so long that she has forgotten your dinner altogether.'

The husband turned a deaf ear, and continued attending to his shop; but when he went into the house and found no dinner ready, it seemed as if all that the bad old woman had said was come true.

He was too sad for words, so they didn't have much of a quarrel, but there could not but be a coldness after such an extraordinary event as a day without dinner.

The husband went back to his shop and mused. The wife sat alone in her room crying; presently the old hag came back to her.

'Well, did you tell him you had found him out?' she inquired.

'No! I hadn't courage to do that. And he was so patient about there being no dinner, that I felt quite sorry to have suspected him. Oh, you who have been so clever in pointing out my misery to me, can you not tell me some means of reconciliation?'

'Yes, there is one; but I don't know if you can manage it.'

'Oh yes; I would do *anything!*'

'Then you must watch till he is quite sound asleep, and take a sharp razor and cut off three hairs from the undergrowth of his beard, quite close to the skin. If you do that it will all come right again.'

'It seems a very odd remedy,' said the wife; 'but if you say it will do, I suppose it will, and thank you kindly for the advice;' and she gave her another cheese.

Then the witch went back to the husband.

'I suppose I was mistaken, and you found your dinner ready after all?' she said.

'No!' he replied; 'you were right about there being no dinner; but I am certain there was some cause for there being none, other than what you say.'

'What other cause should there be?' exclaimed the old woman.

'That I don't know,' he replied. 'But some other cause I am persuaded there must have been.'

'Well, if you are so infatuated, I will give you another token that I am right,' replied the old woman. 'You don't deserve that I should save your life, but I am so goodnatured, I can't help warning you. To-night, I have reason to know, she intends to murder you. You just give some make-believe snoring, but mind you don't sleep, whatever you do; and you see if she doesn't take up one of your razors to stab you in the throat.'

The good husband refused to believe a word, and drove her away. Nevertheless, when night came he felt not a little anxious; and if he had tried to sleep ever so much he could not, for he felt so excited. Then curiosity to see if the woman's words would come true overcame him, and he pretended to snore.

He had not been snoring thus long, when the wife took up the razor and came all trembling to the bedside, and lifted up his beard.

A cold sweat crept over the poor husband as she approached—not for fear of his life, which he could easily rescue, as he was awake—but because the proof seemed there that the old hag had spoken the truth. However, instead of taking it for granted it was so, and refusing to hear any justification—perhaps killing her on the spot, as she had hoped and expected,—he calmly seized her arm, and said:

'Tell me, what are you going to do with that razor?'

The wife sank on her knees by his side, crying:

'I cannot expect you to believe me, but this is really how it was. An old woman came and told me you were making love to a young girl in the shop, and showed me how she was bowing and scraping to you. I was so vexed, that to show you my anger I got no dinner ready; but afterwards, I felt as if I should like to ask you all about it, to make sure there was no mistake: only after what I had done, I didn't know how to begin speaking to you again. Then I asked the old woman if she couldn't tell me some means of bringing things straight again; and she said, if I could cut off three hairs from the undergrowth of your beard, all would come right. But I can't expect you to believe it.'

'Yes, I do,' replied the husband. 'The same old wretch came to me, and wanted me in like manner to believe all manner of evil things of you, but I refused to believe you could do anything wrong. So I had more confidence in you than you had in me. But still we were both very nearly making ourselves very foolish and very unhappy; so we will take a lesson never to doubt each other again.'

And after that there never was a word between them any more.

When the Devil saw how the old woman had spoilt the affair, he took the pair of shoes he was to have given her, and tied them on to a long cane which he fastened on·the top of a mountain, and there they dangled before her eyes, but she could never get at them.

---

[1] 'I sposi Felici.'

[2] 'Esempio,' see preface. 'Esempiuccio,' a termination of endearment, meaning in this place 'a nice "esempio."'

[3] 'Vecchiaccia,' bad old woman.

[4] 'Forma di formaggio,' a whole cheese. 'Cacio,' the proper word for

cheese, is almost entirely superseded by 'formaggio,' which comes from 'forma,' the press or mould in which it is made.

[This is just the Siddi Kür story of the mischief-making fox, which I have given as 'The Perfidious Friend' in 'Sagas from the Far East,' and similar to the first Pantcha Tantra story.]

WHAT HAPPENED IN THE ROOM OF A HOTEL.[1]

THEY say there was a countess who was very fond of her husband, and her husband was very fond of her; and they vowed nothing should ever make the one think ill of the other.

One day the brother of the countess, who had been long away at the wars, and whom the count had never seen, came back to see her just while the count was out.

'Now we'll have some fun,' said the countess. 'We'll watch till my husband is coming home, and then as he comes into the room you just be kissing me; he will be so astonished to see a stranger kissing me, he will not know what to make of it. Then in five minutes we will tell him who you really are, and it will make a good laugh.'

The brother thought it would be a good joke, and they did as she had said.

It happened, however, that by accident[2] the count did not that day as usual come into his wife's room, but passing along the terrace in front of it, he saw, as she had arranged, one who was a stranger to him kissing her.

Then he went into his room, and calling his confidential servant[3] he told him what had happened, and adding, 'You will never see me any more,' went his way.

The countess waited on and on for her husband to come in, full of impatience to have her joke out. But when she found he did not come at all, she went into his room to seek him there. There she found the servant, who told her what the Count had said, and the desperate resolution he had taken.

' What have I done !' exclaimed the terrified Countess. ' Is it possible that I am to be punished thus for a harmless joke ! '

Then, without saying anything to anyone she wrapped her travelling cloak about her, and set out to seek her husband.

The Count had walked on till he could walk no farther, and then he had gone into an inn, where he hired a room for a week ; but he went wandering about the woods in misery and despair, and only came in at an hour of night.'

The Countess also walked on till she could walk no farther, and thus she came to the same inn ; but as she had only a woman's strength the same journey took her a much longer time, and it was the afternoon of the next day when she arrived. She too asked for a room, but the host assured her with many expressions of regret, that he had not a single room vacant. The Countess pleaded her weariness ; the man reiterated his inability to serve her.

' Give me only a room to rest a little while in,' she begged ; ' just a couple of hours, and then I will start again and journey farther.'

Really compassionating her in her fatigue, the man now said :

' If you will be satisfied with that much, I can give you a room for a couple of hours ; but no more.'

She was fain to be satisfied with that, as she could get no more, and the host showed her into her husband's room, which he would not want till ' an hour of night.'

By accident, however, the Count came in that night an hour earlier, and very much surprised he was to find a lady in his room. The Countess, equally surprised to see a stranger enter, pulled her veil over her face, so that they did not recognise each other.

'I am sorry to disturb you, madam, but this room, I must inform you, I have engaged,' said the count; but sorrow had so altered his voice that the countess did not know it again.

'I hope you will spare me,' replied the Countess. 'They gave me this room to rest in for two hours, and I have come so long a way that I really need the rest.'

'I can hardly believe that a lady of gentle condition can have come a very long way, all alone and on foot, for there is no carriage in the yard; so I can only consider this a frivolous pretext,' replied the Count, for sorrow had embittered him.

'Indeed it is too true though,' continued the Countess. 'I came all the way from such a place (and she named his own town) without stopping for one moment's rest.'

'Indeed!' said the Count, his interest roused at the mention of his own town; 'and pray what need had you to use such haste to get away from that good town?'

'I had no need to haste to leave the place,' replied the Countess, hurt at the implied suspicion that she was running away for shame. 'I hasted to arrive at another place.'

'And that other place was —— ?' persisted the Count, who felt that her intrusion on his privacy gave him a right to cross-question her.

The Countess was puzzled how to reply. She had no idea what place she was making for.

'*That* I don't know,' she said at last, with no little embarrassment.

'You will permit me to say that you seem to have no adequate reason to allege for this unwarrantable occupation of my room; and what little you tell me certainly in no way inclines me to take a favourable view of the affair.'

The Countess was once more stung by the manner in which he seemed to view her journey, and feeling bound to clear herself, she replied:

' If you only knew what my journey is about, you would not speak so ! ' and she burst into a flood of tears.

Softened by her distress, the Count said in a kinder tone :

' Had you been pleased to confide that to me at first, maybe I had not spoken so ; but till you tell me what it is, what opinion can I form ? '

' This is it,' answered the Countess, still sobbing. ' Yesterday I was the happiest woman on the face of the earth, living in love and confidence with the best husband with whom woman was ever blessed. So strong was my confidence that I hesitated not to trifle with this great · happiness. My brother came home from the wars, a stranger to my husband. " Let him see you kiss me," I said, " it will seem so strange that we will make him laugh heartily afterwards." He saw him kiss me, but waited for no explanation. He went away without a word, as indeed (fool that I was) I well deserved, and I journey on till I overtake him.'

The Count had risen to his feet, and had torn the veil from her face.

' It can be no other but my own ! ' he exclaimed, in a voice from which sorrow being banished his own tones sounded forth, and clasped her in his arms.

¹ ' Una Camera di Locanda.'
² ' Combinazione.'
³ ' Credenziere.'
⁴ ' Un ora di notte ' ; an hour after the evening ' Ave.'

THE COUNTESS'S CAT.¹

THERE was a very rich Countess who was a widow and lived all alone, with no companion but only a cat, after her husband died. The greatest care was taken of this cat, and every day a chicken was boiled on purpose for him.

One day the Countessa went out to spend the day at a

friend's villa in the Campagna, and she said to the waiting woman :

'Mind the cat has his chicken just the same as if I were at home.'

'Yes! Signora Countessa, leave that to me,' answered the woman; but the Countess was no sooner gone out than she said to the man-servant :

'The cat has the chicken every day; suppose we have it to-day?'

The man said, 'To be sure!' and they ate the chicken themselves, giving the cat only the inside; but they threw the bones down in the usual corner, to make it appear as if he had eaten the whole chicken.

The cat said nothing, but looked on with great eyes, full of meaning.[2]

When the Countess came back that evening the cat, instead of going out to meet her as he always did, remained still in his place and said nothing.

'What's the matter with the cat? Hasn't he had his chicken?' asked the Countess, immediately.

'Yes! Signora Countessa,' answered the cameriera. 'See, there are the bones on the floor, where he always leaves them.'

The Countessa could not deny the testimony of her eyes, so she said nothing more but went up to bed.

The cat followed her as he always did, for he slept on her bed; but he followed at a distance, without purring or rubbing himself against her. The Countess saw something was wrong, but she didn't know what to make of it, and went to bed as usual.

That night the cat throttled [3] the Countess, and killed her.

The cat is very intelligent in his own interest, but he is a traitor.

'It would have been more intelligent,' I observed, 'if he had throttled the waiting woman in this instance.'

Not at all; the cat's reasoning was this:—If thou hadst not gone out and left me to the mercy of menials, this had not happened; therefore it was thou who hadst to die.

This is quite true, for cats are always traitors. Dogs are faithful, cats are traitors.[4]

[1] 'Il Gatto della Contessa.'

[2] 'Il gatto non dissi niente, ma guardava con certi occhi grossi, grossi, fissi.'

[3] 'Strozzato,' throttled ; killed by wounding the *strozzo*, throat.

[4] 'E questo è un fatto vero, sa; perchè il gatto è traditore sempre. Il cane e fedele si, ma il gatto è traditore.'

[Perhaps this tale would have been hardly worth printing, but that the selfsame story was told me as a positive fact by an Irishman, who could not have come across the Italian story. In the Irish version it was its master the cat killed; in the wording of the narrator he ' cut his throat.']

WHY CATS AND DOGS ALWAYS QUARREL.[1]

' Why do dogs and cats always fight, papa ? ' we used to say.

And he used to answer, ' I'll tell you why ; ' and we all stood round listening.

' Once on a time dogs and cats were very good friends, and when the dogs went out of town they left their cards on the cats, and when the cats went out of town they left their cards on the dogs.'

And we all sat round and listened and laughed.

' Once the dogs all went out of town and left their cards as usual on the cats; but they were a long time gone, for they were gone on a rat-hunt, and killed all the rats. When the cats heard that the dogs had taken to killing rats, they were furious against the dogs, and lay in wait for them and set upon them.

' " Set upon the dogs ! at them ! give it them ! " ' [2]
shouted the cats, as they flew at them ; and from that
time to this, dogs and cats never meet without fighting.'

And we all stood round and laughed fit to split our
sides.

[1] 'Perchè litigano sempre i Cani ed i Gatti.'
[2] 'Dàlli ! Dàlli ai cani !'

[Scheible, Schaltjahr I., 375, gives a more humorous version
of this.]

THE CATS WHO MADE THEIR MASTER RICH.

' Ah ! as to cats and mice, listen and *I*'ll tell you something
worth hearing !

'In America, once upon a time, there were no cats.
Mice there were in plenty ; mice everywhere ; not peeping
out of holes now and then, but infesting everything, swarm-
ing over every room ; and when a family sat down to meals,
the mice rushed upon the table and disputed the victuals
with them.

' Then one thought of a plan ; he freighted three ships ;
full, full of cats, and off to America with them. There he
sold them for their weight in gold and more, and *whiff!*
the mice were swept away, and he made a great fortune.
A great fortune, all out of cats !'

[In the 'Russian Folktales' is also a version of the Whit-
tington story, p. 43.]

APPENDICES.

I HAVE done injustice to the part assigned to the horse in French legendary tales by omitting mention of it in this place. Charles Louandre (' Chefs-d'œuvre des conteurs Français,' Paris, 1873, note to pp. 43–4) calls special attention to it and gives us the name of many horses famous in the old French minstrelsy. There was 'Valentin,' the horse of Roland; 'Tencedor, of Charlemagne;' 'Barbamouche, swifter than the swallow;' and many others. But there is no name to the charger in the graceful 'Lai de Graélent,' by Marie de France, whose fidelity is the occasion of his Note. I ought not to have forgotten either, the honours paid him in the Spanish Romances, of which the brave 'Black Charger of Hernando' ('Patrañas') may serve as the type.

APPENDIX B.

MY attention has been called, while these sheets have been passing through the press, to a collection which enables me to subjoin some notes of analogies between the Folktales of France and those in the text. It is entitled 'Recueil des Contes des Fées,' Geneva, 1718; published without author's name, and the stories are much less artificially treated than in the better known collections of the Comtesse d'Aulnoy, de Caylus, Perrault, Madame de Villeneuve, &c.

Monteil ('Traité de Matériaux-Manuscrits,' Paris, 1835) mentions a MS. in his possession, of the year 1618, entitled 'Contes des Fées,' from which Perrault, the least artificial of the French collectors, seems to have drawn his tales. Mayer ('Discours sur l'Origine des Contes des Fées,' Geneva and Paris, 1786) ascribes to him the revival of the knowledge of the existence of popular fairy tales and mediæval romances, and many of our own Nursery Rimes (notably ' Puss in Boots') are simply translated from his versions.

'Prince Rainbow' ('Le Prince Arc-en-Ciel'), the fifth story in the ' Recueil,' contains similar incidents with those in ' Filagranata,' in combination with the introduction of the opening of a nut in place of one of the oranges in my next story. (I have another Roman story in MS. which hinges on the opening of three nuts in the place of three oranges.) In the French story the ire of the bad fairy is excited against the princess who holds the place of Filagranata, by her receiving the name of ' Fairer-than-Fairies' (' Plus-belle-que-Fée'). The bad fairy Lagrée, who is so old that she has only one tooth and one eye, carries her off to an underground palace, where her task is to tend a fire, instead of feeding pigeons. Here she is courted by a prince transformed into a rainbow, whom she finds of course always seated in the sunshine on a fountain. While talking to him, she lets her fire out. Lagrée sends her to get fresh fire from the giant Locrinos, devourer of maidens; the giant's wife takes compassion on her, and gives her the fire, and with it a stone to use in time of distress. Lagrée, in fury at her success, sends away Prince Rainbow. Fairer-than-Fairies escapes, and goes in search of him, taking with her the stone, a branch of myrtle, and her cat and dog; when she is weary with wandering, the stone provides her a cave to sleep in, the dog keeping guard. Lagrée pursues her ; the dog attacks her, and throws her down, so that she breaks her only tooth, and the princess escapes for another stage. Lagrée overtakes her again as she is sleeping in a bower the branch of myrtle has raised for her. The cat makes the defence this time, scratching out her only eye, finally disabling her. After this, Fairer-than-Fairies is entertained in a white and green palace by a white and green lady, who gives her a nut, to be used only in direst need. After another year's wanderings, another white and green lady gives her a pomegranate; at the end of another year, another gives her a crystal vial. Afterwards she comes to a silver palace, suspended by silver chains from four trees. She then breaks the nut ; a Swiss appears and admits her, and she finds

Prince Rainbow in àn enchanted sleep, answering to the kiss of forgetfulness in 'Filagranata.' Fairer-than-Fairies breaks open the pomegranate, all the pips become violins, whose melody makes the prince open his eyes. She breaks open the crystal flask, and a Seiren appears, who sings the tale of all the princess has endured. The prince wakes—the spell is ended. The silver palace turns into a real and inhabited one. They embrace, and are married.

'Incarnat, Blanc et Noir,' in the same 'Recueil,' is very similar to the 'Three Love-Oranges.' A prince walking out in the snow sees a crow. He tries his skill at bringing him down, and the black bird falls bleeding on the white snow. The sight makes him desire a maiden who combines these three tints. Suddenly a voice tells him to go to the 'Kingdom of Marvels,' and that there he will find a tree with splendid apples (they are not expressly said to be golden). He is to take three, and not to open them till he reaches home. Curiosity overcomes him by the way; he opens one, and a beautiful maiden appears; before he can embrace her she disappears. Afterwards, his homeward travels lead him on the sea; the desire to open one of the apples again overcomes him, but though he orders the vessel to be closely covered down all over, the second maiden disappears like the first. He only opens the third on reaching home, and then there comes to him a maiden exactly such as he desired, whom he marries. Afterwards he goes to the wars; and the mother-in-law, who hated her all along, kills her, and. throws her body in the castle moat, and substitutes another woman, a creature of her own. The prince expresses his surprise, but she assures him the different appearance is only the effect of a spell. The prince, however, pines after his own maiden. One day he sees swimming in the castle moat a fish with red, white, and black scales, which he spends all his time in gazing at. The false wife pretends she has an irrepressible desire to eat that particular fish; she is in a delicate state of health, and he cannot refuse her. After that a tree springs up suddenly, which once more presents the three colours. The false wife (inspired by the mother-in-law) demands that it shall be cut down and burnt. He cannot refuse her. Finally, a palace, built of rubies, pearls, and jet, suddenly appears by the side of his own. By unheard-of exertion he gets into it, and there finds in a cabinet his own maiden, whom he recalls to his side.

Another ('Le Buisson d'Épines fleuries') contains noticeable analogies with both the group of 'The Pot of Marjoram,' and that of 'Maria Wood.' The mother of a fairy princess is led to fill the stepmother's part towards her, by her having so lavishly distributed the ointment of perpetual youth, which had been entrusted to her keeping, that none is left for the queen's own use when she desires to have recourse to it to regain the lost affections of her husband, an earthly king. The governess comes to the aid of the princess, and they fly away together with tents and all requisites of the journey stowed away in pearls for travelling boxes (some analogy, perhaps, with the 'Candeliera'). Their adventures bring them across Prince Zelindor, who marries the princess. The vengeance of the fairy mother pursues them in various shapes, till at last she turns Zelindor into a Sweet Briar. The princess is attracted towards the plant, and tends it with the greatest care, without knowing it is her husband. The enraged fairy queen orders her to pluck a branch, and she is obliged to obey. The plant flows with blood, and Zelindor declares she is the cause of his death; at this juncture the husband of the fairy queen, fetched by the benevolent governess, appears. His return reconciles the queen to her daughter; and with an elixir she heals Zelindor's wounds, and restores him to his bride.

Perrault's rimed fable of 'Peau d'Âne' is much nearer 'Maria Wood.' The dying queen binds the king to marry no one who does not surpass her in beauty and understanding. Only their daughter comes up to the mark. Her fairy godmother tells her to ask for the brilliant dresses, and finally for the skin of a gold-coin-producing donkey. The king sacrifices even this. The fairy tells her to put on this skin while she stows her sunbeam dresses, jewels, &c., in a press which she promises shall follow underground wherever she carries her wand. She is made hen-wife in a king's farmyard, and puts on her brilliant dresses on holidays in her private room. The prince sees her through the keyhole, and falls ill because his parents object to the union. 'Peau d'Âne' makes him a cake into which she drops one of her rings. The prince is charmed with the idea of the hand it suggests to him ; his malady increases, and this softens his parents. He says he will marry no one but her whom the ring fits, and thus of course ' Peau d'Âne ' marries him.

The counterpart, in Perrault, to the group to which ' Il Rè Moro' belongs is a very clever, but somewhat artificially told story, called 'Kadour.' Kadour, an exquisitely beautiful princess of Cashmere, is utterly deficient, not in riches, like the chicory-seller's daughter, but in mind. She comes one day to a hole in the ground, and a monstrous figure comes out of it, and offers her the gift of mind, on condition of marrying him in a year. Without knowing what mind is, she has perceived that all her exceeding beauty has been powerless to attract any of the atten-tion she has seen lavished on others, and she gives a sort of stupid consent. The monster tells her that the gift of mind is to be obtained by simply repeating the words, ' O Love, who canst inspire all things; if it needs but to love to lose my insi-pidity, behold I am ready ! '

> ' O toi qui peux tout animer,
> Amour, si pour n'être plus bête
> Il ne faut que savoir aimer,
> Je suis prête.'

In proportion as she repeats these words she is filled with in-telligence; but no sooner is she so gifted than everyone appre-ciates and surrounds her, and she soon falls in love with Arada, the handsomest of her adorers. When the monster returns at the end of the year, and takes her down to his palace through the hole in the earth, she is in great perplexity what decision to make. She perceives that either way she must lose Arada, and says that she cannot give any answer; the monster says he will decide for her, and send her back to her first estate. Her newly-acquired powers, however, give her such loathing of this condition, that she finally prefers retaining her mind even on the terrible condition already propounded. The monster declares himself King of the Gnomes, master of boundless riches, and every kind of luxury and pleasure is lavished on her, as on the chicory-seller, to reconcile her with her situation ; but in this case all in vain. She contrives to let Arada know her unhappy position, that she may have the benefit of his sympathy. The gnome-king punishes her by transforming his handsome person into a duplicate of his own, so that Kadour never knows to which of them she is speaking.

This story is better known under the title of 'Riquet à la Houpe,' under which name it has been dramatised; in this, however, the senseless but beautiful princess has the compensatory faculty of rendering handsome her mind-giving but hideous lover, and therefore the happy *dénouement* is easily worked out. It is also the foundation of 'Beauty and the Beast;' and probably springs from the same idea as that embodied in the Ardshi Bordshi story I have given as 'Who invented Woman,' in 'Sagas from the Far East.'

A sort of counterpart to the story of 'Il Rè Moro' is given under the title of 'Le Prince Sincer,' in Gueulette's 'Fabliaux, ou Soirées Bretonnes,' but this series seems to be but a *réchauffé* of Oriental tales, and not a collection of local traditions, as the name leads one to expect, notwithstanding that he introduces Druids into them. The story I have named forms a link also in some of its details with that in the text called 'I Satiri.' Another of the same series, called 'Le Prince Engageant,' has some analogy with the 'Tre Merangoli di Amore' (The Three Love-Oranges), in a prince finding his bride by giving her a pomegranate while she is transformed as a dragon.

In a note to his translation of the ballad of 'Pérédur ou le Bassin Magique,' Th. de la Villemarqué[1] gives a Breton version of the 'Three Golden Apples' story. Pérédur is induced to abandon the state of retirement in which his mother has kept him, after the death of his father and his five brothers, by seeing Owen ride by, 'seeking the knight who divided the apples at the Court of Arthur.' Upon this the annotator remarks that the episode here alluded to has not been discovered; but, by way of compensation, he supplies the following, which was told him by a peasant of the diocese of Quimper, who could not read, and had received it by tradition from his forefathers.

King Arthur was holding a feast at Lannion, in Brittany; five other kings assisted at it, with their wives and their suite.

---

[1] 'Contes Populaires des anciens Bretons, précédés d'un Essai sur l'origine des Epopées chevaleresques de la Table Ronde.' Par Th. de la Villemarqué. Paris et Leipzig, 1842.

Just as dinner is over Merlin appears, and hands three golden apples to the king, and says they are to be adjudged to the three most beautiful women. There is a great commotion, and blood is about to flow in the dispute, when an unknown knight advances into the hall, mounted on a black charger with so luxuriant a mane that it envelops both him and his rider. The cause of dispute is referred to him for arbitration. He takes up the three apples, and compares their colour to the hair of the five queens, and their perfume to the ladies' breath; but settles the competition, like 'the Gold-Spitting Prince,' in 'Sagas from the Far East,' by disappearing with the prize.

He further quotes, from 'Myvyrian,' i. 151, 152, 155, that Merlin was so fond of apples that he devoted a poem to their celebration, and declared he had an orchard with 147 apple-trees of the greatest beauty; their shade was as valued as their fruit, and was confided to the care, not of a dragon, but of a fair maiden, with floating hair and teeth like drops of dew.

APPENDIX C. p. 195.

IT ought to have been remarked under Note 1, that Abelard's name is spelt Abailard in old French, which brings it nearer the name in the legend.

APPENDIX D. p. 196.

CARDINAL VALERIO, Bishop of Verona (in his 'De Rhetorica Christiana' cited in Ludovic Lalanne's 'Curiosités des Traditions,' iv. 403–4), has a very ingenious mode, among others, of accounting for the amplification of Legends; he says it was the custom in many monasteries to give the young monks liberty as a sort of exercise and pastime to write variations of the acts of the saints and martyrs, and they exerted their fancy in producing imaginary conversations and incidents of a nature consonant with the original story; that the most ingenious and well-written of these would sometimes be placed among other MSS. in the Library, and would mislead readers in later times.

APPENDIX E. p. 208.

CHARLES LOUANDRE ('Chefs-d'œuvre des Conteurs Français,' Paris, 1873) gives an episode out of the 'Voyage d'outremer du Comte de Ponthieu' (a *Roman* of the thirteenth century), which has curious analogies both with this tale of the Pilgrims, with another Roman story I have in MS., and with that of 'The Irish Princess' in 'Patrañas.' Adèle de Ponthieu was married to Thiébault de Domart. They go a pilgrimage to S. James of Compostella to pray that they may have heirs. Robbers overcome them by the way, bind Thiébault to a tree, and ill-treat Adèle. As soon as she escapes from them Thiébault calls to her to cut his bonds with his sword; she, judging it better that he should die than live to blush for her, attempts to take his life with the same blow which severs the cord; he foresees her intention and circumvents it. He does not divine her motive, but yet makes no allusion to the matter till they return from their pilgrimage, then he puts it as an A and B case to her father; the father decides such a woman should die. She is put into a barrel and cast into the sea; the barrel is picked up by merchants who sell her to the Sultan, and she becomes the mother of the mother of Saladin. Meantime her father and husband cannot rest for love of her, they go to search the world over for her. A shipwreck makes them the property of the Sultan who makes a present of them to Adèle. She, recognising them, pretends to be a Saracen soothsayer, and by revealing her acquaintance with their previous history, like the injured Queen in 'The Pilgrims,' brings them to an expression of penitence and of lasting love for her. She then escapes with them and lives happily with her husband, the Pope prescribing to her a certain penitential rule of life to purge her involuntary infidelity.

APPENDIX F. p. 392.

THE centenarian Guillaume Boucher (1506–1606) gives in his 'Sérées' a French story (called 'The Fish-bone') of a quack doctor favoured by luck, to whom he gives the name of Messire Grillo. Charles Louandre ('Chefs-d'œuvre des conteurs Français,' p. 278) points out that doctors hardly ever figure in popular literature before the sixteenth century, though after the Renaissance they became the constant subject of satire; and that thus Molière did little more than collect the jokes at their expense which had been floating during the previous half-century.

www.ingramcontent.com/pod-product-compliance
Lightning Source LLC
Chambersburg PA
CBHW031825270326
41932CB00008B/549